BY LIZA MUNDY

THE SISTERHOOD

Bin Ladin Determined To Strike in US

Bin Ladin Determined To Strike in US

Clandestine, foreign government, and media reports indicate Bin Ladin
since 1997 has wanted to conduct terrorist attacks in the US. Bin Ladin
implied in US television interviews in 1997 and 1998 that his followers would
follow the example of World Trade Center bomber Ramzi Yousef and "bring

Embassies in Kenya and Tanzania in 1998 . . .
operations years in advance and is not deterred by setbacks. Bin Ladin
a . . . . d our Embassies in Nairobi and Dar es Salaam as early
a . . . . members of the Nairobi cell planning the bombings were
. . . . d in 1997.

. . . . . . have resided
. . . . . . maintains a
. . . . . . rs found guilty
. . . . . . citizens, and a

. . . . . . New York

THE
SISTERHOOD

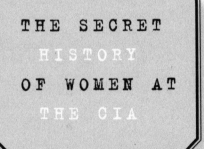

THE SECRET
HISTORY
OF WOMEN AT
THE CIA

LIZA MUNDY

CROWN
NEW YORK

Published in the United States by Crown,
an imprint of Random House, a division of
Penguin Random House LLC, New York.

CROWN and the Crown colophon are registered
trademarks of Penguin Random House LLC.

LIBRARY OF CONGRESS CATALOGING-IN-PUBLICATION DATA
Names: Mundy, Liza, author.
Title: The sisterhood / Liza Mundy.
Description: New York: Crown, 2023. | Includes bibliographical references and index.
Identifiers: LCCN 2023021017 (print) | LCCN 2023021018 (ebook) |
ISBN 9780593238172 (hardcover) | ISBN 9780593238189 (ebook)
Subjects: LCSH: United States. Central Intelligence Agency—History. |
Espionage, American—History. | Women intelligence officers—United States—
Biography. | Women spies—United States—History—Biography. |
Intelligence service—United States—History.
Classification: LCC JK468.I6 M85 2023 (print) | LCC JK468.I6 (ebook) |
DDC 327.12730092—dc23/eng/20230601
LC record available at https://lccn.loc.gov/2023021017
LC ebook record available at https://lccn.loc.gov/2023021018

Printed in the United States of America on acid-free paper

crownpublishing.com

9 8 7 6 5 4 3 2 1

FIRST EDITION

Book design by Barbara M. Bachman

For Anna and Robin,

who make my world,
and the world, a better place

CONTENTS

Part Three: GETTING THEIR GUYS

AUTHOR'S NOTE

THE CASUAL READER, OR EVEN A CLOSE STUDENT OF US HISTORY, would be forgiven for thinking that for most of its existence, only men worked at the Central Intelligence Agency. Not only that: very manly heterosexual men. Countless books exist about America's flagship spy agency—its legacy, actions, errors, achievements—and it's striking how many include the words "man" or "men" in the title. In 1971, when CIA director Richard Helms was trying to persuade newspaper editors that there was virtue in American spycraft, he asserted that "the nation must to a degree take it on faith that we too are honorable men devoted to her service." A later director, William Colby, titled his autobiography *Honorable Men*. Helms's own biography was *The Man Who Kept the Secrets*. Ray Cline, who founded US intelligence analysis during World War II, speaks in his memoir of "the men who made CIA." William Stephenson, the British emissary who coaxed the Americans into creating a spy service to begin with, was *A Man Called Intrepid*. A long-serving agency lawyer named John Rizzo called his book *Company Man*. The journalist Evan Thomas titled his book about the early architects *The Very Best Men*. "Best" was laced with irony. "Men" was not.

Yet fast-forward to today, and you'd be forgiven for thinking women now practically run the place. And one has: Gina Haspel, who served as the first female CIA director from 2018 to 2021. This shift in perception is one part real progress, one part Hollywood fiction. In the 2010s and 2020s, American films and television shows became peopled with fe-

male spies, often blond, usually slim, always brilliant, invariably problematic. The best known is Maya, protagonist of Kathryn Bigelow's
2012 film, *Zero Dark Thirty,* a character based on a group of real women
who hunted Osama bin Laden. There's Carrie Mathison, the bipolar
analyst whose own war against terrorism carries eight seasons of the spy
drama *Homeland.* There's Annie Walker in *Covert Affairs,* Sydney Bris-
tow in *Alias,* Queen Latifah in *The Equalizer.* Not to mention Elizabeth
Jennings, the Soviet sleeper agent in *The Americans,* whose wigs, as one
reviewer noted, are practically characters in themselves.

From scarcely a mention in the historical record to, seemingly, ubiq-
uity: Much has changed, on the surface.

But what resemblance does reality bear to Hollywood's flock of
fierce female spies? Do these women, who sometimes seem as though
they arrived on the scene en masse after the 9/11 terrorist attacks, have
predecessors? If so, who were *those* women; where did *they* come from;
and what did they contribute to American national security? Were
women involved in spying at the CIA—or did they even play key
roles—during the long years when the face of the agency, to the extent
it had a public face, was so relentlessly male? This book sets out to answer those questions, but the short answer is: Did they ever.

And that answer only raises more questions. What talents and skills
did women intelligence officers apply, and were those different from the
men's? How did they operate in a clandestine workplace dominated not
only by men, but, for many decades, by a certain kind of man who filled
the halls at headquarters and the CIA stations around the world: powerful, unchecked, heterosexual, white, often larger than life, not always
picky about principle, manipulative, competitive? How did women
fight to attain a recognized place in a workplace that, by its nature, is
meant to be secretive? What trade-offs had they been compelled to accept along the way? Was there another history, an important history, to
be written about the CIA that places women in a starring role?

One fact about the CIA, as it developed, is that it ran on networks
of male officers—station chiefs and deputy directors and division
chiefs—who gathered in cigar-smoking sessions to engage in what
they called "career planning," deciding who would be director, next, of

what. It's also true that the men undermined one another, and the savvy ones surrounded themselves with team players and loyalists.

As I discovered, however, there was another network at work in these decades, one built by women—a sisterhood, as I would come to think of it, a word the women often used themselves. A picture came into focus, showing contributions from three generations of women—the sum of whose experiences and connections to one another amounts to an alternative, and corrective, history of American spycraft. There was in fact quite a hidden history to tell: The women were there all along, though the agency sought ways to suppress their voices and set them against one another, even as the male leaders relied on their loyalty, their skills at elicitation, their attention to detail, and their insights. It took female spies decades to earn the posts and exert the influence they deserved. These women, like the men, were manipulators and operatives, by instinct and training. During the Cold War and into the modern era, women worked alone and together, laboring in secret, running operations against the adversary as well as—strikingly often—the organization they worked for.

This book tells the story of one of the biggest transformations in CIA culture, from a male-dominated institution where women were seen as typists and sexual playthings to one where women propelled some of the agency's most important successes.

EMBARKING ON THIS RESEARCH, I knew from experience that those whose contributions to history fall under the umbrella of intelligence are especially easy to overlook. I became intrigued by the story of the postwar CIA while writing my last book, *Code Girls*, about women code breakers during World War II. These were more than ten thousand young Americans, schoolteachers and recent college graduates, recruited to do top secret work deciphering enemy communications. These women made real breakthroughs, reading Japanese and German code systems, not to mention Russian and those of many other countries. And yet, after the war concluded, those women's contributions were lost to history; authors and scholars chose to overlook the evidence that came to light as many records became declassified in the

1990s. When *Code Girls* was published, I heard from hundreds of descendants of these women, who were astonished to learn about what their mothers and grandmothers had been up to during the war. They were good at keeping secrets.

I also knew that in addition to the code breakers, there were thousands more women who joined the Office of Strategic Services, the first US spy service and forerunner of the CIA. (Perhaps the most famous of these was Julia Child.) The story of that group felt like the clear beginning of this book. That makes it, in some ways, a natural follow-up to *Code Girls*, which concludes in 1945 with the end of the war, when all but a handful of code breakers returned to their private lives at the behest of Uncle Sam.

For the Allies, World War II was a moment, however brief, however imperfect, of what we now call inclusion, and that willingness to be inclusive was one reason the Allies won. The Germans considered bringing women into the Nazi war machine and decided not to. They felt women belonged at home. So did the Japanese war cabinet.

But progress in the United States, as is so often the case, did not proceed in a straight line. One poignant reminder of what happened after the war came in the form of a note I discovered from 1952, when Ruth Weston Cable, a code-breaking mathematician with the National Security Agency, took out a pen and a small piece of blank unlined paper and—in neat, looping cursive—wrote a reluctant message. With seven months to go before delivering her first child, Cable felt obliged to quit. "To Whom It May Concern," the note read, "I wish to resign my position as mathematician, GS-9, effective December 31, 1952." She added one sentence of explanation: "My time is needed at home to care for my baby."

I think a lot about that note. Ruth Cable wanted to be a mother, but she also wanted to continue doing the public service work she was so good at. The nation, at that time, said no. When a nation deprives itself of half an available talent pool, as America did for much of the 1950s, '60s, and beyond, the consequences speak for themselves. That expertise had to be rebuilt, and it was, slowly and surely, beginning in the Eisenhower years, by a cadre of women operating in the shadows of our nation's spy branch.

———

OF COURSE, WOMEN HAVE been present at the CIA all along. Even in these early years, there were women—not only officers, but secretaries and wives, who all played critical roles—building files, learning secrets about foreign countries and leaders, piecing together relationships, practicing tradecraft, handling assets, and building the internal networks that led from there to here.

These included Jeanne Vertefeuille—you might call her the Miss Marple of Russia House—and her team of female sleuths who exposed Aldrich Ames, an old boy and a traitor who blew the covers and caused the deaths of Soviet agents working for the US. They include Shirley Sulick, the patriotic Black wife of a white case officer, who reveled in outracing the KGB in Moscow. They include Lisa Harper, a pioneering Cold War operative who discovered that feminine qualities carried their own advantages; Gina Bennett, who in 1993 published the first prescient warning about Osama bin Laden; and Molly Chambers, an operations officer who helped find Nigerian schoolgirls kidnapped by Boko Haram. These women made contributions not despite their gender but because of it, using their sex to move around the world unremarked.

Spy work can be fun. That's a big reason people do it. This was true for Mary Bancroft, the wartime right-hand woman and secret weapon of Allen Dulles; Eloise Page, the first female CIA chief of station, who ran a successful operation against men who attempted to unseat her even as she aspired, unsuccessfully, to truly be one of the old boys; Sue McCloud, who fitted the classic spy profile of someone who runs toward danger, not away; Heidi August, who in the 1980s tapped into a wave of global feminism and discontent to persuade foreign women to hand over secrets; and Holly Bond, who joined the CIA in the post-9/11 era, when it had finally admitted gay and lesbian officers. She found that gender helped quite a bit when surreptitiously picking a lock to gain access to a hotel room.

In the 1980s, a generation of women came to the CIA whom I particularly identify with, because I was coming into the workforce—in journalism—at the same time. These women were born two decades or so after the end of World War II. Like me, they (dimly) remember fallout shelters and the 1969 moon landing; they experienced the wave of woman leaders of the 1970s, people like Billie Jean King and Shirley Chisholm, who made, to girls like me, bold things seem possible. They devoured books like Louise Fitzhugh's *Harriet the Spy,* published in 1964, which affirmed the idea that it's okay for a girl to have a sneaky side; and of course the multiauthored Nancy Drew series featuring the intrepid convertible-driving girl detective, with her doting boyfriend, Ned Nickerson. This cohort attended college at the pivotal moment when American women drew even to men in numbers and graduated into a workforce thinking the playing field was level. It was not.

In some cases, women intelligence officers proved effective because they were (and are) extraordinary people; because they have innate strengths that may or may not be related to gender; because they injected fresh thinking; and/or because they gravitated or were steered to roles where their talents emerged as key. But the women who arrived at the CIA in the 1980s also had to endure what we now call microaggressions and unconscious bias, in addition to outright misogyny. That made it hard for the women to be heard, even when what they knew or had noticed was urgent. Discrimination is bad enough at an advertising firm or insurance company; in a national security agency whose job is to predict and warn, the ramifications can be dangerous and literally fatal.

The federal government during the Cold War was more willing than the private sector to hire women, but once the women got to the CIA, they often landed in fields viewed as ancillary. Those very fields—analysis and targeting—would become critical after September 11, 2001, when the world was changed in a day, much as it had been after Pearl Harbor, by terrorists who happened to believe women had no role to play in their organization, nor in public life. In part because of how they had been channeled and discriminated against, CIA women happened to be in key places both before and after one of the signal catastrophes of the twenty-first century.

It was a small group of women at the CIA who first noticed the unusual group of stateless foreign fighters who emerged from Soviet-era Afghanistan—many of whom would become al-Qaeda's foot soldiers. Could it be, I wondered, that one reason the 9/11 attacks seemed to catch America's leaders so flat-footed was because of sexism and women's difficulty in getting institutional buy-in to what they were seeing? That's one of the important questions I sought to answer in the pages that follow.

Being underestimated because of gender (or any other reason) is an advantage when you are a spy on the street trying to move around unobserved. Being underestimated is a problem for everybody when you are a woman (or anybody) in a national security community trying to make yourself heard about something important you have discovered.

WHAT HAS ALWAYS SET the CIA apart from many other institutions is an atmosphere of secrecy, a license to break foreign laws and the recklessness that license engenders; the strange intimacy of spy work; the creation of a world where usual rules do not apply; and at times, the perceived carte blanche to violate the rights and well-being of vulnerable people, including the women who worked there. The CIA is a controversial agency, and always will be. Its mandate is to collect information that foreign governments are trying to hide, to analyze that intelligence and issue warnings and predictions, and to carry out presidential policy with covert actions in other nations. It operates in the shadow realm of clandestine warfare to stave off actual war.

What we are seeing in today's female spies is the trickle-down effect of a decades-long fight to win their place in this environment. This book does not argue that women are better or more virtuous or upstanding. It does show that women were behind numerous intelligence "wins" that have never seen the light of day, and that women made points, papers, and predictions that more attention should have been paid to. They also participated in some of the agency's darkest, most controversial chapters. Along the way, women created their own legacy. Women made discoveries, designed systems. Women were often poised to see things that others didn't. But "every step along the way," said one, Jonna Mendez, "was forced."

Here is the story of how they prevailed, how they spied, how they came together and advanced. Even the women working in today's intelligence community often don't know this history, because so much of it has been cloaked in secrecy.

THIS BOOK IS BASED on more than a hundred interviews, most of them on the record, with women and men who served at the CIA or in related roles. Some interviewees preferred to speak on background and provided valuable context. I also relied on published histories, scholarly papers, declassified documents, and personal writings. Spy work is so fascinating, often so surreal, that many retired officers have a desk drawer containing a screenplay or memoir. I thank the officers who shared these as well as speeches and papers.

In any work about spycraft, an important caveat is that there is much we still do not know. Sometimes the person telling the story was the only person present. Whenever possible, I sought corroboration. Future histories, and more declassification, may clarify questions and events. All names are real names, except in a few cases where the person is still undercover. These instances are made clear. All the people are real. The majority of figures whose stories are profiled in this book are, I believe, honorable women devoted to the nation's service. The work they do is hard—and when they succeed, the public almost never knows.

PROLOGUE
The Promise

November 1985

THE BODY ON THE GURNEY COULD SO EASILY HAVE BEEN HER own.

Heidi August stood in a hospital morgue on a chilly Mediterranean morning—November was a cold month on the island of Malta—contemplating the white-sheeted body of a woman. The sheet was folded back to reveal the woman's face, which was framed by a rich tangle of long red hair. She wore a necklace with a crucifix—the same cross she had on in the photo of her American passport, which Heidi held in her hand. Heidi stood shifting her gaze from the photo to the body and back to the photo. Seeing the cross she'd been wearing the day the photo was taken, now crumpled on her lifeless neck, felt to Heidi almost unbearably moving.

Two days earlier, Heidi knew, this woman had been packing her suitcase in Athens and looking forward to a weekend trip to Cairo. Now she was dead. The necklace provided confirmation to ID the body. That was why Heidi had come to the morgue—to make the formal identification. There was nobody else to do it. The woman had no friends or family in Malta. She had been traveling alone.

Heidi had just come from the hospital's ICU, which was full of burned and injured people. She was running on adrenaline and caffeine, shaken by the events of the last forty-eight hours and by an odd feeling of kinship with a stranger. She had not expected to feel this way about the dead woman. Maybe it was exhaustion. But she didn't think so.

Her task complete, Heidi found she couldn't leave, not yet. She continued to stand rooted to the spot, in the basement of St. Luke's, the island's only hospital, a blocky postwar building that looked particularly out of place here, in one of the most splendid ancient neighborhoods in the Mediterranean region. The hospital stood in the old city, a fortified area preserved from the Middle Ages, replete with sixteenth-century bastions and towers and defensive walls, beautiful stone edifices dating back to the era of the Knights Hospitaller.

The past two days had been endless and strange. First there had been the phone call interrupting Heidi's dinner in a seaside restaurant with Maltese friends. Then the sprint to her car and the race to Luqa airport. Then nearly two days in a makeshift command center where Heidi and two Arab men sat ridiculously close together at a small table, the three of them trading a rotary phone back and forth, taking turns talking to their governments about the hijacked plane on the tarmac. One of her seatmates was a Libyan diplomat, the other a representative of the Palestine Liberation Organization. The two men had not known Heidi was an American spy. They thought she was a capable but somewhat abrasive (she got testy in crises; she knew that) American who worked at the US embassy processing visas. In fact, Heidi was a CIA station chief—as far as she knew, the only female station chief in the world. When it was her turn with the phone, Heidi spoke in Pig Latin to her secretary, Jackie. Spycraft called upon unexpected talents. You never knew what qualities, what tricks learned in girlhood, you would need.

Certainly, a spy was the last thing Heidi August looked like. Petite, with brown eyes and a curly halo of short brown hair, she was thirty-eight but looked a decade younger. Just now she was wearing jeans, sneakers, and a sweatshirt from the University of Colorado at Boulder, her alma mater. The PLO representative, at one point, over food, in one of those weird bonding moments that can occur in crises, had asked about her family. He clearly expected her to talk about a husband and children. She told him she was unmarried but sometimes felt she was married to the president of the United States, or at least to his government. The PLO representative had laughed.

What paralyzed her—the reason Heidi couldn't leave the morgue—were the parallels between herself and this female civil servant. The dead woman was American, like Heidi. She was single, like Heidi. Both women were the same age. Her parents lived in California, as did Heidi's. She was a GS-13, just as Heidi was, a civilian working abroad, self-supporting, protecting US citizens and the national security of her country. She was accomplished enough to have risen to a position of some expertise and to have experience traveling in the Middle East. And how many weekend excursions had Heidi herself taken during her seventeen years with the CIA? How many dangerous situations had she found herself in? How many crowds; how much gunfire?

What struck Heidi most was the woman's poise: the clear-thinking way she had slipped her military ID out of her wallet and hidden it in the seat pocket in front of her once the hijackers started collecting passports. It hadn't saved her, but it had been smart. There was no evidence she had panicked, despite the chaos and terror inside the plane. The hijackers had threatened to shoot a new passenger every fifteen minutes. Heidi knew enough about herself to know that she possessed the same ability to keep her head. During her spy career she had survived coups and uprisings, fled rocket fire. But the difference was that the woman on the gurney was dead and Heidi was alive. She was alive and she had a responsibility to the dead woman.

That year, 1985, had been terrifying. Around Europe and the Middle East, violence against Americans was rising, and becoming more random, more unpredictable, and did not spare civilians or children. In June, just a few months earlier, TWA flight 847 had been hijacked out of Athens en route to San Diego, an event that lasted seventeen days as the plane crisscrossed the Middle East. In October, terrorists had hijacked the Italian ocean liner *Achille Lauro,* and the poor man in the wheelchair, Leon Klinghoffer, had been killed and thrown overboard. And now this: the bloodiest terrorist incident in history, fifty-eight bodies lined up on the tarmac in beautiful Malta.

Heidi sensed, in herself, a profound change. The last two days had given her a concrete goal. Up to now, Heidi's mission, like that of most everybody else in the Central Intelligence Agency, had been to keep Communism in check and stave off nuclear war. She had combated

Communism in Europe, Communism in Africa, Communism in Southeast Asia. Here in Malta, the hospital was staffed by East European doctors, a telltale sign of influence from the adversary. But now something new was occurring. A new kind of threat was rising. Hijackings, explosions. Around the world, networks were forming. Networks of ruthless men whose violence was indiscriminate.

Heidi had seen the woman's killer. He was lying in the ICU recovering from being struck by the pilot—who, escaping from the cockpit, rushed him wielding a fire ax. But there were people who funded and trained the killer. She would find them. She would avenge this woman's death and dedicate her working life to helping to insure something like this didn't happen again.

On an impulse, Heidi August spoke to the body on the gurney. The woman's name was Scarlett Marie Rogenkamp. Heidi wanted to make a promise. *I'll do everything I can to bring this killer to justice,* she told the body of Scarlett Rogenkamp. If people had helped them, she would track them down. Her words, spoken out loud, cut through the cold silence of the morgue.

She would never forget the link she felt to this other woman. The promise would propel her for the next twenty years. Their fates were tied, and Heidi now knew it. She was a huntress. And she was no longer alone. Back at Langley, there were women coming up behind her. There were other huntresses now, too, and they would help.

Part One

THE ASSESSMENT OF MEN

Representation of the world, like the world itself, is the work of men; they describe it from their own point of view, which they confuse with absolute truth.

—SIMONE DE BEAUVOIR, *THE SECOND SEX*

CHAPTER I

STATION W

N THE UNCERTAIN WINTER OF LATE 1944, WITH THE END OF WAR close yet frustratingly distant, a stream of well-dressed men and women filed through the front door of a "drab brownstone building" in downtown Washington, DC. They arrived between eight-fifteen and eight-thirty every morning except Sunday. Before the war, the brownstone had been an ordinary home, but not any longer. The nation's capital had exploded in population over the past two years, as American citizens, foreign officials, and soldiers arrived to serve the war effort. Every available piece of real estate had been snapped up. Barracks-like temporary buildings dotted the capital's green spaces: there were Quonset huts near the Reflecting Pool, even a government office in an old roller-skating rink. Near the Mall, members of America's diplomatic and military corps labored in hulking, drafty offices through which messenger boys rode on bicycles. On E Street, in Foggy Bottom, on an elevated patch of land near the Christian Heurich Brewing Company, another ragged cluster of buildings was shaping up as the heart of the country's espionage establishment.

The brownstone was unmarked—anonymous by design. Bundled against the winter weather, each person entering the building arrived bearing a unique paper card. Inscribed on the small card was a false name, the letter W, and a number. Each day's group consisted of about eighteen applicants, their arrival times staggered so they could be processed one by one. Most had no idea what lay in store, but they knew why they had come. They sought employment in a new wartime agency: the Office of Strategic Services. They were applying to be spies.

Depending on who—if anyone—had briefed them, applicants might have been told to expect a series of tests, during a day that would be "interesting and profitable as well as strenuous." Upon arrival, they were told to present their cards to the "clerk on duty." Yet even that simple instruction was itself a test. At desks inside the foyer sat two officials, neither of whom made any effort to greet newcomers warmly, or at all. They sat silent, waiting for the applicant to make the first move. "Here was a difficult situation," as a report later noted. Some applicants were put off; some were flustered; some became "aggressive and sarcastic." All reactions were noted. If a person asked a reasonable question, such as "Is this the right place?" the question would be "challenged immediately" to throw the asker off guard.

After the candidate managed to present the card, the intake officers introduced themselves. One was a psychiatrist, the other an assistant. They would be today's examiners.

Male applicants were directed to the basement, to change into Army fatigues. The aim was to make each man appear equal before his peers, so nothing would be known of his job, his social class, his military rank, his role in what might be called real life. He would come before the group naked, as it were, shorn of insignia or "ego support." He must try to prove his ability to work with others and his capacity for leadership, if he had any.

Women were taken to another room to remove coats and hats. Since the women were, well, women, no further equalization was thought to be needed.

Applicants received a purple-inked sheet of instructions, fragrant from the ditto machine, and learned they would be graded on comprehension. The instructions were intentionally vague: The psychiatrists wanted to see how recruits reacted to confusion. Some read quickly; others read, hesitated, reread.

The instructions told applicants they'd been called there to assess their assets and liabilities for confidential spy work. They had been in-structed to develop a cover story—a fake identity they could sustain. They were to reveal nothing about their real lives, apart from what they wrote on a personal history form that would be seen only by the exam-iners.

The applicants moved on to room 41, which had been turned into a classroom. Here they found desks, pencils, and copies of a question-naire. They were given one hour to complete it. Questions included their parents' names and places of birth; their family's politics and reli-gion; whether they had siblings and what were their ages. Then the questions became more probing. Which parent did you feel closer to at various ages? Which parent wielded the discipline in the house? Do you often think of your father? If so, is it with affection or resentment?

Applicants answered questions about past marriages, illnesses, and foreign travel. Did they drink alcohol? Had they ever been sued? The questions invited self-reflection or even stoked potential emotional vul-nerability.

If you came into a large fortune, what would you do with the money?

What embarrasses you?

What did you lack most as a child?

After one hour, a staff member called stop, explaining that "the rest of the morning would be tight and the tempo fast." They moved on to a health form—Did they suffer dizziness? bad dreams? headaches?—then a "work conditions" survey in which they were asked how they felt about work that involved danger; lots of parties; a hot, humid climate; responsibility; initiative; monotony; "working in close relations with Negros"; "working in close relations with Orientals"; working "exclu-sively with women"; or "seeing only men for long periods of time." Did they mind dirt? What if they were sent to a region with a lot of malaria, syphilis, alcoholism? Applicants were being considered for work in the global war theater, an array of overseas locations in which one fact held certain: something, probably many things, would go wrong.

After forty-five minutes, a staff member greeted the test takers. This was the security talk. At no time should they reveal their real name. If they recognized another person present, they should not let on.

In the afternoon, they would gather for a group discussion. The first task was to select a problem the United States was likely to face after the war, then arrive at a solution and plan of action. The point was to sort leaders from followers, listeners from talkers. Each part of the day was a test, including breaks.

"Lunch will be served in room 21 at about twelve forty-five P.M.," the staffer told them. "It will probably be announced by the cook shouting, 'Let's go back!'" The official explained: "We have tried to get her to say something more intelligible, but we have better success if we simply tell each class of students what this strange phrase means and let it go at that." They were observed, to see how they reacted to weird behavior.

"You're going to be kept pretty busy today, but you will have occasional brief breaks," the staff member continued. "During these periods we urge you to go to room 31, in which you will find a ping-pong table, some cards, a checkerboard, and some other small recreational equipment. This is your room and you are encouraged to go to it for visiting, rest, and relaxation."

At lunch, the staff noted how people interacted. "Some were uncommunicative and ill at ease," the report noted. "Others found it difficult to talk of anything other than their experiences of the morning. Some competed constantly for the staff members' attention, snubbing or interrupting their fellows."

During breaks—while playing ping-pong or darts—they were observed even more closely. Were they competitive? Friendly? Shy? Aggressive? How did they function in a group? Were they—as instructed—observing one another even as they were being observed?

THE NEED FOR A formal US intelligence service had become clear even before America entered World War II. In May 1940, Germany swept through Belgium and marched into France, where more than three hundred thousand British and French troops found themselves stranded at the port of Dunkirk. England sent fishing boats, ferries, and every other manner of watercraft to rescue them, evacuating close to 340,000 troops—more than one-third of them French—but only after taking disastrous casualties. Heavy equipment, now under Hitler's control, was left behind. Amid the ensuing months of blitzkrieg and occupation, England stood vulnerable and alone. President Franklin Roosevelt needed to know two things above all: Could Britain stand? And, if the United States entered the war, did America have what it needed to win? To the first question, US ambassador Joseph Kennedy, reporting from London, predicted England would be defeated by the Germans.

Roosevelt wanted a second opinion. He sent William Donovan, a New York lawyer and war hero, on a visit to England. Donovan reported that morale was high, under the leadership of Prime Minister Winston Churchill. But America, he warned, did not yet have what it needed to succeed. After spending time with the British intelligence community, he pointed out that the United States had almost nothing in the way of its own spy apparatus, even as it faced "imminent peril." Up to then, US intelligence, to the extent that it existed, had been confined to wartime—George Washington had the Culper Spy Ring; during the Civil War, both North and South used secret agents—then mostly dismantled during peacetime. After World War I, the State Department's small code-breaking operation had been shuttered by a horrified secretary of state, Henry Stimson, who famously sniffed, "Gentlemen do not read each other's mail." The US Navy and Army deployed military attachés who lurked in other countries and reported back on weapons and troop capabilities, but apart from that, American intelligence gathering was thin.

Donovan urged Roosevelt to set up a "central intelligence operation."

The British could not have agreed more. After weathering a prior world war, not to mention centuries of conflict with European nations, the UK had practically invented twentieth-century intelligence gathering, constructing a sophisticated and effective spy agency. England desperately wished to share intelligence with US allies but needed a partner who knew what it was doing. The UK "ran an operation" against its American cousins, sending consultants to persuade Roosevelt to build a spy agency along the lines of MI6. The British model was constructed around the notion that a centralized spy service should be civilian—not military—and draw from a wide swath of skills and people. It adopted the tactic of recruiting amateurs who had been trained as lawyers, businessmen, writers, archaeologists, and historians; who had an appetite for covert action; and who could be schooled in spycraft.

Roosevelt got the point. In 1941 he appointed William Donovan as the "Coordinator for Information," head of an effort to glean intelligence from allied spy services as well as open sources such as foreign newspapers, radio reports, and debriefs of businessmen returning from abroad. But after the surprise Japanese attack at Pearl Harbor, on December 7, 1941, it became clear a far larger effort was called for. America's shortcomings were now tragically apparent. In June 1942, the Office of Strategic Services was created, and Donovan was tapped to run it.

Donovan embodied the kind of man who would long dominate the culture of the OSS and its successor, the Central Intelligence Agency. A decorated World War I officer who after the armistice had insisted on marching with his men, the Fighting 69th, in a New York City victory parade—rather than riding—he was a man of panache, charisma, activity, and grandiose gestures. He was also a snob and a sociopathic womanizer. "Like Nature, he was prodigal, uncontainable, forelooking, and every completed project bred a host of new ones," noted an after-report on the OSS recruiting effort. He was the kind of man who dreamed big and let others fret about details. He ran a loose ship, felt comfortable with chaos, loved paramilitary action, was fascinated by exotic poisons, and spent most of the war away from his desk, preferring "faraway theaters of war," as Ray Cline, a historian who became head of the OSS analytic directorate, put it.

The OSS had one central purpose: to ensure the United States was never again caught by surprise as it had been at Pearl Harbor. To achieve this, it needed to build a network of agents to gather strategic information. It wanted to know about geography, troop movements, enemy intentions. It needed covert officers who could inveigle, taunt, bribe, threaten, cajole, and persuade citizens of other nations to share plans, maps, blueprints. It needed resourceful people who could snap photos from airplanes, worm their way into confidences, write up cables, run networks, forge documents, keep agents safe. It needed people who were not squeamish about how this got done. And Donovan wanted people willing to do the literally explosive work of war. Working with England's new clandestine paramilitary unit, the Special Operations

Executive (SOE), the OSS needed people who could sabotage rail lines, blow up train depots, evacuate downed Allied airmen.

But the OSS also needed workers possessing a less glamorous skill set. The spy service needed brains. It needed trained researchers and analysts, clear-eyed thinkers who could study the intelligence to assess its reliability; keep files; draw maps; provide vital charts for military landings; draw conclusions; and give warnings.

It needed people of action—and people of thought.

As Ray Cline pointed out, the OSS amounted to the country's first "large-scale professional US espionage network ever to operate abroad," even if its spies were not always particularly good at what they did. By late 1943, the OSS was "busily and somewhat haphazardly recruiting personnel without benefit of any professional or uniform screening process," the report said. The new service was recruiting too many people who were well educated or well bred, but "know nothing about working with men or how to look after the welfare and the morale of men under them."

In October 1943, the idea of creating an assessment school was pitched to Donovan at a staff meeting. Donovan, who liked schemes and big new projects, said yes. But recruiting the recruiting staff was itself a challenge. At a time when the US government and private sector were competing for brainpower—every wartime agency needed people who could read blueprints, calculate rocket trajectories, use early computers—the assessment staff was cobbled together from an array of experts that included clinical psychologists as well as animal psychologists; Freudians as well as anti-Freudians; social psychologists, sociologists, and cultural anthropologists—most anybody with experience in studying what made people tick.

The group had to agree on a way to spot talent. They sought to identify people who would be bold and resourceful and to eliminate those who would be "stupid, apathetic, sullen, resentful, arrogant, or insulting." They had to figure out who could work with forgers; send a subordinate on a suicide mission; assassinate a collaborationist mayor of a French village; cope with a situation where a careless agent left behind vital documents that needed to be retrieved. They sought people endowed with "effective intelligence"—people who could get things done.

They wanted officers who were able to cope. Working conditions would be unlike those most Americans had ever known. Recruits had to get along with "members of other OSS units, with the British, the French, and the Chinese, and, not infrequently, with some resistance group in occupied territory."

The assessors spent months trying to grasp the jobs involved. The fledgling spy service needed clerks, secretaries, doctors, historians. For propaganda operations to demoralize Axis nations—posters, leaflets, radio broadcasts—they needed script writers, singers, voice actors, type-setters. They needed paratroopers, saboteurs, pigeoneers, pilots, bomb makers. They needed folks who could run supply chains, live in China, send coded messages, eat foreign cuisine. People who could operate in Algiers, Cairo, Kunming. They needed scholars. People who could read maps. People who spoke Romanian, Albanian, Greek, Danish, Malay, Polish, Korean. People willing to jump from a plane or withstand isolation in a lonely farmhouse while being tracked by the Gestapo. They needed people who could hold their liquor while others got drunk.

They wanted people who could live a secret life; who were not obnoxious; whom others would trust; who were intrepid but not foolhardy. There was no way to know all the challenges that would face the American spy service, some self-inflicted by a US war machine in chaotic expansion. They needed people with "a rather high degree of snafu tolerance."

To find people like this, they borrowed an idea the British army had developed. Candidates were brought together in "leaderless group situations," then tested in a climate of fantasy, role-playing, and manipulation. Some came from the military, where officers kept an eye out for talent. Some were steered by the civilian personnel agency. The OSS employed "the usual and recognized techniques" for recruiting—namely, "vaguely worded newspaper and magazine advertising." But word of mouth was a major source of candidates, too: bored Wall Street lawyers; friends of Donovan and his social set; executives too old for fighting—they came by way of club memberships, whispered suggestions, college ties. "The Harvard connection was the entering wedge," recalled Ray Cline, a Harvard man who, along with his wife, was recruited by the Navy's code-breaking service. He was soon picked off by the OSS.

The OSS then set up secret schools. The first, Station S, was established on a Virginia farm in the foothills of the Blue Ridge. Horse country offered the privacy needed to transform an open-field landscape—streams, pastures, hedges—into an imaginary war ground. For three days, recruits play-acted crises and dramas. In one—the Brook Situation—recruits stood on the bank of a brook, told to imagine it as a torrential river with sheer banks. Their group was a sabotage party that needed to cross the raging waters. Nearby was a pile of boards. Assessors watched as the group debated a course of action. Did they have the skills to tie knots and fashion pulleys? Whom did the group gravitate toward as its leader? In another situation, each recruit was told to build a structure using pegs, poles, blocks, and sockets. Assistants were assigned to "help." Secretly, the assistants had been told to thwart the project by complaining, arguing, and shirking. The assessors wanted to gauge a person's ability to persist despite infuriating setbacks. Recruits were tested for practical skills, like the ability to synthesize fragments of intelligence and write a brief summary in code. They had to endure critiques, manage their emotions. In the evenings, candidates were judged not on how much they drank but on how alcohol affected them. It was not always easy to guess how the human personality would unfold in the heat of the moment.

THE VOLUME OF AMERICANS eager to join America's fledgling spy service proved overwhelming. As recruits poured in, the assessors had to figure out how to evaluate people more quickly. This is where Station W, the rented brownstone, came in. It was here that many scholars were evaluated before heading to the OSS Research & Analysis headquarters at 2430 E Street NW, a cluster of buildings in the Foggy Bottom neighborhood, just blocks from the Potomac River. There, brain workers scoured geographic records to produce maps for the military. They evaluated intelligence; wrote papers; composed biographies of foreign leaders. Academics were recruited from a network headed by

the Harvard historian William Langer; the group included intellectuals, like Arthur Schlesinger, Jr., who would go on to have distinguished
public careers.

"To Station W were sent the highest echelons of executives whose
abilities were better known to the administration or who were too busy
or dignified to spend three days solving field problems, debating, and
composing propaganda at Station S," the after-report noted. But this
did not make them easier to evaluate. Just because they were patriotic
men of business, or pipe-smoking thinkers, or future White House
speechwriters, or members of the Skull and Bones society did not guarantee prowess in the field.

And—Station W processed most of the women.

CHAPTER 2

GET THE FOOD, MARY

WASHINGTON, DC

1943

THE WOMEN CAME BY THE THOUSANDS. AT ITS PEAK, THE OFFICE of Strategic Services employed thirteen thousand Americans, of whom more than one-third, or forty-five hundred, were female, with nearly a thousand of those women serving overseas.

Here again, the Americans borrowed a page from the British. By the start of World War I, the British had hit upon the advantages of hiring women to staff a spy service, plucking wellborn women from the few universities that admitted females, and placing them in desk jobs in the country's spy operation, which was formally known as the Secret Intelligence Service (SIS) but, during the war, came to be referred to as MI6. These brisk and polished women did the paperwork the men needed to succeed. They built files, produced fake documentation, came to know the patterns of foreign agents. They also did much more. Some rose to be top administrators, including Vera Atkins, the logistician on whom Ian Fleming's character Miss Moneypenny is said to be based. Atkins started as a secretary, it's true, but did far more than flirt or take memos. Responsible for the recruitment, training, and welfare of British operatives in occupied France, she rose to become a formidable intelligence officer, managing the overseas spy network. (John le Carré's Russian-hunting Connie—implacable, all-knowing—was another fictional character who embodies many traits of what women did for England's spy service both during and after the war.) Atkins felt responsible for the female SOE agents, accompanying them to secret airfields for missions, offering them suicide pills, calling them "my girls."

Other British women handled agents, ran safe houses, and went undercover to infiltrate groups of Nazi sympathizers. For this on-the-ground spy work, officials looked for women who were not only charming and resourceful, but could channel their charm toward the right people in the right sort of way. One wartime officer, Maxwell Knight of MI5, England's domestic intelligence organization, ran several women in infiltration operations against pro-Nazi organizations and sympathizers, grasping that women, placed with a targeted organization under the cover of being secretaries or clerks, had wide access to information. In a memo, Knight reflected that a female agent should not be too sexy or beautiful, lest she seduce the poor male superior handling her. Nor should she be chilly and undersexed. "What is required," he concluded, "is a clever woman who can use her personal attractions wisely." Knight felt women—though vain, he believed—were more discreet and better at keeping secrets, men more prone to "loose talk."

"Man," he declared, "is a conceited creature" whose desire to impress "often leads him to indiscretion."

The paramilitary SOE operation also trained women who spoke native French and parachuted them into occupied France. Female SOE officers often worked as radio operators, one of the most perilous intelligence-related jobs of the war. Hiding in attics and safe houses, hunted by German vans with direction-finding equipment, they sent vital coded communications to London. These women were uniquely vulnerable: Unlike male operatives, they did not hold a military rank, and when captured were not entitled to the considerations accorded to military prisoners. At least twelve female SOE agents died in concentration camps.

To be sure, female operatives have always existed, but before World War II, they tended to exist on an ad hoc and freelance basis. While women spies are almost always stereotyped as honeypots or Mata Haris—eliciting information via sex and pillow talk—the truth is that they have exhibited range and courage, often by cloaking themselves rather than showing off. The first known female spy for England was the playwright and novelist Aphra Behn, who in 1666 was dispatched to Antwerp by Charles II to talk a Dutch spy into becoming a double agent for the British monarchy. Behn, who noted that her mission was "unusual with my sex, or to my years," reported that "though at first shy," her target "became by arguments extremely willing to undertake the service." Behn, whose code names were ASTREA and Agent 160, became the first former spy buried in Westminster Abbey.

In the United States, Harriet Tubman—self-taught spymistress and logistical genius—ran an extraordinary exfiltration network, evacuating slaves from the South and routing them to freedom under the noses of one of the most ruthless detection networks in the world: white slave-owners whose livelihoods and way of life were at stake. Tubman demonstrated an enduring truth of espionage: The qualities that might seem to work against a given spy can be flipped to one's advantage. Nobody expected a Black woman to be capable and in charge. On something like the same principle, America's first private detective organization, the Pinkerton Agency, built an entire Female Detective Bureau; its head, Kate Warne, had shown up one day to offer her services to Allan Pinkerton, pointing out she could easily pose undercover, since women practically were undercover anyway; nobody expected wives or laundresses to be doing anything that mattered. "Women," she further argued, "have an eye for detail and are excellent observers." In March 1861, Warne, posing as a Southern belle from Alabama—her aliases included Mrs. Barley and Mrs. Cherry—attended secessionist parties and got wind of a plot to assassinate Abraham Lincoln before his first inauguration. The Pinkerton agency smuggled him on a train to Baltimore, disguising him as an invalid, with Warne escorting him in the role of caregiving sister.

It wasn't their sex appeal that made women good spies. Just the opposite, it was their inconspicuousness as well as their social role. Women heard things; they created spaces and occasions where quiet conversations could be had. During the Civil War, Washington-area society women spied for North and South, holding salons and reporting back to handlers. In Richmond, a Southern heiress named Elizabeth Van Lew, an opponent of slavery, spied for the Union; she talked her way into Libby Prison—the Confederate prison for captured Union soldiers—by plying the commandant with gingerbread and buttermilk and posing as a nurse. While projecting the air of a harmless eccentric, "Crazy Bet," Van Lew built a spy network around Richmond, sending her household staff to work as servants for high-ranking Confederates. After Robert E. Lee surrendered at Appomattox, Grant's secret service chief reported that "the greater portion of our intelligence in 1864–65 in its collection and in good measure in its transmission, we owe to the intelligence and devotion of Miss Elizabeth Van Lew."

WILD BILL DONOVAN, IN constant need of people, easily saw the merits of the British model. After one of his London meetings, the new American spy chief wrote the word "women" in his notes about the SOE, and circled it. Word went out. Records suggest the women who lined up to enroll in the OSS were unusually accomplished. Many had achieved career success at a time when most graduate schools, colleges, and high-paying professions—law, medicine, business—were all but closed to them; and when women on average earned a quarter what men did. "The highest incomes before 1940 of the females seen at S and W were well in excess of women's salaries generally and roughly equivalent to the male income distribution for the US," the report noted. An extraordinary 48 percent of the women hired by the OSS had four years of college, compared to just 4.6 percent in the United States overall. Twenty-one percent had done graduate work; 8 percent had PhDs. Some came from wealthy or well-connected families—daughters or wives of Donovan's contacts.

The women of the OSS were also cosmopolitan. One out of four spoke a foreign language fluently, and half had traveled outside the United States. The women were driven by all manner of motivations. The first was patriotism. They wanted to show what they could do, and they wanted to help end the war. They wanted to travel. They wanted to test themselves.

The majority were processed though Station W, the unmarked Washington brownstone. Here, female applicants participated in one mixed-gender test, a game called Ball and Spiral. To take part, applicants gathered around a board featuring a spiral ramp, six handles, and a ball. The challenge was to get the ball to the top. It was a silly exercise, but not nearly as easy as it looked. Most groups failed, and almost nobody did it within the goal of fifteen minutes. Assessors were more interested in behavior than in success. Did one person take the lead? Did two people compete? Did the group hold stubbornly to one procedure despite repeated failure? Did people blame one another? Sabotage one another? Was there "unifying spirit"?

Afterward, applicants were divided by gender. The men were taken to a room containing two raised platforms, ropes, pulleys, and a pair of boards. The men were told to imagine themselves as a scouting party pursued by an enemy force, standing at a blown-out bridge. Below loomed a thousand-foot chasm. A bucket of water was a "water-cooled machine gun" and a pack of paper towels represented "highly secret and valuable radar equipment," which the group needed to transport over the chasm. It was an exciting scenario, one that allowed lawyers and stockbrokers to imagine themselves commandos and war heroes. The assessors saw the bridge-making exercise as a "masculine" building challenge that was "not particularly well suited to feminine interests or special abilities." It had, the report conceded, a bit of a "boy scout" flavor.

So they designed a test "expressly for women." The task was to file papers. Rather than imaginary explosives, the women were given index cards, a file box, a typewriter, ten memos, a file folder, and pencils. Working as a group, they were told to create a cross-referenced system in which memos could be filed, then retrieved, according to the name of sender or recipient. They had thirty minutes. The panel watched. The OSS assessors wanted to see who could design a system that would enable easy access to key records; who could best envision how to link people; and who could work well with others.

They also wanted to see how women reacted to doing menial work that was beneath their talents and skills. They wanted to see how the women handled being undervalued. This was a situation the women were certain to encounter in the spy service. By the time Station W opened, OSS assessors had noticed "there was a definite tendency in the organization to recruit able and intelligent women for relatively simple jobs well below their capacity." It was a tart insight, arrived at because at least one author of the report (in addition to several staff members) was female. That was Ruth S. Tolman, a psychologist who helped write the final 541-page report, titled *Assessment of Men*.

At the outset, the report noted, female OSS applicants had been warned that most, if hired, would end up doing low-level tasks. The role-playing situation provided a chance to study how they handled that indignity. And the testers wanted to observe how the women coped when pitted against one another in a zero-sum scramble for top jobs. In the 1940s, as now, the federal government maintained a "ratings" system in which workers were assigned pay grades, such as CAF-4 or CAF-6. In the role-playing exercise, the women, after completing the filing test, were told to assign the others a civil service grade. Only a few high grades were available.

Discussions ensued, and arguments. "Relatively few recognized the fact that this was only an imaginary situation," the report tut-tutted. "They reacted as though they actually were to be assigned to these hypothetical jobs." In other words: As the assessors sought to predict how all OSS applicants might react to setbacks and snafus, aspiring female spies were tested for a unique frustration, that of being stymied and underused. They were also set against one another, encouraged to compete—and conspire.

To an uncanny degree, *Assessment of Men* predicted what women in the US spy trade would confront for the next eight decades—and the coping methods they would develop. At Station W, bright young women competed for entry-level "secretarial and stenographic positions." As the war advanced, their work expanded to include editing cables, developing maps, stealing code books, breaking into embassies, designing propaganda, writing reports that enabled huge military operations like the D-Day landing. They became guardians of information, organizers and file builders, experts in the habits and backgrounds of foreign leaders as well as enemy agents and landscapes. This army of women pioneered systems of organization and data retrieval that would prove critical as the agency moved from the Cold War to the twenty-first-century practice of tracking narcotics rings, traitors, and terrorists. A direct line can be traced from the women who built files and came to know the secrets, lies, education, movement, and relationships of adversary spies and leaders, to the targeters of today, who have honed the agency's ability to fly drones and track terrorists and enemy commanders.

The women also formed a fractious sisterhood that would take decades to jell. They loved their work even as it consumed them.

IN 2015, I ATTENDED a memorial service for Betty McIntosh, who had served in the OSS in Japan and China. Present that day was her friend, nonagenarian Doris Bohrer, another OSS officer. The two women met long after the war, in a retirement community in suburban Virginia. As a young woman, Bohrer longed to fly airplanes, and she sniffed when I asked her if the OSS work had been exciting. Most women, she said, did paperwork. When war broke out, she'd taken the civil service exam, hoping to defend her country. The OSS hired her as a typist, then promoted her to a desk job, albeit an important one, working in the map unit and studying aerial imagery in advance of the Italian campaign. Sent with an Air Force division to the Adriatic Coast, she scrutinized overhead photographs of Germany, noting train movements and factory construction and looking for places to air drop supplies to OSS officers behind enemy lines. After the war, she signed on with the CIA and finished her career as deputy chief of counterintelligence. McIntosh, the daughter of a sportswriter, had trained as a newspaperwoman before the war. She later wrote two books about her undercover work in Japan and China, working for a somewhat flaky outfit called Morale Operations, writing "black propaganda" to demoralize the Japanese by means of ginned-up flyers and leaflets, and encouraging the enemy to give up by—among other things—persuading soldiers their girlfriends were cheating on them.

In her second book, *Sisterhood of Spies,* McIntosh quoted Donovan as saying women were the "invisible apron strings" of the OSS. It was faint praise, a backhanded compliment if there ever was one. She noted that the women were invariably called "girls," discrimination against them was "obvious," and even though most were as well educated as the men, they were employed as "secretaries, filing clerks, translators."

During World War II, women spies were part of a nationwide moment in which female talent was intensely competed for. A group of highly educated women formed the first predominantly Black battalion of the Women's Army Corps—the first full female battalion sent overseas, it included at least one Puerto Rican and one Mexican woman—and sailed to Europe to deal with the warehouses of mail that had accumulated after the Normandy invasion. While the people of France looked at them with curiosity, the women of the 6888th Central Postal Directory Battalion got their work done with brisk dispatch and ahead of schedule. In Washington, a group of "military mapping maidens" created topographical maps; their charting and geolocation work underpins what is now the National Geospatial-Intelligence Agency, not to mention modern-day GPS. At Aberdeen Proving Ground in Maryland, hundreds of female mathematicians worked as "computers" calculating ballistics and weapons trajectories. At the University of Pennsylvania, a team of six women programmed the Army's first computer, the ENIAC, only to be shut out of the formal unveiling. Grace Hopper, a former Vassar professor, programmed the Mark I computer. A group of Black women mathematicians worked in the segregated section of what would become the National Aeronautics and Space Administration.

In wartime espionage, women confirmed the covert value of being underestimated. The American entertainer Josephine Baker smuggled sheet music out of Paris to Lisbon, using invisible ink to carry messages to Allied fighters planning the North Africa campaign. In Paris, a young Frenchwoman named Jeannie Rousseau de Clarens worked as a translator for a publishing house that was taken over by the Nazis. Fraternizing with her new German bosses, she listened as they mansplained plans for weaponry systems, little suspecting their tiny, cheerfully agreeable helper was a spy for the Allies and unaware that among her gifts was a photographic memory. When she feigned disbelief, exclaiming that the German war machine couldn't possibly have produced the mighty weapons the men were bragging about, they showed her blueprints. The plans were for the V-2 rocket. She passed these plans to the British, who bombed the German rocket factory at Peenemünde. During a trip across the English Channel to meet her admiring handlers at

MI6, she was captured by the Gestapo—a traitor had exposed her—and sent to a series of concentration camps, where she barely survived. Another Frenchwoman, Marie-Madeleine Fourcade, ran a spy network that reported on doings at the shipyards where the Germans housed their U-boats. She, too, was captured—several times—and escaped, in one case by wriggling naked through the bars of a prison window.

In America, women contributed to every aspect of spycraft, both in the office and in the field. The essence of human intelligence—HUMINT—entails taking care of people: ensuring that assets are trained and kept alive. Taking care of people is a fundamental human activity for which women have tens of thousands of years of specialized training. Few were better at it than Virginia Hall, a Baltimorean who in 1940 was spotted in a train station by a British intelligence officer; she had been driving ambulances in France and, as the blitzkrieg swept Europe, was making her way to England. The United States was still neutral, and the officer realized an American woman could travel freely, posing as a journalist, through occupied France. Hall became one of the SOE's most tenacious spymasters, building a network of agents in Lyon, France. Pursued by the Gestapo, she hiked over the Pyrenees despite the impediment of a wooden leg she'd named Cuthbert. When she radioed back to SOE headquarters in London that Cuthbert was giving her trouble, the recipient, unaware she had blown one foot off in a prewar hunting accident and used a prosthesis, thought Cuthbert was a male companion. "Have him eliminated," came the radio reply.

THE UNITED STATES WAS still new to intelligence gathering: In 1943 and 1944, OSS reports drew mostly from the better-networked British. Slowly but surely, though, the OSS's own collection net began to produce. "The star of the show was unquestionably the urbane Allen Dulles," observed Ray Cline, the service's top scholar-analyst. (Cline ran the office of analysis along with several men, whom he cites by name in his memoir, and "with the aid of several Radcliffe girls who wrote well and helped organize the morning briefings for OSS brass" but whom he did not consider worth singling out.)

Dulles, the Princeton-educated brother of Secretary of State John

Foster Dulles, served as OSS station chief in Bern, Switzerland. That country's neutral status made it a refuge for exiles from around Europe. Dulles was a Republican, the son of a Presbyterian clergyman, and, like Donovan, a Wall Street lawyer; before the war, he had been a partner in the New York firm of Sullivan and Cromwell. In Switzerland, his best asset was Hans Bernd Gisevius, a German intelligence officer who was part of a network secretly planning to assassinate Adolf Hitler. Dulles sent a stream of intel back to Washington based on Gisevius's "magnificent" reports.

In point of fact, Gisevius was run by an American woman, Mary Bancroft, who spoke flawless German and possessed the charm, intellect, and listening skills to elicit vital information from a lonely man living a secret life abroad. Two lonely men, actually. Dulles and Gisevius both relied upon Bancroft's counsel. "Both of these men would discuss with me how they should behave in a situation in such a way as to achieve some specific ambition of theirs," Bancroft wrote in a memoir. "The required behavior was quite clear to me and I would tell them what I thought they should do. They would do it, it would work—and the next time they were baffled, back they would come."

Urbane and well read, Bancroft longed as a child to do exciting things, and was disappointed to learn that girls could not become police officers. She was raised in a prominent Boston family, step-granddaughter to Col. Clarence Barron, the publisher of *The Wall Street Journal* and founder of the Dow Jones financial journalism empire, who taught her to think clearly, ask questions, and form her own opinions. After attending Smith College for a year, she left to marry a Harvard graduate, Sherwin Badger, with whom she maintained an unconventional household. The couple lived on the Upper East Side of Manhattan and attended West Side parties where they drank highballs of bathtub gin, discussed "truth," and disappeared into bedrooms. "There was plenty of experimenting with different partners and a general feeling that to suppress one's desires could well be responsible for the alarming increase in cancer," she wrote. A few years in, they divorced, and she remarried to a Swiss accountant, Jean Rufenacht, who was abusive as well as wealthy; when drunk, he slapped her.

When Dulles met Bancroft, she was living in Zurich with her daughter and Rufenacht, who left on business for long stretches.

Allen Dulles, a serial adulterer, was, like his boss William Donovan, sexually unfaithful to an almost pathological degree. His sister, Eleanor, estimated he had "at least one hundred" affairs. He first met Bancroft at a bar in Zurich. She was already an intelligence officer without knowing it. Fluent in several languages, Bancroft had been recruited by an American acquaintance to analyze the speeches of Hitler, Goering, and Goebbels, as well as articles in the foreign press. Unbeknownst to her, these reports went straight to the Coordinator of Information, the predecessor to the OSS. On their first meeting, engineered by a mutual contact, Dulles as a matter of course tried to seduce her; after she put him off, they chatted about furnishing his apartment and she offered to rent him linens. He came to pick them up and hit on her again; again, she rebuffed him. She playfully guessed his briefcase combination, which was his house and street number, a surprising lapse for a spymaster.

Dulles offered her a job and assumed she would succumb to his advances. "We can let the work cover the romance, and the romance cover the work!" he said, according to her memoir. He added words with which many women are familiar: "Because you're you, I am going to pay you only the minimum." Dulles knew there would be a postwar accounting and did not want to be found overpaying a woman he was having an affair with.

A natural analyst, Mary Bancroft at first drew on newspaper articles, speeches, and radio broadcasts—open-source intelligence—providing Dulles with reports he would fold into his nightly cables to Washington. On one early assignment, she chatted with close friends who had been to Berlin, Hamburg, and other German cities and wrote a "mood piece" that delighted Dulles; it confirmed casualties from an RAF attack on Gestapo headquarters in Brussels. He eagerly awaited her analyses of foreign sources; she considered these bland, but America was so hungry for information that Washington regarded it as "hot news." He also expected Bancroft to pinch-hit as a waitress at meetings: At one encounter with her and Gisevius, he barked, "Get the food, Mary!"

Dulles called her at 9:20 every morning; they had a private code that consisted of slang and outlandish made-up names. She also met with his contacts. She called it "stroking the people I saw for Allen." In espionage, this is called handling. By 1943, Bancroft was working full time for Dulles. She often found herself in settings with people from all over Europe and the world. She listened to gossip. Dulles, like everybody in the OSS, was new to the spy business, and Bancroft seems to have intuited some key principles before he did. When he complained Hitler was getting many facts wrong in his speeches, Bancroft, who had read *Mein Kampf* in the original German, explained the "Nazi theory of propaganda," pointing out that it had "nothing to do with presenting facts accurately" but was "an appeal to the emotions of the German people": a Big Lie.

She also explained aspects of human sexuality to her boss, who for a man of the world seemed startlingly naïve. Once, they started discussing the Nazi criminal code, which criminalized homosexuality. "What do these people actually do?" Dulles asked her. "'Don't you know?' I asked in astonishment. Allen shook his head. 'Do you want me to tell you?' I asked. 'If you know,' said Allen, looking skeptical. So I took my courage in my hands."

When she finished explaining to him sex between men, assuring him same-sex couples "do different things just like everybody else," he was "red in the face" and told her she should be ashamed, but said, "I'm glad to know." Another time, she told him the Hungarians thought Dulles was gay and having an affair with his male secretary. She also reported that Gisevius had told her "The real bond between Himmler and Heydrich was that they had once been 'involved' with one another." These facts of life came as news to Dulles. "He is a gentleman," his butler told Bancroft. "He understands nothing!"

Her housekeeper, Maria, a native German, showed Bancroft letters from her brother-in-law, who reported that "there are no more aluminum spoons in Germany." Dulles called the housekeeper "the Wehrmacht" and always wanted to know what she thought. Bancroft's husband slipped her tidbits and put her in touch with Yugoslavs. He didn't mind that his wife was having sex with the spy chief; in fact, he was flattered. As Dulles expected, Bancroft by now had acquiesced. On her weekly visits to Bern, they'd have drinks and dinner, discuss news, and "engage in a bit of dalliance" before she made her way through darkness to her hotel. Like many a male leader before and after, Dulles understood that having a tip-top right-hand woman working on his behalf—brilliant, unconcerned with her own advancement, sexually available when he needed an outlet—was, for him, win-win-win.

What little has been written about Bancroft portrays her as a red-lipsticked honeypot. In truth, Dulles was the aggressor. In her memoir, she describes a morning when he rushed into her Zurich apartment knowing her husband was away and her daughter at school. "By chance, the maid was out at the market. His hat pushed back on his head, his pockets stuffed with newspapers, he said, 'quick!' Without any further preliminaries, he added, 'I've got a very tricky meeting coming up. I want to clear my head.' Feeling it was too risky to go into my bedroom, we settled in on the living-room couch. In scarcely more time than it takes to tell the story, he was on his way again, pausing in the doorway only long enough to say, 'Thanks! That's just what I needed!'" The maid returned within moments, and Bancroft, rattled, vowed not to cooperate with that kind of impromptu head-clearing again.

Bancroft knew her ability to listen served a vital purpose for a pressured man on whom the fate of the free world rested. In a detail that is almost too good to be true—but is true—she happened to be in analysis with Carl Jung. The psychoanalyst knew of her spy work and said it was her role, as a woman, to give powerful men someone to talk things over with. "Men like Allen, very ambitious and holding positions of power, needed to listen to what women were saying and not go off the deep end" was her summary of what Jung told her. For their part, Jung and Dulles were almost comically fascinated by each other. Bancroft helped Jung write a letter to Dulles, and then helped Dulles write his response. She referred to it as "all this corresponding with myself."

Dulles confided in Mary Bancroft in a way he did not to his own wife, Clover, with whom he settled into a long-distance marriage of convenience. Dulles called Clover an angel and did not tell her anything about what he did. He seems to have regarded a wife as chiefly a vehicle to a man's advancement; Bancroft noticed that once, when a mutual acquaintance became engaged, Dulles wondered why a man would marry a woman who didn't seem "useful." Being shut out pained Clover, whom Bancroft described as vague and otherworldly. Clover was worldly enough to enjoy being the wife of a prominent husband, however. She confided to Bancroft that they had terrible fights. And when Clover Dulles came to Switzerland on a visit, she sized up their relationship right away. "I wanted you to know I can see how much you and Allen care for each other," she told Bancroft, "and I approve!" The two women conspired to look after Dulles. Bancroft saw herself as "far less idealistic" than Clover. "I knew his dark side . . . and it didn't bother me in the least."

Bancroft played a similar, if nonsexual, role with her German asset, spending long hours with Gisevius under the pretext of translating his memoir. He did not realize she was reporting their encounters back to Dulles. She played into his self-importance; he was puffed up enough that it seemed reasonable a woman would want to immerse herself in his life story. His role as a double agent—employed by the Abwehr but secretly conspiring to assassinate Hitler—was so dangerous, he didn't feel it would be ethical to have a wife or girlfriend. He told her "it would mean a great deal to him to be able to discuss his ideas with a woman." So voluble were his confidences that Bancroft took a helper: Elizabeth Scott-Montagu, a British friend who had driven ambulances in France until she had to flee the Gestapo. The two women drew him out. They would "focus our entire attentions on the author, and off he'd go. Into his fascinating stories that were so useful in giving helpful insights into the personalities and intrigues of the Nazis."

The intelligence, gathered in no small part thanks to Bancroft's efforts, helped cement the reputation of Allen Dulles. He would go on to become the foundational director of the CIA.

AS OFFICERS IN EUROPE and Asia developed their tradecraft, other American women pioneered the analytic methods that proved one of the war's real and lasting intelligence achievements. Among these was Cora Du Bois, who in 1942 joined the Research & Analysis branch. A renowned anthropologist and open lesbian who had spent time in Indonesia and Ceylon—at the time, enough to make her a relative expert in the South Pacific—Du Bois first worked in Washington, extracting all the "dope on which we can lay our hands" about population, geography, and fortifications along key Pacific area coasts. Confronted with thin file-keeping at the Navy's hapless Office of Naval Intelligence, she sought out missionaries, travelers, Dutch and British colleagues, and anyone else who knew the shoreline, producing reports that helped enormously as Americans mounted dangerous amphibious landings in an effort, successful, to retake landmasses in the Pacific and Asia.

In 1944, Du Bois found herself traveling from San Francisco to Bombay on the SS *Mariposa* with hundreds of male GIs and a handful of civilian women. Nine of the women were OSS personnel, among them Julia McWilliams, a gregarious Smith College graduate hired as one of Donovan's clerks. Tall Julia—as Du Bois fondly called her shipmate—was a jolly colleague, a party lover who "retained her sense of humor" and proved a "lovely mad woman, you know, when she gets sportive." In Kandy, Julia McWilliams would meet her husband, Paul Child, a State Department mapmaker. After the war, she accompanied him to Marseille, where Julia Child found her calling as the chef who brought French cuisine to the American kitchen.

For her part, Cora Du Bois fell in love with Paul Child's assistant, Jeanne Taylor. The foursome would remain friends; the Childs settled in Cambridge, Massachusetts, where Du Bois in 1954 became the first tenured female professor in the Faculty of Arts and Sciences at Harvard. During the war, Du Bois rose to become chief of SEAC, the Southeast Asia research and analysis branch, the only woman to head a branch of the OSS. Working with local sources, she created an "unexcelled map service" for planning Allied invasions and landings. Known for crisp, acerbic cables, she enjoyed the work "more than any I have ever set the hand to." Her successor wrote, "I have no illusions about being able to do the job as magnificently as Cora did."

At war's end, Du Bois received the Exceptional Civilian Award, and joined the State Department, which inherited the OSS research branch. There, analysts in her office perceived the importance of unexploited colonial regions and foresaw the peril of US involvement in Vietnam.

Du Bois also personifies the postwar brain drain. After the Japanese surrender, exclusion—not inclusion—became the order of the day.

During the power struggle between the FBI's J. Edgar Hoover and the architects of the CIA and State Department, Du Bois and Jeanne Taylor were witch-hunted out of public service. In 1947, Taylor was compelled to resign because, as a young artist, she had voted for a Communist. In 1948, the FBI launched a "full field investigation" of Du Bois, at a time when more than four hundred homosexuals in the State Department were "fired or harried into resignation." The FBI file for Du Bois, who never hid her relationship with Taylor, noted she was "single" and living with a woman.

AFTER THE WAR, WOMEN faced much pressure to resume their roles as mothers, helpmeets, and housewives. Wartime ads had exhorted women to serve the war effort—"The more WOMEN at work the sooner we will win!" read one of many posters—and after the war, the same propaganda urged them to depart the workplace "as you promised," in the words of one newsreel, to free up jobs for returning men.

America's spy apparatus concurred, to a point. The OSS was dissolved (technically, absorbed into the State Department) with the thinking that peacetime required less in the way of intelligence effort. But soon enough, the Cold War called for more—much more. In 1947, after an interim year as the "Central Intelligence Group," the Central Intelligence Agency was created by an act of Congress. A few inept early directors emerged from the US military and disappeared quickly— Rear Adm. Sidney W. Souers lasted from January to June 1946, Lt. Gen. Hoyt S. Vandenberg a bit longer, replaced by Admiral Walter Bedell "Beedle" Smith, who somewhat righted a wobbly ship. The agency grew fast. By the 1950s, under the ambitious and well-connected Allen Dulles, the workforce reached an estimated ten thousand people, half its modern size of approximately twenty thousand. For a decade, it continued to hum along in a hodgepodge of buildings and old barracks in Foggy Bottom and the National Mall, with buses, the "green beetles," shuttling between them. These included I, J, K, and L buildings— wartime temporary buildings clustered near the Reflecting Pool and containing vast stores of physical records, invisible behind barred windows through which the women who kept them peered out. Before trips abroad, officers paid visits to Central Processing, where fake passports and travel papers were dispensed by "old broads," as one hardboiled case officer dismissively called them. "There seemed to be no way to jar the spinsters into any sort of priority action," this case officer complained, saying that any time he went to the Records Integration Office, he had to "wait hours for girls" to run biographical traces on prospective assets.

Upon its creation, the CIA was instantly one of the most important spy services in the world. Directors complained about how tough it was to find good men—ignoring the obvious truth that, for the corps of officers, the agency confined the search to men who were white, (mostly) wealthy, and straight. In Hoover's Washington, gay men and lesbians were shut out of federal service. The scrutiny was merciless in intelligence work, reflecting the belief that men who had sex with men were vulnerable to blackmail. People of color often were steered into administrative jobs. Recruiters avoided "inner cities," and security officers torpedoed applicants with "nonstandard" backgrounds.

But the women did remain, or many of them—ubiquitous, and in some cases powerful. Like Wall Street, Detroit, and Madison Avenue, the agency needed women to type letters, keep files, take dictation, build archives, edit reports, and communicate between headquarters and the field. Women ran the finance and personnel offices, developed budgets. Recruiters for clerks and typist positions sought young white women from places like Pennsylvania and West Virginia; it was thought that single women from nearby states would be willing to leave their families to live in places like the Meridian Hill Hotel for Women. Once they were married, it was assumed they would resign. The women briskly amassed quite a bit of knowledge, and not just about spycraft. They learned a lot about the men—not only typing their correspondence, but often composing it—and put that knowledge to use. Like le Carré's Russian-hunting Connie, the women were careful. Suspicious. Perceptive. Cranky. Women worked in the public affairs office, fielding calls from the public, listening sympathetically to job seekers as well as cranks and paranoiacs who thought the CIA was eavesdropping on them through tooth fillings. Regardless of their real name, the women of public affairs signed all correspondence "Grace Sullivan."

Any number of men built careers on the work of women in the back office. And the jobs to which women were relegated were often more important than acknowledged. It may or may not be true that women are more patient than men. What is true is that women were believed to be more patient, and thus were steered into jobs requiring attention to detail. "Patience, thoroughness, skepticism, and tireless review of data are the marks of a good counterintelligence officer," observed Ray Cline. Counterintelligence entails identifying attempts by foreign spy services to penetrate the agency. It "depends on records: understanding who is in touch with whom," Cline noted. Women built a huge brain, records of who knew whom and who had been spotted where.

IN THOSE EARLY DAYS of the CIA, women's spying was rarely acknowledged, often unofficial. As the years went on, however, and the agency became one of America's leading instruments of foreign policy, women fought their way into the spy corps. They made major contributions in an era when the fight against Communism was paramount, and the survival of the United States was existential. Women believed in the mission. They brought unique gifts and they made unique sacrifices. Women spies during the Cold War almost never married. Even fewer had children. Not because they didn't want to. Women who aspired to serve abroad were told to forgo having a family, whereas for men, having a wife and children was encouraged. Wives participated in the mission, helping husbands elude surveillance and cultivate the cover story of a normal American diplomat leading a normal American life.

It was exquisitely tough for aspiring female spies to rise within these structures, at a time when what we today call institutional sexism was everywhere practiced. At CIA's training academy—the Farm—women in the 1950s, 1960s, and 1970s were denied training and certification for jobs that involved actual intelligence collection. "Men were the case officers, and women were the reports officers," one CIA officer told me, describing a rigid division of labor whereby men ran spy rings, recruited assets, and handled them, while women sat at desks, editing and often rewriting the reports they filed, and reining the men in—or trying to.

Even when doing the same work as men, women were expected to do it more cheaply. A friend of mine, a former case officer, described the agency's tactic of hiring women from elite colleges and making them secretaries, which lasted well into the 1980s. "You have to understand," he said, "the women didn't matter."

The women also had to contend with an atmosphere of reckless sexual infidelity, for which Donovan and Dulles set the standard. Women staffers were sent from desk to desk to get people to sign off on cables; on days when they were perceived as especially fetching, they'd be dispatched around for colleagues to gaze upon. One of the early architects of the CIA's clandestine service, Tracy Barnes, told his secretary that men join the CIA because "they crave constant danger and for the sex." According to William Colby, the "romantic activism" of Barnes's colleague Desmond FitzGerald "produced great dinner talk." In postwar Washington, it took a lot of sexual activity on a man's part for it to be considered noteworthy. FitzGerald was behind the agency's many, often bizarre, efforts to assassinate Fidel Castro and embodied what Colby called "the macho atmosphere of secret operations." Colby himself—despite his own reputation as "the choirboy"—was always assessing how women looked. In his memoir, the US diplomat Clare Booth Luce was "extremely attractive," Vietnam was full of "wonderfully pretty women."

The women, no matter how bright or experienced or capable or ambitious, usually started out typing and filing. At first, the records of the CIA were kept on 3 x 5 cards, and it was women who typed these or handwrote them. Name traces—a search of records to see who does what and who knows whom—are essential to spy recruitment; women kept those records and knew their depths and secrets. They built the classified database that became the foundation of the agency's modern high-tech tracking technologies. "Whether the counter-espionage file was a simple card file, as it was initially, or a vast computerized research bank, as it became in CIA, it was impossible to conduct any foreign intelligence collection or to analyze hostile intentions toward the United States without building such a set of records," noted Ray Cline.

And, because they understood the importance of relationships, the women—eventually—began to develop relationships with each other. This took a while and was often discouraged. But over time, they sought solidarity and, sometimes, solace, and learned to join forces. They warred, thrived, and fought an institution that was more than willing to fight back. They would form a sisterhood—and they would win their place.

CHAPTER 3

THE CLERK

TRIPOLI, LIBYA

September 1969

THE APARTMENT HAD BEEN FURNISHED BY THE DIRECTORATE of Plans—lavishly, considering its only occupant was a twenty-two-year-old clerk. Airy, with tile floors and high ceilings, it occupied the entire second floor of a two-story building painted a pale green against the North African heat, with gay orange latticework on the balconies and stairways. Inside, the heavy Western furniture was somewhat at odds with the seaside aspect, but it was Heidi August's first place of her own, and its very existence amazed her.

Just months earlier, Heidi had been living in a rental near Columbia Pike, a gritty corridor of Arlington, Virginia, in a three-story brick building that had been hastily constructed, twenty-five years earlier, to house women workers during World War II. Her three roommates had no idea what she did for a living. Every day, she commuted ten miles to the Central Intelligence Agency's headquarters, now located on a 258-acre tract of countryside in McLean, Virginia, once sleepy farm country near the Potomac River, where the spacious campus—also known as Langley, after the neighborhood it dominated—was close to Washington but far enough to feel discreet and safe from nuclear annihilation.

Now here she was in Libya, with a giant apartment all to herself and a secret office steps from the Mediterranean Sea. The dramatic change of circumstance had come courtesy of Tom Twetten, a mild-mannered clandestine officer who had briefly been her boss back at headquarters. It was Twetten who told Heidi about an opening for a clerk in Tripoli Station—a kind of Girl Friday, employed to assist the men in the station with tasks like making coffee and filing cables. After she applied for the job, and got it, Twetten ushered her into his Mercedes and drove her along the George Washington Parkway to a discreet little Georgetown furniture shop, where the agency had some sort of account.

She would like Libya, Tom, who proved surprisingly adept at select-ing fabric swatches, assured Heidi as they picked out what seemed to her a vast quantity of items. Coffee table, dining room suite, side chairs, beds, rugs, curtains, mirrors—it all went on the government tab. Libya was peaceful and cheap, he told her. The CIA would find her a place to live and pay her a housing allowance, so she'd be living rent-free. She could shop on the local economy and buy discount items at the Amer-ican military PX. Libya was a good place for a girl who wanted to travel—it bordered Tunisia and was a short flight from Europe. The Libyan king, Idris, was an obedient ally, installed by the Allies after the war. The CIA would retain ownership of her furniture and keep it for whatever clerk succeeded her.

Sure enough, Heidi's things had arrived in Libya around the same time she did. The agency even shipped her seafoam-blue stick-shift VW Beetle. The furniture included a full suite for the guest bedroom— from which Heidi's friend Joanie was just now emerging. The two had met during clerical training in DC. Joanie worked as a clerk in Tunis Station—a quick one-hour flight from Tripoli—and, like Heidi, was making her first overseas tour. Heidi had visited her earlier in the sum-mer, and Joanie had flown for a return visit over the three-day weekend.

Today was Monday, September 1, 1969—Labor Day in the States. The weather was insufferably hot. Now, over the buzz of the air-conditioning units, Joanie raised her voice to be heard. She seemed excited.

"I hear gunfire," she said, as Heidi remembered it later.

HEIDI'S LIVING ROOM OPENED onto a balcony, so the women went outside to see what was happening below them in the street. Directly across the alley was the building that housed Libya's state-run television and radio stations. The women could see men with guns and office workers being dragged into the street. "Holy crap," Heidi thought. She had never seen a coup, but this was exactly what she would expect one to look like. In the event of a takeover, rebels would need a means to communicate with the citizenry and proclaim their power. If this was the case—if the Libyan monarchy was being overthrown—it amounted to a CIA intelligence failure of the first order.

Heidi thought quickly. The CIA's chief of station, Art Close, ran a clandestine office out of the US embassy building in downtown Tripoli, where agency officers worked undercover. The agency also maintained a small second office about eight miles outside the city, on Wheelus Air Base, where Heidi worked. Bordering the sea, with palms and the Tripoli skyline in the distance, Wheelus was the largest US military base outside the United States. Built by the Italians in 1923, it had been used by the German Luftwaffe to fly bombing sorties during the early years of World War II. In 1943, the Allies liberated North Africa and took possession. As the Cold War heated up, the US Air Force began stationing McDonnell-Douglas RF-4C Phantom II fighter-bombers on the base, in the event of war with the Soviet Union.

The air base was a city in its own right, boasting a beach club, a radio and TV station, a bowling alley, movie theaters, and a high school where members of the military and American oil executives sent their children. The CIA had its own base in a compound near the edge. Better defended than the embassy station, the base office held the most sensitive papers. Evenings, it was Heidi's job to lock them up in one of the station's twelve safes: hard copies of classified cables and memos as well as carbon paper and typewriter ribbon. She emptied trash cans and put the contents in burn bags; she burned the bags. She filed, typed, shredded, and did whatever else was needed to help the men with their mission of countering Soviet influence in Africa, retaining Western access to Libya's shallow oil wells, and watching over the cooperative king. His wife, the queen, liked to shop at the PX, which closed for everyone else during her visits.

Like most of the CIA's Africa stations, Tripoli Station was small and short-staffed, and already her duties were expanding. The administrative officer had gone on home leave for two months. Before he left, he had taught Heidi to operate the darkroom and develop film taken by the officers or handed over to them by assets. He had also taught her to use the station's coding machine.

So busy was the base that Heidi was not sure what went on in the main office downtown. The two staffs were not supposed to have contact. She had seen Art Close only once, when he slipped into the base office on a visit. Her immediate boss was the chief of base, Ray Monahan, an old Africa hand who was also a recovering alcoholic. Heidi sensed he might have traded one addiction for another. There was a slot machine in the NCO club on base, where Monahan could often be found, a Gauloise cigarette hanging from his mouth. Mornings, he had Heidi drive the new cables across the base, and read them aloud while he played the slots. Heidi knew this was an insecure way to treat top secret intelligence, but it didn't seem her place to object.

Heidi, along with a secretary—the only other woman—was the lowest-ranking member of the station hierarchy. Now, as she and Joanie stood on her balcony, it occurred to Heidi that they might be the only people in the US government who knew a coup was in progress in Libya. The men lived in a residential neighborhood with homes large enough to house families and servants. Heidi lived closer to town. There was no point phoning the US embassy; nobody would pick up on a federal holiday.

She had been given Art Close's home number in case of emergency. It seemed to her that a coup qualified. She dialed the number, introduced herself, and said, "I work for Mr. Monahan. I think there's a coup going on."

"You're at home?" the station chief asked. Art Close was a World War II veteran who came from a long line of Princeton men. To Heidi he was unto a god. When she told him yes, he replied, "Can you get to the car?"

"I wrecked it yesterday," Heidi admitted. This was true. The day before, she and Joanie had borrowed the station's Volkswagen and driven south to a region occupied by the Tuareg, a nomadic Berber tribe. As they were heading back from a day of sightseeing, a truck came barreling around a curve and Heidi swerved to avoid a head-on collision. The VW had tumbled down a hillside, the roof getting closer to their heads with each roll. When they came to a stop, there was silence. A recent acquaintance, an American teacher named David, was sitting in the backseat. "Everybody okay?" Heidi asked. They made their way uphill, picking up passports and pottery from the debris field. A man came along and drove them back to Tripoli in a minivan, refusing to accept any cash. After getting checked out at the hospital on base, Heidi and Joanie made spaghetti and drank red wine. Heidi had not worked out if she was going to have to pay for the car.

Close, however, did not seem surprised by the revelation that the station's shared vehicle had been totaled; car accidents happened in Africa all the time. "Do you have your own car?" he asked. Heidi told him she did. He told her that if she could get out of her garage, she needed to get to the base and start burning papers.

Heidi grabbed a toothbrush and the car keys. Joanie said she'd come, and the two women got in the car and made their way through the commotion on the street. It was frightening—the first time she had heard gunshots fired in anger—and exhilarating.

On the way, it occurred to Heidi to stop by the home of the Air Force colonel in charge of the base. When there was no answer at the front door, she followed the smell of bacon to the back and knocked on a screen door to the kitchen. The colonel emerged. Heidi introduced herself and told him there seemed to be a coup going on and they might want to close the base. She told him she had to go, and, she recalled, "I left him and he was just sort of speechless."

A CLERK'S JOB WAS not what Heidi August had expected when she applied to work at the CIA. Granted, the first time she wrote to inquire about employment, she was eleven and the year was 1958. As a girl growing up in Arizona, where her father ran the family shoe business and her mother ran their home, she developed a keen interest in the world beyond Tucson. Her parents subscribed to *Newsweek* and other periodicals of the day, and she was intrigued by articles about the Central Intelligence Agency. This was a time when the agency enjoyed free rein to combat Communism with a mission that was roughly threefold: to collect information about the plans and capabilities of foreign countries; to analyze the intelligence and inform the president and national security community of what was happening or likely to happen; and to engage in covert actions to execute the president's policy in ways that couldn't be done openly. The American public was largely supportive of this secret work, if ignorant about what, exactly, it entailed.

"The need for clandestine covert action to fight the Cold War was accepted as an article of faith," William Colby would later put it in his memoir, and "the CIA had carte blanche to liberate Europe from the communist yoke." In addition to recruiting and handling foreign agents, the CIA was wielding secret influence by purchasing and running corporations and foundations, publishing fake newspapers, buying off political parties, and receiving, as Colby put it, "unqualified backing" from the American public, enabling years of "explosive growth." The US president had a say over operations, and what he said was: yes. By and large, the press took a benevolent approach; a 1953 *Time* magazine cover story on Allen Dulles noted that he was a "scholarly, hearty, pipe-smoking lawyer" with the "cheery, manly manner of a New England prep school headmaster" who "runs the agency smoothly and with apparently inexhaustible energy" and "spends as much time as possible with his wife" at their "handsome shore place on Long Island."

What Heidi read in the newsweeklies sounded enticing. She formed the notion that she would like, as an adult, to live in Paris, and the CIA might be a way to get there. She didn't know anybody who worked for the federal government, apart from an uncle who worked as some sort of economist at the State Department, a job that sounded boring. Heidi enjoyed imagining herself in exotic locales where dramatic events took place. Another uncle sometimes visited Cuba to gamble; he and his wife happened to be in Havana on January 1, 1959, the day Fidel Castro shut down the island's mob-run casinos. The way her uncle told it, lights started flashing, soldiers crashed in, and everybody was ordered to leave. He was holding a lot of chips and lost a lot of money. Heidi thought it would be thrilling to find herself in a place at the very moment when history was being made. She wrote the CIA a letter and received a brochure explaining how to become a clerk-typist.

Ten years later, during her senior year at the University of Colorado at Boulder, Heidi attended a job fair. That year, 1968, was one of anguish and turmoil, one of the strangest, most unsettling years in the second half of the twentieth century. America's escalating involvement in Indochina; the assassination of Martin Luther King, Jr.; the ensuing riots, the TV footage of Washington, DC, on fire; billows of smoke from behind the US Capitol—it was shocking and terrifying, and would only get worse as the year progressed, with the assassination of Robert Kennedy in June. By then, the public bloom had somewhat gone off the Central Intelligence Agency's rose. In 1961, the infamous Bay of Pigs mission had ended with Cuban exiles stranded on a beach being slaughtered, abandoned by the US government that had sent them to overthrow Castro. The failed operation made the CIA look like "bunglers," as Colby put it, exposing the extent to which, in their unchecked freedom and high-handed arrogance, the men of the spy agency had led it into misguided foreign covert actions, including assassinations and the overthrow of democratically elected leaders. An exposé in *Ramparts* magazine revealed that as part of its proxy war with the Soviet Union, the CIA was funding, and aspiring to control, student organizations devoted to mutual understanding and world peace. On the East Coast, CIA recruiters now might be bodily ejected from campuses. Things had not yet reached that point at Boulder, which, while experiencing protest and unrest, remained a party school with great skiing nearby. At any rate, nobody prevented the CIA from setting up a recruiting booth; or maybe most people didn't notice.

HEIDI DID. AS A graduating senior and a political science major, she remained keenly interested in living in Europe. The question remained: how to get there. In 1968, Heidi's female classmates were mostly planning to get married, work as schoolteachers, or both. Newspaper classified ads were still divided into men's jobs and women's. Women's work consisted of teaching, nursing, secretarial work, or writing articles for a newspaper society page. Feminism was emerging—in 1963, Betty Friedan's *The Feminine Mystique* had set off strong reactions in American kitchens and bedrooms, introducing the notion that domestic life was not the be-all and end-all of a woman's existence—but the culture had not yet caught up. Law and medical schools awarded few spots to female applicants, and job opportunities in those fields were few.

For a young woman, there were three ways to find work overseas. The most obvious was as a stewardess, glamorous work that offered lots of travel but also came with height, weight, and age requirements, not to mention marital ones—stewardesses had to be single—making it a temporary pursuit, not a career. Another way was as a secretary to a corporation with offices overseas. The third was government service. To Heidi, this seemed the best option. At the job fair on the Boulder campus, she approached the booth and inquired. The recruiter handed her a brochure. Heidi looked down and saw that it was the same clerk-typist pamphlet she had gotten in the mail ten years earlier. Then the recruiter turned back to her male classmates.

Heidi applied anyway. She didn't hear anything, so after graduation she went to San Francisco, where her parents now lived, and worked at the front desk of the Hilton Hotel. After about a year, she got a call from Washington: The agency had completed a background check and offered to hire her as a secretary at the GS-4 level. She would have to pay her way to the East Coast. She flew herself to Washington, purchased the seafoam Beetle, found a room in a boarding house near Dupont Circle, then moved into the apartment near Columbia Pike in Arlington.

Her first week at the CIA, Heidi had been directed to an office building in Rosslyn, Virginia, a suburb on the Potomac River across from Georgetown. Rosslyn was an urban cluster designed to be a city of the future, by planners who thought that in the future, humans would want to cross surface roads and highways by means of elevated walkways that loomed thirty feet in the air, accessed by stairways that were dark, remote, and dangerous for a woman walking alone.

The CIA maintained offices in several anonymous buildings in this concrete outpost. In one, Heidi found herself seated in a windowless room where she and dozens of other young women were taught to fold maps. The maps, unclassified, depicted cities and regions around the world and were used by operations officers in foreign stations who needed detailed knowledge of geographic features, potential meeting places, and street layouts. The maps came off the printers in big sheets. It was the women's job to hand-fold them according to a pattern that Heidi would, as it turned out, never forget. After a half day, Heidi went to the supervisor to complain. She said it had been her understanding she would work at CIA headquarters. The supervisor, a woman, told her to sit down and keep folding.

She eventually realized that the map folding room was a holding pen where the women were put to work while their security clearances were completed. After hers came through, Heidi was assigned a lower grade than she expected. Since she did not know shorthand, she was hired as a clerk at the GS-3 level, rather than a secretary at GS-4. But at least she would be working at headquarters.

The entrance to CIA headquarters off Route 123 was easy to miss, just a small, discreet entrance flanked by bushes and trees, with a sign outside that read BUREAU OF PUBLIC ROADS. Heidi drove to the guard gate and gave her name, then parked and made her way along the leafy and tranquil campus, walking through the entrance with a feeling of awe. She found herself standing in the grand lobby of the spacious headquarters envisioned by Allen Dulles, who wanted a relaxed, cerebral, campus-like aspect, though he was never able to enjoy it firsthand. After the debacle of the Bay of Pigs, it had been thought best to replace the war hero with a new director, John McCone, who retreated from covert operations and focused on building the agency's technical capability as America moved into the era of the space race and U-2 spy plane.

Outside the building was a statue of Nathan Hale, the Revolutionary War spy. Inside was a statue of William Donovan. On one wall was the biblical passage from John, "And ye shall know the truth and the truth shall make you free." Embedded in the floor and impossible to miss was the large granite seal of the CIA: an eagle, a shield, and a sixteen-point compass star. Somebody had told Heidi you got in trouble for walking over the seal, so she walked around the edge for several days, until she realized she had been pranked.

Heidi found her way to the personnel office, where she was informed she had a temporary assignment to Africa division's North Africa branch, which included Tunisia, Morocco, Algeria, Egypt, and Libya.

"There must be some mistake," she said. There was not.

NOW HEIDI'S GOAL WAS to reach Wheelus before whoever had seized power did. At the entrance, she told the guard a coup was likely in progress, then sped across the base to the compound. As part of her clerical training, Heidi had watched a black-and-white "emergency destruction" video. The idea that it might fall to her to burn out a station on her first assignment had seemed implausible, and she found herself wishing she had paid more attention. She asked Joanie what she remembered from the video; the answer was, not much. Joanie, a math major in college, had helped Heidi get through the bookkeeping portion of training.

Heidi had locked up classified material before the start of the three-day weekend, and now a dozen safes had to be unlocked. Heidi and Joanie started grabbing papers and carrying them to an incinerator that stood outside, in a little breezeway between the office and a nearby warehouse. The women started shoving in papers. Before long, the incinerator broke. It has been on its last legs and the coup situation finished it off.

Heidi did remember there should be a drum for burning classified papers. They hunted around until they found a key to the warehouse. Inside, they picked their way through a tangle of equipment until they found the drum, sure enough, elevated on a pallet in the back. It was a heavy steel barrel with a grate on top, lined by a thick fuse coiled inside like a fat black snake.

Heidi also remembered the fuse should not be lit in an enclosed space, so the women found a forklift. It took some more hunting to find the keys, and then one of them clambered into the forklift, eased the drum off the pallet, and drove the forklift to the open-air courtyard. They dropped the drum and resumed grabbing papers, taking whole files and dropping them in flat. They lit the fuse, placed the grate on top, and—waited.

Nothing happened. By stuffing the papers tightly, they had created a solid unburnable mass. The two women unloaded the files and started wadding pieces of paper and tossing them in. The wind picked up, and top secret documents began flying and getting stuck in bushes.

It was about then that they noticed the *thwap thwap* of helicopter rotors. The Libyan air force had taken to the skies. Were the pilots participating in the coup or fending it off? It was impossible to tell. Either way, flames would be visible for miles. The two women could be seen from the air—and shot. They took the files and locked themselves into the fortified station vault.

Presently the men showed up, along with their wives and children. The officers had heard about the coup on the shortwave. There was an air, now, of panic. The men managed to drag the drum closer to the door, and Heidi showed the kids how to wad papers. "Don't read it," she said. "Just crumple it." They slept in the station for several nights. Joanie stayed until the rebels reopened the airport. Then she flew back to Tunis.

The coup had been led by an Air Force officer named Muammar Qaddafi. The son of a Bedouin goat and camel herder, whose illiterate parents worked hard to get him an education, Qaddafi as a young man had come to deeply resent the British presence in Libya and the postwar rule of a corrupt, lazy king beholden to powerful Western oil interests. An adherent of Arab nationalism, he aspired to socialism and organized a cabal of like-minded officers who took advantage of the king's family vacation abroad. The coup started in Benghazi, the royal capital, at dawn. What Heidi witnessed was the uprising as it spilled over into Tripoli. Despite the commotion she witnessed, the takeover turned out to be bloodless.

The coup came as a shock to the Nixon administration, who had had no inkling that the pliant, pro-American king was about to be toppled by a son of the Bedouin desert. For more than forty years, Qaddafi would be one of the world's leading sponsors of terrorist attacks against Western nations. If the CIA station had been doing its job, Heidi later reflected, the officers she worked for would have cultivated sources in the Libyan air force. After all, the Libyans were sharing the base. Qaddafi himself had taken an English language class there. "We were flying blind," Heidi recollected. She kept asking the men: *Why didn't we know?* They shrugged and couldn't give her a clear answer.

For eight months, Tripoli Station existed in limbo. Art Close, the station chief, had some sort of nervous collapse and had to be medevaced home. Even before the coup occurred, the Pentagon had agreed to withdraw from Wheelus. It took almost a year to work out a withdrawal plan. The CIA base office continued to function. There was more, not less, to do. With Close's departure, the station had a handful of men—and Heidi. At five foot three, with a quiet but forthright manner and a gift for logistics, she was smart and alert. As a young white woman, she would be taken for a tourist, teacher, or student.

One day, one of the case officers approached Heidi and said he needed help with a job he thought she'd be good at. He drove her around the administrative capital, showing Heidi the park benches and other locations where he would leave dead drops. A "dead drop" is a means of communication between a case officer and an asset, or between officers of cooperating intelligence services. He showed her how to roll a coded message, insert it into an empty ginger ale can, and place it under a bench. The ginger ale was a foreign brand. She noticed the same brand in the refrigerator in the apartment of her dark-haired British boyfriend, Michael, who lived across the street. She realized Michael was likely an undercover intelligence officer. He might be in touch with someone at the station where she worked. She knew better than to ask.

During the day, Heidi performed her clerk duties and practiced tradecraft. In the evenings, the station officers partied and had dinner. She was not a drinker, but most of the men were. Overseas, the agency made sure liquor was cheap and always in stock at the PX. Qaddafi, however, declared no alcohol could leave the base, and Libyan soldiers began checking cars. To thwart the regime, Heidi's colleagues ran a clandestine operation to get some of their liquor cache past the inspectors. Still at the base was a huge jeep left over from the desert campaigns of World War II. The jeep had two auxiliary fuel tanks, which, when empty, proved perfect for stashing bottles. Two bottles fitted in each tank, so they could get four bottles out with each run. To Heidi, "this was just huge great fun."

AFTER EIGHT MONTHS, THE United States departed Libya, and so did Heidi. Soon she received a cable saying she was being posted to Germany. Finally, Europe! As of March 1970, Heidi was assigned to work as a secretary in Bonn Station. She was detailed to the "liaison" branch, which cooperated with European intelligence agencies. It was hard to imagine a more important posting than Bonn, where West Germany's main CIA station was located (later, it would move to Berlin). Bonn provided a base for spy missions against East Germany and Communist-controlled Europe and was tasked with staving off a much-feared Soviet incursion through the Fulda Gap. To Heidi, an assignment to Germany sounded like something out of a John le Carré novel. And in fact, that's exactly what it was: Bonn was where le Carré set his novel *A Small Town in Germany,* published the year before she got there.

She arrived during a May snowstorm. Collecting her beloved VW from the port of Bremerhaven, she found the car had been stripped of its engine somewhere between Africa and Europe. After a few weeks, she felt bored out of her mind. Bonn was a huge station. Working there was like working at headquarters, and not in a good way. Her branch alone boasted four or five secretaries. The secretaries dressed up for work every day. In Libya, she had worn jeans. Heidi sat among the other prim young women, a nobody among nobodies. She lived in an embassy compound along the Rhine River and dated a Marine guard. She spent her days typing reports, filing, making coffee, and answering the phone for the branch chief, a stuffy man who wore a three-piece suit. The secretaries called him Mr. Peepers.

She was elated when a small office was opened in Düsseldorf, with a slot for an "operational support assistant" to handle finance and communications. She applied and was accepted. By now she had a new VW, purchased with the insurance money from her old one. Düsseldorf, a center of international finance, was prosperous and bigger than sleepy Bonn. Her new boss was Hans Jensen, a World War II aviator who had been a gold medal rower at the 1948 Olympics. He was a charming man with a lovely wife and a welcoming household. "He wasn't too smart, but he was a real gentleman," Heidi remembered.

When Heidi arrived, Jensen said he did not know anything about finance or communications. "I'll just leave this all in your hands," he told her.

In Düsseldorf, the CIA had an "inside office" within the US consulate, consisting of Hans Jensen and Heidi. There was an "outside office" consisting of several NOCs—spies working under nonofficial cover, which meant they were embedded in the private sector and had no diplomatic protection. Heidi took care of the NOCs. She learned to "vanish" expense accounts, disguising what was spent and who was spending it, a CIA bookkeeping task blandly termed "financial management." She handled coded communications, a time-consuming job that required mastering the idiosyncrasies of a huge encryption machine. To encrypt cables so adversaries (or host governments) could not read them, the station used something called a one-time tape. Messages were punched onto a strip of paper, with holes that functioned as a kind of binary Morse code, then encrypted by means of a "key tape" that created a third, different stream of holes. Sending a cable took hours of slow typing, but Heidi enjoyed the challenge. She would encrypt a cable and pass it to the embassy, where the message would be dispatched, to be deciphered on the other end.

She worked in Düsseldorf for two years. Her boss's health was not good, and he was often absent. Even when Jensen was present, she "literally ran the office."

Jensen often mentioned how nice life was in Scandinavia, so after her tour, Heidi put in for Helsinki, to work for a station chief named David Whipple. The job was as the chief's secretary and administrative officer, agency-speak for "You have to coddle the chief of station."

A lot of chiefs needed coddling—in the sense of needing smart right-hand women to take care of details. This was the era of larger-than-life CIA station chiefs, knocking around the world with money in their pocket, a mission to fight Communist influence, and a mandate to break the laws of other countries. They were men with big personalities, charismatic, eccentric; they tended to be funny, outrageous, and often drunk. Among the best-known Cold War station chiefs was Alan Wolfe, a snobbish and incisively witty man who spouse-swapped when he was chief of station in Kabul, Afghanistan, where Wolfe and his first wife, Nancy, socialized with the archaeologist Louis Dupree and his wife, Annie, in an atmosphere of expatriate intrigue. In the mid-1960s, the couples decided they would prefer to be married to each other's partners, so they switched. Wolfe, according to one secretary, had little interest in women unless they were "exceptionally intelligent or exceptionally sexy." There was Burton Gerber, a Moscow station chief and éminence grise known to throw staplers and whatever else was ready to hand; secretaries rolled their eyes, in a workplace culture where flinging things—typewriters, coffee cups—was by no means out of the ordinary. There was Duane "Dewey" Clarridge, a Russian-speaking alumnus of Brown University who favored white suits and polka dot ties.

Heidi's new boss, Whipple, was a World War II veteran who had played football at Dartmouth. Upon finding out she'd gotten the job in his station, she sold the VW, got a Fiat, and had it shipped to Helsinki.

On home leave in DC, she heard that Whipple wanted to meet her, so she dropped in on the Scandinavian branch of European Division. The secretaries and clerks often traded intel on bosses, so Heidi asked around. "Well, he's kind of an acquired taste," she was told. Still, nothing she had heard prepared her. "I go there and there is this really strange guy with a shaved head and he's wearing a three-piece suit. He kept pacing the floor, and while he was talking to me, he kept rubbing his head and smoking his pipe." He told her that he and his family would be on home leave in the States for two months; she'd be welcome to stay in their house upon arriving in Helsinki. She should keep in mind that the maid ate only tomato soup and there must always be some on hand. "So then he goes up to Cape Cod to finish his home leave and I'm thinking, *This is the weirdest dude.*"

Whipple sprinkled his food with a huge amount of pepper; he loved spicy food and had a wickedly sharp sense of humor. "I always thought David was a little bit crazy," Heidi said. "He could drink an unbelievable amount of wine, and as he got older, he lost the faculty to control it." He'd served in Hanoi, Rangoon, Bangkok, and Katanga—the former Belgian Congo—among others. Heidi found it perplexing that he had moved around the world with such dispatch, given how difficult he found it to get around his own neighborhoods. Her new boss was the kind of person who knew only one driving route to work. "David was sort of helpless. He couldn't do anything for himself," Heidi recalled. His wife, Carolyn, ran his personal life; Heidi ran his work life. He was senior and crusty and could be "kind of nasty" to junior officers, but that didn't bother Heidi. "We got along really well. I wouldn't take a lot of his bullshit. We got to be really really good friends."

Whipple taught Heidi to write an intelligence cable. She would bring him a typed draft, return to her desk, and get a call saying the chief wanted to see her. "I'd say fine, walk into the office, and get hit with this huge wad of paper." Whipple would take the draft, crumple it, and throw it at her. "He would say it was shit, start over, three or four times till you got it right."

Her cables got better. Heidi became an honorary Whipple family member. At dinner he would critique her job performance and she would take his advice. Helsinki Station was important; Finland was a corridor for defectors and assets exfiltrated from Soviet-occupied countries, and Heidi kept track of safe houses in which they could be debriefed. One day, Whipple instructed her to enter a certain apartment, wait until she heard a knock, open the door, collect an envelope, and come back. Heidi set out. It was snowing heavily. She reached the destination, an old European apartment building. She took a rickety lift, found the apartment, put the key he'd given her in the lock—and nothing happened. The key didn't work. She returned to the elevator cage, where she could hear the lift ascending; the agent emerged. "I'm sort of standing there, he didn't know me from a hole in the wall," said Heidi, who asked, carefully, "Are you looking for Dave?" The agent said yes, and she took the message. Whipple had made a sloppy mistake. Back at the office, she took the keys and threw them underhand onto his desk, in return for the cables she'd had thrown at her. Whipple looked up, startled. "Hey, Buster, you gave me the wrong keys," she said.

She liked the work—"It was a quite responsible job, again heavy on the finance"—and she liked her quarters in a guest house on the estate of a Finnish family that ran a beer company. "Whenever I would go home on leave or something to see my parents, I would go see my friends, whatever—I just couldn't describe my life to them at all. And I couldn't identify with anything they were doing."

ONE SATURDAY HEIDI GOT a call from Whipple, asking her to come into the office. He had gotten an eyes-only cable from headquarters. It was 1974. The United States was at the height of its involvement in Indochina, the other great battleground between America and Communist powers. Things were not going well, to put it mildly, and the agency's Cambodia presence was hanging on by a thread. Whipple, who spoke French and had served in Hanoi, was being summoned to serve as chief of Phnom Penh Station.

Heidi said she would be sorry to see him go. No, he said, she didn't understand—it was an unaccompanied tour, meaning families could not come. He was allowed one assistant. He wanted Heidi to go with him to Cambodia.

Up to then, Heidi's career progression could be traced by the cars she purchased. In Germany, she'd sold the VW and bought the Fiat. In a showroom in Bonn, she had seen an unusual Volvo sport wagon, put her name on a list, and got a call saying one was hers if she could come up with $4,800. She sold the Fiat, took out a loan, bought the Volvo, and flew to Gothenburg, Sweden, to take possession. The car was gold and the clutch was stiff. Perched on a pillow, she drove it through a rainstorm back to her place. She loved the car and was loath to leave it. She could not go to Cambodia. "Where are your loyalties?" Whipple demanded. She told him her mother had been diagnosed with breast cancer. Whipple said he would stop in San Francisco and reassure her parents. He made good on his word. "He is the strangest guy I've ever met," her father told her. "But he's very smart and he reassured us that if they decide to have an evacuation, that you'll be on the first plane." Heidi's mother, who was having a bone marrow transplant, urged her to go.

Heidi went to Cambodia as Whipple's logistical alter ego. "My only purpose in being there was the care and feeding of this man." She gave orders to his servants, talked to the cook if he was having people for dinner. They worked twelve hours a day, seven days a week, trying to keep Cambodia in the hands of an elected but chaotic and increasingly corrupt government with whom the United States was allied. "The corruption was just unbelievable, and the Communists were coming down from the North. We had people all over the country, we had these little two-man bases." Every week another village fell. Heidi followed the collapse on the map as the Khmer Rouge drew closer.

On December 31, 1974—New Year's Eve—Heidi was driving home from a party when the sky lit up. It was the beginning of a four-month siege of Phnom Penh. They put fencing around the windows of the US embassy. The CIA office was lined with sandbags. Outside, walkways were covered with corrugated roofing. During intense bombing, embassy officials would take cover. Heidi recalled the US ambassador, John Gunther Dean, pushing people out of the way in his haste to reach the basement. Whipple would stay in his office, smoking a pipe, writing. "I'm not going anywhere," he told her. Heidi stood in the doorway. "I said, all right, I'll explain it to Carolyn."

In the spring, Congress did an end run around the administration to shrink the American presence. The embassy head count was reduced to two hundred, then to fifty. Heidi and David Whipple and a communications officer were the only people left in the CIA station. Heidi and the ambassador's secretary, Beverly, were told to move into the embassy club, a kind of country club the US embassy maintained in an old mansion. Five military attachés moved in because "we don't think you should be alone." The attachés were good-looking, and that part was fun. "My mother's going to kill you," she told Whipple. In truth, she wanted to stay, to see how the siege would end.

There were a lot of items in the communal freezers, including turkeys, and the ambassador decided the time had come to thaw them. Heidi and Beverly organized the dinner, laying out a complete Thanksgiving in April: twenty-five people on one side of a table, twenty-five on the other. They lit candles and opened canned sweet potatoes. The ambassador gave a toast.

The time came for final evacuations. Three helicopters stood ready. The CIA station had an obligation to evacuate local assets. When the agency's top Cambodian asset, a senior government official, showed up with his wife and children, Whipple turned to Heidi. Whipple had promised to get the family out. "How are we going to do this?" he asked her. Cambodian nationals who worked for the embassy were allowed to depart on refugee flights into Thailand, so Heidi forged the names of his wife and children onto the rolls. The asset would leave by helicopter later. She rode with the family to the airport; shots were fired at the SUV as they raced across the runway. "Foot to the floor, foot to the floor," she remembers shouting as they hunkered in the back. The children cried hysterically. "I kept saying 'It'll be okay, it'll be okay.'"

Heidi and her boss were among the last to leave. Whipple insisted on finishing his pipe. They climbed into the back of a truck and jiggled along in darkness to a soccer field. She departed Cambodia under live fire. As the Marine helicopter descended toward a Navy warship, Heidi found herself clinging to a pole, watching through a cargo opening as the ocean got closer.

For her efforts during the evacuation, Heidi was awarded the agency's medal for valor and sent back to Helsinki. (Whipple was posted to Portugal—to, as she laughingly put it, "protect Portugal from the Communists.") In Helsinki, the new station chief, Bill Simonsen, turned out to be a nice man who left all the cable-writing to Heidi. Helsinki Station had many assets but too few case officers, so Simonsen also assigned Heidi to handle an asset with "unbelievable access to North Koreans." Working with an officer in Copenhagen, they ran an operation against North Korean diplomats—who were selling duty-free items on the black market to finance the regime—and got them ejected. Heidi was promoted to GS-7. Reunited with her Volvo, she got an offer, agreed to sell it, and bought a Mercedes. Her boss, Simonsen, called her in. "You really are much more capable than what this job normally calls for," he said, and suggested she consider becoming a case officer.

What he was proposing was all but unheard of. In the mid-1970s, there were only a handful of women among the case officer ranks of the CIA. Case officers were the elite of the elite, like astronauts or fighter pilots. It was widely believed women could not do what the men did: could not persuade a foreign asset to hand over secrets, could not work in male-dominated cultures, could not keep themselves safe on the street. In each class at the Farm, a group of thirty or forty clandestine service trainees might include one or two female aspirants. Those women had usually been specially recruited.

Heidi, in contrast, was on the "nonprofessional track," a constrained, one might say dead-end, channel. Nonprofessionals were clerks, secretaries, and desk officers. People hired into that track did not often jump to the professional track. But here Simonsen was, proposing that Heidi join the ranks of the men she worked for. The suggestion reawakened a dormant goal that Heidi—in her naïveté—had made when she entered on duty. On her first day of work, she had been handed a chart of the civil service pay scale, printed on a little card. The scale started with GS-1, the lowest grade at which workers were hired, then moved to GS-2, GS-3, and so on, showing the salaries for each grade as well as pay raises associated with intermediate "steps" 1 through 9. The first side ended at GS-8, and so did the nonprofessional track. When Heidi flipped the card over, she saw that the scale went from 9 to 15. "And then I understood that there was more after the 15. Those were the super grades." On the flip side, salaries went into the thirty thousands. Heidi's goal was to make it to the flip side.

At Simonsen's urging, European division agreed to sponsor her for a slot at the Farm. In July 1977, Heidi was reassigned to headquarters to prepare for conversion to professional officer status. While she waited, she worked as a name tracer on the Turkish desk. As a former clerk trying to switch tracks, she was what was called a "retread." That was a dismissive term for someone who had not been recruited into the elite cadre of trainees but was trying to claw her way up from below. The implication was that an old tire would never be anything but an old tire; the Farm certification was just a thin veneer of rubber, layered on. It was a slur against women who changed tracks or aspired to. Heidi would be entering the Farm alongside more than a dozen classmates. Many had master's or law degrees or had worked in the private sector. Just one, apart from her, was female. Heidi had only a BA.

Before Heidi left the Turkish desk for the Farm, the head of the division called her in to say one more thing. In Heidi's case, it would not be enough to pass the training. To become a case officer, she had to finish number one in her class. If she failed, she would remain on the non-professional track and spend her career doing support jobs. Headquarters set this standard because she started out as a clerk. And because she was a woman. "They didn't believe I could do the job."

So, she called the only person she knew who could—and would—help her.

CHAPTER 4

THE DIPLOMAT'S DAUGHTER

1966

HURRYING TO CLASS ONE DAY IN THE SPRING OF 1966, LISA Manfull paused at the big, checkerboard-type bank of glass-fronted mailboxes, to see what might be waiting in hers. Lisa was a senior at Brown University, where female undergraduates had historically been part of Pembroke College, a kind of women's annex whose centerpiece was a gloomy red-brick building from the late nineteenth century. Though the sexes took classes together, female students were required to live in a separate dorm where matrons kept an eye on their conduct. With only a few phones in the dormitory, posting and receiving letters was the women's chief means of communication with the outside world. Every day brought envelopes; flyers; tickets; notes from professors or admirers or parents; and, for seniors like Lisa Manfull, missives from graduate schools and prospective employers, sorted into numbered boxes, each with a knob and a small clear window.

As she opened her box, Lisa's eyes widened at the sight of a letter—one she wished to keep hidden from her classmates. She had asked the sender to omit the return address, but as usual, the sender had its own ideas about how it wished to proceed. Brown was a self-consciously progressive and rather hothouse Ivy League environment, where classmates debated Sartre and Camus, read German philosophers, used words like "egocentric," fell asleep in library carrels reading Henry James or *The Animal Mind,* studied and smoked cigarettes simultaneously, pondered "the fragile relationship between the student and the university," and, in the words of the yearbook editors, considered themselves "nerve-racked" while, in "an atmosphere of intense competition," they did differential equations and built card towers out of computer punch cards. They also inclined toward judgmentalism. As sock hops were giving way to sit-ins and an era of student activism, a few signs on campus had appeared protesting America's involvement in Southeast Asia. Government careers, with their taint of establishmentarianism, were falling out of favor.

Lisa slipped the letter in her bookbag and headed to class. She had a decision to make and preferred to make it without scrutiny. The letter had been sent by the CIA.

APART FROM HER GENDER, Lisa Manfull in 1966 was a shoo-in to enter the CIA's elite spy training program. It is hard to think of a twenty-one-year-old who was better qualified. Brown, where three-quarters of undergraduates were male, had been a fertile source of OSS officers during World War II, a legacy that quietly continued in the decades that followed. When Dewey Clarridge, an alumnus, arrived at CIA headquarters in 1955, he realized that "the entire place was staffed with people from Brown." Even now, as the nascent protest era materialized, professors on the Providence campus—like those in Cambridge and New Haven and Princeton—kept their eyes open for prospects, who would find themselves called in for a chat, or contacted after their names had been passed to the personnel office at Langley. Almost always, the candidates were men. But Lisa Manfull was a standout—so much so that, as she approached her graduation, she had begun to be covertly recruited. Her gifts were impossible to ignore.

In part, her distinctiveness derived from an unusual, almost precocious air of worldly sophistication; despite being American, Lisa at twenty-one spoke English with a vaguely French accent. Cropped hair—a shorter, sleeker style than the usual undergraduate bouffant or bob—framed a slim face with an intense, alert aspect: What the French would call gamine. Most Pembrokers wore cardigans, knee socks, and loafers; Lisa favored French couture, stitched by her mother from designer patterns. An air of faint exoticism was not an affectation but rather the natural result of having spent her girlhood as a diplomat's daughter in Paris, making her way along foreign streets and coming of age as something of a stranger in a strange land. In 1952, when she was six, her father, Melvin Manfull, had been summoned to help rebuild Europe, implementing the Marshall Plan from an office in the Hotel Talleyrand. Lisa and her younger brother found themselves nestled in a Pan American Clipper Constellation, and, upon landing in Paris, bundled into a hired car that swept them to the elegant apartment on the Avenue Victor Hugo where they would live for six years. A literal child of the Cold War, Lisa had spent her formative years absorbing the sense of public duty that went along with her father's career in international service.

Melvin Manfull, a protégé of the diplomat Averell Harriman, had pursued a career with the US State Department at a time when America was celebrated as the engine of democracy and liberator of Europe. His wife, Suzanne, served as a vital, if unpaid, accessory, a role that was expected of wives. State Department officers at that time received an annual evaluation in which one of the categories they were graded on was whether their wives served as satisfactory assets. Wives were expected to dress appropriately; to socialize relentlessly; to volunteer selflessly; to represent the United States to their utmost. If a wife faltered, so did her husband's career.

Suzanne Manfull was a former ballerina, a Southern belle, and a conscientious partner to her husband. Before Lisa's eyes, her mother began to transform. In France, Suzanne Manfull shed her quaint Mamie Eisenhower–type wardrobe and acquired a closetful of Parisian suits and dresses. To Lisa, she seemed a new person, almost a stranger— when she was home, which wasn't often. Rebuilding Europe was a full-time job. Both of Lisa's parents were often away for twelve or sixteen hours at a stretch. That was when Lisa began to develop her capacity for self-reliance.

Lisa's parents hired a former actress—Mme Fournez-Garufor—to tutor her in French vocabulary and pronunciation. They enrolled Lisa in L'Institut des Filles de Marie Auxiliatrice, a convent school where she sat in the back, comprehending little. Gradually, she began to pick up on what the French girls were saying, and what they were saying was that she was a little American snot nose. Within a few years, French had become Lisa's first language.

Her childhood had, however, been often lonely. There were no big American backyards to drift into, no spontaneous nighttime games of Kick the Can. Rather, Lisa would go outside and jump on her pogo stick, alone. Her seventh birthday party was celebrated not with raucous friends playing Pin the Tail on the Donkey, but with a hat-shaped cake and a tiny bottle of champagne.

It was also a self-consciously public childhood: Lisa's mother made it clear that America's reputation depended on the perfect conduct of Lisa and her little brother. At parties, the siblings would be trotted out to speak French in their high-pitched children's voices. An obedient child, Lisa was also an attentive one. In their building, the concierge was a Muslim man, a Moroccan, whom tenants treated with disregard. Everyone, that is, except her parents. One day, he asked them if he could show Lisa the Grand Mosque of Paris. They said yes, and he did. Her parents wanted to expose her to other beliefs and ways of thinking. A Jewish friend invited Lisa to a Friday Center—"She was afraid to ask me because there was such prejudice in France against Jews"—and she went. As a teenager, she read the Qur'an.

On holidays, the family rented a small house in Catalonia. During one visit, Lisa noticed the same man lurking wherever they went. The Spanish government suspected her father of spying and had assigned a surveillance officer to watch him. Lisa wrote a report on the man's patterns. The house had a balcony and one day she dropped the report, written in her best Spanish, on his head. "I did it," she recollects, "because I resented the man surveilling."

After six years in France, the family returned to the States and her mother gave birth to another boy. While her parents fixed up a house, twelve-year-old Lisa went to Gonzales, Texas, where her grandfather worked as a doctor. Lisa arrived wearing a little gray suit and a hat, fiercely admonishing her brother to put on his gloves. Her Southern grandmother had no idea what to make of the stiff, French-speaking children who arrived on her doorstep. Her grandmother was mortified when the Texas school district placed her in remedial English, but Lisa felt delighted; her peers were Mexican girls whose warm Catholicism reminded her of the convent school for which she now felt nostalgic. Her English got better, as did her Spanish. When she rejoined her parents, in Washington, she was tested and put into ninth grade at Wilson High School, skipping middle school altogether. That made her two years younger than most of her classmates. Wilson was a fine public school with students from many countries, and she added Russian to her repertoire. She ran with the bookworms, the nerds. She could never figure out why she wasn't part of the popular crowd from Chevy Chase; why boys didn't ask her on dates.

That's when she realized that some ordinary things would not come easily—like fitting in. Robbed of a typical American childhood, she had been given something else: the ability to function, no matter where in the world she was dropped. Upon graduation, she took the Russian and Spanish prizes. She was offered a Foreign Service scholarship to Barnard but chose Brown, where she majored in linguistics and studied Mandarin Chinese.

Brown was a rigorous school, intellectual without being truly broadminded. The student body tended to be cliquish. Most other girls were not friendly. Holidays presented a dilemma. Her father was usually posted abroad, and Lisa often had nowhere to go over Thanksgiving and Christmas. Pembroke closed over the holiday break, so she couldn't stay at school either. The few Black girls on campus were the nicest, and sometimes invited her to their homes. She made friends outside school. She dated older men. "I just made my life outside the college. I wanted to be just one of the girls, but it didn't work out."

IN 1963, LISA'S FATHER was posted to South Vietnam, as political counselor at the US embassy in Saigon. It was a high-level posting at a bleak time, just before the United States would embark on a tragic incursion that would taint its global standing and cost tens of thousands of lives. Some months after her father's arrival, President Ngo Dinh Diem, the dictatorial leader whom the United States had supported, then discarded, was murdered. His assassination was followed by a series of short-lived governments and military coups. At first, Lisa's father had supported the policy of containing Communism in Asia; but by 1965 he changed course and opposed America's military buildup. "His career went into the toilet" is how Lisa put it. "He nearly lost his job."

For Lisa, though, the tragedy of America's coming war in Southeast Asia resulted in "two really incredible summers in Vietnam." Visits to see her parents were among the high points of her life. Her parents lived in a French-built compound with high walls, tile floors, and a pool. They threw parties that attracted soldiers of fortune, architects of US policy, diplomats, South Vietnamese officials. Journalists like Neil Sheehan and David Halberstam were making their names and calling her father at all hours. Members of President Johnson's Georgetown brain trust came and went. Lisa visited Hue, the ancient capital, at the invitation of a Vietnamese girl who had attended a branch of the convent school Lisa went to in France. Her friend's uncle was a Saigon cinnamon king who deployed his private army to escort the two young women to a beach resort, Cap San Jacques, where he owned two villas, side by side, which he occupied depending on which way the wind was blowing. Immensely wealthy, he lectured her about the disadvantages of free trade and the virtues of monopoly.

At Brown, Lisa had written a paper on the Cao Dai, a Vietnamese political religious sect. Upon meeting a general in the sect's private army, she managed to convince him she was a world expert on the Cao Dai. He invited her to give a talk to the faithful in Tay Ninh Province, and she accepted, eager to see their temple, with life-sized statues of "saints" including Joan of Arc and, implausibly, Victor Hugo. One of her father's officers drove her to the airport, or rather, tried to drive her. A road blockage turned out to be another coup in progress, so the officer turned back, to her fury.

She was—she discovered—the type of person who ran toward conflict, not away. She worked with a social welfare group trying to get Buddhists and Catholics to cooperate on projects such as orphanages, and the difficulty taught her about the bitter depth of religious conflict. She spent a night in an abandoned whorehouse near the Perfume River in Hue. It was, she says, a "very stimulating summer."

So stimulating that she took a year off from Brown to figure out where she fitted into the world. Her father had been reposted to Europe, lodged in a hotel with no room for family members, so she hatched a scheme to study Spanish in Guadalajara. Her mother joined her, as did her brothers. They enjoyed six months living abroad without embassy obligations. They lived as ordinary Americans and it was fun. When her dad took a position at the Imperial Defense College in London, the family moved to be with him, and Lisa felt she got to know her mother and father. They seemed to her extraordinary people, and she began to realize what her upbringing had imparted. Her mother always told her to be a good American, and from her father, she was "hardwired on this idea of duty."

By her senior year, Lisa knew she wanted a career in public service. One of her professors had another idea, securing funding for her to pursue a PhD in comparative literature at Yale. Much as she loved languages, however, a scholarly life held little appeal. Another option was working as a translator for the State Department, where her father had gotten her an internship the summer she was seventeen. If she tested for fluency in French, Spanish, and Russian, State would bring her in as a GS-13. But working as a translator felt machine-like to Lisa, and unimaginative.

She never knew how she came to the CIA's attention. Lisa figured a professor may have spotted articles she wrote for *The Brown Daily Herald*. Like her father, she initially felt the United States had a role to play in pushing back Communist influence in Asia; like his, her views evolved away. But when she wrote some op-eds, her classmates decided that Lisa, a liberal Democrat, was a "right-wing nut." In retrospect, she thinks the qualities that set her apart are what sparked the CIA's interest. "I think part of what they saw was somebody who'd lived abroad, who spoke all these languages, and who was active in defense of policy."

Hence the letters in her mailbox. So attractive was Lisa as a candidate that the CIA sent two recruiters, one from the Directorate of Intelligence, which was responsible for generating reports for policymakers in Washington. The other emissary came from the Directorate of Plans—the clandestine service. Lisa knew something about espionage and covert action. In Vietnam, some of her father's political officers were undercover CIA agents. "I certainly got to know the spooks," recalled Lisa, noting that their long hair and rakish demeanors sometimes gave them away.

The quintessential image of the CIA officer in Vietnam was the fictional Alden Pyle, the misguided implementor of American exceptionalism in Graham Greene's *The Quiet American*. And in real life, the CIA's operational legacy was not one to be proud of. The agency's covert arm allowed itself to become a tool of the Nixon administration and of Secretary of State Henry Kissinger, who was interested in action and not in "incomprehensible reports." The American spooks moved throughout Southeast Asia, making payoffs, executing commando raids, fixing elections, and implementing the infamous Phoenix program—a paramilitary campaign to root out Viet Cong agents that turned into a massacre of thousands, including civilians. CIA analysts, however, had a respectable track record; by 1975, CIA director Colby was warning the administration that America would lose. Agency estimates of unwinnability were more accurate than those of the Department of Defense and the White House, even if their dire estimates were received coldly by an administration that, as Colby put it in his memoir, had "an intense, almost *macho* American determination not to lose the contest with the Communists."

THE TWO CIA RECRUITERS who came to Brown did not impress Lisa. They competed even as they remained cagey about the jobs on offer. It was suggested she start as a secretary, which appalled her. She took a battery of tests in a set of trailers near the State Department in Foggy Bottom. She purposely failed the typing exam even though she typed well and had "my own little shorthand," a private code consisting of Chinese characters, stenography, and symbols of her own devising. Next, the DI dangled a job "counting troops"—working as a low-level analyst, studying images of military installations in China. But analysis, like academia, didn't appeal. Analysts had to brief policymakers, and presentations were not her strength.

Lisa was born, she felt, to clandestine spy work. She knew how to melt into a crowd. She was not easily intimidated or put off; she knew how to deploy foreign languages like a native speaker; and, from her parents, had absorbed two key traits. Her mother taught her how to create a new persona and inhabit it. Her father exhibited a fierce work ethic that Lisa inherited. She would need both. If hired by the clandestine service, she would be assigned a cover job with the State Department or some other plausible agency. Her real work would be performed after hours.

The job Lisa wanted was as a case officer, also known as operations officer—the agency's term for spy. Being a case officer was by far the most sought-after job at the CIA. The work entailed spotting foreigners with access to secrets and persuading them to hand those secrets over. It entailed negotiating and persuading. It meant looking after the lives and safety of sources, known as assets or agents. It meant creating a false identity and living a secret life. It meant dispensing large sums of cash, bags and stacks of it, in return for information and cooperation. Nights would be spent meeting assets in cars and hotel rooms, followed by hours of scribbling notes and writing cables. Case officers were like rainmakers in brokerages or law firms; they were expected to land top clients. Most were required to make a major recruitment at least once a year. Being a CIA case officer was the ticket to advancement at one of the top intelligence agencies in the world, at a time when the threat of nuclear war with the Soviet Union defined American life.

The job also imparted freedom and independence. Case officers were employed to convince people to commit treason. They enjoyed great latitude in deciding how to achieve that. It was their mission to befriend strangers, spot their vulnerabilities and appeal to their venalities; dangle schooling or medical treatment or cash, offer to help children or parents or spouses to persuade them to spy. It was not easy work, but Lisa knew she was cut out to do it. But by aspiring to become a case officer, she was taking on an even tougher challenge than she knew. At the CIA, there were jobs for men and jobs for women. Lisa wanted the men's job. The cost of that undertaking was something she would have to find out for herself.

Upon her graduation in 1966, she went to visit her parents while a background check was conducted. Her father was now deputy chief of mission at the US embassy in Brussels. There, the formidable US ambassador's wife needed an American to represent the embassy at Le Bal des Débutantes, an international debutante ball, so she drafted Lisa, who reluctantly slipped into a white dress. To occupy her time, Lisa took Chinese lessons and dabbled in Japanese.

While in Europe, Lisa got a call saying she had been accepted into the CIA's February 1968 career training program. She would be part of a select group of spies in training. She relocated to Washington and presented herself at Langley. She was hired as a GS-7. One of her first discoveries was that the men were brought in as GS-8s.

CHAPTER 5

FLAPS AND SEALS

RURAL YORK COUNTY, VIRGINIA

1968

S PY TRAINING HAD EVOLVED IN THE DECADES SINCE WORLD War II and the brownstone in Washington, but retained much of the spirit of role-playing and fantasy honed at the wartime "stations" set up by the OSS. Lisa Manfull's first weeks with the agency were spent at headquarters in Langley. She and her fellow recruits signed loyalty and secrecy oaths, filled out paperwork, and took classes on national security. Then they traveled south to "the Farm," also known as Camp Peary, a residential installation on a military base in eastern Virginia. Under the tutelage of former case officers, recruits took the wobbly baby steps of tradecraft. They practiced the classic cycle of "spotting, assessing, and recruiting": learning how to recognize a likely prospect; how to develop a relationship, set up a meeting, talk the prospect into betraying his own country. They learned how to pass a message, how to devise a surveillance detection route, or SDR—a circuitous way to approach and leave an encounter, to ensure they were not being followed.

According to many accounts of the Farm written over the years, in a course called "flaps and seals," recruits steamed open envelopes, slit pouches, and mastered ways to read other people's mail. They learned how to pick locks, bug hotel rooms, approach a safe house. They built radios, donned disguises. They listened to Russian defectors talk about life in the Soviet bloc. They practiced "bumping"—striking up a conversation in a bar or grocery store to make a contact. At watering holes in nearby Williamsburg, Virginia, they recruited instructors put there as plants.

At the end of training, top CIA officers would woo them. The Directorate of Plans was divided into geographic divisions: Africa, Latin America, European, Near East, Far East, and so on, each with its own personality and reputation. The most sought-after division was Soviet bloc—later named Soviet and Eastern Europe—whose officers operated in Moscow and Communist-controlled areas. These countries were known as "hard targets" because they had top-notch spy services of their own. Once recruited into a division, you'd likely spend your career there. Graduation from the Farm was a pivotal, life-altering moment.

And it was a moment when old-boy connections became the order of the day. Twenty years into its existence, the agency had distinct cliques—the Greek Americans, the Ivy Leaguers, plus the geographic divisions themselves—and the men in each looked out for one another. The heads of divisions were among the most powerful people at the agency; they were known as the barons. During training, word would trickle up to Langley about which recruits were doing well at the Farm, and the barons would visit, to glad-hand and win the best ones over. "The division chiefs were the feudal lords," Lisa recalled. "They would come down for kind of spotting and assessing sessions, and they would try to recruit people they wanted. Well, nobody's recruiting the women."

When Lisa started in 1968, the case officer trainee corps was almost entirely male and white. Recruits had already been winnowed, beginning with a secretive recruiting effort directed at certain people with certain backgrounds. Extensive testing—psychological testing, a polygraph or lie detector test, background checks—provided another means by which recruits could be eliminated without recourse. During the polygraph sessions, applicants were aggressively queried on their sexual behavior, desires, and preferences, to unnerve them and to weed out anybody who was homosexual. These were known as "lifestyle" questions, and they were relentless. To be gay or lesbian was grounds for disqualification. Nobody argued. The security office, which conducted the background checks and kept an eye out for infractions once an officer was hired, tended to be staffed by white men who skewed socially conservative. Lisa came to know a man, a clandestine officer, who was homosexual but did not act upon his desires. He never married or partnered. He just didn't have sex. Even then, the men in charge looked askance at him. He was never made chief of a station. He could have run one, standing on his head. But he did not present as sufficiently masculine. The only thing worse than being a womanish man was being an actual woman.

And in the almighty Directorate of Plans—soon to be renamed the Directorate of Operations—the bias against women was openly expressed. Nobody hid it. The view was that there were some skills, like clerking and typing and filing and record keeping, women were good at; and others at which they were not. Common wisdom held that women lacked the fortitude for recruiting assets and had an especially hard time in patriarchal cultures. "Not too many women are suited to the way of life of a field case officer" is how one case officer put it in a 1973 pamphlet, given that the job entailed meeting "spooky agents in back street hotel rooms."

The sentiment was pervasive and nobody was ashamed of saying it, recalled Jonna Mendez, who worked in the technical office developing spy gadgets like tiny cameras and hidden microphones—the real-life version of Q in the James Bond novels. Case officers visited her office to learn how to use the gadgets, and Mendez was the one who taught them. "They just didn't think a woman could run an operation," said Mendez. "They didn't think a woman could *start* an operation." The case officers even doubted Mendez's own ability to train foreign assets to use CIA technology, telling her that assets likely wouldn't listen to a female instructor.

As her own Farm training proceeded, Lisa began to realize that the recruiters had deceived her. Having lured her in, the Directorate of Plans was steering her into a female channel. In her class, just five recruits were women. Most were there to train as analysts in overseas stations, where they would evaluate information and write papers for the Directorate of Intelligence. Others were being trained as reports officers, who, while they did work for the Directorate of Operations, were not spies. This sacred division of labor in the clandestine service— men as case officers, women as reports officers—reflected the culture at overseas stations, where, as one reports officer put it, "men worked out- doors, and women worked indoors."

Which is not to say that the indoors jobs weren't important; they were. The whole point of collecting intelligence is to write it up and pass it along to people who need to see it and are authorized to do so. After each meeting with an asset, a case officer was required to file two reports: one summarizing the intelligence imparted, and another de- scribing the asset who supplied it. These went to a reports officer, who would edit the language, strip out details that might reveal the identity of a source, put it into standard format, perhaps even rewrite it, and if necessary, instruct the case officer about what constituted intelligence and what did not. Reports officers would consider field intelligence alongside "all source" intelligence, which consisted of reports from headquarters, foreign partners, the military, US agencies, and other CIA stations, not to mention the local press. The reports officer could rate the likely accuracy of the new information, often appending a "sta- tion comment," a gloss or annotation. Was the information good? Bad? Was the asset likely lying? The reports officer would transmit the report to headquarters, where another reports officer decided who should see it. Relevant parts would be distributed to analysts, policymakers, the Justice Department, the Pentagon, the National Security Council, and what is known as the "First Customer": the president of the United States.

Alongside the reports officers, there existed many, many women in other support roles. These included clerks, desk officers, and women with even more specialized positions; "rovers" were crisis handlers who flew in, like Mary Poppins, to fix things in overseas stations. As one ops officer put it, rovers were hyper-competent types who could "be what- ever the station needed," spending five or six months filing cables or smoothing personnel misfires or putting expense accounts into order. The rovers were stoic women who could land anywhere—Cape Town, Cairo—and fill any job. They carried huge designer handbags, because what else were they going to spend their money on? They were almost always single, because what husband would follow a wife from pillar to post? The women supporting the clandestine services were "brides of the agency," as the phrase had it.

Of the female jobs, reports officers were among the most high-level. Reports officers—inevitably, women—functioned as editors. It was their job to remain objective and cold-eyed; to look for gaps and contradictions; to package the product and vet it; to receive instructions from headquarters about what else was needed and tell the case officer what questions to ask his source at their next meeting.

It was their role to push back—den mothers in a workplace where it was understood boys would be boys. In the espionage business, problems were bound to arise. The opportunities for bad information were myriad. Because of quotas and performance evaluations, case officers had a strong incentive to exaggerate the merits of an asset and were not above making up a report from whole cloth. Assets had a strong incentive—money—to keep producing even when there was nothing to produce. Back in Washington, policymakers had a strong incentive to cherry-pick intelligence that enabled them to do what they wanted. Had a case officer become overattached to his source and begun insisting everything the source asserted was gospel truth, a malady known as falling in love with your asset? Reports officers were the main line of defense, pushing back against all these pressures and temptations.

It was the women's job to make sure "somebody was not feeding us a line of crap," as one reports officer, Amy Tozzi, put it. Tozzi had been hired into the clandestine service a few years before Lisa Manfull. During a career that took her through Latin America at the height of CIA's notorious involvement in coups and assassinations, Tozzi had a frontline view of what the men were up to. Fluent in Spanish, she had been recruited as a secretary, despite being, as she put it, "overtrained." She served in Argentina, where "the coups were so frequent, the generals would just call one another up and say: Which side are you on?"

In another posting, it fell to Tozzi to inform a case officer that an asset of his, a colonel, had retired and was using newspaper articles to flesh out his reports. Tozzi knew this because she spoke Spanish and took the time to read the local papers. She had one chief of station who told her to go easy on the case officers, and stop browbeating them for so much accuracy, to which she replied, "Do you want the facts? Or do you just want to pay for crap?"

THESE—REPORTS OFFICER, ANALYST, CLERK—were CIA jobs to which women were accepted. Promotions would come more easily if Lisa Manfull let herself be swept along the well-carved female channel. The thing was, Lisa didn't want to work in the female channel. She wanted to use her native gifts. She also understood that the sacred division of labor stemmed not just from bias but from self-interest. In the CIA's postwar structure, the pyramid of jobs was wide at the bottom and sliver-thin at the top. Case officers belonged to a tiny fraternity. Only a select few would become chiefs of station. Even fewer would become barons or occupy top jobs on the seventh floor of headquarters. There, in expansive offices with views of the Potomac River, the men conspired with and undermined one another, competing for the choicest jobs. They had the best parking spaces, the lushest carpets. In meetings, they didn't have to hold so much as a pencil; others took notes. They weren't about to let women make the competition tougher. More than any other directorate, operations—the clandestine service—was a stronghold of masculinity.

"Nobody wanted a female. They told me women cannot do operations, women cannot recruit," recalled Janine Brookner, the other woman in Lisa's class who aspired to case officer status. Brookner had arrived at the Farm with a master's degree in political science from New York University and an unusual (at the time) life situation: She was a single, divorced mother with a young son. And, like Lisa, she was determined to go overseas as a spy. But it wasn't just men who deemed women unfit for operations work; the personnel office, staffed by women, concurred. "I went down to the career management office and told them what I wanted to do," said Brookner, who talked to a counselor. "She was like: 'You're not going to be a case officer.' This was *another woman.*"

Lisa Manfull, like Janine Brookner, set out to prove them wrong. She did well during Farm training—better, she sensed, than expected. Her supervisor seemed flummoxed. Without explanation, she was sent for extra psychological assessment. In evaluating recruits, psychologists looked for traits like charisma, sociability, tolerance for ambiguity, and willingness to take risks. Lisa didn't know any other trainees who had to sit with a shrink for an extra three days. The verdict was: qualified.

And so the agency played a trump card. Unseen authorities cut short Lisa's training. After she completed the "short course"—a one-month course known as ops familiarization, designed for lower-level staffers— Lisa was told to return to headquarters. "I was not allowed to finish the course.... And you can't get an assignment as a case officer unless you've been certified."

Her classmate Janine Brookner ran into similar problems. Brookner completed the full course and passed, only to find that no division chief would hire her. Baron after baron said no. Far East. Africa. Europe. "Nobody wanted me." So Brookner found herself in a dingy office in the basement of headquarters, working under protest for an operation that was illegally spying on American dissidents, including students and civil rights activists, in violation of the CIA's charter not to spy on US citizens or engage in domestic operations.

The winsome promises of the recruiters had come to naught. Lisa went into limbo, stuck handling cables and reports. "I was really just like a leper." She did well but found nobody to help her. She could see young men her own age being mentored and taken to lunch by more senior men. She had no clique, no network, no helping hands extended.

AS LISA WAS TRYING to make her way in the clandestine service in the early 1970s, there was not yet a sisterhood to tap into. Heidi August encountered the same thing. No female barons, no female station chiefs, and few female case officers. At headquarters—as in overseas stations— there were multitudes of women but few in positions of true authority. Women worked turnstiles making sure employees had the requisite badge to enter a classified area. Women procured passports; women handled expense reports.

And women guarded vaults of top secret files. At headquarters, at that time, most work spaces were not secure. Officers had to keep their own papers in individual safes; security officers patrolled at night and checked. The only truly secure spaces were rooms known as vaults, and these were where the classified paper records about people and operations were kept. These archives were windowless rooms that, like a bank vault, were themselves safes. Tiny, miserable places to work in, they were obscure spaces illuminated only by electric lights. And yet, they were literally the brains and memory of the Central Intelligence Agency. The women who worked in them—ostensibly insignificant people who rarely left to so much as visit the cafeteria—knew everything about the most top secret operations. They were called by a jumble of titles, including intelligence analysts, intelligence operations research analysts, or IORAs, and, later, staff operations officers, or SOOs.

The names and acronyms changed, in part because no term easily encapsulated the crucial role the so-called vault women played. They analyzed operations: Is a source good, is he being handled properly, what information about an operation do officers working another operation need to know? They kept records dating back to the days of the OSS, with hard-won biographical information about foreign scientists, politicians, military commanders, and agents. The record-keeping women wore tennis shoes, since they were on their feet all day; hence their other belittling nickname: sneaker ladies. Their footwear was a marker of sorts, setting them apart from the rest of the female workforce, who felt obliged to wear heels. But the sneakers were also, in a way, a disguise, masking their importance and even power.

The vault women were not friendly. Some were spouses of officers. Many were fearsome. In the Soviet division, as well as east Asia and China, the most highly classified information was known as "restricted handling," or RH. It was kept in wooden drawers. A desk officer, dispatched by a boss to get information, would approach and ring the doorbell. A vault woman would materialize. The officer would present a signed form. "They would kind of snatch the form from you," recalled one operations officer, Mia McCall, who, like most clandestine service recruits, worked on the desk before doing her own Farm training in the 1980s. The officer would wait, peering into the space, which "had nothing electronic other than the lights." No typewriters, even. Everything was handwritten on index cards and legal paper. The women were like mushrooms; they seemed to thrive in low lighting. The vault woman would place a call, verify permission to access the documents, then pull them, place them in an envelope, and grudgingly hand them over. "Those vault women were legends," McCall said. "Guardians of the sanctum sanctorum."

Granted, their power was local. "They were kind of—shunned isn't the right word, but looked down on," McCall added. "We were respectful to their faces, but not behind their backs."

In truth, the vault women were key. Their work was labor-intensive and low-tech. It consisted mostly of processing paper. They created a niche that no man wanted, but it was a much-needed niche even so. They could also be found in "back rooms," which were secrets parts of a division that nobody talked about. Case officers might occasionally hear senior leadership saying, "That's got to go into a back room," and they'd find that a case they were handling had been taken away. Usually, this was because something about the operation was controversial from a counterintelligence point of view—a traitor or mole—or it was simply a really sexy operation. The vault women would know; but they weren't telling.

The vault women also provided critical background on the adversary. Their biographical files helped case officers suss out connections, determine who went to the same university; who belonged to the same clubs; whose children attended the same school; who was a suspected officer of the KGB. "Let's say, I met some guy in Poland whose name was Pawel So-and-So," recalled Mike Sulick, an operations officer who spent much of his career working hard targets, before rising to head the clandestine service. When considering a potential asset, he relied on the vault women to tell him what he needed to know. There was a great one named Ruth. "They'd have the 3 x 5 cards and say, yeah, his father was in the Polish intel and he beat up prisoners or something." The vault women had "library type memory before there were computers."

In effect, the vault women *were* the computers.

FAR OUTNUMBERING THE VAULT women, however, were the sea of women secretaries. "You could come in with a master's degree in French, and they would put you into the typing pool," said Jonna Mendez. "The first job was to get out of the typing pool."

So interchangeable did the women at the agency seem to the men hiring them that mistakes were made. In 1954, Lee Coyle was a graduate of Rosemont College, a Catholic women's college outside Philadelphia. Her father—knowing that a college diploma, for a woman, was no guarantee of getting a job—sent her to secretarial school. Coyle and her sister both applied to the CIA. Coyle's sister couldn't type. They went to the application office in Manhattan. Having passed her own test, Coyle returned and posed as her sister. Both were hired. Coyle went on to work in information management, turning the 3 x 5 cards into computer files.

The agency had myriad ways of ensuring that most women who got out of the typing pool did not get far. It seemed to Lisa that things went okay for women who stayed in their lanes; having a few women in top administrative jobs seemed to be a way to satisfy Washington regulators that women were being advanced. But to anybody who looked closely, it was clear they weren't being advanced equally. What women did exist at high levels were tough and remote, and far less encouraging than the male mentors—and they did exist—like the ones who valued and encouraged Heidi August. As Lisa Manfull was making her way, some men suggested she look for a female mentor. But she found that most senior female clandestine officers were discouraging, even condescending. Some suggested she pursue a less fraught path, like reports officer. Others "were genuinely concerned that [becoming a case officer] would ruin my life. They were really trying to protect me."

If men in the clandestine service benefited from "a grapevine of 'here's a job here; there's this there,'" the women "thought they were doing you a favor by telling you not to do it," Lisa found. "They loved it, but they thought, it's so hard, I could do it, but others can't." One of her contemporaries, case officer Mike Kalogeropoulos, noticed that most of his women colleagues "never got a break from any female." Instead, they "just spiraled along on their own."

CHAPTER 6

YOU HAD TO WEAR A SKIRT

I N THE 1960S AND 1970S, WHEN HEIDI AUGUST AND LISA MANFULL were getting started, the topmost female officer in the CIA's clandestine service—a tiny, effete woman named Eloise Page—was by far the most unhelpful to her younger female colleagues. This could be because Page, after many hard years of service, felt frustrated by having her own abilities and intelligence collection dismissed; or because she absorbed the truth that men were the institutional power source that mattered. It could be because she feared being perceived as a feminist. Or it might just have been because she was a snob.

Whatever her motivations, the fact remained that Eloise Randolph Page, a Richmond-born blueblood who for many years was the only female GS-18 on the operations side, was seen as a person who did not extend so much as a white-gloved pinkie to help the women coming along behind her. Having started in World War II, Page was one of the many OSS secretaries—in her case, assigned to Wild Bill Donovan himself, who liked to recruit from highborn families and must have been delighted that "Eloise," as everybody called her, came from not only one such family, but two. At the time, there were few snobberies more potent than the snobbery of FFVs, or "first families of Virginia." The Randolphs and the Pages—her forebears—were two of the oldest white families, with roots that went back to the origins of the commonwealth, and to slavery. "She was a classy woman," as one female officer put it, "who belonged somewhere on a plantation."

Born in 1920, Page boasted the perfect pedigree of the Southern upper classes, spending a year at Hollins College, a well-regarded women's college in Virginia's Blue Ridge Mountains, followed by stints at the University of South Carolina, where she studied French, and Baltimore's Peabody Conservatory, where she studied music. With those two quintessentially feminine subjects under her cinched belt, she completed the trifecta by attending Rice Business College, one of myriad entities that trained women as typists and executive secretaries. Upon America's entry into World War II, Page spent a couple of years keeping Donovan, a terrible administrator who said yes to everything and everyone, organized and on track.

In 1945, her responsibilities were broadened and her calling discovered: She traveled to Belgium to join X-2, the only OSS unit granted access to England's top secret "Ultra" code-breaking dispatches of German communications. There, Page helped identify adversary agents and keep track of them, helping build a priceless roster of names of some three thousand known or suspected spies—"all individuals who had been reported by anyone to be engaged in espionage," as analyst Ray Cline put it—for Axis countries and others.

Page thus helped lay the foundations of an enormously valuable cache of records detailing the identities, aliases, and backgrounds of spies working for hostile nations. In the process, she advanced America's still-nascent skills at "counterespionage" or "counterintelligence," navigating the complex, hall-of-mirrors world of double agents and spy-versus-spy dealings. She also worked with Swedish, French, and Belgian counterparts to track Nazis and make sure they did not get away. This required building liaisons with foreign allies—another unsung element of spy work. Both liaison work and counterintelligence were jobs toward which women tended to be steered. It was work that was critical to the agency's need to know who it was dealing with, but not nearly as prestigious as on-the-street recruiting.

After the war—when many women were told to leave and make room for returning veterans—Eloise Page hung on, employing her wide acquaintance with scientists and academics to track technical advances and help wage a central contest of the Cold War: the scientific competition with the Soviet Union. On October 4, 1957, Page was serving as chief of the Scientific and Technical Operations Staff when the

Soviets launched Sputnik, the first artificial satellite, a world-changing piece of technology, slightly bigger than a basketball, that shocked the American public and exacerbated anxiety about Soviet nuclear capabilities and the much-feared "missile gap." The news media portrayed the Sputnik launch as a failure of intelligence while members of Congress accused the CIA of being "asleep at the switch." In fact, the real story was more complicated: The actual failure was that of a male-dominated bureaucracy to listen to what a woman was trying to tell them.

According to an internal CIA study declassified in 2013, Page's office had compiled "dozens" of reports about Soviet plans to put a satellite in space, sourced from her "high-level contacts" in the scientific community. By May 1957, the agency well knew a launch was to occur, and roughly when. "It was to be between September 20th and October 4th," Page later stated in an interview. "We had everything else there was to know about it. We had the angle of launch, we had the date." But despite vigorous efforts, she could not get a gatekeeper—Jack White, head of a major committee in the Office of Scientific Intelligence—to accept what she was hearing. He dismissed the intel as Soviet disinformation. Page visited him to try to change his mind, warning him that "we are going to have an intelligence failure." She bet White a case of champagne that the launch would occur, and after it did, she said, "You should have seen my office." Full of champagne. Her office wrote a bang-up after-action report, and she received a letter from OSI saying that the information in it was "essential and indispensable."

After weathering frustrations like these, Page shared the irritation of other female colleagues who were struggling to make their way. It was in these initial years of the postwar era, with spy work institutionalized and so few top jobs available, that the convenient idea took hold: that women could neither handle nor recruit. At a town hall meeting in 1953, a discomfited Allen Dulles found himself peppered by questions from women wanting to know why so few of them had risen above the GS-15 level. To placate them, Dulles—perhaps also prodded by his sister Eleanor, who was working at the State Department—convened an all-female group to study the problem of discrimination. The effort was known, in all seriousness, as "the petticoat panel." Given just a few months to complete a study, the panel found that men they interviewed were fully willing to share views that "women won't travel," are "more emotional and less objective," are not "sufficiently aggressive," and "can't work under the pressures of urgency." Leaders and supervisors readily opined that women almost always quit because of marriage or family, and men "dislike working under the supervision of women." One of the most dismissive was Richard Helms, a future CIA director, who at the time was chief of operations for the clandestine service and deplored the "constant inconvenience factor" of female clerks who came and went. The inspector general, Lyman Kirkpatrick, saw the women's complaints as "gripes." When the panel sought employment statistics, the institution claimed that hard numbers were "classified" and would be provided but only if "closely held." It was a brilliant move to torpedo the report: "Closely held" meant few people saw the results. That the panel had been convened at all was "quickly forgotten."

IN SUCH AN ENVIRONMENT, it was remarkable that Eloise Page rose as high as she did. That she succeeded was not only because of her persistence but because she had spent enough time in back rooms to well know the darkest corners, and secrets, of Langley. At the CIA, there exists a critical concept to appreciate: the "hall file," a collective consensus that is unseen, unacknowledged, and key to any officer's career. Simply put, a hall file consists of the remarks people make about one another during casual conversations in the hallways. The hall file, not the personnel file, in many ways determines a CIA officer's career, because of the lying that goes on as a matter of course. At the spy agency, it's understood that supervisors will stretch the truth in personnel reports, assuring the head of some other section that this or that person did well as a way of getting rid of a problem employee. If you really wanted to know whether somebody was a good officer, you had to know their hall file. You had to ask around. You still do.

Eloise Page managed to learn the hall file on everybody, a skill she cultivated from the start of her OSS tenure. Secretaries, after all, did much more than type. They drafted correspondence and took calls from bosses' colleagues, wives, children, mistresses, enemies, and friends. They knew who was angry with whom and who was undermining whom and who was having sex at lunchtime with a woman not his wife. One former secretary recalled that she paid all her boss's bills, "wrote his mother a letter every week," and knew how much he spent on therapy sessions.

Eloise Page likewise knew everything about Wild Bill Donovan. And there was a lot to know. As one OSS officer, Rolfe Kingsley, put it, "you knew to have women at the receptions Donovan attended. He'd take care of the rest of it."

"I had the goods on him, and I played it for all it was worth," Page told female officers in a rare meeting where she seems to have let down her hair, conversationally if not literally. Some of the women in attendance later reminisced about Page during a lively 1992 question-and-answer session, a transcript of which (with last names redacted) was declassified in 2013. "She had the pictures on somebody," one case officer marveled. Meaning: incriminating photos.

Such confidences were rare; in general, Eloise was known for her lofty isolation. "She did not go out and fight for us," said Lee Coyle, who felt Page was insulated by her own sense of self-worth. Her family consisted of her mother, whom she took care of, and two dogs, always a matched pair. Coyle sometimes ran into Page shopping with her mother at Garfinckel's, an upscale DC department store. "She was always beautifully dressed," Coyle recalled, but in a fusty old-fashioned way, with white gloves, which she wore in the office. She made a point of being called Miss Page and insisted her middle name be pronounced Ran-DOLPH. She employed a Black chauffeur whom she called "dear Walter."

Apart from knowing secrets, the key to her advancement was making herself unpleasant. "Some women were just so tough, people were afraid of them," observed Jeanne Newell, a staff operations officer who crossed paths with Page. "They were promoted to get rid of them. Instead of firing them, promote them to make them somebody else's problem." People knew the sound of her heels clicking down the hall, and feared it.

For all her apparent power, though, Page remained at a disadvantage. She exerted influence from a bureaucratic position rather than an operational posting. In a world that ran on hall files, this, too, imparted stigma: Everybody knew staff jobs were worth a bucket of warm spit, to borrow John Nance Garner's vivid description of the role of vice president. As she rose through the administrative hierarchy, Page gained wide say over operational budgets. Hers was a puissant position in that she controlled the purse strings: Any baron who wanted funding for a covert operation had to get the go-ahead from Eloise. "She scared some of these men to death," remembered Lee Coyle. "They were afraid to go into her office."

"She was in a position like J. Edgar Hoover to make or break a person," said an operations officer, Mike Kalogeropoulos. "She knew where the bodies were buried. She knew the real story about everything. Nobody touched her."

From where Lisa Manfull sat, Eloise Page was everything she did not want to become. "Eloise Page was an Olympian management figure rather than a bona fide operations officer. If she had been on the operational lines, no one knew about it. If she helped other women officers, it was not apparent."

A YEAR AFTER BEING courted by the avid recruiters, Lisa found herself waiting to see if she would ever get assigned overseas. Working on the desk at Langley, she had to navigate an office environment in which men—or some men—saw their female colleagues and underlings as having been hired for their own pleasure and entertainment. Headquarters was rife with sexual innuendo and advances, not to mention sexual paraphernalia. Pornography, in the world of spycraft, was a common means of what is known as "elicitation," particularly in places and cultures where sexually explicit material was not easily obtained. "When you are trying to recruit someone in sub-Saharan Africa," Dewey Clarridge, Lisa's fellow Brown alumnus, noted, "you can count on the attractions that are hard to come by there—particularly gourmet food, fine liquor, and the latest videos (especially pornographic videos)." He continued, "If you are trying to get a diplomat or local citizen to your home as part of a recruitment effort, inviting him over for some good

Scotch, locally unavailable, and a private screening of 'Debbie Does Dallas' is a good technique."

And porn became a means of harassing incoming women, a tactic that endured for decades. In the 1980s, when a young Californian, Pamela McMaster, started in the operations center, her co-workers posted a sign, festooned with *Playboy* centerfolds, saying, "Welcome, Pam, to your first night shift." McMaster, whose father was in the military, was not easily offended and merely told them to take it down. But the next day, she was summoned to her supervisor's office and told "This can't happen," as if she were to blame for the obnoxious greeting.

Among the many published histories of the early CIA, there is one anecdote that gets oft repeated. With variations, the story goes like this: After World War II, when the CIA was operating out of the cluster of buildings near the Lincoln Memorial, one male officer happened to have a window overlooking that of a colleague in the building next door. He gazed out when the colleague was—depending on the version—either taking off his secretary's clothes or having sex with her on his desk. The observer dialed an internal number and watched the couple jump apart. "This is the voice of God," he said. "And I see what you are doing." Whether the story is true doesn't matter; the fact that it's oft repeated shows that office sex was assumed to occur as a matter of course. And people thought it was amusing.

And so, women—secretaries, clerks, case officers—had to navigate a workplace in which they were assumed to be, on some level, playthings. When one case officer, at the Farm, was told the desk officers had given her the pseudonym "Fallex," she decided not to object, and put up with being Miss Fallex for the duration. When she wrote her first cable as a case officer, describing a meeting with an Egyptian colonel, she noted that the meeting went well, and she saw opportunities for further contact. Her supervisor cautioned that the desk officers would guffaw at what they saw as loaded language and that she should avoid expressions like "further contact."

Women could turn down advances—most of the time—but certain expectations were beyond their control. "There was one particular deputy director of operations who wanted to see our legs," Lisa Manfull remembered. "When you went to brief him, you had to wear a skirt." CIA staff had to walk around a lot. Cables were ranked as classified, secret, or top secret, and, with a cover sheet stapled to the top, had to be circulated for people to sign off on. The more problematic the cable, the more likely a good-looking woman would be assigned to take it around. One time, Lisa Manfull was wearing a clingy knit suit. Her boss said: "Look, we're going to have trouble coordinating this cable. Go shake your butt at so-and-so." Lisa disliked being circulated like a box of office candy, but "I didn't dare say anything."

The expectation that women would serve as flings and office wives was common throughout Washington, where power imparted a sense of droit du seigneur. In Congress, senators like Lyndon Johnson, John F. Kennedy, and Gary Hart and representatives like Arkansas's Wilbur Mills—the chair of the House Ways and Means Committee whose girlfriend, an Argentinian stripper who went by the name Fanne Foxe, famously jumped out of his car during a traffic stop and ended up in the Tidal Basin—were some of the more conspicuous philanderers of the twentieth century's second half.

But they were by no means the only ones. At CIA headquarters, a young officer named Bonnie Hershberg interviewed in the mid-1970s for a job in the plans and budgeting office of the Directorate of Intelligence, where she found herself working for an analyst "infamous for his affairs with a number of secretaries, all of whom he eventually married." She sensed a "huge amount of sexual tension" in an environment where female underlings were arrayed like contestants. Another boss told her "right off that he liked to be around pretty women, particularly pretty, smart women, and he would make sure if I were willing to come and work with him for a year or so and get the budget up and running and help with all these staff kind of jobs, that he would make sure I had a shot at management." He was a sexual harasser, and the other men in the office made fun of him for it. Hershberg felt she had no choice but to put up with his comments; she was a single mother and this was her career. She put up with it when he put his arm on her and asked who she was going out with. He chose to mentor her, which meant that when he picked her to head a task force, the men on the task force didn't respect her authority. In a "Lord of the Flies environment," she would call a meeting and nobody would show. Later, she was hired for a branch chief job by a man who said he picked her over others "because I want you." It was only years later that she realized he meant it literally.

There were men who were allies and others who were predators—"creatures," one case officer called them—and the former did not rein in the latter, in part because they did not realize how far things went. In the mid-'80s, Dick Stolz, head of the clandestine service, met with a group of women who had submitted questions to him. At the end, he asked his own question: Had any of them experienced sexual harassment, and if so, would she please raise her hand? Every hand went up. Stolz was appalled and embarrassed. "You could just see the flush go from his collar right up to his hairline," remembered one participant.

"Sexual harassment happened all the time. You knew who they were," Lisa said. At the CIA, each man had his own special hall file that only women contributed to and kept track of.

But the double standard was impossible to fight. The CIA differed from virtually every other federal workforce in that sex was part of the official discourse, an aspect of people's personal lives that the agency considered its business and got involved in. Beginning with the polygraph, the CIA asserted a right to inquire about sex lives—"they asked all sorts of questions to rattle me," Lisa remembered—and continued to do so during an officer's career. The security office monitored conduct. For instance, any officer having sex with a foreign national (that is, somebody who was not an American citizen) had to get approval from headquarters. One-night stands were okay, but anything involving "close and continuing" contact had to be reported. It was obvious that men got more lenient treatment. "If you went in and you reported—you said, 'I met Maurice, I think we're going to sleep together, I want to report him,' well, you would just be hammered by security," said Lisa Manfull. "But the guy who comes in and says, 'I've met Fifi and we're going to have a little fling,' maybe it's just the one time, two times—the men who had affairs within the station, married or not, never were called to task."

This dynamic was confirmed by a longtime officer, Patsy McCollough, who was hired in 1977 as an armed security guard and rose to work in the personnel operation, where she witnessed, and vocally objected to, a double standard that lingered into the 1990s. "If a male went overseas and said he wanted to marry a foreign national, part of the process is they have to write a resignation letter while the person is getting a security background check," said McCollough. Male case officers usually got the green light, and women often did not. For men, all sorts of heterosexual alliances were winked at, including threesomes. "I remember one guy who actually had his maid and his wife living with him when he came back. In a romantic situation."

The peril of the "honeypot" is the purported reason why the agency exerts a say over sex lives. In the honeypot scenario, a philandering officer opens himself (or herself) to blackmail, or other kinds of targeting, by a foreign intelligence service. A new fling, for instance, might casually ask for the list of phone numbers in a CIA station. McCollough observed that people in the security office "felt like the women were weaker" and "automatically assumed the women were not as strong-minded and will allow themselves to be used."

Then again—echoing Maxwell Knight's wartime neither-too-hot-nor-too-cold prescription for self-presentation—women who didn't cater to prevailing notions of femininity became suspect for a different reason. "When women started wearing pants," McCollough noted, "everybody accused them of being gay."

Some women played along, or tried to. One trainee Lisa knew had an eye-poppingly flagrant affair with a top supervisor at the Farm; the twosome went AWOL for days. The same officer had an affair with a chief of station who liked to have nooners in his office. People could hear the thumping. The female officer, though a good one, became a pariah. For a man, promiscuity was okay and opportunities abounded in a clandestine lifestyle in which secret meetings were normalized.

Then again, dating men from the private sector presented its own peculiar challenges. Men in the 1960s and 1970s often weren't accustomed to girlfriends who worked, much less girlfriends who couldn't reveal what their work entailed. Nor was a husband likely to follow a wife to an overseas posting. For a female CIA officer who wanted to date or marry, the obvious option—often, the only real option—was to marry a colleague. Then, as now, the CIA became exhibit A for what sociologists call "endogamy," the formal term for marriage within a clan or tribe or other small and closed community. What was less obvious were the career costs for the woman who exposed herself to a hall file identity as the trailing, and therefore less important, spouse.

LISA MANFULL CERTAINLY WAS not yet aware of those costs and the extent to which they would impact her. As she bided her time while awaiting an overseas posting, her desk work led her to cross paths with a case officer, David Harper, who was handsome, bright, engaging, and a few years older than she was. Within a year, they were engaged. Lisa envisioned the two of them building a joint career and a life of shared service. But when she reported their engagement, as required, she received a phone call from the head of the career training program at the Farm. Far from congratulatory, he was livid.

"I got screaming phone calls saying I betrayed the course," recounted Lisa, who was shocked when told she should repay the $30,000 that American taxpayers had put into her training. The official assumed that, once married, she would quit. Ignoring that the agency had cut short the full course she expected to be offered, he "expressed a tremendous sense of betrayal."

Many other women were butting up against the same assumptions. Around this same time, another promising trainee, Jeanne Newell, was recruited out of the University of Wisconsin. Assigned to the records section, Newell was assured she could apply to train as a full-fledged analyst after two years, with the promise of a slot at the Farm and a posting overseas. She did her stint and was accepted to the Farm. When she reported being engaged, however, her Farm slot was revoked. Newell was told the agency "did not want to waste their training dollars on someone who was going to quit when they got married or had kids." Four years later, the marriage ban was lifted, so she reapplied. But by then she was pregnant, and a man on her career panel—a father several times over—became visibly angry that she had the effrontery to present herself for consideration. Once again, she lost her slot. Newell made her career working part time as a staff operations officer.

In July 1974, an economist named R. Jennine Anderson wrote to *Ms.* magazine to relate her own ordeal. Anderson had earned a PhD in economics from the University of Virginia, and when she went on the job market, "The only blatantly sexist recruiting practices I found" were at the CIA. Her interviewer expressed concern upon learning she was married; "they assumed that my career was secondary to my husband's, and they did not want to spend money processing my application." When she said she and her husband had agreed her career would come first, the interviewer scoffed: "Famous last words." She described a gender-conscious aptitude testing system, in which the women's test had a pink cover and the men's had a blue one. Behind the pink cover, she encountered questions like "Do you prefer household magazines or fashion magazines?" and "Would you rather be the wife of a research scientist or the wife of a rancher?" Not to mention "Would you rather spend a lot of time putting on makeup or go out without makeup?" or "Would you rather cook or sew a dress?"

WHATEVER THE ASSUMPTIONS OF the people controlling her career path, the fact was that Lisa Manfull had no intention of quitting. She wasn't ready to start a family and couldn't wait to begin the spy career she aspired to. She assumed she and her husband would take jobs at the same overseas station, traveling in tandem. Her next inkling that the agency did not share this assumption occurred a year after her hiring, when, eligible for a routine promotion and the pay raise that came with it, she was denied. "They thought I didn't have a career ahead of me," said Lisa, who ran into her classmate, Janine Brookner, who was infuriated on Lisa's behalf, but not surprised. "There was just blatant discrimination," Brookner later recalled. "I said, 'Lisa they can't do that . . . you tell them no, that was a commitment they made. You did very well, and you deserved that promotion.'"

RATHER THAN TANGLE WITH personnel, Lisa embarked on quiet talks with a European chief of station willing to employ both her and her husband. She and David Harper married in September 1969. Her father, posted in Belgium, insisted it be a "big embassy wedding." The ceremony turned into an affair of state with hundreds of guests. A man in knickers carrying a silver mace led them down the hall of the Hôtel de Ville, to a civil ceremony with a woman in a tricornered hat officiating. Her mother made a fuss because the groom had brought a light-colored suit, and being stubborn, refused to change. A bigger crisis followed: When it emerged that her father might be appointed ambassador to the country where they were hoping to work, they ran into a nepotism problem. One or both would likely work undercover at the embassy. So, the agency nixed that assignment.

Instead, David Harper was posted to Copenhagen, a station that did not have a case officer job for Lisa. CIA operational slots were precious and few, and it was universally accepted that a husband's career took precedence over his wife's. Lisa received word that she had to resign and give up her security clearance. This was standard practice: As a 2003 report pointed out, in the 1950s and beyond, "it was automatically assumed that a woman was no more than an adjunct of her husband" and that "women were expected to go LWOP [leave without pay] or resign when their spouses were transferred overseas." Lisa's heart sank. The agency had created the very situation it accused her of planning. She didn't want to quit. She was made to. Her only option was to go overseas as a "dependent." It was, she said, "very tough on me."

Winters in Denmark were dark and bleak. To maintain a professional identity, she initially took a job as a conference interpreter. But she was officially a diplomat's wife, and diplomatic wives were not supposed to compete with the local workforce. The only job she was allowed to keep was as social secretary to the US ambassador's wife. She found herself critiquing menus; attending to correspondence and double-checking titles such as "Her Serene Princess"; and making sure her boss didn't wear the same outfit twice.

She kept hoping a slot would materialize at Copenhagen Station, enabling her to get her spy career back on track. Instead, the station chose to avail itself of her free labor as a wife. Copenhagen Station began sending Lisa out under "housewife cover," the term for a woman whose very inconspicuousness made her useful.

Lisa's pro bono spying duties began on a rainy night when the station needed to pass an urgent message to an asset. Her husband was busy, so the station insisted Lisa strike out in his stead. "It was a miserable night and the asset in question was a miserable guy," Lisa recalled. "Nobody wanted to meet him." She went, deploying the tradecraft acquired during her single month of Farm training. Her execution was flawless despite the man's attempts to seduce her. "I went out in the rain and the dark and spent three hours trying to figure out if somebody was on me. Usually, if you're a housewife, nobody is on you." She completed the assignment, and found herself getting more, as—in her eagerness to jump-start her career—she proved willing to take the jobs nobody else wanted.

The station did not pay her, and would not hire her, even when slots arose. There was no other wife with Lisa's qualifications, so it was hard to see who would object. But "people came and went and there was no job for me." Instead, management expected her to contribute as a spouse—unrewarded, unrecognized, with no write-up in her personnel record, because as far as the agency was concerned, she no longer had a personnel record. At least, not one that mattered.

CHAPTER 7

HOUSEWIFE COVER

W HAT LISA MANFULL HARPER HAD STUMBLED UPON IN Copenhagen was the other secret category of women who kept the CIA running: wives. In this regard, once again the CIA was much like other government agencies, not to mention the world at large. Into the 1970s and even the '80s, wives continued to be seen as working extensions of their husbands. Lisa's own mother experienced it in the diplomatic corps. In greater Washington, political wives—Pamela Harriman, Lady Bird Johnson—were a potent force, forming committees, hosting lunches, pouring drinks, joining clubs, building alliances, and lubricating the social channels that helped husbands (and wives) advance. In the military, wives had many duties and observed a strict hierarchy depending on the rank of the men they married.

But this was even truer at the CIA. Wives incurred taxpayer expense; wives were flown overseas, wives had to be housed and fed. If the agency could recoup some of that outlay by commandeering a wife's time and talents, so much the better. And the truth was: Being a wife provided great cover. There was so much that wives could do to help. At cocktail parties, the wife of a case officer could be dispatched to sidle around to the wife of a potential asset, chat her up, cadge an invitation to dinner, crack open the door to a recruitment. Wives were expected to host elaborate "developmental" dinners, often on short notice. In the spy business, entertaining is key. The home is usually where the case officer has initial meetings with the asset. "It's quiet," says Lisa. "You control the area; and you can get to know them."

Other situations were even more delicate and urgent. At any time of day or night, a wife might find herself face-to-face with a "walk-in"—a "volunteer" with vital intelligence to impart, who wanted to offer himself as an asset. Her case-officer husband might be away on a mission. "You answer the door, and it's a Russian wanting to defect," Lisa offered by way of example. "What you do in that critical time really affects whether this guy is going to be snatched by a bunch of thugs. The smart husband has prepared his wife for this eventuality. Who do you call at the embassy? What is the code word you say? What do you do with this guy? How do you respond if you see somebody outside?"

It was an open secret that many senior CIA officers had built their careers with the help of effective wives. Ray Close, a chief of station in Saudi Arabia and the Middle East, got lifelong backup from his wife and high school sweetheart, Marty. Director William Colby's 1978 memoir is full of grateful praise for his own wife, Barbara. In an early posting to Sweden, he worked under State Department cover and Barbara "jumped into the job of the junior diplomat's wife with her typical enthusiasm and charm." She made a wide circle of friends, convincingly presented herself as a diplomat's helpmeet, and "did much to shore up my weak cover." In Vietnam, her "warm and outgoing personality" carried them through dinners and receptions. She saved him from falling too deeply into the "cult of intelligence" and was "determined to maintain a normal life for us and the children." She helped him stay sane.

Wives could be particularly helpful in the very male-dominated societies where women were said to be at a disadvantage. The beauty of housewife cover was that it relied upon women's lower status. Whatever a housewife was doing—grocery shopping, strolling the baby, sunbathing by the pool in an embassy compound—it surely wasn't important. If she reached down to pick up a dead drop, who would notice? The more patriarchal the culture, the more a wife could get away with. And wives who were uninterested in spy work didn't always last: One baron discarded his first wife in favor of a reports officer who was much more engaged with the work. "It happens," the second wife told me.

Wives were true partners in the toughest postings: hard targets such as the Soviet Union and other Communist-controlled areas. In those "denied areas," the saying went that a case officer needed a QP wife and a QP dog. QP stands for "quasi-personnel," meaning something—like a car—that the government owns but lets the case officer use. In these places, ceaseless surveillance was part of the kabuki ritual of Cold War espionage. The KGB and other adversary spy services had deep vaults of their own and conducted assiduous research to know which American diplomats were actually spies. A known or suspected CIA case officer was tailed at all hours. Three or four KGB officers might converge on a single American case officer the minute he pulled out of a garage or parking space. The goal was to prevent the CIA officer from doing the one thing he had come to do: communicate with Soviet assets. Here again, a wife was key. Not only did a female companion make a man less conspicuous, but an alert wife could help spot a tail and shake it off. As the saying went, two sets of eyes were better than one.

In denied area postings, the bulk of a case officer's job was physical, low-tech, exhausting, and time-consuming. For American case officers operating in places like Moscow, a huge amount of their working hours amounted to trying to break free of surveillance. Sometimes, the goal was to execute a dead drop, leaving or picking up a message nestled in a fake rock or tree trunk. Sometimes the goal was to leave a coded signal such as a chalk mark on a mailbox. Sometimes, the mission was to execute a "brush pass," an encounter where a message or payment could be handed off. Even harder was a "car toss" in which the officer would fling a message out of a car, in a bottle or other projectile, aimed at a bush or other pickup site. With a wife to help, these things became more feasible. The wife might make the toss. Or she could drive the car so her husband could toss at the precise moment where a bend in the road caused the surveillance car to lose sight of them.

To prepare for postings in areas like the Soviet bloc, China, and Cuba, case officers took an intense six-week "internal operations course" conducted in a city like Washington or Baltimore, where students were tailed by FBI agents, disguised, who did surveillance for a living. Wives took the course as well. "They put the pros on us," said Mike Sulick, who served two tours in Moscow—as deputy chief of station and, later, chief—and whose wife, Shirley, also underwent the training. The FBI surveillers were amazing. They could imitate anybody: a homeless person in a field jacket, a decked-out suburbanite shopping at Nordstrom.

During training, women often proved better at detecting surveillance. Women are always, on some level, alert to interlopers, with keen antennae for strangers in their personal space.

This was true of Shirley Sulick, who would urge Mike to pay attention to shoes. Surveillance officers might change clothes during a chase, but it was hard to swap out footwear. If two people appeared sequentially wearing the same shoes, it was likely one person: the surveillance.

ALL IN ALL, A COMPETENT and willing wife was a case officer's most important asset, and Shirley Sulick, who died in 2021, was one of the best. The Sulicks were an early biracial couple. Mike is white, from a Northeastern Catholic upbringing, and Shirley was Black, with roots in North Carolina and work experience in New York politics, where he met her. Shirley's exuberant charisma and good nature were crucial to Mike's well-being as well as to his career trajectory. On early postings in Japan and South America, she entertained Bulgarians or Russians or anybody else he invited home. For a lot of wives, "If they haven't been overseas before, whether it's Tokyo or Peru, whatever, it could be daunting," Mike told me. But no aspect of overseas work was daunting for Shirley. Still, entertaining could be exhausting: Many guests did not speak much English, and conversation was halting enough to tire out even the most gracious hostess. Shirley was elated when they went to Moscow and she could put the dinners aside and concentrate on pleasures like evasive driving. "This," she said, "is my wheelhouse."

Shirley, who also worked as a secretary to the chief of station during their first tour, had a heavy foot and enjoyed messing with their Soviet counterparts. "She loved surveillance," remembered Mike, who had bought her a mink coat, for the cold, that enhanced her panache. "I'm going to go out and play with the boys," she would tell him. With that, she'd be off on a drive. Often Mike would go with her; she'd look in the mirror, evaluate the tactics of their pursuers, give them nicknames like "White Hat." There was a method to her madcap forays. She would try to flush out the Soviets by turning and doubling back. "You act like you're going out on a casual errand, nothing much, a trip to the store, you just sort of wind and meander," as he described it. "You have a certain number of turns so you see who turns with you; you channel them into somewhere where you can separate them from other cars. If you don't see them after a while, you start driving up and down the streets, turning around." Another goal was to ensure the KBG did not learn their patterns. They would take turns at the wheel, so the KGB got used to seeing Shirley driving.

Working in a denied area made for a constrained marital existence, since the apartment was bugged and the only place they could speak freely was a vault at the office. But there were ways to exploit the lack of privacy. At one New Year's Eve party, Mike Sulick pretended to get very drunk, and Shirley propped him up as he staggered home. Knowing the Soviets were listening, he slurred his words and demanded that she bring him Irish coffee. His surveillers assumed it was safe to sleep in on the following holiday morning. Instead, Mike got up early and struck out unobserved.

There was a ritualistic quality to some of these interactions. If an American CIA officer was apprehended, he would sputter that he was a diplomat, demand to speak to a consular officer, and get ejected from the country. His cover was blown, but he didn't get hurt.

For a Soviet asset, the consequences were infinitely more dire. "They're putting their lives in our hands," Mike said. Getting close enough to pull off a brush pass was especially risky. The case officers preferred to operate "in the gap," which meant shaking off surveillance altogether. So Shirley would drive, circling until Mike could do what was called "drop a foot": jump out of the car. It was so exhilarating that one time, when he broke free, "it was minus 20 degrees, and I didn't even feel it. I was just so, 'I'm free. I'm free at last!'"

Wives could also assist with dead drops. Shirley Sulick made a point of carrying a huge purse, out of which she would let fall a pencil or lipstick. Reaching down to retrieve it, she could pick up a message. They'd go on a picnic or tour a church—"They probably thought we were all very religious"—and Mike would make a big production of taking a photo. While the KGB officers watched him, Shirley would go around the side and pick up whatever had been placed there.

WIVES WERE VALUABLE AND men were encouraged to get one. And "wife" was how the agency now saw Lisa Manfull Harper. She worked under housewife cover for three years in Copenhagen: unpaid, unpromoted, frustrated but willing to accept whatever scraps of work came her way.

Then in 1974, her husband was posted to Africa, where the Cold War was being furiously contested. The agency had spent much of the 1950s and 1960s concentrating its efforts in Europe, expending resources on covert actions intended to liberate Communist-controlled countries and prevent Communism from spreading to others, like Italy, seen as vulnerable to Soviet influence. The agency fought a propaganda war—printing posters, funding political parties, buying newspapers, planting op-eds. The agency also endeavored to train exiles from Soviet-occupied nations and send them back into their home countries with the aim of fomenting uprisings. But when Soviet tanks quashed the 1956 Hungarian revolution, hope faded of rolling back the Soviet presence in Eastern Europe. The playing field for the great game shifted to the so-called Third World, where the powers competed for influence and resources.

And in Africa, Lisa Manfull Harper found the environment gave her more room to maneuver, because stations were small, and needs were great. When it came to espionage, the agency didn't much care about the local and regional governments. "African political developments should have been on our list of priorities, but they weren't," Lisa recalled. "The only thing that counted in Africa was, if there was a coup, you wanted to report it fast." The real draws were the Cold War adversaries: China, East Germany, Eastern European nations including Hungary, Romania, Yugoslavia. And, of course, the Soviet Union, which had officials embedded in African institutions.

In Africa, the goal was to cultivate assets in—say—the local finance ministry, to find out who the Soviet agents were and what they were up to. The CIA also wanted to sell democracy and the US standard of living to African nations; persuade African leaders to vote with the West at the United Nations; and encourage the country to be pro-West, rather than pro-Russian or nonaligned.

Africa—where there was a "great need to cover the intelligence, and they were willing to take a chance on women"—would provide a new opportunity for Lisa to make her mark.

In their first posting, to Burundi, Lisa worked under housewife cover, this time on a contract basis. She got a modest paycheck at the GS-4 level—a big demotion from her hiring grade of GS-7—with no benefits, no accrued leave or pension, and no chance of being promoted. Pushed off the career track, she nonetheless felt grateful to be working. Targets were accessible, not walled off by huge bureaucracies like the one Heidi August had encountered in Bonn Station. "The first time I went out to meet an agent, at the top of a hill with a winding road, my agent was drunk and managed to drive his car into a ditch," Lisa recalled. "I got him out of the situation without blowing our covers and set a next meeting on flat ground." The local pool of expatriates was a rich source: Foreigners living abroad still had ties to their home countries. Lisa met a Russian speaker from an exiled aristocrat family, a "fabulous man" who wouldn't be recruited, officially, but was the kind of chatty person she could rely on for tips about targets, saying things like, "You know Yvonne from the embassy is drinking a lot at the local bar." She got to know the community; diplomatic staffs mingled. "All these little places were just perfect places to acquire assets."

And it was fun. For Lisa's thirtieth birthday, her husband threw her a party and set up a stereo speaker loud enough to be heard by neighbors. A goat was roasting; hundreds of people came. Suddenly their house was surrounded by troops and shadows; dogs started barking. None other than Michel Micombero—the country's de facto dictator, who had a weekend home nearby—walked in, declared himself a "guest everywhere in this country," and proceeded to knock back drinks. He toasted Lisa by sharing a Burundi proverb. "He got everyone in a circle, and he said, 'Remember, Madame David, you can never lift your shoulder above your ear.'" She asked someone what it meant. The reply: A wife should always remain subservient to her husband.

The president stayed all night. Nobody could leave until he did. At seven A.M. he departed. After that, he dropped by often to say hello. The second time he did, they called the US ambassador, David Mark, and invited him over. This time, the president stayed all day. Afterward, Mark told Lisa and David Harper that they were welcome to meet him on their own from now on. The ambassador also took professional notice of Lisa. Burundi had been a Belgian colony, and her French came in handy. The ambassador "began to use me unofficially to go and talk to people." Her husband seemed piqued. "I could feel just a little resentment already that I was doing something that was not in my charter," Lisa said. The ambassador would send her to talk with this or that person; she would write it up, and off it would go as an embassy missive. "Our relations as husband and wife suffered from the fact that I was so active professionally," she reflected. "There was a kind of a sense of competition."

Lisa was now working three jobs. The combination of being a CIA wife, a State Department wife, and a CIA contract employee led to collisions. At an event at the German ambassador's residence, diplomatic wives were supposed to put cookies in bags for the Christmas party. Lisa told the US ambassador's wife she didn't have time to do it. "She got furious at me, and she made a big scene." She realized it would be better to get her own cover job. A 1972 State Department directive had decreed that wives could no longer be drafted as free labor, but it didn't matter. Traditions were traditions. She found a job teaching English and liked it.

Marriage, for her espionage career, was both hindrance and asset. Tutorials from her husband helped compensate for the training she had been denied at the Farm. But marriage meant that Lisa's "career was always number two." Still, Lisa valued their time together. "Her husband, she pointed out, was my protector. If you have to do really sophisticated operational activity, there's no one better to do it with than your spouse. You look natural together in a car. It gives you access to places. I wouldn't have gotten the assignments at first that I got if I hadn't been married to him."

She meant "protector" literally. Being married protected her from overtures from male colleagues—at least it protected her in the local station, where her husband worked. It was different when she was sent on TDY—a short tour elsewhere. Sex with colleagues did not have to be reported to the security office. Whenever Lisa traveled, she had to fend off men at the station who saw her as a freebie. "It happened mostly when you were defenseless," she said. "Where I was stationed with my husband, they never would have dared."

On one assignment, Lisa went to a meeting where a colleague was supposed to turn over an asset to her. The "turnover" is a fraught moment when an officer says goodbye to an asset and introduces the new handler. Lisa showed up at a hotel and entered the room where the turnover would take place. To her horror, her colleague was poised to strike—at her. "He chased me around the bed. Literally chased me. Saying, Oh, my wife's understanding, blah blah blah." What they should have been doing—what she had expected—was talk about the meeting and check for surveillance. Instead, "he wanted to get me to bed and do a quickie." She dodged him, saying what she always said: "I love my husband, I don't fool around, sorry."

WHEN THE TOUR IN Burundi concluded, in 1977, Lisa was again obliged to resign. This was the norm for contract wives; each posting ended with a formal resignation. If the wife was offered work in the next station, she came back at the same grade. A contract wife might travel the world and remain a GS-4. But Lisa wanted more. She had been working in the field for six years. She was sick of scraps. Back at headquarters, she inquired whether Africa division would offer her a case officer position, but the only paid position on offer was as a French-English translator.

So, Lisa did something unusual: She jumped ship, seeking work in another division. Since she spoke some Russian, she signed on with the Soviet and Eastern Europe division, which hired her to brief defectors. She found the conversations fascinating—and instructive—but longed to do the spy work she had signed up for. Chatting with a personnel officer, she was given a piece of quiet advice, woman to woman: Petition to go back to the Farm. And take the long course, with the hope that the passage of a decade had cracked open the door to fairer treatment.

The woman's name was June Sworobuk. She occupied one of the myriad female positions at headquarters dismissed as unimportant. Lisa appreciated the advice but wasn't convinced. She didn't want to go back and do baby steps. She was past that. Sworobuk knew better. She explained that Lisa would never be taken seriously unless and until she was certified. "She said, 'Look, you have to show that you can do it.'"

———

AND SO, TEN YEARS after she started, Lisa Harper returned to the Farm to obtain what she had been denied: full certification. Her husband remained in Washington, so she commuted. It was exhausting: weeks of intense coursework followed by weekends spent driving more than two hundred miles on traffic-clogged I-95. The Farm had not changed much. There were more women than in 1968, but not many. Then again, at least she was being permitted to take the full course. More than that: Living in a dormitory among students ten years younger than she was, Lisa conceived a goal: to graduate number one.

She set out to master the system and game it. Gaming things is what CIA case officers do. To "case officer" something, or someone, is a verb at Langley. It means: to size up and manipulate a situation or a person. The Farm, she knew, was a structured place. It was important to obey the rules. The instructors had to follow strict guidelines. Trainees were graded on how they handled writing cables. They were graded on what techniques they used to meet assets; how well they recruited; how adeptly they collected intelligence, how well they wrote it up, how well they followed the reports format.

Lisa's strategy would be to follow the rules—and know her audience. Plenty of Farm instructors were mediocre officers, substance abusers fresh out of treatment, or both, and there was a reason they were warehoused in Williamsburg. The instructor corps was not the best and the brightest. They tended to be older, sometimes back on contract after having retired, which meant they were likely to have old-fashioned biases against women. But Lisa showed them respect. She listened. She did what they said. She played dumb: Asked if she had already done a certain exercise—had she ever written a cable?—she would say no, and please would they show her how.

As a wife and a contractor, Lisa was what was known in agency parlance as an "internal": a lower-level employee trying to move up. It was like being called a "retread." In the fine-drawn hierarchy of the elitist spy service, "internals and people who had been contractors were second class citizens," and everybody knew it. That, now, was her hall file.

There was one instructor, Greek Orthodox, with old-school notions, who clearly resented the female students. In one role-playing exercise he provoked her to anger, and she took the bait. "I just got so mad at him. Then he wrote me up that I could never do this, and I could never do that. He was trying to say—he did this to a whole generation of women—that we couldn't do it." He was cruel to a female recruit who suffered from multiple sclerosis. "He really was trying to destroy her."

Lisa regretted walking into his trap, but she figured out the system and aimed to max the grades. Along the way, she fended off classmates who were also gunning for top marks. "There was one guy who claimed that I was an alcoholic—and I'm not—just to discredit me. There was another guy who would ask to partner with me on exercises and try to embarrass me. They figured me out as their competition, and they were trying to take me down. It was such a dog-eat-dog world."

Lisa set out to build alliances with the other women. She began organizing meetings in the sauna at the Farm, or sometimes in a person's room, to strategize. For the group, the advantages of working together outweighed the temptation to compete. And Lisa wanted to lift the other women up. "I was also really working hard with the women that were not quite making it. That was really important to me." A couple of men joined their meetings, too, and a class solidarity began to develop. The group set out to case-officer the faculty together, predicting when the surprise exercise would occur.

At the Farm, it was a known tradition that the class would have to deal with a walk-in—a foreign agent who wanted to defect to the United States. Lisa studied the calendar and figured out when the walk-in would happen. She was correct. The class was accused of bugging the instructors' meeting. At the Farm, bugging an instructors' meeting was seen, in its way, as impressive.

When the session ended, Lisa Manfull Harper finished first. Based on the grades for each exercise, she had the highest score. Word got around back at Langley. "When I was number one, people were just amazed. By God, a contractor, a female contractor! I became a commodity. I mean, I became somebody that maybe you wanted to have in your division."

———

LISA REMAINED THE TRAILING spouse in her marriage—but at last, with full operational accreditation. In 1979, her husband was assigned to a station in Ethiopia and Lisa was able to expand her own clandestine portfolio, working with assets and perfecting her methods. The work itself—the spy work!—was every bit as exhilarating as she had hoped. And she excelled at it.

Newly emboldened, Lisa began to develop her own style of spycraft, one that drew on her feminine qualities. As she had anticipated, case officer work united "all the different little talents that I had. I always liked working a crowd. Because you're in this big crowd, and who is going to be that person who's going to produce intelligence? It's all about who's got the goods and how can I get to them." Her childhood had well prepared her.

As a woman, she felt her caretaking instincts helped. She enjoyed the relationships and respected the assets she worked with. "You became really good friends with these people." Lisa knew that outsiders often thought of CIA assets with scorn, "as something maybe almost unclean." Not so: "These are people that want the US government to know, and they can't do it overtly." She took pains to be honest with her assets, and she learned to stop an operation if her instincts told her something was amiss. "Maybe the production's down or maybe the person is not as careful as he or she should be."

Compassion proved a "powerful tool" and helped her build trust and protect an asset's safety and well-being. She deployed what is now called emotional intelligence: the ability to intuit feelings. She found that men in Islamic cultures felt surprisingly comfortable sharing confidences with a woman in private; the men felt curious about her, a working Western woman, and found it a relief to let down their guard. A female spy could subtly adopt a familiar role. "In Arab culture, the mother is just totally revered. The trick for the female case officer—this is in any type of patriarchal society whether it's Islamic or African or whatever—you have to negotiate your position. So, you have to analyze what relationship is going to work." She might assume the role of a mother figure, or daughter figure, or a pupil seeking instruction. "It sounds cold-hearted but you're in the business of manipulation."

She adopted other roles, too: confidante and even marriage counselor. At one point, Lisa was assigned to handle an asset whose cover had been blown through no fault of his own. The asset had been evacuated and resettled. His wife had not come with him. The agency had a responsibility for the man's upkeep regardless of whether he still had value as an asset. He did still have access, and Lisa's job was to keep him producing. But with the change in his circumstances, the man sank into depression. "I would go to our safe house, and he'd be lying in bed not wanting to get up," Lisa recalled. "I'd have to talk him through his depression. Sometimes I would go to a pay phone and call his wife" and tell her what a hard time he was having.

Far from being disadvantaged, Lisa found that "cultural biases worked in my favor." She was less threatening to a nervous target; less likely to be suspected of spying; less likely to attract surveillance. It remained inconceivable to many foreign intelligence services that women could be full-blown spies. She learned to take advantage of what she called the "guilelessness factor." She could ask personal questions and enjoyed dreaming up creative ways to elicit information: tarot cards, for example, and palm readings. She discovered kinship with foreign women. At one function, a female official turned to her unexpectedly and said, "Look, Lisa, I know who you are. I won't be recruited, but I'll help however I can."

The role she avoided was the one that women are most often suspected of: She never set out to seduce. She avoided meeting in "love hotels" or any boudoir-type setting. "You really have to be careful if you do any kind of flirtation. It's a double-edged sword. Because you as a case officer must maintain control."

She also came under more scrutiny from her own supervisors—she was more closely watched by headquarters. This, too, was not a bad thing. She was extra careful never to do anything under the table. She did not falsify reports or cheat on finances. "It's very easy to make up stuff. You can't do it. You'll get caught." In her day, case officers enjoyed "tremendous latitude to make operational decisions and to control funds up to a certain point. The people that weren't honest and didn't keep track of the money really paid for it."

The pleasure of the work made up for a decade of being thwarted. The better Lisa got, though, the more treacherous the terrain became. Women in the 1980s began coming to clandestine work in greater numbers, and not all were as collegial as Lisa. In Africa, she was working on one obvious target—low-hanging fruit—when another wife began recruiting him, and accused Lisa of stealing her asset. The other woman got her own case officer husband to talk to the chief of station to try to take the asset away from Lisa. "It was very awkward," said Lisa, "and I hadn't expected that." Lisa prevailed, but "made a mortal enemy in this woman."

Lisa and David Harper's final Africa posting was to Senegal, where she worked as a case officer with a State Department cover job. Once again, the US ambassador singled her out for her linguistic skills, and she became the "ambassador's pet," his trusted interpreter for visiting delegations. But she was surprised when he asked Lisa to cook a dinner. He was hosting people from China; he wanted good American food and said his own cook couldn't make it. Lisa truthfully said she had a conflict. "My interests come first," the ambassador asserted. She refused.

The dinner incident aside, she and the ambassador had "an excellent relationship," and Lisa could sense that her natural aptitude for spycraft was creating a problem in her marriage. As one case officer, Paula Doyle, put it, Lisa Manfull Harper was emerging as a "rock star," the "true package," a skilled and exceptionally gifted clandestine operative. People were taking notice. As part of her cover job, she reported on local labor. Normally it was a low-profile assignment, but "it happened to be a time when labor became an important factor in the country's stability." Her contacts were good, and Lisa's cables to Washington gained wide attention.

Her husband, Lisa sensed, was taken aback. "I had all that time off and he just hadn't bargained on how quickly I'd advance and how well I would get along with other people. That's one thing that being a Foreign Service brat does for you—you settle in fast. You just arrive at a place, and you know what it's going to take to get your health going, get the household organized, you know how to run staff and servants, you can pretty much tell what it's going to take to be a woman in that society and to make it work."

Now that they had similar jobs, the competition between the spouses became explicit. She and her husband were standing at a cocktail party, and "it's like a movie, this guy that we knew about, and we sort of were interested in, walks up to us and says, 'Meet me at such and such a place in two hours. I've got something to tell you.'" Her husband made the recruitment, for which he got credit; Lisa, being less conspicuous, did the handling. "This gets to be very tricky," she reflected. "Your promotions are based on the operations you run, the intelligence you produce, the number of people you are able to recruit. If your husband is taking all the good cases, you're going to suffer."

Lisa believed in making her own opportunities. Her attitude was: Expect nothing from the system. Ask no special favors. Play it straight. Don't complain. Cultivate a reputation as an all-around officer. If your station chief sends back-channel messages telling headquarters he doesn't want a woman (as one of hers did), win him over. Write up extensive contact reports. Remind him you speak five languages. Don't play sexual politics.

In the clandestine service, she knew she had to be careful not to be seen as an angry reactionary or conspirator. "Being perceived as a feminist was the kiss of death."

LISA HAD LEARNED HOW to watch out for herself, but she also learned the power of collaboration, and continued to look for ways to help others. So when Lisa Harper got a call from Heidi August, embarking on her own stint at the Farm in the class of 1978, she was glad to help. Years later, Heidi remembered why she turned to Lisa as her own training got under way, with such high stakes and consequences for her own future. The two women had crossed paths in headquarters, and it was clear to Heidi that Lisa Manfull Harper, unlike Eloise Page and others, was the kind of colleague who embraced solidarity and understood the advantages of creating a network. Lisa, Heidi recalled, "was very friendly. She was the kind of woman who would assist another woman. And so, I'd see her sometimes on the weekends and I would be describing a certain problem at the Farm. And she had been through the same thing a couple months earlier and she was giving me kind of a heads-up: Be prepared for this. She was very helpful." The time she called Lisa at her home, Heidi recalled that Lisa responded in her usual agreeable manner, but Heidi could hear her husband in the background. "He got angry because she was helping. He said, 'I don't approve of this.' And he tried to snatch the phone away." Lisa hung on and continued talking.

AND SO HEIDI AUGUST, like Lisa, set out to finish number one at the Farm. In her case, she didn't have a real choice; it was her only path to case officer status. Her peers were well educated and capable, but they didn't have Heidi's on-the-job training. Assigned to write a cable, some of her classmates took hours—days—to master the format. After years of having David Whipple crumple up cables and throw them at her, Heidi "could do it blindfolded." But Heidi didn't lord it over anybody. They sat in classrooms doing assignments, sometimes quite late—recruits couldn't take work back to their rooms—and if she finished early, she made runs to a nearby McDonald's and brought back food to share. Her classmates vaguely knew she had been in the agency for a while, but nobody asked much, and she did not provide details.

Heidi aced the recruiting scenarios, the report writing, the role-playing. Having burned out a station, having evacuated a war zone in a helicopter, having run operations against hard targets, she, like Lisa before her, finished first in her class. Heidi had done it. She was headed for the flip side of the pay grade card.

The head of European division congratulated her. But he had a word of caution. Calling her in, he warned her: "Heidi, there is no mommy track for Cat B women." "Mommy track" was an emerging term for working mothers who were perceived as having downshifted their careers, working part time or not as single-mindedly. What he was saying was: not permissible. The work of a spy did not leave time for maternal duties. If she wanted to succeed, she must forgo children. This didn't come entirely as a surprise; among the women case officers Heidi was aware of, there were fewer children than she could count on both hands. (When Lisa Harper did her own count in the 1980s, among two hundred female case officers, there were eighteen children.)

Still, to hear it expressed so bluntly did come as a shock. But Heidi was part of the sisterhood now, and she had to make trade-offs.

CHAPTER 8

THE HEIST

O N HER FIRST CASE OFFICER ASSIGNMENT, HEIDI AUGUST FOUND herself up against the world's most sophisticated diplomatic apparatus and the spies who navigated within it. The CIA's Geneva Station had several missions in a global city where the United Nations housed many big agencies—the World Health Organization, UNICEF—in the splendid Palais des Nations, an edifice near Lake Geneva. In the late 1970s and early 1980s, one of the station's tasks was keeping track of Soviet agents occupying high-level UN cover jobs. Another was to discover what Soviet allies like Ethiopia and Cuba planned to propose in meetings, to give a heads-up to the American delegation. Still another was to recruit foreign officials who would return to their home countries and ascend to important posts.

In short: The UN presence in Geneva was a happy hunting ground for spies from all nations, a place full of targets. Sooner or later, many would end up in the coffee lounge at the UN building, a vast space with an espresso bar and tables where backroom conversations hummed along. The first time she walked in, Heidi could smell the opportunities along with the coffee. Heidi's cover job was "assistant to the US political counselor" in the American delegation to the UN. This made her a third secretary. At the UN, secretary is not a job but a rank. There are first and third secretaries, and these are important people. The third secretary was usually a young person a few rungs up from a clerk. When a delegation wished to offend another delegation, the third secretary was deployed to sit at the microphone as the "insult." Being the insult was fun. Being female made her more insulting. It was part of the theatrical, public side of diplomacy, and she enjoyed it.

She enjoyed the clandestine side even more. And she had one advantage: Her former boss David Whipple had taken over as station chief, so she was reunited with her pepper-loving, hard-drinking boss, now in his late fifties and crusty and sharp-tongued as ever.

IN PREPARATION FOR THE Geneva posting, Heidi had undergone French language training and done much self-guided reading. Her cover-job portfolio included nuclear proliferation and human rights. Inheriting an African asset who schooled her on disarmament, she had him over for regular dinners and he sat at her kitchen table and tutored her. He was a short, round, cheerful man who wore silky shirts and bell-bottom pants and had a wife and children back home. After their sessions, she would hand him an envelope of cash and he would head out clubbing.

"Don't get in trouble," she would tease him.

Heidi's reading included essays by the Italian journalist and feminist Oriana Fallaci. Heidi wanted to develop her skill at elicitation, and Fallaci struck her as a useful model. The Italian writer could get anybody to say anything, especially men. In an interview with Iran's Ayatollah Khomeini—the cleric who assumed power after the America-backed shah fell, marking one of the CIA's greatest twentieth-century intelligence failures—Fallaci had gotten a rise out of her interview subject when she criticized the cleric's retrograde policies regarding women, flinging off the headscarf she'd worn to the interview and calling it a "medieval rag." From her reading, Heidi developed a new appreciation for the role that women's issues were assuming globally, including in regions where women's enlarged ability to study and work collided with a rising strain of religious fundamentalism that sought to suppress these changes. And she intuited the related role that women—with their twin impulses of aspiration and dissatisfaction—could play as assets.

Her aha moment occurred in diplomatic meetings where the side seats were full—she noticed—of women. They were clerks, assistants, secretaries, scribes. Many high officials present might regard them as interchangeable, but here, Heidi perceived, were targets hidden in plain sight. In ten years with the agency, she had never seen an American case officer attempt to recruit a female asset. And yet Heidi, having served in the role herself, well knew the kinds of "wonderful files" clerks and assistants had access to.

That's when her idea was born.

She would specialize in recruiting women. Women who were taken for granted, underpaid, disrespected; women with access to files. Whatever resentments women harbored, whatever mistreatment they suffered, Heidi would be happy to offer payback.

Heidi shared this idea with Whipple, with whom she'd had many arguments about the feminist movement in the United States. Whipple mentored Heidi because he liked her and saw her skills and work ethic, but he deplored organized feminism and hated Gloria Steinem. "He was dead-set against the women's liberation movement," and, when she pitched her plan, "thought I was nuts." Heidi pressed her point. Nobody was pursing female targets and the station was missing a lot.

"It's your career," he told her. If Heidi August wanted to waste her time, "that's your problem."

AS PART OF HER COVER JOB, Heidi sat on a human rights committee, and one day she found herself sitting next to a member from China. She invited her seatmate to lunch. The two women began taking walks, and the Chinese woman revealed that she had a husband and child, who were not allowed to visit her in Switzerland. Keeping family members at home, as virtual hostages, was one way Communist countries prevented civil servants from defecting. The woman was unhappy, and Heidi asked more about her background. The woman confided that up to now, the only Americans she had met were the nuns who educated her as a girl. She recalled the convent school fondly, reminiscing about songs by somebody named Foster. Heidi realized that she was talking about Stephen Foster, composer of "Camptown Races" and "Oh! Susanna," as well as "Old Black Joe" and other racist tributes to the antebellum South. She managed to obtain some cassettes and gave them to the woman. She might as well have given her a brick of gold bullion; her new friend was that overjoyed. This small gesture confirmed Heidi's instinct that there was an untapped lode of aggrieved women waiting for somebody to listen to their problems, and they might not be too hard to win over.

HEIDI'S NEXT BREAKTHROUGH CAME in the form of a cable from Paris, alerting Geneva Station to a person with access to an artifact the station had been trying for years to obtain. The Paris officer had met the person—a woman—at a party; she worked for a foreign government with offices in Geneva. He didn't know much else except that she played squash. Whipple passed the tip to Heidi. Part of being a good case officer was coming up with ways to bump somebody, and Heidi began thinking: How could she do this? An idea occurred.

There was a well-known squash club in Geneva, so Heidi inquired about joining. Whipple agreed to pay the membership fee, so Heidi bought a racket and started taking lessons. When the female players had a tournament, she scanned the roster and, sure enough, saw the target's name. Heidi asked the front desk if she could switch her locker to a centrally located spot. Before long she was sitting on a bench when she sensed a form approaching. It was her target, a vivacious young woman a few years junior to Heidi. They said hello; the target sat down and began to chat. Heidi confided that she was a novice and didn't quite get how a backhand in squash differed from a backhand in tennis. The woman said she would be glad to show her. Heidi said she was free the next day.

Her target was from an African country. She was white, and the only woman in her office. Her litany of grievances was long, legitimate, and centered on being treated as a servant. She was expected to make tea, clean, and serve men who never included her in conversations, meetings, or parties. They worked her at all hours and refused to pay overtime. "She was royally pissed off."

She was single and had no one to vent to, so she vented to Heidi, who was familiar with the common reasons why people betray their country. Money was—is—first and foremost. Other motivations include helping children or parents with education or medical care or housing. Also: ideology, narcissism, heroism, and a real wish to help the world. And, often, vanity. Case officers don't hesitate to stretch the truth and explain that the president himself is hanging on the asset's every report.

Now Heidi sensed another motive: revenge.

Soon she and the target were spending time not just on the squash court, but in cafés and on quiet sidewalks, having lunch and taking walks. Six months went by. Seven. Eight. Her target relaxed, evidently thinking that "if anything was going to happen to me with regard to this friendship with Heidi it would've happened by now," Heidi reflected. "She was becoming more and more comfortable in this role of confiding in me and telling me things that she probably shouldn't have been telling me. She knew it. I knew it."

As Lisa Manfull Harper put it, admiringly, Heidi August's "methods were feminine." Heidi was friendly, Heidi was empathetic, Heidi was cheerful and straightforward. And, Heidi was patient. She had seen case officers try to recruit assets on a first meeting. "You've got to be crazy" to try a cold pitch, she believed. She knew her first impressions were good ones. "I could tell within five minutes of the first meeting if somebody was worth my time." But it helped to proceed slowly enough to make a real connection.

After nearly a year, Heidi figured the time had come. When she confided that she worked for the CIA, her target "thought it was kind of cool." The act of recruitment is an intimidating one. A lot of new case officers drop out at that point, unable to make the hard ask. Heidi pressed ahead. Having told the asset who she was, she told her what she'd like her to do.

COMMUNICATIONS SYSTEMS ARE THE crown jewels of national security. No country gives away the secret of how it protects its communications—the machines and devices for creating codes and ciphers. Encrypted systems are how top secret conversations are sent. To surrender your communications system is to bare your national soul: plans, intentions, negotiations, alliances, troop movements. During World War II, code breaking was a key to Allied victory. The Allies broke the Enigma, the small but complex machine by which the German military enciphered its communications, and they broke Japanese military and naval encryption systems. The ability to read Axis messages was critical to winning the Battle of the Atlantic against the German U-boats; the Battle of Midway, against the Japanese navy; and other critical engagements including the D-day landing to liberate Europe. After the war, the US code-breaking force evolved into the National Security Agency, which continued to eavesdrop on adversaries—and, sometimes, allies.

It fell to the CIA to help by stealing code books and machines (and, later, computer codes, hardware, and software) that gave access to systems. Breaking into an embassy was part of the CIA's stock-in-trade. It could take a year to organize a break-in, sometimes with help from a host nation. Heidi, back in her clerk days, had operated US encryption machines. Other countries had similar devices. But each country employed its own key or "control" systems: numerical settings, tapes, and other devices that contained the method for encrypting and decrypting messages. Whatever format it came in, the encryption key changed regularly, making it impossible—in theory—for one nation to read the intercepted messages of another.

Unless they had the encryption key.

This is where Heidi's new asset came in. Geneva Station had long been trying to get access to the cryptographic methods used by the government her asset worked for. The thing the CIA wanted was a slender piece of technology that held the key. Heidi's asset operated the machine in her office. Heidi wanted the asset to remove the device long enough for CIA technicians to make a copy. She made her pitch. Heidi offered to pay the asset a regular amount. She knew the asset wanted to buy her parents a better home. The woman agreed.

Heidi would come to think of recruitment and handling as akin to pumping up a tire. Over lunch or drinks, an asset will agree to work for the CIA. Afterward, the air will go out of the tire; the asset's confidence will deflate; the case officer must pump up the asset's resolve. A few days later, the new asset called, and Heidi could tell by the tone of her voice that she was reconsidering. Heidi talked her back in.

Next, Heidi had to figure out how to steal the technology and put it back. First, they would need a concealment device. The CIA's technical office specialized in making those. Purses, briefcases, and wallets—reconfigured to have a secret compartment or false floor—were popular means. "What about a tennis bag?" Heidi thought, musing. The asset played tennis, and a tennis bag was roomier than a squash bag. Heidi bought two identical tennis bags and sent them to Frankfurt, Germany, where the CIA had a quiet arrangement with a certain shop. The Frankfurt technicians ripped apart one bag and used it to make a hidden compartment in the other. "They did a beautiful job, the technicians."

Now she had to find a place where the CIA's technology team could copy the device. She started hanging around in the neighborhood near her asset's office. She homed in on a hotel: small, unobtrusive, cozy. Guests had their own key to the front door, allowing them to come and go unobserved. The theft would take place on a Sunday morning. She found a weekend parking place; her car had diplomatic tags, so she couldn't park too close. She ran through the plan countless times in her mind. Weekends, she would do dry runs. By the time they were ready for the real thing, "I've been over it so often, I could recite it in my sleep."

She had to dream up a reason why her asset would be in the office on a Sunday, in case a co-worker appeared unexpectedly. "What was she doing there? We had to give her a cover story. Either she was on her way to play tennis or to come back. We're going out for dinner, and she forgot that she put her wallet in the office on Friday. Everything had to have a good cover."

Heidi instructed her asset to carry the tennis bag often. "Use it. The more people that see you with this bag, the better." The asset asked if she could keep the bag. "I said, 'Well, yeah, because we're going to need it again.'" The key changed every couple of months, and so did the device.

She also had to get her plan approved by headquarters. Every operation had to be signed off on by the operations directorate, sometimes by the CIA director. "It was what we call a 3,000-mile screwdriver from Washington," Heidi remembered. "Sitting there, trying to fine tune whatever it was anybody wanted to do." Headquarters had lots of questions. "They start nitpicking: Well, who else has instant access to that particular building? What's the cover story?"

And she had to convince her boss, Whipple, who was not yet persuaded. "I said, 'If I didn't think this would work, I wouldn't propose it. I know it's a gamble. Everything we do is a gamble.'"

When a CIA operation goes bad, and becomes public, it's called a "flap." Flaps are a big deal, especially in a high-profile station like Geneva. If the operation failed and the asset was caught, there'd be hell to pay not only for Heidi, but for her boss, who could lose his career. Whipple had never met the asset. He had to trust Heidi. "I will bring home the bacon," she assured him. "Don't worry."

"Are you sure you still feel strongly about this?" Heidi remembered him saying. "I said, 'Yeah, I do.'" In the risk-benefit analysis, the potential upside was enormous.

Whipple was planning a trip back to the States. He told Heidi he would go back early to talk to the division head involved. "I will argue this case," he told her. "If something goes wrong, I will retire."

Heidi also had many conversations with her asset, who was running by far the biggest risk. "If this thing goes south, I'll end up on an island, breaking rocks for the rest of my life," her asset told her. "And you'll get to go back to McLean, Virginia."

"You're absolutely right," Heidi recalled saying. She knew all too well what could happen to a spy who got caught; governments advertise the consequences to prevent others from flipping. She reminded the asset that the other outcome—success—would be good for her, good for her parents, good for mankind. "You've got to trust me," she said. At the same time, "I felt an enormous sense of responsibility."

A polygrapher flew in to make sure the asset was on the level—a routine part of vetting an asset. The polygrapher remarked that he had never polygraphed a female asset.

"Well," said Heidi. "Welcome to the world."

THE NIGHT BEFORE THEIR first theft attempt, Heidi stayed at the asset's house. She brought a book, figuring she'd have a hard time sleeping. (Later, her friend Mary Margaret Graham, a fellow case officer, would teach her to do needlepoint, for distraction during operations.) Restless in the guest room, Heidi began to wonder how her asset was faring, nerves-wise. She crept near the main bedroom door to listen. She could hear snoring. Snoring! "She was cool as a cucumber."

The plan was that the asset would drive to her office and go inside. Heidi would follow and park. The two would meet on the street and Heidi would relieve her of the tennis bag and hand it off to the technicians. "It went exactly as I thought." The asset unlocked the office building, disappeared, emerged. "She walked out with her tennis bag, met me on the street. We walked over a few blocks away to the hotel where the technicians were and went up in the elevator. She never saw the technicians, and they never saw her. The door opened. I went in and dropped the bag. We waited in the room. It took them about maybe ten minutes to copy what they needed to copy. All I saw was the bag when it came back out." The asset returned to her office and emerged, still carrying the bag, unruffled but in a hurry. She had a tennis game to get to. Heidi was astonished by her sangfroid. "Sure you don't want to go somewhere and have a drink?" asked Heidi, who felt like she could have used one. "No, no. I'm late for my match," said the asset.

Heidi went back to her apartment and took some bacon from her refrigerator. She put the bacon in a baggie. Whipple lived in the suburbs of Geneva, in the hills amid splendid vineyards. Heidi drove to his house and rang the doorbell. His wife answered the door, and she asked if he was home.

"I went inside, dropped a little bag of bacon on his breakfast table," Heidi said.

"I said, 'We got it.'"

THE OPERATION LASTED FOR more than a year. Heidi and the asset developed a mutual understanding and respect that bordered on genuine friendship. The asset was a firecracker and Heidi liked her. They were two single women far from their homes. And they shared a passion for cars. Geneva hosted an international car show. They met one day not long after that year's exposition. "You'll never guess what I saw at the Geneva car show," the asset told her.

"A car?" Heidi suggested.

"It's a little Alfa Romeo," she said. "I know I have the money."

Assets must be scrupulously careful when it comes to spending. Nothing is more likely to arouse suspicion than abrupt outlays. In this situation, Heidi did not hand over cash. Instead, the agency made a quiet deposit into a secret account. "Here's the problem," Heidi said. "You show up at work next week in this beautiful car. The first thing that your boss is going to say is, 'Where in the hell did she get the money for that car?'" So Heidi constructed a complex way for her asset to obtain a loan by means of a bank in Geneva and make the car purchase seem routine.

But Heidi wanted to give her something more. One way to keep an asset engaged is to provide something to look forward to after the next operation. Plus, Heidi really wanted to thank her. The asset had always wanted to see America. She was a fervent admirer of President Ronald Reagan and seemed somewhat in love with him.

"Okay, after this next round, what we're going to do is we're going to go to the States," Heidi told her. "We're not going to travel there together, but we're going to meet up in the States. I want to show you my America."

This required another operational plan. The asset had friends in Canada and flew to visit them. Then she took a bus over the border into New York. "No one could trace the fact that she was going to the United States," said Heidi. They visited New York City and saw the World Trade Center. "She wanted to see where Abraham Lincoln was shot, so we went to Ford's Theatre in Washington." They tooled down to Key West, turned around, and meandered back up the coast. The asset flew back to Geneva with no one knowing her Canadian vacation had included a two-thousand-mile detour.

AT THE END OF her first tour, having pulled off a "unilateral agent acquisition operation"—a recruitment made without help from any foreign government or intel service—Heidi August received a special commendation for an important first recruitment and, a year later, a promotion to GS-9, and shortly thereafter, GS-10.

She also received a cable.

THE CABLE CAME FROM headquarters. It was 1982, and CIA director William Casey wanted to offer Heidi something she never envisioned. He wanted to make her a chief of station. More than that, he wanted her to open a new station, in the Mediterranean region. She thought it was a joke. Once she realized it was a serious offer, she felt tempted. But—station chief? Was she ready?

She asked Whipple, who said she wasn't ready. If she accepted, he thought it was going to be a huge failure and "I'd regret it for the rest of my life."

I'm not ready, she told headquarters.

She received a cable back within twenty-four hours. Reading it amounted to a life-changing moment. At age thirty-five—nearly fifteen years after Heidi had been brought on as a clerk, obliged to pay her way to Washington, and consigned to the map-folding room—she, through her own ingenuity and cool-minded performance, had achieved something she herself never expected. She had made it to the other side of the card, and then some. The cable stated in no uncertain terms that she, Heidi August, was hereby ordered to take up an assignment as station chief.

CHAPTER 9

INCIDENT MANAGEMENT

By the time of Heidi August's promotion—more than thirty years after the CIA was founded—the number of female station chiefs could be counted on one hand. The first woman sent to head a major overseas CIA station was none other than Eloise Page, who in 1978 traveled to Athens to take over as station chief there. "You would have thought the world was going to end," recalled Eileen Martin, a CIA officer working in the inspector general's office, who heard the chatter in the halls and beyond. "The reaction was so strong; it was like, Oh my gosh, how can this happen, this is a disaster, this can never be!" It was bad enough when a man from the Directorate of Intelligence became chief of station; case officers hated being bossed around by analysts, who, they felt, had little true grasp of what they did. Far more appalling was the idea—nay, the reality—of a female chief. And while it may have been, at least in part, a gesture toward equality or a reflection of Page's talents and deserts—the officer who promoted her, John McMahon, was seen as well intentioned when it came to women—in Page's own view, her appointment represented a shrewd risk-benefit analysis by male rivals who wanted her out.

Nearing sixty years old, Eloise Page, the former OSS secretary, was dispatched to the Farm almost four decades after she started her career during World War II. "She was five foot one, and skinny," recalled Mike Kalogeropoulos, who was beginning his own operational career at the same time. A recent graduate of Columbia University, he'd been recruited while working behind the wallet counter at Macy's. Kalogeropoulos found himself standing at the firing range behind a woman old enough to be his mother. "She fired and the gun flew right out of her hand. She went flying into the mud." Page got up and tried again. Kalogeropoulos was deputized to "hold her shoulders as she shot, so she wouldn't fall backward. I'm about two hundred pounds, six feet tall, I'm holding this yellow-haired woman pointing down at the firing range."

Rather than thank him, Page, upon learning his name, remarked that his surname was too Greek, and he should change it to Kellogg.

Kalogeropoulos's first posting was to Athens, so he ended up working for Page. She liked him, and he liked her; over sherry on Fridays, she shared her understanding of why she'd been sent abroad. The men "were trying to get rid of her," she told him. In her former position overseeing policy, staff positions, and funding, she enjoyed, they felt, too much power. The barons resented her ability to approve or reject their budget requests and disliked having to come to her and grovel.

Men at headquarters had been pressing Page for years to go overseas, she told him. She had no real desire to serve in an overseas capacity and was able to put them off, saying she had to care for her aged mother. When her mother died, however, the pressure intensified. "They said, 'You have to go, or we'll cashier you,'" Kalogeropoulos remembered her saying—meaning that they would find a way to ease her out altogether. The barons offered her one of two stations: Canberra Station, which consisted mostly of working with Australian counterparts, or Athens, which was more "operationally vibrant," to put it mildly. Athens Station was a hard, risky assignment. Three years earlier, Athens station chief Richard Welch had been murdered by left-wing terrorists waging a guerrilla war against the right-wing Greek regime. He was succeeded by Clair George, another bigfoot chief who later would become implicated in the Iran-Contra scandal and convicted of lying to Congress. "It was a horrible time in Greece," one covert officer recalled. The top job here was not one for the faint of heart. "She picked Athens just to show them up," said Kalogeropoulos.

But the men at headquarters were setting her up for failure. Or so they believed. Greece was a patriarchal culture, and there were fewer women more conventionally feminine, and conventionally Anglo-American, than Eloise Page. She hated olive oil, detested lamb, favored sherry and cocktails over retsina or ouzo. So outlandish was the prospect of this diminutive high-church Episcopalian operating in a macho culture, the barons knew she would fall on her face, and they looked forward to watching. All these years, she had been telling them what they could and could not spend their money on. "They all hated her guts," observed Kalogeropoulos, who had been privy to the invective.

To everyone's surprise, the Greeks embraced her. They called her Auntie and relished her supple, well-mannered ways. Conventional femininity turned out to be a plus, not a minus. A background of finishing schools and old-Virginia hospitality stood Eloise Page in good stead; she had spent her life among men and knew how to charm and disarm them. They saw her as someone to pamper and take care of. "They did the same thing that they did with me," said Kalogeropoulos, who found himself dealing with Greek officials who respected his position and found his youth endearing. "I was twenty-two. They took me under their wing as 'the boy.'" They reacted the same way to Page. "They liked her because she was very nice to them." In Athens, he said, "she was extremely genteel, we had cocktail hour every Friday, in the office." And she was easily put under cover.

She was as quirky as the other station chiefs of her generation, however, and many aspects of her behavior were as, or more, egregious. In Athens, there was a Black family who helped take care of her residence; one of the children, a boy of eight or nine, was required by Eloise Page to salute anyone who entered. It was racist and objectionable in the extreme. The US ambassador was appalled. Page didn't care. And she ignored directives from headquarters if she disagreed with them. In 1978, headquarters ordered overseas case officers to write "contact reports" to build the database maintained by the vault women. The case officers balked. They hated writing. Page told headquarters that Athens Station would not be filing those reports. "It really just showed you the clout this woman had, headquarters would tell her to do something, and she'd say no."

Even as the Greeks embraced Page, the men in Athens Station chafed under her leadership, or some did. When her deputy—an alcoholic—died on the job, the men liked to say he was so scared of Eloise that it killed him. So, the men did what comes naturally to case officers; they ran an operation against her, working with allies back in Langley. As a ploy, Page was summoned to headquarters to sit on a panel. During her absence, an emissary from Langley paid a visit to Athens Station. The emissary called the station's officers in, one by one, and solicited criticism of her, assuring them he himself would replace her as chief.

"This bozo shows up, trying to get dirt," said Kalogeropoulos, who was warned by a mentor not to get involved. But his colleagues hastened to bad-mouth her. They said "she was inexperienced, she didn't know squat, really trying to nail her to the wall."

When Eloise returned, she called the staff into the secure room and divided them into two groups. One group consisted of those who had ratted on her; the other, those who had not. She turned to the rats and "proceeded to tell everybody what they had said. It was supposed to be confidential, and she just—it was just incredible," Kalogeropoulos remembered. After that, he said, two case officers left the station. "She threw them out."

None of this made her a revolutionary. Like her colleagues, Page knew how to protect her turf. She came from the same elite background as many of the men she worked with, and shared their outlook along with their tactics. A hard-line anticommunist, she was right-wing to the point of being blinkered. When the conservative Greek government fell in 1981, and socialists took over, Page "wouldn't let us report on it." The radio silence out of Athens Station amounted to an intelligence failure. On election night, she served fried chicken on a Wedgwood platter, hung banners, and declared victory. "She was so pissed off," said Kalogeropoulos. "That was the only flaw. She was very much aligned with the old-timers. Communists and socialists, she hated their guts."

In that sense, Eloise Page belonged to the same old guard that tried to sabotage her. At its founding and for decades afterward, the thinking at the CIA held that wealth was a desirable quality in an officer, in that it made him—or her—immune to mercenary interests. But wealth and social status create their own ideology. Page (though her family fortune had declined) bought into the institutional worldview, and the institution scorned her.

After three years, Page completed her tour in Athens. Upon her return, the seventh floor shunted her back into desk jobs. She was assigned to coordinate policy with the larger US intelligence community, working from a well-appointed office downtown, where she sometimes wrote cheery notes to her own secretary, Joanne Richcreek, using shorthand. It was a cushy job that amounted to being put out to pasture. She went on to serve at the Defense Intelligence Agency, but never again in operations and never again at Langley.

She did, however, employ operational tactics in her personal life. For years, Page headed the volunteer altar guild at Christ Church Episcopal, one of the oldest churches in Georgetown. She lived nearby on P Street. When Rev. Stuart Kenworthy took over as rector at Christ Church in the 1990s, the altar guild was down to a dwindling handful. Most members had quit to escape Page, who tyrannized them and monitored their conduct, reproving women who wore pants suits to Sunday service. It was the altar guild's duty to look after the church silver and ceremonial vessels. One after another, members came asking Kenworthy to depose her. Eloise Page ably case-officered him; he would try to talk her into resigning, and "she would go from this formidable personality to almost this little girl," hanging her head as if he was taking away her one pleasure in life. She hung on for some time with this canny tactic. Finally, he screwed up his courage and said, "Eloise. It's time to share the wealth."

But she did sometimes prevail in their interactions. When one of her beloved canine companions died, she begged him to preside over a funeral at her home. "We don't do dog funerals," Kenworthy gently told her, explaining that it would denigrate funerals for humans. But he agreed to say a few words. When he went to her home, he saw a full-sized grave—a "perfect rectangle" dug by a prominent Georgetown doctor—and a yard full of mourners. Kenworthy thanked God for the goodness of creation but stopped short of a full-fledged eulogy. He had to admit, the dog operation was well played.

———

WHEN HEIDI AUGUST STARTED her case-officer career in Geneva, she worked a few countries away from another formidable predecessor: Sue McCloud, a clandestine officer who served as a chief of station in Switzerland and Stockholm. Like Page, McCloud rose through the ranks owing to stoicism, personal sacrifice, and a knack for logistics; unlike Page, she relished overseas service and sought it out. But McCloud, too, was seen as someone who did not befriend younger women; when Heidi was posted to Geneva, she never heard any kind of "atta girl" coming from northern Europe.

Like Eloise Page, Sue McCloud came from an affluent background—in her case, immensely so. Her father, an athlete at the Naval Academy, was serving as a flight officer on carriers in the Pacific during World War II when her mother, raising two daughters in picturesque Carmel-by-the-Sea, California, became frustrated by the absence of any store in which to buy clothing for teenaged girls. With a bit of her own money, Mrs. McCloud founded one that "took off like gangbusters," as her daughter Sue put it. Sue McCloud majored in political science at Stanford, graduating in 1956 and proceeding to the Graduate School of International Studies in Geneva.

McCloud in 1959 was unable to find work except as a secretary at Crown Zellerbach, a paper and pulp company in San Francisco, where she served as "interpreter" for Richard Zellerbach, listening to phone calls for her boss, who was deaf but read lips, and mouthing to him what was said. After several years, she got a late-night call in her apartment from somebody named Jack Winter, who claimed to be a CIA recruiter. He invited her to take a test. Some of her male friends got the same call, so she went.

Hired in 1963, Sue McCloud was sent to the Farm at a time when the focus was on training operatives to maneuver in Cold War Europe. The grounds included full-fledged replicas of Eastern Europe border crossings, complete with jeep patrols and guard dogs. The CIA trainees wore military uniforms, in case an unfriendly spy service was taking a photo from overhead. Out of some seventy trainees, McCloud recalled, just six were female. Two quit. Another became a reports officer;

another, an analyst. The only aspiring case officer among the women, McCloud was allowed to parachute from a jump tower but not out of an airplane.

Upon completing her training, McCloud found herself in the thick of sixties-era covert action: Having been active in the Stanford under-graduate body—"I could talk student stuff"—she was assigned to take part in the agency's propaganda operations; specifically, the effort to penetrate the international youth festivals that were an artifact of the era, and stack their ranks with anticommunist young people. Among her assets was none other than Gloria Steinem. Given that the Soviets were doing the same thing, McCloud thought the effort made sense— "It worked fine until it blew up," she reflected amiably during an inter-view. She then worked her way up through the operational directorate, serving in Tokyo and other stations.

McCloud's reputation, like Page's, was fearsome. After Mike Kalo-geropoulos finished his tour in Athens, he put in for Stockholm and began getting back-channel warnings about taking yet another job with a female chief of station, particularly this female. "You really don't want to go out there and work for this woman," his mentors told him. But he took the job, and Sue McCloud liked him just as much as Eloise Page had.

Like Eloise Page, Sue McCloud remained unmarried. The men were hard on her; in cables, they gave her unflattering code-nicknames like Sumo. Sue was hard on them. People would arrive at their desks to find yellow paper with writing scribbled everywhere. They called McCloud's missives "yellow rain," and lived in fear of her wrath and her detailed instructions. "Every morning you'd go into your desk, long sheets of paper, did you do this, did you do that," said Kalogeropoulos. McCloud, he said, was "demanding" as well as "operationally brilliant." In many ways, for all its mystique, what a case officer's job requires are the skills of a modern-day event planner: resourcefulness, problem solving, and the ability to make things happen. In 1980, she helped exfiltrate six Americans who had taken refuge in the Canadian embassy during the Iranian hostage crisis, as part of the caper immortalized by the film *Argo*.

McCloud had drive, talent, and gravitas; what she did not have was a network of women to help her advance. Hence, her intimidating persona. Obliged to fight her own battles, she "left bodies in her wake, some of whom deserved it," said one admirer who noted that she was undermined by "a couple of men" who saw her as competition. "Sue, if you'd been a man, you'd be sitting in this chair," McCloud recalls being told by Ted Price, a head of the clandestine service. She chose to take it as a compliment. When I interviewed her in 2020, she remarked that she was in the job for the intellectual challenge, not the status, and "they gave me a lot of recognition in the end." Even so, she acknowledged that when she was making her own way, "women were second-class citizens" who had to work "twice as hard" to win a place.

And for all her perceived reputation as a woman who did not help women, McCloud did what she could. Among her gestures was a series of brown bag lunches where senior women met with younger ones. Men came as well: "They had some of the same concerns that women did, about family and various things, but they didn't feel that they could talk to their male counterparts without jeopardizing their positions." She helped women selectively and sometimes secretly, though her offers weren't always welcome. Mike Kalogeropoulos founded a mentoring network and observed that McCloud would offer to mentor younger women, only to be turned down by junior officers who gravitated toward the true power center: men.

But when she saw an opportunity, McCloud pounced. "My whole experience with her, and all my conversations, was about how she wanted to get women into the agency," recalled Mia McCall, a former case officer who helped McCloud with an operation while still a college student in the mid-1980s. "She's the reason I'm in."

McCloud, whose career responsibilities included talent spotting, set up every part of McCall's application: the medical exam, the polygraph, the interviews. Everything went well. They were "both stunned" when McCall was denied. As they discussed it, McCall recollected one interview when a man, a retiree working on contract, asked when she planned to have children. "I said something like, 'Well someday, but that's not what I'm thinking about right now.' He snorted and smirked and said, 'That's what you say now, but you will leave us halfway through, and all of this would have been a waste,' and he was very condescending."

When McCall repeated this, McCloud was "apoplectic."

"A couple weeks later, she came back to me and said, you're going to get a second chance to interview."

McCloud had gotten the man fired.

"She was very proud of herself. She said, 'Of all my operational accomplishments, you've now been behind two. You've helped me get rid of one more chauvinist preventing women from getting into the agency.'"

"This is what Sue McCloud means to me," said McCall, who marvels at how hard it was for early women ops officers to acquire power, and how vigilant they had to be to keep it. "If we spent half as much time operating against foreign threats as we do operating against each other," McCall reflected, "we'd be a hell of an intelligence service."

AND NOW HERE WAS Heidi August, not yet forty, opening a station in the Mediterranean region from scratch. Much of its work would involve monitoring activity out of Libya, which, in something of a coming-full-circle situation for Heidi, was led by Muammar Qaddafi. In the years since she'd borne witness to his ascendance, Qaddafi had become one of the world's biggest supporters and financiers of global terrorism, which was on the rise in Europe and the Middle East. Up until recently, terrorism in Europe had been the preserve of radical left-wing intellectuals—Communist and Marxist sympathizers using bombs, gun battles, and kidnappings to protest fascist influence.

Now, terrorism was reaching a new level. Several Middle Eastern groups were driving an unprecedented series of hijackings and bombings in which Americans, including CIA officers, were among the targets and victims. On April 18, 1983, the agency suffered its worst loss of life when eight of its people at the US embassy in Beirut died after a truck bomb was detonated by Hezbollah, the Lebanese militant group; in October that same year, 220 US Marines died in Beirut in a separate attack on their barracks. In 1984 and 1985, one airplane hijacking succeeded another. The Abu Nidal Organization, a radical wing of the Palestine Liberation Organization, was emerging alongside Hezbollah as the most dangerous terrorist group in the world. And Heidi was stationed in the region where much of this violence was taking place.

Nor did she have much in the way of support staff. In her new role as chief, Heidi presided over a tiny station tucked into an American embassy so small that it fitted into one floor of a bank building. The station consisted of Heidi and one secretary. (She requested that the city where it was located not be named, because it would expose a small number of embassy employees to the suspicion of being CIA officers. In diplomatic circles, this is a pastime called "guess the spook.") But the fact that the station was small didn't take away from the satisfaction of knowing she was chief, every bit the peer of the influential men she met at annual station chief conferences, which resembled gatherings of tribal chieftains.

Heidi also relished serving as the voice of the CIA at "country team" meetings. Overseas, a country team consists of the US ambassador and deputy chief of mission, the heads of the embassy's political and economic sections, the military attaché, other top officials, and the CIA station chief. The group gathers weekly to trade information and strategize. Separately, the CIA station chief holds private chats with the ambassador, to disclose operations that might blow up in somebody's face, metaphorically and literally. Omitting names or details, the CIA chief relates what the station is working on, whether local authorities are helping, and what a plausible storyline could be for the public affairs office in the event of a flap.

"I thought it was going to be great fun to do that kind of stuff," said Heidi. Her station was in a cosmopolitan city through which every target in the world traveled—from Europe, Africa, the Middle East. "It was like walking into a candy store. And the social life there was big, so you always saw everybody." When former CIA director William Colby heard she was opening a station, he invited her to go sailing with him and Barbara, who was delighted the CIA would have another female chief. Heidi joined the Colbys for dinner in their apartment, where another OSS veteran, David Blee, advised her to be picky and patient. "You've got three years to do this, don't do it all in six months. Be very methodical in what it is you're doing and prioritize your targets. Not so much who you get along with best, but who do you think has got the keys to whatever kingdom you're looking for."

HEIDI APPRECIATED THE GUIDANCE. Her cover job was as US consul, processing visas. From her desk, she saw the names of everyone applying to enter the United States. Her CIA role was not declared to the local government, which had been so penetrated by Libyan agents that to declare her would have been to declare her to the Libyans. In 1985, she set out to organize a training exercise on the island of Malta, a former British colony, now independent, that occupied a key location in the Mediterranean Sea, with an ancient history as a way station during the Crusades, and a crossroads between the Christian and Islamic worlds. The island had its own complex politics: Though formally nonaligned with either the Communist Soviet Union or the democratic United States, the island skewed pro-Palestinian and anti-Israeli. Anti-American sentiment was strong. Close to both Europe and Africa, it was a plausible locus for a plane hijacking.

Heidi's job was to set up the training and make contacts within the Maltese police department, without people knowing the CIA was behind the exercise. She developed a course called Incident Management in which FBI agents flew over to lead several days of training in how to handle a hijacking. The agency's Rome Station was deeply affected by terrorism and helped sell the idea to the Maltese hosts. A deal was struck: The FBI trainers would come up with a hijacking scenario, and Maltese officials would handle it in real time.

Heidi sat in on the session, ostensibly representing the US State Department's visa-processing unit, just a harmless lady functionary who handled passports and was there to report to Rome. As a trained operative, she was also there to recruit. She scanned a list of potential Maltese participants and spotted some she wanted to target as internal assets—people who could tell her whatever they couldn't tell her in their official capacity. One was a young investigator, a smart, personable guy with training in forensics. The other was the police officer in charge of the traffic section, who could slip her the license plate numbers of diplomats. She made sure they were included. Heidi had her own small entourage that included her secretary and an Arab-speaking officer there to help target a certain Libyan. The officer was a twentysomething alumnus of the University of Virginia. His father had worked for the CIA, and he'd grown up in Beirut. Unlike Heidi, he had been ushered into the clandestine service, a legacy hire. She and her team took the Maltese officials out for dinner, and the Maltese returned the favor. She got to know the forensics investigator, and "engineered for myself a dinner at his house so I could meet his wife and his two little kids."

Heidi had developed a modus operandi when working with married male assets. She took pains to befriend the wife, making it clear she would meet often with the husband, but not to worry—there would be no fooling around. The tactic worked well. She liked being around families, especially children. At this point in her adult life, Heidi knew her career would always take precedence over marriage, a life state she saw as best avoided for any woman officer who wanted to advance. She knew a husband's career always came first, and that wives had a chance to shine only if the marriage ended—in divorce, or sometimes, as did happen, death. And in the case of divorce, ex-wives could be—and were—sabotaged by ex-husbands who had risen higher and were better connected at headquarters than they were.

Being single enabled Heidi to handle a two-job lifestyle. She never had to worry about kids expecting dinner or a husband feeling neglected. But she did miss children and enjoyed spending time around them. The Maltese officials were gracious to her. A month after the training, they were all friends, and "everybody sort of goes home."

HER WORK TOOK HER to Malta often. She rented a small apartment in Mdina, a fortified medieval town in the island's center. On November 23, 1985—a Saturday before Thanksgiving—she went to dinner in a new seafront restaurant called the Lanterna. She had mentioned to the US ambassador she was excited to try it. Telling him her dinner location turned out to have been a good idea. "I'm sitting at this lovely table with my Maltese friends and the owner of the restaurant comes over and I was the only non-Maltese at the table. He said, Miss August? And I said, yeah? And he said, you have a phone call." He ushered her to the telephone at the front desk.

She picked up the receiver to hear the voice of the US ambassador. An Egyptian plane headed from Athens to Cairo had been hijacked. The plane had just landed at Malta's Luqa airport. There were three Americans on board. Heidi returned to the table, made her apologies, put down cash to cover her bill, and left. Outside, she took off her high heels and started running barefoot down the street. Back at her apartment, she wriggled out of a cocktail dress, changed into Levi's and a UC Boulder sweatshirt, and packed a small bag including a hairbrush and toothbrush. She also grabbed a pack of Carlton 100s and her diplomatic neck badge.

Earlier that night, Egyptair Flight 648 had taken off from Athens. Ten minutes in, three Palestinian men hijacked the plane and ordered it diverted to Libya. Passengers were told to hand over passports. Reaching into his back pocket, an undercover sky marshal instead pulled out a gun and shot the lead hijacker and killed him. A shoot-out ensued; a bullet penetrated the fuselage and the plane lost altitude and began losing fuel. The Egyptian pilot managed to touch down at Luqa. When Heidi got to the airport, the US ambassador was waiting. The hijackers were demanding fuel. "And he said, 'The world is inside of this plane. You've got Palestinians, you've got Americans, you've got Israelis, you've got Greeks, you've got Egyptians.'" The Maltese prime minister, Karmenu Mifsud Bonnici, had rushed to the airport to negotiate with the hijackers—exactly what should not happen. Negotiations, she knew from the training session, should be done by professionals.

The United States had no jurisdiction over the hijacking and how it was handled. Heidi's only responsibility was the welfare of the Americans on board, but she resolved to influence events to the extent she could. Running up the steps of the control tower, she encountered the investigator she had recruited coming down. They had an official relationship but also met in clandestine sessions. Like Heidi, he was worried that Malta had become a "stationary aircraft carrier" for Libyan agents, and that his own government wasn't doing enough. Pausing, he asked if this was part of the training exercise. She replied, "As far as I know, this is real."

He said, "Oh, Jesus."

There was nobody at CIA headquarters in charge of handling terrorism events as they unfolded. The lone officer who dealt with terrorism, Charlie Allen, mostly reported to the national security community. Heidi was on her own. She needed a command post. On the ground floor was a bare room containing an old rotary phone. The US ambassador said she and some others could use it. She asked what he meant by "others."

"He said, 'Well, you're going to be joined by some other diplomatic people there who have citizens in that plane.'"

Chairs and a small table were brought in. Her tablemates consisted of the head of the PLO office in Malta and the head of the Libyan embassy on the island. The governments the two Arab men worked for would never sanction their meeting with Heidi in her cover job, nor would the US State Department permit her to meet with them. And yet here they all were, side by side by side.

The three exchanged business cards. Heidi shared cigarettes from her pack of Carltons. From an operative standpoint, it was a rare chance to make contacts. "I had wanted to meet the PLO guy in the worst way. I mean, it was a great operational advantage to me." But it would be impossible for her to talk on the phone without her tablemates hearing.

The person she most wanted to talk to was Dewey Clarridge, now chief of European division, who had weathered the terrorist surge during his tenure as station chief in Rome. Using the phone to call her secretary, Jackie, she quietly asked, "How's your pig Latin?" Her secretary, working out of Heidi's apartment in Mdina, said it was rusty but usable. She and Heidi continued talking, using a garble of English slang and pig Latin. At her direction, Jackie and the UVA-grad-junior-officer set up a Bearcat scanner that Heidi had bought in the States, tuning it to the frequency of the police, the ambulances, and the airport. They could hear what was happening and relay it to her, which was vital, since the Maltese were telling her little. They sent cables to headquarters and relayed questions to Clarridge, who cautioned that the plane should not be permitted to leave the ground. He suggested flattening the tires. Instead, Heidi put in a word with the investigator, who got Maltese officials to put small trucks in front of and behind the wheels, using the cover of darkness to block it in.

She got the sense that Clarridge was jealous she was there and he wasn't.

The terrorists wanted fuel so they could fly to Libya and negotiate for the release of some terrorists who were imprisoned. The Maltese refused to provide fuel until the passengers were released. The terrorists warned they would start shooting a passenger every fifteen minutes. On the scanner, Heidi's team could hear the pilot warning that they were serious and pleading for fuel. A Maltese doctor was permitted aboard and emerged, shaken, reporting that two wounded flight attendants would bleed to death if untreated. The flight attendants and eleven passengers, all women, were allowed off. For a moment it seemed possible that the rest would be released.

But inside the plane, the terrorists called the two Jewish passengers, and the three American ones, to the front. They shot a Jewish woman, Nitzan Mendelson, and threw her body onto the tarmac. Heidi's assistants heard the gunshot on the scanner and let her know. Heidi went upstairs and found a small men's room with a hand-cranked window and a door that locked. On the way back, she ran into the investigator; she told him they couldn't stop the unfolding nightmare, but when it ended—however it ended—they should find out who had financed it, who had trained the hijackers, and whether more attacks were planned. He assured her he would help.

The second Israeli woman, Tamar Artzi, was shot and thrown onto the tarmac. Still alive, she crawled under the plane and hid. Fifteen minutes later, an American man, Patrick Baker, was shot, but he was tall and the shooter couldn't get a good angle. Baker, after falling, played dead until he felt it was safe, then got up and dashed under the plane, unseen by the hijackers, and was rescued.

So, Heidi thought—they were shooting the Americans. Back in the little command post, the Libyan had vanished, and the PLO representative seemed depressed and helpless; there were Palestinians aboard, including women and children. He talked about his life and family, and asked Heidi about hers. Her secretary called to say the hijackers were negotiating for food. A second American, Jackie Pflug, was shot and her body was thrown onto the tarmac. She was alive but nobody realized it. She would lie on the ground for five hours.

A US embassy driver had delivered to Heidi a pair of binoculars, which she hid under her sweatshirt. She went back to the bathroom, climbed up on the sink, and looked out. The cabin door of the plane opened, and a tall woman emerged. A hijacker ordered her to kneel and shot her in the head point-blank. Her body made the long drop to the tarmac and lay still. It was the third American, a woman.

The Maltese prime minister was handling the negotiations, but Egypt was in charge of any hostage rescue attempt, since the hijacked plane was Egyptian. The US ambassador called Heidi upstairs and confided that a group of Egyptian commandos was en route. The US Army Delta force had been providing Egypt with hostage rescue training. A group of those soldiers was on board. Heidi asked whether anybody had told the Maltese there would be US soldiers arriving on Maltese soil. Formally nonaligned—neutral when it came to the two great powers—Malta would never permit American uniformed soldiers onto the island. She urged the ambassador to let Egypt know the US soldiers must be dressed as civilians.

Heidi wanted to be planeside when the C-130s landed, to make sure the US soldiers could help the Egyptian rescuers practice. Two planes, camouflaged, landed in near silence; Heidi figured the engines had been altered by special forces to make them less noisy. The planes were far enough from the hijacked airliner to be invisible to the terrorists. One plane held equipment. The other held a team of young Egyptians, who filed out wearing jeans and sneakers. Behind them were three American officers in uniform. Heidi was standing with a Maltese protocol officer. "And the head of protocol went, 'Wait a minute, what is this?'" recalled Heidi. "I said, 'Well, I don't know, let me go ask.' I mean, I knew, but I had to play stupid."

She found an Egyptian colonel and asked whether anybody had instructed them to put the Americans in civilian clothes. He said no. The head of protocol refused to let the Americans off the plane, except a major general who was told to go straight to the US embassy. Heidi was alarmed to see wooden crates containing a powerful explosive, Semtex-H, being unloaded off the other plane. It seemed like a lot.

It was now day two. Still posing as a visa lady, Heidi accompanied the Egyptian team into a hangar. The commandos looked tired and bored. "I see a kid sitting by himself at the table, one of the rescue guys." He spoke some English, and Heidi asked him if the team had ever rescued hostages from an airplane. He said no. The team handled hostages trapped in buildings. They traded off weekends with the team who did airplanes. This happened to be their duty weekend.

Heidi went back and talked to one of the US advisers. "I want to make sure I understand this," she recalled saying. The group had never been deployed before. Their training had been restricted to buildings. He said that was right.

When she communicated the situation to her secretary and the junior officer, the UVA grad ventured that it "could turn out to be a real goat fuck."

The Egyptian team devised a plan to storm the aircraft by posing as food suppliers. Then they changed their mind and decided to blow a hole in the luggage bay. "The hijackers had used neckties to tie the inside of the doors so they couldn't be opened. They were thinking they were going to blow their way into it from underneath."

The rescue went horrifically awry. The explosives went off in the rear of the plane, vaporizing one of the terrorists. Inside the plane, Omar Mohammed Ali Rezaq, the sole remaining hijacker, pulled a grenade pin with his teeth and rolled it down the aisle. Another explosion followed. The pilot left the cockpit and hit Rezaq with a fire ax. "We heard all this shouting and guns going off," Heidi recalled. Human forms began fleeing the plane and the Egyptians were shooting. It was dark and hard to see.

After twenty minutes of "just sheer mayhem," the shooting stopped.

Fifty-eight passengers lay dead, many shot by the commandos. Others died of smoke inhalation. The dead included all seven children who had been on the plane. Maltese firemen began to line up bodies on the tarmac.

The Maltese prime minister called a press conference, announced that all the hijackers were dead, and urged officials to go home. "My thought is, what do I do with these wounded Americans?" recalled Heidi. "And the dead one? Now I had to put my State Department hat on." She left to get some sleep. The PLO representative insisted on walking her to her car. She was the first American he had met. He told her he would like her to come to his home for a meal and meet his family. She said she would like to do that.

Back in Mdina, her two assistants had checked into a hotel, and she had the rented apartment to herself. The place was unheated.

Heidi had been given the passport of the dead American woman, Scarlett Rogenkamp. She had been a civilian employee of the Air Force, working at an airbase in Athens. For the long Thanksgiving holiday, Rogenkamp had decided to visit Cairo. When the hijackers began checking passports and papers, she had done something Heidi felt was "quite clever": She slipped her military ID into the seat pocket in front of her, so hijackers wouldn't know she worked for the US military. Her passport identified her as a tourist.

The task fell to Heidi to call Rogenkamp's mother, who lived in Oceanside, California. She wrote a script on a legal pad. Then she dialed the number. "And I didn't know what to say. I didn't know how much she knew. I didn't know if she knew that her daughter was going to Cairo for Thanksgiving. I had no idea."

Heidi introduced herself as being with the American embassy at Malta. "And I said, 'I'm not sure anybody from the State Department has been in touch with you yet.' 'No.' I said, 'Well, I have some very sad news.' I said, 'Your daughter, Scarlett . . .'"

The hijacking was not yet on the news. "She said, 'Well, I know she was going to Cairo for the weekend,' or something like that. I said, 'Well, there was a hijacking and unfortunately she didn't survive it.' I didn't give her any of the details. I said, 'But I will take care of getting her back to California.'"

Heidi and the US ambassador had agreed to meet the next morning in the intensive care unit of St. Luke's hospital. When Heidi got to the ICU, she found the ambassador sitting with the head of the hospital, who pointed to a patient hooked up to IV lines. The figure in the bed was the remaining hijacker, Omar Mohammed Ali Rezaq. "And the question was, what do we do with the hijacker? Because the Libyans started jumping up and down that they wanted him."

Heidi relayed the situation to Dewey Clarridge, who, she says, replied: "No, we're going to come and we're going to kidnap him."

"I said, 'Dewey, I don't think that's going to be possible. How do you intend to do that?' I said, 'He's hooked up to life support. You would have to break into this hospital.' He said, 'No, but you've got to keep him out of Libyan hands.' She eventually grasped why the Libyan ambassador had been in the control room even though there were no Libyan passengers on the plane. He was there to protect the interests of the terrorists.

She met with the Maltese investigator. A passenger had reported the hijackers were seen sitting together in the departure lounge in Athens, wearing suits and carrying briefcases. He proposed searching the charred overhead bins for the briefcases. Heidi thought this was a long shot. Several days later, the investigator invited her to dinner, and there were the briefcases. They went through them. There were maps of Athens; little marks about their meeting places; a bank that was circled. "So we had people in Athens go to the bank and get the story. It was money that had been transferred from Yugoslavia." The investigation pointed to Abu Nidal. The investigator provided her with the hijackers' full names and photocopies of their passports, and she ran name traces.

The investigator debriefed Rezaq. Heidi funneled questions.

The question became: What would the Maltese government do with Rezaq? After recovering from his injuries, he was put on trial in Malta, convicted, and sentenced to twenty-five years in prison. Meanwhile, Heidi had a more immediate problem: how to get the body of Scarlett Rogenkamp home. Rogenkamp had been a civilian employee at the US Air Force Contract Management Center at Tanagra Air Base, outside Athens. Technically it was the Air Force's responsibility to see that her body was returned. But when Heidi called the base commander in Athens, he asked if there was a "fund site"—a pool of money to pay for transport. Heidi had no idea. "The question is, are you going to come pick her up, at least take the body to Heathrow where I know you have planes going every day?" He didn't know. "He said, 'I don't think we have any provision for this, particularly because it's a civilian.' So, I said, 'Well.'"

Once again, a problem outside her purview became Heidi's to handle. She called Ernest Flamini, an official at British Airways, who had been at the dinner table with her. She told him she needed a favor. She needed to get a body to California. The body was in the morgue, and she would take care of the paperwork. He advised that she didn't want the passengers on an outbound flight to see a coffin being loaded, and offered to have the coffin taken in an ambulance to the airport. It would be good, he said, if Heidi would accompany it. She said she'd be happy to.

Flamini explained that the coffin should be transported to one of the airport hangars. "And what we're going to do is, we'll pull the plane out, and then the plane goes into another hangar where they partially back it, so that the passengers don't see anything, they're all facing this way, and everything's going on behind them." Heidi contacted the hospital to get a shipping coffin. The next day, "we had it all arranged."

UP TO THAT POINT, the body of the American woman had seemed abstract, a distant form Heidi had seen falling. She was not prepared for the emotions she would feel seeing the body up close. "They pulled back the sheet, and there was this nice-looking gal." As with her intrepid car-loving asset in Geneva, she felt a connection with this unmarried civil servant. The dead woman's face was swollen and there was blood matted in her hair.

It occurred to her Rogenkamp's coffin should be wrapped in an American flag. The next day she obtained one, never used, from the embassy storeroom. "And I get there, and Ernest is there, the British Airways guy, he's a Maltese, lovely people. And I'm carrying the flag. I said, 'Ernest, you know how to do this?' He said, 'No, but I'm sure we can figure it out.'" They found a bungee cord and attached the flag. "They bring out a little airplane vehicle, a little teeny thing, that had like a conveyor belt on it, it was used for conveying luggage up into the plane. So we put Scarlett on the little conveyor belt in her coffin, and they backed up this plane."

Heidi put her hand on the coffin. She leaned over and once again assured the dead woman that she would track down the mastermind who caused her death. The horror of the past forty-eight hours had shaken and transformed her. She resolved to commit her career to fighting terrorism. The agency needed a better way to stop attacks and protect human life. "I'm going to make a career out of this, because this is just getting under way here, and I don't want to go through this again."

Fighting Communism remained the agency's central mission. Terrorism was not a career-making field. But—people were dying. Families, public servants, children. "I knew we had no way of combating any of this, so there had to be a better system. We had suffered so much of losing American tourists in airports in Europe because of terrorism incidents. So I just thought, there's got to be a better way to do it."

She lifted her hand off the coffin. And up the conveyor belt Scarlett Rogenkamp went.

CHAPTER 10

THE VAULT
WOMEN REVOLT

1980s and 1990s

THE CIA HEADQUARTERS BUILDING GREETS VISITORS WITH A lofty ground-floor portico topped by an angular roof, peaked and folded downward like origami. Above, more than five hundred vertical windows line the east façade, which runs parallel to the Potomac River. Seen from the air, the footprint resembles the letter H: The east and west wings form the long sides of the H, connected by two shorter cross pieces. Inside, the result is a lot of long corridors, and corners around which colleagues can materialize abruptly.

Walking down one hallway, in the 1990s, Jonna Mendez spotted an officer approaching. He was an old-school ops guy—louche, often drunk, and notorious among the women for describing the sex acts he would like to commit upon them. As they drew closer, Mendez braced.

Jonna Mendez had started out at the CIA in the early 1960s, as a secretary. Fresh out of college, Mendez was working as a bank teller in Germany when she befriended a group of young Americans who came to cash paychecks every week. They were convivial to the point where she soon had the same employer they did. Back in the States, she found herself working in the CIA's technical office, still located in Washington, on a hillock in Foggy Bottom, the agency's historic heart. Across the street was 2430 E Street, the legendary address of Allen Dulles, where a sign blandly read BUREAU OF NAVAL MEDICINE. The technical office employed a thousand wizards who developed spy equipment—tiny cameras, hidden microphones, coding machines, poison pens.

The denizens of the technical office did not share the reverence for the men of the operations directorate that so many others did. It was their view that case officers tended to be hapless at using gadgets. "We used to call the case officers James," said Mendez. "We would say: James is going to lose it, he's going to break it, or it's going to break on its own." The goal was to design spy gear sturdy enough to withstand mistreatment by the Jameses. Within two years she rose to become secretary to the director of the office. "It was a quick climb to the top. When I got to the top, I discovered it was a dead end." Out the window she could see the rooftops of the Smithsonian rising above the National Mall. She told her boss—a quirky, brilliant, good-hearted man—that she planned to quit and go to work there.

To keep her, her boss offered to enroll her in a photography training course. Soon Mendez found herself on a runway south of Washington, clambering into a small plane with open doorways. Once aloft, she wore a harness and dangled outward, learning to hold a long-lens 35 mm camera while using a microphone to call requests to the pilot. "I would say: 'See that pickup, the one going down the dusty road—can we get down low enough so that I can photograph the license plate?' That's what I really consider my first day at CIA."

Mendez became a photo operations officer: taking photos and training officers, and their assets, to snap images of papers, people, and military installations—how to steal secrets without getting caught. The work gave her great satisfaction, not just the technical challenges but knowing she was protecting assets who were putting themselves at risk on America's behalf.

Around the same time Heidi August found herself sitting on a bathroom sink watching a hijacked plane burn up on the tarmac, Mendez became aware that espionage was becoming more deadly. During the 1980s and 1990s, "the targets that we were working against were changing from traditional espionage targets to terrorism, and to narcotics, and counternarcotics. We were starting to work against totally different groups of people, a more criminal element. It wasn't so much about diplomatic cocktail parties and chatting up people from another embassy. There was a lot more danger. The risks were bigger."

Mendez took many training sessions, and these began to include classes in self-protection. She took courses in defensive driving, escape and evasion, shooting. Working against drug traffickers, she many times thought she might get shot. In Latin America, going to work at a US embassy, she'd be picked up in an armored car, with cars in front and behind full of men with guns. "The protocol was, you've got three minutes to get into this car, we'll stay three minutes and leave."

And male case officers became more aware of how their own gender put them at risk. In the early seventies, she said, many Jameses thought disguises were silly; that started to change when it became riskier to be "identified as that American man." Wigs and mustaches began to serve almost as a form of body armor. Walk-ins presented a new level of danger. The walk-in might have valid knowledge of a threat, or he might be "some random terrorist wanting to see what the inside of your embassy looked like, and see who came down to meet him."

Protocol dictated that someone had to meet a walk-in, and men became more willing to don disguises to do it. Business began to boom in her section of the Directorate of Science and Technology. "We were doing all kinds of R&D, developing new materials, things that were more comfortable, went on easier, quicker, things that you could breathe in in a hot, humid, sticky climate, things that wouldn't melt, hair glues that wouldn't go limp, hair color and skin color and on and on." For Jonna, sitting in the director's chair, "It was kind of an exciting time."

It was also a time when a new generation of women entered on duty, with specialized degrees and training. One of these, a chemist named Trish, happened be walking beside Mendez the day she was making her way down the long corridor of the headquarters building. As the officer—his name was Bill—approached, Mendez prepared to ignore his comments.

This officer was hard to ignore. "He's famous—like a construction worker on a crane. You'd walk by and he'd whistle and yell, say 'here's what I want to do!'" And sure enough, "we're walking, he's saying, 'you two beautiful ladies, you know what I would like,' and he starts in on that. And Trish just looks at him and says 'Fuck off.'"

"He was just stunned," Mendez recalled. "He was just stunned. I'm sure that he hadn't heard that before, from a woman, especially from a pretty young woman. I almost fell over. And I thought, 'Oh, okay, it begins. She's the fresh—not going to put up with the crap.' And I do believe that there was a little bit of a sea change."

IN THE 1980S, THE Central Intelligence Agency was enjoying a hiring boom. Recruits included women who had a different life experience from Lisa Harper, Heidi August, and Jonna Mendez. These women had played sports and benefited from Title IX, the federal law guaranteeing equal funding for women's athletics; they had lived through the sexual revolution and gone to coeducational colleges. They entered the espionage business expecting to be treated as equals.

The agency itself, meanwhile, had undergone a series of beatings. The 1967 exposé in *Ramparts* magazine made public the extent to which the CIA had co-opted so-called independent entities, like newspapers and student groups, and broken the law by spying on American citizens. In 1961, the disastrous Bay of Pigs operation had exposed the lack of competence and judgment in covert operations and led to the resignation of Allen Dulles. In the early 1970s, Watergate soured the public on Washington, presenting the spectacle of Howard Hunt, a former CIA guy, providing the Watergate burglars with absurdly cheesy disguises. In 1974, the investigative journalist Seymour Hersh published a blockbuster exposé in *The New York Times*—"Huge CIA Operation Reported in U.S. Against Antiwar Forces, Other Dissidents in Nixon Years," read the headline of the lead story of the December 22 edition—revealing the CIA's domestic spying and its surveillance of the antiwar movement. These flaps amounted to an annus horribilis for the CIA. In 1975, the "Church-Pike hearings" unfurled in Congress, day after day in which the post-Watergate class of newly elected members flexed their muscles and began to exercise oversight of the intelligence community, for really the first time in US history. Two congressional committees, chaired by Frank Church (D-ID) in the Senate and Otis Pike (D-NY) in the House of Representatives, sought to expose and seriously rein in abuses by the intelligence agencies, not just the CIA but also the FBI,

IRS, and NSA. Abuses included the wiretapping and bugging of American citizens including journalists and Supreme Court justices; harassment of American citizens; and, at J. Edgar Hoover's own behest, wiretapping of Martin Luther King, Jr., by the NSA and by the FBI. Abroad, the agency had toppled regimes; fomented a military coup against Salvador Allende, the democratically elected president of Chile; enabled the assassination of General Rafael Trujillo Molina in the Dominican Republic. And so on. One major upshot was the creation of the House Permanent Select Committee on Intelligence and the Senate Select Committee on Intelligence.

During the hearings, the director at the time, William Colby, whose scholarly horn-rims and earnest rectitude earned him the nickname Choirboy, surrendered records of CIA covert operations—what became known as the "family jewels." Colby admitted to Operation Chaos, the surveillance of antiwar and dissident groups; "the buildup of substantial files on Americans"; surveillance of journalists; experiments with mind control drugs and LSD; and assassination attempts of foreign leaders.

In 1977, a new director, Stansfield Turner, resolved to clean house. A technocrat who favored signals intelligence and satellite imagery, Turner eliminated more than eight hundred positions—the notorious "Halloween massacre"—making him hated by the workforce over which he presided. Reports officer Amy Tozzi recalls explaining to the director why they were having trouble getting information out of Cuba; when you fire so many officers, she told the former naval commander, you must rebuild your covert sources. President Jimmy Carter's administration inflicted indignities large and small upon the whole federal workforce: thermostats were turned down during the energy crisis, and people drank hot chocolate to stay warm.

A rebuilding had begun under Ronald Reagan, who fixated on the potential for mortal combat with Soviet Russia, what he called the Evil Empire. A federal hiring freeze in 1982 was followed by a surge of hires. Equal Employment Opportunity laws now applied to the federal government, and at the CIA, the impetus to hire women was spurred by an uneasy sense that people were watching—or trying to. With Congress trying harder to extract statistics, women were hired in numbers. The institution still found ways to delay promotions and make them feel unwelcome. Black men and women were steered into the human relations department, inflating the numbers without giving Black employees true opportunities to advance in their chosen fields.

While Heidi August and Lisa Harper were overseas, showing what women could accomplish in spy work, a set of operations was unfolding at Langley, overt and covert, to change the culture. In some ways, headquarters was a tougher environment than overseas. There was more competition, less independence, less freedom to maneuver, more knives out. But as women at headquarters pressed their case, the CIA sisterhood, disorganized as it was, grew and, in its own way, prospered.

SOME OF THE FIRST change efforts came from fed-up backroom workers—the oft-scorned vault women. One was Lee Coyle, who in 1954 had taken her sister's typing test as well as her own. Coyle rose to head the "information management" office, which managed the 3 x 5 cards. These were the proceeds of years upon years of recruitment, elicitation, and research, one of the most valuable sets of intelligence records in the world. In Coyle's case, the paperwork appealed to her and so did the hours. Her household needed two incomes, like many in the Northern Virginia area, where neighborhoods in Vienna and Reston were so thick with CIA employees that, if your car broke down, you could hitch a ride to Langley with a neighbor. Coyle took the night shift so she could spend days with her kids.

Even in a female-dominated office, the top managers were men. The women were vulnerable to sexual predation: Coyle can't forget the branch chief who, while seated next to her, lifted her dress and put his hand up her leg. "I was—I couldn't move, just couldn't move, could not move. I did nothing, except, from that day on, I never wore a dress again." At Christmas, the branch chief would grab her staffers and pull them under the mistletoe. "He would French-kiss them, and they would tell me how disgusted they were. And I to this day fault myself for not going to the rooftops to complain about that, and to put him in his place."

But to complain would have been pointless. The Equal Employment Opportunity office was located offsite and "considered laughable," Coyle recalled.

By the 1980s, Coyle's office had begun converting hundreds of millions of paper file cards into digital records. "To get people to trust the computer" was a massive effort. The women in her office—mothers, grandmothers—proved adept. But the women didn't get promoted, or not as often. For Coyle, the last straw came when management "brought in a young man" from the Directorate of Intelligence who she suspected was a castoff somebody wanted to off-load. He arrived two grades below her, and soon was promoted over her head. "I took that as a case to equal opportunity, and I won that one. I did get my promotion, and I got a lot of money, so I bought a mink coat." After a career in support positions, she reflected that "we had to fight for everything."

One of the first real shots over the bow had occurred in 1977, when a staff operations officer named Harritte Thompson quietly brought a complaint to the Equal Employment Opportunity office. Staff officers constituted the sturdy backbone of the Directorate of Operations. "Tee" Thompson was the best of the best, and everyone knew her, recalled Heidi August: a hypercompetent, good-natured officer who worked in the Near East division. It was staff officers' job to run interference between the field and—well, everybody. They were a vital subset of the sneaker-lady corps. Sometimes running between the directorates, staff officers would send and receive cables, work with analysts to find out what new intelligence was needed, consult archives, run traces, send dispatches.

Thompson's suit showed that even when men and women held the same job, women made less and got promoted more slowly. Her supervisors said she was "indispensable" and had an "encyclopedic knowledge of operations." They repeatedly recommended her for promotion, but every time her file went before the agency's all-male promotion panel, comprising high-level officials from all directorates, she was denied. She remained stuck "in grade" as a GS-14, doing jobs intended for a GS-15 or GS-16. After ten years without a promotion, she filed her complaint. It asserted that she had been denied the training to advance or go overseas. She had been denied essential courses, depriving her of a key credential.

The agency fought the complaint for three years. In the hush-hush, need-to-know environment of Langley, almost nobody knew Thompson had filed it. So, Tee Thompson escalated her objection. At the urging of her white male supervisor, she filed a lawsuit—the first EEOC complaint that became a full-fledged discrimination suit against the CIA. Her 1979 suit charged that the agency had willfully violated the Equal Pay Act of 1963 by paying Thompson less than it paid male employees for equal work under similar conditions. It argued that women were given less training and the training they got was inferior. The suit pointed out that a 1978 study by the Directorate of Operations found women were very underrepresented in the higher grades, women waited longer for promotions, and there was a "widespread bias" against operational use of women.

The affidavits confirmed what Lisa Harper and Heidi August well knew: Many men believed "women could not run agents," as one put it in a deposition. The Jameses cited women's second-class status in many regions—Latin America, Africa, the Near East, and Asia—to argue that women officers could not work effectively overseas. They felt women were of little use as assets because "women in these countries seldom have access to information of value."

The agency settled Tee Thompson's suit the same year it was filed, grudgingly, arguing that the court was "stacked against us." Thompson received $3,898.23 in back pay, which was all she had asked for. She did not request damages, did not seek publicity or speak to the press. She just wanted to show that ending bias would make the agency better at its mission. Those colleagues who found out about her lawsuit learned of it long after the fact. She was granted retroactive GS-16 status, retired in 1989 as a member of the Senior Intelligence Service, an SIS-4, and received the Distinguished Intelligence Medal.

"It was absolutely brilliant," says Jonna Mendez. "None of us, none of the women, none of the other employees knew that she was suing them, and nobody knew that she won. She was the one that put the CIA on notice." Under the terms of the settlement, the DO was required to revise its promotion criteria, enormously benefiting other women and their ability to advance.

OTHER WOMEN DROVE CHANGE using their own levers of power. The 1980s and 1990s saw a series of internal woman-led operations that, in their own way, proved as momentous as a blown-up bridge or severed phone line in Nazi-occupied France. One of the most impactful was masterminded by the agency's most venerated unpaid helpmeet: cheerful, warm, gracious, well-mannered Barbara Colby. The quintessential CIA wife, Barbara Colby had gamely spent decades in service to American national security, supporting her husband, William Colby. After starting out in World War II as a member of the Jedburghs—joint British-American paramilitary units—Bill Colby rose through the postwar clandestine service, serving in Europe and then Vietnam before becoming CIA director. Their son Carl thinks it was Henry Kissinger—maybe Richard Helms—who described Barbara Colby as "the most loyal CIA wife *ever*." It was Barbara Colby who laid and detonated the bomb that exploded one cherished, if unspoken, tenet— that CIA wives owed their country everything and their country owed them nothing.

For many years, despite all that overseas wives contributed, they were not entitled to benefits if their husbands divorced them. And even at the best of times, being a spouse exacted enormous strain. Married couples had little privacy, especially in places like Cuba and Moscow, where bugged apartments meant arguments about kids or money or sex had to be taken to the embassy and hashed out in a copper-lined room. Barbara Colby, like many agency wives of her generation, was accomplished and well educated—a graduate of Barnard College, she was friends with high-powered dynamos like Eileen Ford, head of the famous modeling agency; competed on a game show in which she showcased her knowledge about the Brooklyn Dodgers; and dated Jack Warner, one of the Warner Brothers—but once married, her own world was replaced by a life of "reflected glory," as Carl Colby put it. Unlike some wives who became disaffected and whose disillusionment affected their husbands' promotions, Barbara was "not resentful."

And in the early years, covert work in Europe had a certain flair;

wives were like Ingrid Bergman in *Notorious,* glamorous accomplices at glittering dinners and secret colloquies. "Who are we tonight?" Barbara Colby would whisper gaily, going out. By the Vietnam War, things became harder and more morally complex. It wasn't fun any longer. In the early 1960s, as station chief in Saigon, attempting to organize villagers to defend themselves, William Colby cultivated a close relationship with the US-installed leader, Ngo Dinh Diem. There is a photo of Barbara and William Colby and two of their children meeting with Diem, a year before he was shot in the head. "We bore some share in this tragedy," Barbara Colby reflected in a documentary that Carl Colby made years later. "Things went wrong somehow." Bill Colby became chief of the Far East division; returning to Vietnam, he oversaw the Phoenix program, an effort to combat the Viet Cong insurgency. The program turned into what "felt much more like an assassination program," as Senator Bob Kerrey, who went to Vietnam in 1969, put it, though Colby disagreed. Posters in Washington compared Colby to Heinrich Himmler.

At that time, the men who ran the agency, many of them still former OSS officers and Jedburghs, were like the "Knights Templar," as Carl put it. They loved what they did. They stuck together. And they made the norms. Since the days of the OSS, it was accepted that for men, being married was no impediment to fooling around. All sorts of heterosexual shenanigans were winked at. The phrase "geographic bachelor" was a term to describe married case officers who, on unaccompanied tours, enjoyed affairs with local women, female colleagues, or both. It was common for divorced officers to remarry while serving abroad, sometimes to Asian women they believed would be more subservient and compliant. There were even instances of men threatening physical harm on wives who wouldn't grant a divorce.

During the mid-1970s, Barbara Colby set out to shift the balance. Well connected and social, she had her own ready network of accomplices. Wives of prominent men enjoyed considerable soft power on Capitol Hill, which they'd spent more than a century amassing. The Senate Wives' Club was run by influential women who often also ran their husbands' offices, and, like Maine's Republican senator Margaret Chase Smith, sometimes assumed political office after their husband died. The Congressional Club included wives of House and cabinet members; these women often handled their husbands' correspondence, raised money, helped write speeches. They knew how legislation got passed. As President Lyndon Johnson had put it: "The wife—your wife—is the most important asset you'll have." Knowing this, Barbara Colby threw her weight behind federal legislation to ensure that every ex-wife of a government employee who spent significant time overseas received part of her ex-husband's pension. Much like a spymaster running a network, Barbara Colby summoned CIA wives and ex-wives to gather the intelligence she needed to make her case. As part of what might be called Operation Justice for Ex-Wives, Barbara Colby invited Lisa Manfull Harper to her elegant riverside apartment, to hear about Lisa's experiences working unpaid under housewife cover. Barbara Colby "was wonderful. She was a real patrician. This was a woman who cared and was smart and knew the levers of power," Lisa recollected. Barbara Colby also had strong ties with Foreign Service wives, who were natural allies.

And the thing was, the powerful men of Capitol Hill also liked her. She would sail into the offices of Mississippi Democratic senator John Stennis, say, or Patrick Leahy from Vermont, using her charm and her unofficial, but real, status. She had the kind of winning manner that drew them in; and the ability, as Carl put it, to "come in for the kill." She wasn't taking no for an answer. The law, passed in 1980, was sponsored by Pat Schroeder, the Democratic congresswoman from Colorado, a working mother who would also be a prime force behind the 1993 Family and Medical Leave Act, the first US law to guarantee job safety for workers who took time off to care for children, parents, or other relations. The law that Barbara Colby helped bring to fruition was a win for all trailing spouses, including, eventually, men.

And William Colby supported it. "My father and his crowd, they didn't have any problem with this," said Carl, pointing out that his father never forgot the bravery of female couriers in wartime occupied Norway, who carried messages and faced Nazi reprisal. Everybody knew that CIA wives had been badly treated; how could they object? When, in 1984, William Colby sought a divorce and married a younger woman, diplomat Sally Shelton, it came as a surprise to many, including

Barbara. "My father is all for this legislation, then divorces her," reflected Carl Colby. "It's sort of an irony."

But even after passage of the law, a challenge followed: ensuring CIA ex-wives learned about the new benefit, and how to get it. Many of their former spouses worked undercover, using pseudonyms. An ex-wife might call headquarters, give the name of the man she'd been married to, and be told, "Never heard of him." So the former Mrs. Colby ran a follow-up operation. For this, Barbara enlisted Martha Peterson, a CIA wife who had become a bona fide operations officer, and was all too familiar with what wives put up with in tough overseas postings. Back in the 1970s, Martha Peterson's husband, John, had worked as a paramilitary officer in Laos. As a newlywed, Martha Peterson traveled to southeast Asia having no idea who her husband worked for. In Laos, she was put to work in the station alongside other wives who were "typing, filing, shredding, and pouching and putting pins on a map." The wives were paid at the GS-4 level. Martha Peterson had a master's degree from the University of North Carolina at Chapel Hill, and work experience teaching and in the travel industry. Everything about the way wives were treated she found "offensive."

In 1972, John Peterson was killed in a helicopter crash. He had left his assets to his parents, and his devastated widow needed to support herself. The CIA offered her a job as a secretary and another as assistant to a married chief of station who made it clear he wanted an on-the-side sex partner. She turned both jobs down.

An agency friend suggested she apply for the clandestine service. And so Marti Peterson entered career training a few years before Heidi August and Lisa Harper. When one Farm classmate suggested she take notes in a meeting, she told him, "Up your ass." Her graduation occurred at an opportune moment—for her—when the CIA was becoming aware of a major problem in Moscow Station. The KGB had done such a good job of identifying CIA officers in European stations that by the time these officers showed up in postings to Moscow, their faces were known to Soviet counterparts. The CIA needed blank slates. Who better than a CIA widow? Someone who did have training but lacked an archival portfolio. In 1975, the division decided to try Marti Peterson out as the first female case officer in Moscow.

Marti Peterson was exactly the tabula rasa Moscow Station needed. She arrived in November 1975, working a cover job in the State Department's consular office. Her real job was handling Aleksandr Dmitrievich Ogorodnik, a vital CIA asset who had volunteered as a walk-in in South America. His code name was TRIGON, and he provided a priceless trove of material, cached in fake rocks, fake tree stumps, and other dead-drop devices.

The first female American spy in Moscow, Peterson pulled off her assignment better than anyone could have imagined. She created the cover persona of "Party Marti," presenting herself as a ditzy consular staffer, the Marlo Thomas of overseas service, just a carefree single gal who stamped visas and loved socializing and sightseeing. This cover gave her the perfect excuse to travel freely, communicating with TRIGON and casing sites. Just thirty, and single, she recalled that "I followed the female pattern. I went to wine and cheeses, I had girlfriends, we went out in my car to see churches. And I dated Marines. I fit the profile of being a young single woman, out for you know, fun." She sipped cocktails at Spaso House, the US ambassador's residence; grabbed beers at Marine House; went to stairwell parties in the US embassy, a big old yellow building in Moscow. Embassy employees had apartments on the lower floors and perimeter. On stairwells with big landings, "we would bring the ironing board out and set that up as a bar and then whoever had an apartment right there would open their door and bring their speakers out and that was our party."

Her male colleagues were certain she was being surveilled. She was certain she wasn't. They checked. She was right.

Martha Peterson handled TRIGON for nearly two years. In the summer of 1977, however, a traitor exposed this irreplaceable asset, and the KGB arrested him. Under interrogation, he committed suicide by taking an "L-pill"—that is, poison—hidden in his pen, which the CIA station had provided at his own request. On July 15, 1977, his arrest not yet known, Martha Peterson headed to pick up a dead drop. The KGB ambushed and grabbed her, then arrested and interrogated her at Lubyanka prison, expelling her the next day. Her photos made the international papers.

Peterson's cover was blown and she was sent home, but not before proving how effectively women could operate in denied areas, underestimated, unseen, and, often, unsurveilled. Upon her return to the United States, Peterson built a career at headquarters, training officers working in areas like Cuba, Eastern Europe, China, and Moscow. After remarrying, she went to work in a unit that provided support to CIA families. It was an office job with reasonable hours that gave her time with her children. The family assistance office had an advisory board on which Barbara Colby sat. With her long years of committed service, Barbara remained an integral part of CIA culture: high-spirited, beloved, and great fun.

Barbara Colby recruited Peterson to mount the second phase of Operation Justice for Ex-Wives, and inform former spouses about the benefits to which they were entitled. "We hatched the idea that we would have this conference or this one-day meeting on headquarters property in the bubble"—a secure auditorium on the front lawn of headquarters, white and striated, like a giant igloo—"and we would invite all the ex-wives," says Peterson, who in her capacity as liaison to CIA families was perfectly positioned to access the necessary databases and pull the necessary strings. They drew up a list and, as they say, reached out.

Thus arose a remarkable scene on the premises of Langley: ex-wife after ex-wife driving onto campus, being waved through security, making her way to the bubble. "We had, like sixty ex-wives," Peterson remembered, happily. One male CIA officer had four wives, as she recalled, and the two they could locate attended. She and Colby gave out information on health care, pensions, and other perks. "We spent all day doing this in the bubble. It was marvelous. And I knew Personnel was cringing."

The following Monday morning, Martha Peterson got an irritated call from the seventh floor. By then it was too late. The operation had succeeded.

CHAPTER II

MISS MARPLE OF RUSSIA HOUSE

MCLEAN, VIRGINIA

1995

DURING HER STINT IN HEADQUARTERS, MARTHA PETERSON also received periodic visits from a trio of women with questions about aspects of spy work in Moscow. Nobody knew what the women were working on, and they didn't say. The women were taking part in a quintessential backroom operation, one with enormous import and repercussions. They benefited from the anonymity of their job and the fact that they seemed, to many, like standard, run-of-the-mill vault women, just some nondescript sneaker ladies doing something with paper or records somewhere. The trio worked in counterintelligence, investigating the one thing every spy agency fears: penetration by an adversary service. In this case, the adversary was the KGB. Just as the CIA endeavored to turn Soviet officers to spy on America's behalf, the Soviet Union did the same. The doubling-back could get confusing even for the spies: In 1985, Vitaly Yurchenko defected to the United States but then famously stood up and walked out of Au Pied de Cochon, a Georgetown restaurant, returning to his Soviet masters. The KGB was not the only spy service that aimed to recruit CIA officers as assets—other adversaries did, too—and counterintel was central to repelling such incursions. But like other backroom endeavors, counterintelligence was painstaking, low-visibility, and trended female.

The three women, Jeanne Vertefeuille, Sandy Grimes, and Diana Worthen, worked for Paul Redmond, a curmudgeon known for his temper, flirtatiousness, and tendency to surround himself with women who worked hard and smart. Redmond's team was conducting "the first computer-assisted counterintelligence investigation in CIA history," an operation that would become a watershed moment in the agency's annals—and expose the many, in this case fatal, weaknesses of the old-boy culture.

In the summer of 1985, the CIA's Moscow Station discovered to its shock and consternation that Soviet assets were disappearing, one by one. These hard-won assets turned out to be the victims of "wholesale arrests, imprisonments, trials, and executions" by the KGB, as Jeanne Vertefeuille and Sandy Grimes put it in a memoir, *Circle of Treason*. These were devastating losses for the CIA as an institution and personally for the officers who handled the assets. Those who learned of the losses were forced to consider the unthinkable. Could there be a mole within the CIA? Somebody cold-blooded enough to provide the KGB with the names of Soviet agents working for the American spy service?

The women, together with a colleague, Dan Payne, provided the backbone of the team assigned to find the traitor, and they persisted through years of failures, false leads, and dead ends. Nobody could have been better qualified in terms of having the staying power to sift through data, the brains to know what it meant, and a long-simmering disgust at the sexism to which they themselves had been subjected and the status quo that perpetuated it. The head of the trio, Jeanne Vertefeuille, was a spiritual descendant of the wartime women of Station W: astute, well educated, and long consigned to jobs well beneath her. She resembled Agatha Christie's Jane Marple in that, as a woman of a certain age, people underestimated her keen intellect and shrewd assessments. "She was always kind of looked upon as kind of like a weird duck," recalls Heidi August. "She was very much like an old schoolmarm type person. She wore these kind of longish skirts and she was unmarried and one of these people who . . . could tell you more about the Russians and their families than the Russians could tell you." Mike Sulick, station chief in Moscow, said Vertefeuille was, however, a "riot" at a bar.

Jeanne Vertefeuille's career had unfolded as a classic tale of gender-related slights. Upon graduating from the University of Connecticut in 1954, she had been eager to work overseas, and for that, a CIA recruiter at her college job fair cautioned she would do well to "acquire secretarial skills." Vertefeuille, fluent in German and French, realized that "the only criterion" that mattered was typing. So she enrolled in a business college where she learned to type and take shorthand. Hired by the CIA, she started out doing clerical labor, consulting purloined directories of North Korean scientists and typing short biographies on 3 x 5 cards. Interviewing for a permanent position, she sparred with her examiner about the merits of Chiang Kai-shek and "whether one could characterize the Communists as agrarian reformers." Having "studied Far Eastern history in college," she "knew more about the subject than my examiner," but despite this—or perhaps because of it—she was posted as a Girl Friday at an outpost in French West Africa.

She served two tours in Africa, loved it, but ran into the inevitable glass ceiling. In Africa division, it was "policy (freely expressed in those days) not to promote women above GS-7," so she took a posting in Helsinki, where women, for no clear reason, could attain a GS-9. Her assignments included updating the station's REDCAP notebook, a kind of biographical binder that contained "a comprehensive listing of all the Soviet officials" in the region. Tedious work, but educative. After four years in Finland, she noted that women now were being permitted to apply for career training, and in 1966, became one of seven women at the Farm in a class of nearly seventy trainees. Case officers had to be certified in the full course, and like Lisa Harper after her, she was limited to the short one. So she became chief of the lowly "biographics branch" of what became the Soviet and Eastern European (SE) division, processing "thousands" of name traces.

There she put the tedium to good use. Vertefeuille began to study Russian and worked translating and editing material provided by Soviet defectors and by Dmitri Polyakov, a GRU general who was a vital CIA asset. She became chief of counterintelligence production, editing all the papers and reports.

Along the way, she became friendly with Sandra Grimes, a 1967 graduate of the University of Washington who had met with similar sexist assumptions. In 1970, applying for professional status, Grimes had been asked "when I planned to get pregnant" and told that "motherhood would end my career." In response, Grimes asked her examiner when he planned to have his next child. Despite this impertinence, she passed. She, too, joined the Soviet and Eastern European division, bringing her into Vertefeuille's orbit. In January 1986, she was called in by Burton Gerber, a former Moscow Station chief, and "listened in stunned silence as he recounted loss after loss of the division's Soviet assets." The roll-up of CIA assets had begun. Polyakov disappeared. The damage caused by these losses "was inexpressible."

Grimes called in Diana Worthen, a graduate of the University of New Mexico who joined the agency as a secretary-stenographer and now was an analyst. The three women began to computerize thirty-plus years of counterintelligence information, and in 1991, the mole hunt began in the back room they opened. They brought in two other experienced women, Sue Eckstein and Myrna Fitzgerald. Their work space was "a vault within a vault, consisting of a maze of several small rooms in a far corner of the basement of the new headquarters building."

Considering a long list of suspects, the backroom team homed in on Aldrich "Rick" Ames, an undistinguished case officer whose behavior up to then had been standard for a straight white male officer who was mediocre, problematic, and insulated by the old-boy Teflon coating. Ames was a legacy hire whose father worked for the CIA. In 1969, he married an analyst, Nancy Jane Segebarth, whose abilities were superior to his. Segebarth, despite having a higher grade than her husband, had been assigned to "a routine job that did not match her talents" and resigned to take better-paying work in the private sector. Ames continued his agency career, where his smarmy behavior and heavy drinking raised not a single eyebrow among his male colleagues. When he was posted to Mexico, his wife, unwilling to leave her job, did not go. A geographic bachelor, he started appearing at parties with a girlfriend, Rosario.

Only one operational colleague found his misbehavior beyond the pale: Lisa Harper's Farm classmate Janine Brookner, posted at New York Station, which targeted the United Nations headquarters. When Ames went on temporary assignment to that station, his lack of caution shocked Brookner. Ames, a narcissistic blowhard, was talking recklessly about operations and taking Rosario to a safe house in Manhattan. Brookner sent a warning to headquarters, but it was ignored. "He should have been fired at once," a clandestine services officer was later quoted as saying. The following year, Ames began spying for the Soviets, revealing the names of KGB officers who were CIA assets. Divorced, he married Rosario and went on a three-year posting to Rome.

When they returned, Diana Worthen, who knew the couple, "noticed a substantial change in their lifestyle." They bought a large house in a "posh section of north Arlington" and embarked on lavish renovations. Ames bought a new Jaguar for himself and a Honda Accord for Rosario. But it was a small detail that sent Worthen's bullshit detector quivering: Rosario's remark that they were "ordering window treatments for every window." An ordinary CIA officer would have ordered curtains over time, room by room, as paychecks permitted. Where was all that money coming from?

Sandy Grimes began to construct a chronology of Rick Ames's whereabouts. Intended as a short timeline, her chronology "ended up a text-searchable word-processing document more than five hundred pages long." The team combed records looking for Ames's true name as well as cover names. They recorded the times he badged in and out of headquarters, his smoke breaks, the rare days he arrived early. They looked at his evaluations, his reported contacts, times he met with contacts but did not report it. They scrutinized bank and credit card payments.

"In August 1992 Sandy hit pay dirt," the women's memoir notes. Grimes saw three correlations between meetings with a known Soviet officer and subsequent deposits into Ames's checking account. The instances occurred in May and July 1985, around the time when the CIA started losing its Soviet assets. It was an epiphany: "Rick is a goddamn Russian spy."

Ames was keeping an eye on them and made a point of crossing paths. Noting his "condescending attitude toward women," Grimes and Vertefeuille wrote that "we had the distinct feeling that he was pleased to know that it was two women that were heading up the investigation of the 1985 compromises, because it would be easier to outwit us." The day Sandy Grimes started in the Counterintelligence Center, Ames approached and "asked her about her new assignment." When she told him, "Rick immediately began a lecture on the most basic tenets of a counterintelligence operation." He mansplained, to the female investigators, how to conduct an investigation.

Despite the evidence, it took a long time for Sandy Grimes's warnings to be heeded. FBI officers joined the hunt and proceeded to focus on a different culprit. Two years went by as the bureau pursued a chimera. But the evidence mounted and proved overwhelming. On February 21, 1994, Rick Ames was arrested for having caused one of the most catastrophic and tragic security breaches in the history of the CIA. The FBI tried to take credit for his arrest, Vertefeuille and Grimes wrote, giving "the impression that they had done all the real work." The CIA was criticized by Congress—for taking so long.

None other than Jeanne Vertefeuille was hauled before a closed session of the House Permanent Select Committee on Intelligence, feeling, as she put it, like a "sacrificial lamb." The memoir relates how one member, Dan Glickman, saw fit to ask her, "What makes you think that you were capable of leading a CI investigation?" She left "not only furious but downhearted." Their boss, Paul Redmond, got a medal; Vertefeuille got a less prestigious award; Sandy Grimes received a still lesser one. Both Grimes and Vertefeuille boycotted the ceremony in protest.

CHAPTER 12

WHAT ARE YOU GOING TO DO WITH THE BOAT?

LATIN AMERICA AND
MCLEAN, VIRGINIA

1990s

T HE AMES CASE EXPLODED INTO PUBLIC AT THE VERY MOMENT when America was undergoing a much wider reckoning over toxic behavior by malefactors like Ames who long had enjoyed power and old-boy protection. The mid-1990s amounted to a nationwide moment when women in many sectors struggled to raise awareness of just how bad things could be and just how entrenched the opposition was to their advancement; and, to change things.

The televised 1991 confirmation hearings of Supreme Court nominee Clarence Thomas had set the reckoning in motion. A lone woman, Anita Hill, assumed her place at a microphone accompanied only by a glass of water, her extended family seated behind her as she described the sexual harassment she had allegedly endured in her government job. An all-white, all-male US Senate Judiciary Committee listened with incredulity as Hill related her ordeal as a young attorney at the Equal Employment Opportunity Commission—of all places—where her boss, Clarence Thomas, allegedly subjected her to comments about pornography, sex with animals, pubic hairs, and oral sex.

It is hard to understand why the senators were so perplexed, given that behavior like this had been an open secret in Washington for as long as Washington existed. In the archives of the US Senate, there is a hair-raising testimonial to what the culture of Capitol Hill once permitted: an oral history by Bobby Baker, secretary to the Senate's Democratic majority and fixer to Lyndon Johnson in his role as Senate majority leader. Baker evoked a scene that was nigh-on medieval. Senator Burnet Maybank, he said, drank "half a tumbler of bourbon" when he awoke; Senator Clyde Hoey would call a woman over to "try to play with her breasts." Senate pages were deployed to buy condoms; Jacob Javits was a "sex maniac" caught by his postman "on his couch having a sexual affair with a Negro lady."

Even in the 1990s, two Democratic senators, Chris Dodd and Ted Kennedy, reportedly engaged in a game of "waitress sandwich" at La Brasserie, a DC watering hole.

Despite the evidence everywhere around them, the senators at Clarence Thomas's hearing were so skeptical that they asked Hill to repeat the more prurient details. Thomas was confirmed.

The spectacle provoked a voter backlash. In 1992—the so-called Year of the Woman—four new female US senators joined Maryland Democrat Barbara Mikulski for an all-time high of five women senators—out of one hundred. The small band helped bring about another upheaval when attention shifted to Oregon senator Bob Packwood, a moderate pro-choice Republican. During a landmark trial, more than *seventeen* female staffers and interns came forward to testify that Packwood had sexually harassed and assaulted them. Packwood had kept a diary of some of these endeavors, admitting he had "made love" to twenty-two aides and had a "passionate relationship" with "probably 75 more." It was a pivotal moment in one of America's most sacred institutions, as the boys' club ejected one of its own. Facing expulsion, Packwood resigned. That same year, the election of President Bill Clinton led to another sex-related spectacle; much like Packwood, Clinton was a deeply flawed ally to the women's movement, a pro-choice politician who made much of his support for women, including his own wife, then First Lady Hillary Clinton, even as he was having affairs and allegedly preying on female aides and civil servants.

In Washington, the rules were changing and people began to feel confused and panicked. In CIA headquarters, conversations occurred about how to get women promoted faster. Something was created called the "13 to 14 panel," an effort to place women in feeder positions that would make them eligible for higher grades. A report was compiled called "the Glass Ceiling study," which comprised damning statistics, showing that women filled 40 percent of professional positions but only 10 percent of jobs in the Senior Intelligence Service, and that they typically capped out at GS-14, while men rose much higher. Women, Blacks, Asians, and other minorities, the report showed, were unfailingly consigned to lower grades. But the study, like most reports and commissions, achieved little beyond permitting the institution to claim it was studying the problem and puzzled by how in the world it had occurred.

SO WOMEN TOOK THINGS into their own hands. Heidi August and her friend Mary Margaret Graham started comparing notes. Heidi by that time had cemented her commitment to counterterrorism: After the hijacking in Malta, she went on to open a station in Dublin, Ireland, where she learned to appreciate Baileys Irish Cream and collected intelligence on ties between the Irish Republican Army and Muammar Qaddafi, who was supporting the IRA out of a mutual hatred of the British. From there, Heidi had served as base chief in Jerusalem during the first Palestinian intifada. She lived in an Arab neighborhood in East Jerusalem, on the second floor of a compound owned by a Palestinian pharmacist with six children. The children were very fond of Heidi, and she was very fond of them.

Like Lisa Harper, Heidi took advantage of her gender when working undercover. "Okay, who wants to go for ice cream?" she'd ask the kids when she needed to do a small safe maneuver, like make a call from a public phone booth. She'd sail out under nanny cover, a two-time CIA station chief posing as a children's caregiver. To reach meetings with assets, she hitched rides in the druggist's van. It was safer than driving around the West Bank in a car with US diplomatic tags. During this same time, Mary Margaret Graham, who started her own career as a nanny for the household of a US general, had emerged as a respected operations officer. Her only career hiccup occurred when she became engaged to a Scotsman and was obliged to go on leave without pay pending his background investigation. When she complained to her boss about how long the investigation was taking, he asked why she had not had her fiancé fast-tracked. The agency did it all the time for men, he told her.

Mary Margaret Graham and Heidi August decided to chart the top fifty overseas positions and realized how few were filled by women. "Once you chart something like that—holy cow," said Heidi. They agreed to "reach down into our particular offices" to bring up talented women. Heidi focused on a clerk who would go on to become a case officer and chief of station. Mary Margaret Graham became a champion of many women, including a promising officer named Gina Haspel.

And in 1994 and 1995, as the Ames case was bursting into the public view, two high-profile lawsuits threw the agency into further disarray, plunging the sisterhood of female officers into chaos and disagreement even as they brought about true change.

THE FIRST INVOLVED JANINE Brookner, a case officer who entered career training in 1968, in the same class as Lisa Harper. I interviewed Brookner in December 2020, when she was suffering from kidney cancer in its advanced stages. Petite and stylish, wearing a leather bomber jacket, she received me in her airy, richly decorated townhome in Georgetown, overlooking the Potomac River. She was gracious even as she awaited news of her eligibility for a transplant. She had two white Maltese dogs, Tony and Cleo, so tiny and spoiled they had to be lifted up the single stairstep separating the dining area from the living room. She died a few months after we spoke.

After graduating from the Farm, Brookner was offered jobs as an analyst and a reports officer; when she turned those down, she was placed in the illegal headquarters job so "super-sensitive" she could not be told what it was. Ushered into the bowels of headquarters, she found it was the infamous domestic spying operation, "working with the FBI against US students and US students abroad, Black Panthers, even nuns." She did it under protest, she told me, telling her supervisor that spying on fellow citizens was not why she joined the CIA.

Looking for an escape route, Brookner landed a posting as a case officer in the Philippines, where the station chief was not happy to see her. He forbade her to do real case officer work and assigned her to read newspapers and brief him. So Brookner sallied forth on her own, paying for her own developmental dinners, attending parties, meeting "all kinds of people who were legitimate targets, from the presidential palace to the Communist Party," writing up contact reports on targets. Her chief signed the reports and ignored them.

After nine months, a new chief arrived, George Kalaris. When he learned she had been assigned to sit at a desk, he was incredulous and asked whether she could recruit some of these people whose names and numbers she had recorded. She surprised herself at how quickly she succeeded. "I asked this guy if he would work for the agency and work for me. I thought he would say yes. I was young and naïve, and it was my first recruitment. And he said, 'Can I think about it?' And instead of saying, 'Yes, take your time,' I said, 'Can't you tell me now?' And he said, 'okay.'"

Kalaris began trumpeting her achievements. "He would sit there, and we'd have weekly meetings, and he would praise me, okay the gold star for this week goes to Janine." When it came time for Brookner to take her next posting, she had lots of offers. She took a slot in Thailand, a badly run station where, she told me, the married chief of station had left his family and was having a messy affair with a female case officer who had moved in with him. Brookner also served in the New York office, where she flagged the conduct of Rick Ames—to no avail.

In 1988, Brookner had begun looking for her next posting. There was an opening for a station chief in Jamaica, which was "known as a very, very difficult station." The island had a crime problem; there was no good schooling. A recent chief had left under a cloud, she said, when his wife totaled their car coming back from a rendezvous with her lover. There were rumors of group-sex parties; morale was bad. "But it was the only station I could get that was decent size and had good operations, a good-sized budget, a chance for me to prove myself as COS."

It was tough to put together a staff, given the hardships. She found a deputy who recommended a female colleague. The woman had an iffy record but claimed "she didn't do well in the last assignment because she worked for a male chauvinist pig." That seemed plausible, so Brookner hired her. Going in, she knew she had at least five problem staffers. "I thought I could work with them. I worked with difficult cases before. I thought I was a good manager."

From the get-go, trouble surfaced. The female case officer got drunk at a party and started bad-mouthing the CIA. Brookner reported the security lapse. Another staffer was cheating on his finances. She made him repay the money. Another put a gun to the head of his security guard and "threatened to kill him if he ever caught him sleeping." Brookner confiscated the weapons. Then one morning, as she was sitting by her pool enjoying a cup of coffee and a moment of peace, the telephone rang; it was the wife of her deputy chief of station, "sobbing and crying." She came to see Brookner and said the deputy chief "had been beating her up since [we] got married." He had choked her until she passed out. The wife was Bangladeshi. There was a court case, and Brookner testified on the wife's behalf.

Returning to Langley, she took language training in preparation for becoming chief of station in Prague. But in November 1992, the Prague job was withdrawn. Brookner found herself relegated to a cubicle with no window or telephone. She was called to see the inspector general, where she was told a complaint had been filed. She was being accused of sexual harassment and drinking. Her former subordinates in Jamaica Station accused her of wearing "brief shorts and thin T-shirts," of wearing "no perceptible underwear," and of dressing to make "some men believe she might make a pass" at them. They complained she had cooked a Thanksgiving turkey on office time.

The inspector general bought the accusations and enlarged them, writing in a December 1992 report that Brookner was a drinker and "sexual provocateur" and should be denied the Prague posting. When her former boss, George Kalaris, found out, she said, he and his wife recommended a lawyer and urged her to sue. "That's how it started," Brookner recalled. "I never ever thought I would or intended to or could imagine suing the CIA."

On July 14, 1994, Brookner filed a federal sex discrimination lawsuit, contending she hit a "glass ceiling." The suit asserted that her former staffers were out to get her; that she had been denied the Prague promotion because the deputy there said he would not work for a woman. She was undercover, so the suit identified her as Jane Doe Thompson. A front page story in *The New York Times* broke the news about the lawsuit and also broke her cover. "By all accounts, Janine Brookner was a terrific spy" was the first sentence.

Brookner read it and burst into tears. The article included effusive words of support from top officials: Kalaris said she had made key recruitments and single-handedly changed his ideas about women's value as case officers. "I'm surprised these allegations could gain any credibility or momentum," the US ambassador to Jamaica at the time she served, Glen Holden, told the *Times*. The inspector general's staff had not bothered to interview him. "I was proud of her, and I think our country should be proud of her." There had been mistakes in the IG report; a DEA official who the CIA said had accused her of groping him at a 1990 Christmas party filed a statement swearing that "Ms. Brookner was not drunk at the Christmas party, that her conduct was beyond reproach and that no one from the C.I.A. inspector general's office had ever contacted him to verify the report." Brookner received "all this mail and telephone calls from people supporting me." Her mailbox and voicemail message bank were full. "People were calling from all over."

The CIA damage control experts fought back. An analyst named Susan Hasler had just begun a stint as a speechwriter in the public affairs office. Hasler listened in shock as men in public affairs—old hands at disinformation—set out to fan the worst rumors about Brookner. "I saw the DO, this group of retired DO guys in action," said Hasler, an observant person who writes novels and pays attention to details. "Case officers—one of the things you do is learn to manipulate foreign press, plant things." Janine Brookner had run afoul of the old-boys network, and "they decided to trash her in the press."

"Everyone knew the DO was guilty as sin," said Hasler. At a lunch with two male public affairs officials, one asked, "Why don't they just do the right thing and settle with her?" The other, she said, replied: "The lawyers think they can win it. They're going to discredit her."

The agency did this, she said, by slut-shaming Brookner in quiet conversations with members of the news media. Public affairs would "issue stiff statements on their inability to comment on an ongoing court case," while clandestine officers "spread salacious and false gossip."

The director at the time, James Woolsey, was, as Hasler put it, "perhaps one of the Agency's [most] hapless directors." Others describe him as "feckless." Woolsey was appointed by Bill Clinton, who was seen as uninterested in intelligence and certainly was uninterested in Woolsey. During his tenure, from 1993 to 1995, Woolsey was unable to get meetings with the president he served. When a man named Frank Corder crashed a small plane onto the South Lawn of the White House, staffers at Langley joked it was Woolsey trying to get in to see Bill Clinton.

For sure, Woolsey was not qualified to handle this amount of shit hitting the fan. *The New York Times* pointed out that since the agency's inception, only ten women had held top posts in the operations directorate. The clandestine service "has long been a male domain," it noted, saying that women and members of minorities had been concentrated in lower pay grades; and "in the years 1985 to 1990, white men were promoted faster and further." Women held 12 percent of senior posts in operations, analysis, and administration, up from 6 percent a few years earlier.

The CIA settled in November 1994, giving Brookner a cash payout. Three high-level officers went on *60 Minutes* to deplore the behavior of their colleagues toward women.

Her cover blown, Brookner resigned. She enrolled in law school and specialized in discrimination cases against federal agencies. Sitting in her living room, she expressed pride in her agency service, saying she had made "some fantastic recruitments" that were "very significant to the planning and the intentions of the future of the US government."

Overall, she thought the CIA "has been a force for good" but has used secrecy to deflect accountability. "The agency has done some really bad things, and they can cover up because they are 'secret,' and everything's a secret. I have sued the agency many times now. They can cover up all kinds of things, and they do. That's the first thing—you cover up, you obscure. They're very difficult. At the same time, they've done some wonderful things, some fantastic things." But, she said, "for women in the beginning, it was a very difficult place."

AND NOW THE SISTERHOOD rose up en masse. As Brookner was pursuing her own case, a group of two hundred female officers brought a class action lawsuit arguing that the entire clandestine service imposed a pattern of discrimination. The suit originated in 1986, when ten women filed complaints with the agency's Equal Employment Opportunity Office. Procedural issues led the class action suit to be filed again in December 1992. The suit involved promotions of women in "Category B," the undercover case officers. "The plaintiffs were pretty unusual people, strong individuals, for sure," the attorney in charge, Martin Schneiderman, told me.

Similar suits had been decided or were under way at many federal agencies and elsewhere. At the National Security Agency, a woman named Renetta Predmore-Lynch had brought a class action lawsuit in the 1970s that called attention to discrimination in promotion and overseas opportunities; she won. At the State Department, a class action suit by an officer named Alison Palmer was resolved in favor of female State Department employees. At State, women had been channeled into "cones" of expertise, such as economics or administration, and kept out of others, such as political or military analysis, that led to becoming ambassador or deputy chief of mission. Class action suits rocked major journalistic outlets, too, including *The Washington Post*, *The New York Times*, and *Newsweek*.

At the CIA, the lead class action plaintiff, who filed suit under the alias Marjorie Conway, was a case officer who at one time had worked with Janine Brookner in New York. Conway was a funny, outspoken, flamboyant woman, prone to spike heels and married to a senior officer who was highly regarded. "She would wear very colorful clothes, she would wear hats that matched—purple hats, purple clothes—and dresses that had slits up to here," said Brookner. "I would have a party and she would come, just sit there, entertain everybody, she's very funny and very personable." According to Lisa Harper, who knew her, Conway was "brilliant."

At the time, the general counsel of the CIA was also a woman, Elizabeth Rindskopf Parker. Female case officers recall an unforgettable meeting that Rindskopf Parker convened in the bubble. "She thought she could just get rid of the class action by calling a meeting and telling everybody to go away," said Brookner, who was struck by the sight of so many women clandestine officers, normally far-flung, sitting shoulder to shoulder. "Elizabeth gets up there to talk, and basically says that there was nothing to this, and you're not going to get anyplace."

Brookner watched officials sitting near the general counsel. "You could see the body language, the men, the career management person, they were moving away from her, as she was talking."

And then the class agent got up to speak. Conway was "outspoken and very funny," Brookner said. Rindskopf Parker told her to sit down and be quiet, not realizing the speaker was the class agent. Conway began talking more loudly; a murmur went through the audience; the meeting took on a life of its own. Rindskopf Parker and Conway began wrestling for the microphone as the audience watched. What some knew was that the class agent, Marjorie Conway, was born with a missing arm—a disability she had overcome so successfully that she could play tennis—and used a prosthetic one. They waited in horror to see if the arm would detach. But the arm held.

The vision Conway floated was dark, paranoid, and plausible. The suit held that the CIA had over five decades refined a culture of fine-tuned discrimination. Women who aspired to be case officers were steered toward being reports officers; those who insisted upon becoming case officers were denied promotions. Female officers were set in competition with wives, who were fed the line that they, too, were case officers in all but title. Women in administration were rewarded for preserving the status quo. Men in power on the seventh floor would claim they had no idea any of this was going on, and they were shocked, shocked, to hear it was. One husband, acting as a mole, reported that men in meetings referred to pretty women as "tomatoes." The power structure found myriad ways to set women at odds: wives versus secretaries versus reports officers versus female case officers.

All sort of emotions exploded. "It seemed like a bunch of angry women," said Paula Doyle, who recently had been recruited from the

State Department and remembers being summoned—"It was kind of like, all females, come to the bubble"—and not wanting to go. She just wanted to settle into her job. But she went, and saw "lots of women in the bubble, and the unnamed protagonist was on the stage . . . and I didn't have enough background to know what was right or wrong." Doyle was married to a man twenty years older, retired and content to be the trailing spouse, enabling her to work as a case officer and have children. "I was a mother many times over by then, and it was very divisive, the name-calling and the stories." It wasn't that she didn't believe the stories—"I know what it feels like to work for a dick, or a guy who thinks you are too pretty"—but her own MO had been to "work more than the other person and get ahead."

Brookner recalled it as the moment the women of the clandestine service truly came together. "All the women started talking, and talking to each other. By the end of that meeting, everybody was sitting here, and standing there and talking, and telling everybody else her experience, and a bunch of women signed up for the class action." It was "all of a sudden this whole camaraderie developing before your eyes."

The Cat B suit settled in 1995. "The Central Intelligence Agency, in a clear admission that it has discriminated systematically against its women secret agents for years, said Wednesday that it has agreed to settle a class-action suit filed by several hundred women clandestine officers," the *Los Angeles Times* noted. "The settlement requires the agency to provide $940,000 in back pay and bestow 25 retroactive promotions to victims of what lawyers for the women call a pervasive culture of sexual discrimination." After two decades of suits—from Harritte Thompson to the unnamed Marjorie Conway—the agency had been flushed from cover.

THE VETERANS KNEW WHAT would happen next. "This is going to go down on somebody's record somewhere," Heidi August remembers telling Mary Margaret Graham. The class action leaders would be punished. "They're going to have the names."

And she was right. The federal government was supposed to exercise oversight for four years, to prevent retaliation—but they couldn't stop hall files from being edited and revised. "They won, but they really didn't," reflected Mike Kalogeropoulos, a case officer who witnessed meetings at which the women who led the suit were discussed. "We knew who they were. When their names would come up from assignments, they would say, 'She's a Cat B.' They promoted some of them, but they never really got very far. We really didn't like it at all. It's not an organization that takes this type of dissent very well."

"They were punished. Nobody wanted them," agreed Lisa Harper. Lisa chose not to join the lawsuit, not because she feared retaliation but because she felt she didn't deserve a cash settlement. "Honestly, by the time they came around, I was doing fine. I didn't deserve [compensation]—I'd fought my battles."

The suit did have a long-term positive impact, ensuring that women could get the training they needed. Derogatory terms like "retread" faded away. Management looked around for women who long ago should have been promoted. One was a case officer, Ellie Duckett, whose father, Carl, had been deputy director of the Directorate of Science & Technology. Ellie Duckett was gifted, well liked, and hardworking, but unlike, say, Aldrich Ames, her legacy status had gotten her nowhere. Now people were asking why Duckett was not a chief of station or otherwise tapped for leadership. Duckett became chief of station in Budapest, but the advancement came too late: She stepped down after being diagnosed with an aggressive form of breast cancer.

LISA HARPER HAD ALSO been promoted, thanks in part to a quiet act of sisterhood from an unexpected quarter. In the early 1990s, the Directorate of Operations needed a station chief in a Central American country. (Lisa asked that the country not be named, so as not to compromise assets she worked with.) Suffice it to say that a decade of covert operations, Cold War proxy battles, corruption, arms trading, and drug-fueled violence made it a challenging assignment. Things were "going really, really badly." The mission was to facilitate the peace process.

The way Lisa heard it: A promotion panel discussed who could handle the station. Present happened to be Sue McCloud, who floated Lisa's name. She thinks that's how she came into the job. "But it's also because none of the guys wanted to go into that hornet's nest. I got the job, I'm convinced, because no man wanted it. They knew it was going to be awful."

But she was grateful for a chance to serve as chief of station—and thankful to the woman who put her name forward. Lisa Harper admired Sue McCloud. "She took absolutely no shit from anybody."

Lisa by then was divorced herself. The competition with her husband had become increasingly stressful, and after they returned from Africa, Lisa spent a solo tour in Paris while he served at a station in the Far East. It was exhilarating, to do her own work, cultivate her own assets, without the added burden of wifely duties. Lisa lacked a helpmeet of her own and needed to hit the ground running, so her parents came to furnish her place. Single women didn't get asked out to dinners and parties as often as single men did; rather than bemoan the unfairness, she befriended male colleagues in the State Department and asked to go as a plus-one to diplomatic parties. Their wives didn't mind; embassy wives were glad for a break from dinners and receptions that invariably turned into one long series of toasts to *liberté, égalité, fraternité,* and the wartime spirit of Charles de Gaulle. She endeared herself to her own CIA colleagues by spreading the invitations around. It was a highly successful tour. By the time she returned, it was clear her marital separation would be permanent.

During her own divorce proceedings, Lisa had been obliged to remain in the Washington, DC, area. Management ensured she take a position off the premises—in effect, exiled—so as to not cross paths with her ex-husband. Lisa went to Capitol Hill as a CIA liaison to Congress. It was not ideal from a career-track perspective, but she got to know the ins and outs of the House and Senate, which had an often-contentious relationship with the intelligence community they now were responsible for overseeing. It was experience that came in handy. She learned to keep a diary in her own personal code, so that if a lawmaker denied being briefed on an operation, she could point out the day and time when the briefing had, in fact, happened.

———

THE CIA IN CENTRAL AMERICA in the 1990s was emerging from one of its most notorious periods, a time of aggressive covert action at the behest of the Reagan administration, which was bent on defeating and unseating Communism in Central America. In El Salvador, for example, the US government backed a right-wing government against left-wing rebels, a devil's bargain that involved working with execution squads and other human rights violators. A rogues' gallery of administration lawbreakers and end-runners sold arms to Iran, and the National Security Council's Oliver North, acting in violation of US law, used the money to fund the Nicaraguan "contras," right-wing rebels fighting the Communist regime. The CIA trained and aided the contras, bombed the Managua airport, and, in 1984, mined Nicaraguan harbors.

Lisa during her career steered clear of illegal operations and knew well what had happened to her covert-action-happy colleagues. While in Europe, she had been approached by a colleague "famous for skirting the law" who sought her help with a sketchy operation. Lisa asked whether he had written approval from the CIA director; when he said no, she refused to help him. Another time, she was deputy in a station where the chief asked his officers to do a secret favor for a friend working for a private defense contractor. Lisa pulled them aside and told them not to comply. Don't make a fuss, she advised. Don't quit. Don't fall on your sword. Just say it's the weekend and you don't have time. When her boss asked about the favor, she covered for them.

Now she was being called upon to clean up a mess. Upon arrival in the station over which she was to preside as chief, Lisa found the situation worse than anticipated. Her predecessor had set traps for her. He canceled the lease on a house she was planning to move into, in a tight housing market. "He turned the men in the station against me," she said, portraying her "as some kind of radical feminist." He urged the men in the station to ask for reassignment. One did. She was being set up to fail by colleagues who "wanted to prove that a woman couldn't run this."

One of her first leadership tests involved a boat the station owned for "E&E": escape and evacuation. Her predecessor had taken the boat out and there had been a mishap and "the whole station nearly died." When she arrived, the question everybody wanted answered was: What would she do with the boat? "Half the men—the macho men that liked to go out fishing and drinking on the boat—wanted to keep the boat," she remembered. "And the other half, the ones who nearly died mostly, didn't."

The boat became a headquarters fixation. "I used to get these really super-classified eyes-only cables. And you know, you think it's going to be about matters of state. No." Instead, the cables wanted to know: "Are you going to keep the boat or not?" Lisa got rid of the boat.

Then there was an old Vietnam-era helicopter that some Jameses wanted to use off the books. She refused to let them. "People were always testing to see if I'd bend the rules. And of course, when I didn't, some of them got even more angry." She knew she was under scrutiny, including from Congress. Once, she was at a conference in Miami and got summoned back when a US senator paid a last-minute visit; by the time she arrived via helicopter, the senator was "already drunk" and insisted on an assistant sitting in who didn't have a security clearance. When she barred the assistant, the senator threatened to call "your boss"—the CIA director—and she said, "That's a great idea."

Endemic violence had not abated now that the war was over. As an American official, she said, "everybody was after you. One side was after you to kill you, and the other side was after you to kill you. And then you had the people that were wanting to kill you just because they wanted your car and your money." She lived in a house fortified by concertina wire; at her door was a "guy with a very serious weapon."

She had to spar with the US embassy to get that level of protection. The US ambassador had several bodyguards but refused to give her a bodyguard of her own "because peace was breaking out and it would look bad." She told him it would be unfortunate if she had to start carrying a gun and created a diplomatic incident by shooting somebody. "I'm not going down in this country," she told him. "I'm not going to die here." It was how you had to talk. She got a driver and a bodyguard.

Even so, she could never relax. Her job required going to parties

with local officials; people drank; late at night it got even more dangerous on the roads. "You never stopped your car. You never stopped at a
red light after midnight," she said. "Some nights when I came home, I
didn't know if I was going to outrun the guys in the pickup trucks behind me. I had one corner to turn, and I'd start honking on the horn,
and the guy—my guard—would open the door and I'd go in."

Being a case officer is stressful under the best circumstances; just
walking out the front door requires hypervigilance and constant checks
for surveillance. Being a station chief in a country emerging from civil
war—the pressure was immense. The one opportunity for relaxation
was romantic. Lisa had a boyfriend, a "good-looking fellow" related to
a former president of the country. "He wasn't the love of my life," but
she enjoyed his company and the peace of his family's lakeside retreat.
She had to approach the US ambassador—the one who didn't want to
give her a bodyguard—and report that they were about to have what
the CIA called "close and continued contact." She also reported the liaison to headquarters, which did not object. "I was very careful that he
not know anything that he shouldn't know."

The relationship gave her access to the ex-president, who liked to
stop by her house for muffins. In clandestine operations work, it's impossible to overstate the role played by food. "He was a man who loved
to eat," said Lisa. "I made muffins for him, and he would come by for
breakfast. I've got my muffins, and his bodyguards would wait outside,
so it was a private meeting." She insinuated herself to the point where
"some nights, they would say, 'We're going to talk politics, and we're
going to say some things'" and treated her as if she were one of them.
"After a while, they trust you."

As the war wound down, slots were taken away in her station. Even
so, "we managed to pull off what's been a lasting peace, and the reporting was good, and I am so proud. That's what you stand on, that even as
I had to get rid of all these people, our reporting was good. Some of the
people we worked with were really bad people. We had to get permission every time our officers went out to meet one of these bad people.
We had to get special permission to do that. By the way, the person who
met the most dangerous guys, the real hard, hard guys, was a woman.
She was savvy, she was impeccable in her tradecraft."

so impeccable was lisa herself that, around the time that the Category B lawsuit settled, she was made chief of Latin America division. A baron. The agency's first woman baron. From being an unpaid spouse, working cast-off assignments under housewife cover, Lisa Harper had ascended to become the first CIA baroness.

"I think it's because when I was COS, there was a whole series of awful things, and I did it," she reflected. "I also think that the DDO at the time wanted to make a point about women . . . He thought, 'Well, Lisa's had all these years of experience. She deserved it. She's ready.'" In addition to the chief of station position, she'd served as deputy in a South American station where a bomb went off in the city where she was serving. Her adept handling of that emergency had enhanced her hall file but aroused the competitive instincts of the station chief, who'd been away. She'd also, at one point, been assigned to debrief a high-ranking foreign official. It was a plum assignment, well executed, that again attracted jealousy and retaliation; she found out through a back channel that a colleague, eager to put the source to a different use, had reported that Lisa was having sex with the asset. She protested and had the false accusation removed from her file. She well knew how people at Langley could play hardball, and had more than proved her merit.

Now—as the almighty baroness of Latin America division—Lisa set up shop in headquarters. She had a secretary; she supervised case officers, desk officers, station chiefs. She looked forward to working with her fellow barons and with the head of the clandestine service, Ted Price, who had backed her. It was a hard job but a glorious one, a chance to get big things done. "I expected that as a division chief, I would have a really collegial relationship with everybody."

Instead, she was frozen out. She got fifteen minutes a week with Price, who seemed to be distancing himself from the discontent. As the agency aspired to right wrongs and make up for lost time, the Jameses felt Lisa Harper had been unfairly advanced. What the men who promoted her "hadn't understood was just the depth of feeling," says Lisa. "People ignored me. Basically, I did my job, and I think I did it well, for as long as I stayed there. But I wasn't part of that group of senior people.

I never got invited to people's houses. Once I became a division chief, nobody invited me. It was like I was in splendid isolation."

Other women could see what was happening. Men had been doing succession planning—or some had—and their plans didn't include a woman competitor coming out of left field. "There were plenty of men who said [Lisa's appointment] was because of Cat B," said Paula Doyle, a case officer who knew how wrong those men were. The sisterhood had been elated by the elevation of Lisa, an ally to so many, and they eagerly watched to see how she fared. "Lisa got ahead by doing the work that needed to be done, in environments where men did well and not so well," said Doyle. "Lisa was a rock star during her career. Nobody in LA Division questioned the qualifications of Lisa Harper. She had the last word. Even so, she was so ostracized."

"She was treated like garbage, from my understanding," said Mike Sulick, a later head of the clandestine service. He still found it upsetting. "If you're a division chief you feel like a god. It's terrible when you get treated like that when you're a division chief."

Lisa felt worn out and sick. A few years earlier, suffering a dizzy spell from an inner ear infection, she had fallen down a staircase in Panama and hit her head. She had never taken time to recover. In one Africa station, she'd been evacuated owing to exhaustion. She could feel the headaches coming back. She consulted a doctor who told her that if she followed his regimen for a year, she would recover. She needed to see to her own well-being.

She stepped down, gave up her barony, and retired. "I wasn't there long enough to really get the guys on my side," she said. "I would have, because I always did in the end."

THE OLD GUYS HAD won a battle. Women's hard-won victories of the mid-1990s attracted backlash, and Lisa Harper became a victim in a long-running contest. But there would be a second baroness three years later: Heidi's friend Mary Margaret Graham, with a handful of senior women behind her, poised to lead. Communism was rolled back, thanks in part to the service and sacrifices of Lisa's generation. In the aftermath, though, another menace materialized in distant Afghanistan, in the form of men preaching religious jihad. In the CIA's other major directorate, a group of women began tracking this menace well before others noticed it. Another sisterhood was forming, a community of female analysts focused on an enemy the women would endeavor to outthink.

Part Two

LADIES DOING ANALYSIS

One of the oldest debates
in history [is] the one
between the intelligence
officer who, after an
event occurs, points to
the single report that
predicted it while the
intelligence customer
complains that he was not
alerted because the re-
port was buried among so
many contradictory re-
ports.

—WILLIAM COLBY,
HONORABLE MEN

CHAPTER 13

THE FIERCELY ARGUED THINGS

AS A GIRL GROWING UP IN THE 1970S, SHARP-EYED CINDY Storer liked making her own maps. Her parents bought her a giant map of the world, which she thumbtacked to her bedroom wall and marked up with pens. A visual thinker, Cindy didn't stop at geography. She mapped whatever intrigued her—novels, newspaper articles, wars. She drew the voyage of Captain Nemo and his submarine *Nautilus* in *Twenty Thousand Leagues Under the Sea*. Her uncle flew helicopters in Vietnam, so she traced the course of the Vietnam War to see what he had been through.

Cindy had an eidetic memory—a photographic recall—for maps. She liked to chart movements over time. She liked heights and depths and contours. She liked outer space. When she was five, her family relocated from Long Beach, California, to Hampton, Virginia, a coastal community home to Langley Air Force Base and a NASA research facility. Hampton was a good place to grow up. Cindy collected space patches, went to the beach, and attended air shows. But most adults worked for the military, which meant families cycled in and out, and so did friends. Girl Scout camping trips were a godsend, the intricacies of compasses and orienteering a respite from always adjusting to ended friendships and trying to make new ones. The details of the physical world, in many ways, were easier to read than the minds and personalities of people.

In college, Cindy discovered math came as easily as mapping. She aced calculus, which surprised her, then blew through higher math and astronomy. "I can't believe I understand this," she thought. She loved puzzles—any kind. But her greatest love was for US history and politics, in part because so many men in her family served in the military, including her uncle, her father, and her grandfather. She majored in government and wrote her senior thesis on America's entry into Vietnam. Cindy would have joined the military herself, but a freak accident in her early childhood—her family was driving to a camping trip when a truck carrying chlorine gas caught on fire on a freeway—damaged her lung capacity and disqualified her for military service. She went looking for another way to serve.

In 1986, her senior year at the College of William & Mary, Cindy visited the career services office, where the CIA and the National Security Agency each maintained a mailbox for prospective recruits. She dropped her résumé in both. William & Mary, the second-oldest US college after Harvard, was chartered in 1693, and began admitting women in 1918. With Washington a little more than 150 miles away, and the naval bases of Virginia Beach and Norfolk nearby, many students came from homes where public service was part of the household culture. And though most students didn't know it, the agency had a shadowy presence among them. The CIA's clandestine training facility, the Farm, was also nearby, and the cobblestone streets and crowded taverns of Colonial Williamsburg's historic district provided a handy setting for recruits to practice brush passes and dead drops.

When the CIA contacted Cindy for an on-campus interview, she went expecting a man in a suit and was surprised to find herself chatting with a friendly, long-haired woman wearing a Laura Ashley dress—the puff-sleeved frock every young white woman in America aspired to own in the early 1980s, as if the height of femininity meant looking like a Welsh milkmaid. Cindy had a pink linen Laura Ashley but never would have dared to wear it to a job interview. "What a cool place the CIA must be," she thought. The NSA made her an offer, but she chose the CIA based on the lady recruiter in the Laura Ashley dress. "I saw her, and I was like—Damn! I really want to work for this place!"

Later, it occurred to her that she never laid eyes on that woman again.

ENTERING ON DUTY IN 1986, Cindy Storer was given a choice of assignments. The Directorate of Operations wanted to make her a reports officer, but Cindy didn't think her skill set lent itself to work in the clandestine service. Her true home, she felt, lay with the Directorate of Intelligence, the group of elite thinkers who carried forward the legacy of clear-eyed analysis pioneered by Cora Du Bois and others during World War II. The analysts were the officers who read the intelligence collected, considered its contents, placed it in a wider context, consulted many other sources, and wrote top secret reports that informed the projection of American power.

At the CIA, the two best-known directorates—the DO and the DI—might as well be two different agencies. That was certainly true in the 1980s, when Cindy was choosing her path. The operations people work undercover, collecting intelligence and engaging in covert actions to carry out presidential policy. Analysts in the Directorate of Intelligence (today known as the Directorate of Analysis) do not carry out policy. Rather, they aspire to help good policy get made. Analysts, ideally, deliver clear and unbiased insights. Their job is to speak truth to power as it resides in the nation's capital, especially but not only to their principal audience, the president of the United States.

The central goal of the analytic corps was, and remains, to prevent another Pearl Harbor—another deadly surprise. Analysts are supposed to see around corners. They do this by reading, writing, and ferociously debating what gets written: a process known, antiseptically, as "review." In a sense, the analytic directorate is one big publishing house, producing a massive, private, classified body of work. The guiding philosophy is that the president doesn't care what a lone analyst like Cindy Storer thinks; the president wants to know what the CIA thinks as a collective body. Every analytic piece is a "corporate product." In that sense, the analytic unit represents the true end point of what the CIA was created to do, though the ops people do not tend to see it that way. There is much rivalry between the two.

When Cindy came on board, analysts and operations officers did not mix. They ate in separate cafeterias and used separate databases, and each referred to the other as "the other side of the house." By selection or self-selection, the two sides of the house attract distinct types to their ranks. The ops people are often (though not always) adventurous and risk-taking, skilled at logistics and winning trust. The analysts are careful and reflective, good at reading data and debating what it means. If an ops person needs a fake identity for a last-minute assignment overseas, they will grab what papers exist and say don't worry, they'll improvise. An analyst will sweat the details in advance, conjecturing all the scenarios in which something might go wrong and painstakingly planning how to react. If an analyst smells flowers—the joke goes—he or she will look around for the funeral. The other joke is that you can tell an extroverted analyst because, while talking, he or she looks at your shoes instead of his or her own.

The Myers-Briggs personality test is taken seriously at the CIA. Analysts tend to be INTJ, which means introverted, intuitive, thinking, and judging. The culture encourages arguing, often brutally. God help you if you are a thinker who has feelings. And analysts can be hard to polygraph. Asked, say, whether she has ever wanted to kill somebody, an analyst will consider the question from many angles. Do I want to kill that person? Well, on some days, sure. Very much so. But not on other days. Or I wouldn't kill them, but I do hate them.

"Ops people are always confident, only occasionally right," is how one officer put it. "Analysts are never confident, and almost always right."

Cindy had studied the agency in college and concluded that the thinkers on the DI side had a better track record than the doers on the ops side. For all the mythology around World War II, OSS operatives— she felt—too often behaved recklessly, and their inexperience got people killed. The analysts, in Cindy's view, did a better job. Cindy felt the same held true in Vietnam: The thinkers outdid the doers. She appreciated that the agency had to engage in covert operations; that the president needs somebody to do jobs the US military can't or won't. But she wanted to work with the thinkers.

And thinking carries heavy responsibility, as Cindy would learn. History can be understood lots of ways, but one way to understand history is to look back at events that occurred abruptly, without warning, after which the world would never be the same. In the ancient world, Hannibal's crossing of the Alps and emergence onto the plains of Italy in 218 BC, which surprised the Roman Army, was one. In the modern world: the Great Stock Market Crash of 1929. The Japanese attack at Pearl Harbor. The Tet offensive, in Vietnam. The fall of the Shah of Iran. In the intelligence business, unforeseen events are known as "discontinuities," and they are what an analyst fears most. The big thing that happens—the big thing it was your job to predict, and you didn't. Or you did, but you couldn't persuade the policymaker to accept it. Or you did predict it, but nobody gives you credit; and for the rest of your life—seriously, the rest of your life—you blame yourself.

As an analyst, you must win people over. Warning entails not only spotting a problem, but convincing colleagues that your prediction is right and that it matters. To be effective, an analyst first needs to persuade her branch manager. The branch officer needs to persuade the division chief, who needs to persuade the office chief, who needs to persuade the editor of the President's Daily Brief. It's not enough to spot something; you need to sell it to a formidable array of gatekeepers.

By definition, somebody will be the very first person to spot a new phenomenon, and in the 1980s and 1990s, at the CIA, that person was increasingly likely to be female. Seeing something early gives the president and the national security community—known as the "policymaker" or the "customer"—more time to react. But it's also risky and frustrating. The policymaker often doesn't want to believe the worst until the worst is upon him. Or her. The policymaker is never ready to make the huge changes needed to combat a rising threat, nor sell them to a skeptical American public. On December 7, 1941, despite two years of war in Europe, America did not yet have the battleships and bombers needed to prevail in World War II. What followed was two years of catch-up, and many tens of thousands of consequent Allied deaths.

To get the policymaker to react, an analyst must woo a skeptical bureaucracy, a struggle during which there are endless opportunities for failure. It's much like the "ball and spiral" game the wartime OSS used during assessment exercises at Station W. When a group of people is working together in a tricky uphill challenge, the ball can drop at any point—and likely will. In the 1980s, incoming women like Cindy Storer found themselves channeled into lower-level jobs that made them among the first to see new security threats—but as they endeavored to get the ball to the top, they struggled to find allies to help it get there. The women tended to be high-achieving and self-critical, prone to wonder: *Why won't anybody listen? Am I not doing a good job? Am I going about it incorrectly? If I'd been louder, better, clearer, would history have changed? Would people have lived? Was there something wrong with me— or something wrong with the people who didn't listen? What if I had written a single word differently?*

ON THE SURFACE, it might appear that by the time Cindy Storer got there, the Directorate of Intelligence was more female-friendly than the Directorate of Operations. Discrimination among analysts was not as blatant. But the DI was a subtle and, in its own way, merciless place. It had a pecking order, and every insider knew which were the most elite desks to work on. The "harder" the topic and higher-visibility the account, the more difficulty women had getting hired on to it. Those who did often found there was no path to the very top jobs. For years, the analytic directorate had just a handful of high-ranking women. Each got there by forging her own path, and each was intimidating and unhelpful to younger women. One, Helene Boatner, the sister and daughter of military generals, started in the typing pool and rose to become head of economic analysis. "With Helene, you were on your own," said one female analyst. "She would smash you as soon as anybody else."

At the DI, the genders traveled in groups, like schools of fish. For decades during the Cold War, the male analysts swam toward prestige units like the Office of Soviet Analysis, or SOVA, and important sub-units that looked at topics like Soviet politics, Soviet economics, and the Soviet military. Female analysts were steered toward more obscure regions, like, say, Uruguay, and softer topics like, say, consumer goods. Gender was one of many factors in the algorithm that determined credibility. Other variables included the region, the topic, and what might be called the historical provenance of the unit.

To understand how provenance factored in, consider the Office of Leadership Analysis, a unit created to produce in-depth studies of foreign leaders. Historically, the analytic directorate relied for background information on a kind of "vault" of its own, a library and research unit called the Office of Central Reference, which was staffed by researchers whom an analyst could call if, say, he needed to know everything about the T-72 Soviet tank or the person who designed it. At OCR, the lowest-level staffers were "indexers" who read materials—photographs, cables—and appended key words and codes, so the material, after being filed, could be retrieved. The indexing unit was called the Head of the Line. The indexers were careful to say they worked in the H-O-L—spelling it out—but everybody else liked to call it "the Hole," to let indexers know their place. A notch down on the pay scale, jobs in central reference went to women, or men who had dead-ended and washed up there.

In the mid-1980s, about the time Cindy was entering on duty, OCR was being phased out as the research records became computerized. Some staffers were diverted to a new IT office. Others joined the all-new Office of Leadership Analysis, or LDA, which was unique in that it was created around a function—assessing leaders—rather than a geographic region. There was much grumbling about whether an entire new office was needed, but the detailed profiles the analysts of the LDA produced quickly became one of the best-read products in the building. Policymakers loved them. Who wouldn't want to read a well-written biography of an emerging autocrat, as opposed to, say, a dry paper on the future of the German economy? LDA positions paid as well as other analytic positions, but because the jobs carried the taint of the old OCR, men often didn't want them. The result was a vacuum into which women poured, knowing leadership analysis was a place where they could do interesting work and might rise to become a manager, or more. Women in other offices who had hit a ceiling rushed toward a big new unit that offered headroom.

The success of the LDA's papers led to anxiety and resentment. Leadership analysts were scorned by regional, political, and military analysts, much as a reporter for *The Economist* might scorn a reporter who works for *People*. Leadership analysis got a reputation as a less rigorous, soft track—assessment lite.

And so, the overall analytic cadre developed a hall-file way to dismiss the unit. LDA, they declared, stood for Ladies Doing Analysis.

BUT THE LADIES PROVED their value, earning respect as well as enemies. In 1980, an obscure agriculture secretary named Mikhail Gorbachev became the youngest full member of the Soviet Politburo, and by 1990 had been elected the executive president of the Soviet Union. As Gorbachev ascended, Robert Gates, the head of the intelligence directorate, wanted a definitive paper on a figure who was something of an unknown quantity. When Gates asked LDA to write it, this sent shock waves through the Office of Soviet Analysis, whose analysts felt *they* should write the Gorbachev paper. The controversy was the beginning of "an awful lot of conflict," one analyst recalled. "There was a lot of discord, fighting, because all of a sudden, we were able to do stuff that before we hadn't done."

The conflict introduced the ladies of leadership analysis to CIA review process at its most combative: what one LDA analyst called "the fiercely argued things." In the DI, written products must be "coordinated." That is, they are collective products that must be run through a complex mill of review. An analyst writing on a topic that intersects with the work of another analyst must get that colleague to sign off, or "chop," on the paper, before it can be published. When the ladies of analysis wanted to write about any Soviet leader, they had to get sign-off from SOVA, but SOVA was often, now, too pissed off to chop. The fearsome Helene Boatner, who was made head of LDA, sought to protect her own standing and would not go to bat for her staffers. "Helene was not into helping us at all," said an analyst who developed an eye twitch from the stress of trying to coordinate her papers.

In the Directorate of Intelligence, power struggles like these were quiet but truly ruthless. So many factors went into an analyst's hall file.

Are you a pain to work with? Do you write fast? Can you brief—that is, are you exciting to listen to? In what office did you start? Did you come through, say, LDA? These qualities all matter when trying to get colleagues to buy in to your analysis. Winning buy-in can mean being second-guessed and challenged in a way that's thoughtful and productive; or being nitpicked, thwarted, and undermined. A cold-blooded colleague might hold off signing off on a paper and secretly write her own version first. A day of coordinating could, as one analyst put it, make you want to "poke your eye out."

In the 1980s and 1990s, a generation of female analysts entered on duty who were well prepared and enjoyed the self-confidence that came with numbers. The CIA is what's known as a "greedy institution." It sets out to inculcate loyalty, and, like a controlling spouse or partner, seeks to isolate the individual in a closed and peculiar world. The weird and prolonged onboarding process—waiting for a background check, receiving a cursory letter from somebody named Grace Sullivan, finally getting a vaguely worded job offer—it's all intended to make the initiate feel grateful, chosen, confused, and determined to measure up. The incoming women felt that way. They were happy to have arrived and anxious to prove they belonged.

The mid-1980s had marked a robust expansion of the CIA, as a hiring freeze gave way to a big bump-up during the tenure of director Bill Casey, who led the agency from 1981 to 1987 and, like Ronald Reagan, was prepared to fight the Cold War by most any means necessary. Women began applying to the analytic corps who were more likely than they had been in the past to have degrees in disciplines like political science and economics. Congress was paying attention and asking for diversity numbers. But it's one thing to admit women; it's another to assign them career tracks. Incoming women analysts often got marginalized and diverted into side channels, of which LDA was one. Others included offshoot units around the Washington, DC, area, in dingy workspaces left over from World War II.

And so, as the women of the operations directorate worked to prove they could bring gifts and grit to spycraft, a group of female analysts fought a parallel battle—to persuade policymakers a global pivot was taking place. Working at the ground level, they often were positioned to see things the people at the top couldn't, but lacked the seniority and stature needed to make their perspective prevail. The women paid close attention to a foe that happened, in its own way, to be paying close attention to them and the changes they represented. The establishment's failure to respond to that foe would forever mark the lives of the women who had warned about it.

That foe was a terrorist organization called al-Qaeda.

CHAPTER 14

FINDING X

ND SO IT WAS THAT CINDY STORER, AFTER ORIENTATION, found herself groggily carpooling to her new workplace in southeast Washington, DC, some fifteen miles from headquarters in McLean. Under a program to accommodate the surge of new staffers, she lived with a CIA family in Falls Church, Virginia, while seeking a place of her own. Each morning Cindy arose before the sun did, zipped herself into one of three new suits—purchased from outlet malls and JC Penney—and slipped into stockings and pumps. She rode with colleagues to a converted gun turret factory near the Anacostia River.

The bland-looking structure was known as Building 213, but the official name was the National Photographic Interpretation Center. Its location along a forlorn stretch of M Street SE on the outskirts of the Navy Yard compound provided unassuming cover for the activities that took place inside. Washington, DC, was in the grip of a crack epidemic, and broken glass often littered the sidewalks outside the building, as bored guards from the General Services Administration watched over the parking lot—sort of. The neighborhood was so sketchy that people in the office were discouraged from walking to a nearby McDonald's; a shuttle took them instead. One of Cindy's officemates did walk occasionally; coming back one day with his badge half-tucked into his breast pocket, he saw a drug dealer emerge from a townhouse, glance at him, and say knowledgeably to a companion: "No, man, that's not FBI—that's CIA." Cindy opted to eat in the cafeteria, which had mediocre food but good hot cookies.

Inside NPIC, the halls smelled of fixers and solvents. The center had been created in the mid-1950s, evolving out of the Navy's World War II charting efforts to support amphibious landings. It now existed to interpret aerial photos taken by the agency's fleet of overhead surveillance technologies: satellites as well as spy planes like the SR-71 and the U-2. The project had blossomed under the tenure of John McCone, who, upon taking over as CIA director in 1961, sought to distance the agency from covert action and applied himself to winning the space race. The NPIC, he believed, would play a key role. Early satellites ejected a bucket of film, which dropped by parachute to be hooked by a spy plane streaking underneath at fifteen thousand feet. An enormous amount of film accumulated—literally miles of it—and NPIC pioneered the field of imagery analysis, employing experts to study what showed up in the buckets. Cindy, like her colleagues, got to work very early to study the morning's film and report on its contents by the time the all-source analysts at CIA headquarters got to their own desks at eight-thirty. The "all source analysts" at Langley were, to her, unknown and unseen; all she knew was that they enjoyed higher security clearances, access to more sources, and therefore, higher status than she had.

By the time Cindy got there, NPIC analysts and their counterparts at CIA headquarters had developed an intense rivalry. NPIC's signal achievement had occurred during the Cuban Missile Crisis in October 1962, when an "air defense team" of imagery analysts keeping a close eye on Cuban military installations noticed "long canvas-colored cylindrical objects along the edge of a field," according to an institutional history. The objects were Soviet missiles. Unfortunately for the all-source analysts, this conclusion flew in the face of a recent paper some of them had written, expressing doubt that the Soviets would deploy strategic missiles in Cuba. The NPIC people got it right, and the all-source people resented being outdone. It was the first use of imagery analysis to verify a diplomatic agreement and won the agency much justified acclaim. But it also exacerbated tensions between Langley and Building 213, where the NPIC staffers suffered disputes of their own. Imagery analysts often came from the military and brought service rivalries with them. "Mike's boys" warred with "Gordy's boys" in disputes both comical and fierce. Aerial images were often grainy, their interpretations open to, well, interpretation. When one faction created an "elaborate theory" that some circular objects were rocket motors, another group insisted that the items in question were discarded tires.

Beset by complex rivalries, NPIC by the 1980s had become cliquish and isolated. Midlevel leaders were "mediocre," and the majority were white men. An inspector general's report found the office marked by favoritism, factionalism, and discrimination; there were only about twenty Black analysts, fewer women, and "none of the women in the analytic group were in any leadership position."

Into this marginalized community sailed Cindy, who was excited to learn her craft. Her first day, she found herself assigned to a branch staffed by men whose careers dated back to Vietnam. Branches at the CIA have around six to eight people. One, her assigned mentor, showed her around. Imagery analysts worked at light tables, which were desks with a flat glass surface on which a photo image could be placed, illuminated by a light from below. The imagery analysts peered through a magnifying scope shaped like binoculars, which were almost too wide for Cindy's face. Her branch had a lone WANG computer: a small box with green letters blinking on a black screen, and a light pen she could jab at the screen to give a command.

During the tour, her mentor slid open a drawer of his desk, revealing his cache of Swedish pornography. Cindy was being tested and knew better than to appear shocked.

Not long after, she got a call from an officer at the Pentagon who sounded taken aback to hear a female voice. He asked to speak to her predecessor. "Whatever you need to know, you're dealing with me now," Cindy told him, and hung up. The official called back and apologized.

BUT THE WORK ITSELF, Cindy relished. There was nothing like opening a fresh brown paper packet of film—the 7 x 14–inch envelope would be on her chair every morning, with a hard piece of plastic to keep the film from being damaged—and removing the precious contents, a photograph thinner than a saw blade and meaningful as a medical X-ray, showing the surface of the earth and what things were upon it. She enjoyed a front-row seat to history, studying images of countries whose military installations the United States was keeping a close eye on. She was a tiny but very important cog in a huge Cold War operation. Her job was to help ensure that the Soviet Union and its allies abided by agreements, such as the INF treaty, to reduce the world's stockpile of nuclear missiles. "Trust but verify" was how President Reagan put it. Cindy was one of the verifiers.

Despite their peccadilloes, the men Cindy worked with in the NPIC were good teachers. Cindy came to think of them, almost fondly, as "the curmudgeons." They went on at length, and with passion, about the difference between a tank and an armored personnel carrier. Her eyes became more expert. She was assigned to look at Soviet missile systems but couldn't share that fact with colleagues, unless they were "read in." NPIC analysts were told not to speculate on one another's projects. She moved on to look at Nicaraguan ground forces when the United States was opposing the Sandinistas. She was not a clandestine operative and could tell friends and neighbors she worked for the CIA, or "the government," but couldn't share many details beyond that. People usually knew enough not to ask.

The curmudgeons taught Cindy how to think strategically—big picture—beyond counting tanks and artillery pieces. It was her office's task to figure out, first, what *are* these images, and second, what do they portend? "We should be able to find X," the curmudgeons would muse, based on seeing Y. They'd turn to Cindy and say: *Look for X*. She would go off, find X, come back. For her, finding things was so easy. NPIC was known for crafting "stories" to describe a weapons system. The men taught her how to construct a chronology, to show changes over time. A key part of the job entailed looking at older images and comparing them with the latest ones. She learned to recognize shadows cast by big new antennae arrays, or raw ground scraped for construction. Communications are often the first thing established when a base is being set up. Once you learn about communications, Cindy realized, you can't go to the mountains and enjoy the scenery. All you see are antennae.

Not only did Cindy get to read maps, she got to make them. Some days Cindy would sit on the floor, lay out a map, shade portions, take it to a laminating machine, and make a display. There were fun side projects. Once a year, NPIC would look at a plot of ground on Mount Ararat in Turkey at the behest of a member of Congress obsessed with finding Noah's ark. When the office started beta testing a Windows computer system, Cindy was assigned to try to overload it. "I'm like, really? You're going to pay me to break the computer? This is awesome!"

She devised her own strategic plan. She would do imagery analysis for five years, then move to the Directorate of Intelligence as an all-source analyst. NPIC was a backwater, and she didn't want to spend her whole career there, but she savored the work and made the most of it, taking night classes toward a master's degree and soaking up information in an office with a bunch of older men who weren't going anywhere and a bunch of twenty-two-year-old women who might or might not be.

MORE NEW WOMEN CAME in all the time. They were roughly of Cindy's age and background. One day, in 1989, a bus from headquarters arrived with four new women aboard. As one member of the quartet, Kristin Wood, remembers, the new group, already friends after their bus ride, were a walking, talking example of the kind of female analyst the CIA in the 1980s was looking for: all Caucasian, all brunette, all brown-eyed, all with big hair and bankers' suits and Aigner pumps and blouses with string ties or pussy bows, all patriotic and eager to serve. Wood grew up in a farming community in California; another, Jennifer Matthews, had attended a small Christian college in Ohio. The women had lunch together every day, chatting about their lives as twentysomethings in the big city. When Jennifer Matthews went for her first waxing appointment, she arrived the next day dramatically limping and, laughing, warned them it was painful.

There were men coming in as well, CIA hires as well as trainees from other agencies. In one training class, a male contemporary from the Defense Intelligence Agency developed a habit of evaluating Kristin Wood's daily outfits. She'd be sexier if she wore higher heels, he whispered to her, or if her hair were longer. You're never going to get a man, he warned. "Lucky me, if you're what's available," she retorted.

The new recruits had nerve, but they weren't prepared for the lingering wolfish culture of the workplace, where office parties were taken seriously, and drinking at the parties started early and ran late. Bosses, otherwise admired men, would get drunk and proposition or try to grope them. Wood formed a career development group to help women figure out how to make their way. Most eye-opening, for her, was to listen to her Black colleagues talk about being "shoved into support and administrative roles" and how hard they had to fight to carve out a career path. "Hearing what these women went through, it was shocking," she recalled. "If it was hard for us to be seen as credible it was doubly hard for them to get opportunities."

With their fresh eyes and well-honed study habits, the younger women sometimes saw things the curmudgeons didn't. When Kristin Wood's branch got its first IDEX—a clunky but exciting machine that enabled analysts to play with an image digitally—a few of her colleagues monopolized it. They spent two days scrutinizing an image that had them stumped. "Why don't we ask *Kristin* to look at it," one of the senior analysts said, as Kristin Wood walked past. He was being sarcastic. Kristin looked. "It's a test stand," she told them—a stand for testing rockets and motors, proof of a certain country's nuclear proliferation into a certain other country. Her manager took the hot piece of intelligence to Capitol Hill. Wood got no credit beyond knowing she had seen something they did not.

They also learned that every analyst matters. One Sunday, Wood came in to check on an African country in the throes of civil war. She opened her film packet to see troops advancing on a rebel base where the CIA had officers stationed. Imagery analysis wasn't yet seen as a tool to support operations—that would come with the Persian Gulf war—so there was no protocol for acting quickly. Deeply alarmed, Kristin called around until she found somebody in the agency's twenty-four-hour operations center who could get the word out. The next morning, the base had been wiped out. The officers—her colleagues—had escaped. "Never underestimate the difference a day makes" was the message she took. Also: If one analyst missed something, there wouldn't likely be somebody else to find it. And people can die.

The women also learned what it felt like to have their insights dismissed. Cindy Storer was assigned to a top secret project and found herself charting the entire missile system of a very hard target. Her ability to comprehend the program surprised even her. She was not, however, allowed to write up her findings. Only all-source analysts could publish. She had nobody to intervene or make her case. Her unit was later criticized for failing to identify the development she had spotted. It was seen as an intelligence failure. Cindy expressed her distress and learned she had begun to develop a reputation for being emotional.

EVEN SO, HER FIVE-YEAR plan proceeded on course. After three years, Cindy rotated to CIA headquarters, where she was assigned to an account in the Near East South Asia office. In the Directorate of Intelligence, offices are the largest units, with hundreds of officers, somewhat like divisions on the ops side. Analysts in NESA focused on a sweeping horizontal band of north African and Asian countries, from Morocco to Bangladesh and everything in between: India, Libya, the Middle East. The pay hike enabled Cindy to upgrade her wardrobe with a couple of silk suits, and pay the mortgage on a house in a woodsy neighborhood in north Arlington, Virginia. She sang in the choir at St. Andrew's Episcopal Church, felt part of a supportive community of friends and neighbors, adopted a rescue dog, became a Girl Scout troop leader, bought a used Mercury Sable. It was not a beautiful car but it could fit a lot of Girl Scouts. She could drive to McLean in twenty minutes.

It was a fulfilling life; she loved her work. At headquarters, she parked the Sable in one of the remote lots and walked happily to her office. As she settled into her new responsibilities, Cindy's route often took her along the ground-floor corridor that displays the "directors' portrait gallery," a row of oil paintings depicting the historic lineup of CIA directors. Clattering along in pumps, Cindy walked past Allen Dulles, looking sober and world-weary, graying features composed with a benign dignity that belied his eventful romantic life and what Mary Bancroft called his "dark side." She passed John McCone, whose focus on technology was in some ways responsible for Cindy's career, and successors including Richard Helms, who, for all his talk about honorable men, was convicted of misleading Congress about agency misadventures in Chile; William Colby, respected but also resented for handing over the family jewels ("A quick man to put on a hair shirt," as one analyst tartly put it); and Stansfield Turner, never forgiven for his purge of the clandestine service. And so on and so on: an unbroken line of white men of varying degrees of competence and integrity. Bill Casey in 1987 had been succeeded by Judge William Webster, charged with restoring rectitude and moral order after the excesses of the Central American misadventures. To his mind, moral order included decreeing female employees must wear high-heeled pumps even in the parking lots, an edict that women like Cindy, who had to walk a long way from her car, did not appreciate. Webster in 1991 was succeeded by Robert Gates, the rare director who emerged from the analytic corps and was rumored to return unsatisfactory writing samples to the unfortunate author stapled to a burn bag.

The portrait gallery gave way to the cafeteria and then a passageway to the building where Cindy's unit was located. The building, known as new headquarters, was occupied in 1988 and formally completed in 1991. An impressive construction of steel and glass, it had a soaring four-story atrium, spy planes hanging overhead, and a long white escalator that crisscrossed its way from the main entrance on the fourth floor. There were two six-story office towers that faced the twin wings of the old headquarters, with the atrium, gleaming and light-filled, between the towers. New headquarters had been built into a hillside, and anybody who entered through the main fourth-floor entrance would take the big escalator to lower floors. People coming from original headquarters could cross the atrium and enter that way. For all its modern touches, new headquarters felt cheesy to those who worked in it. Leaks developed, and it was found to suffer from "sick building syndrome," a vague term for a building whose problematic ventilation caused wheezing and headaches. The place had a clammy feel, and people preferred to work in OH, as they called old headquarters.

But here Cindy was.

By now, virtually every room in headquarters was a secure vault. Each day, Cindy punched in a code to enter the space that housed NESA, which consisted of rabbit warrens of analysts busily producing reports about events taking place in their assigned region of the world. She passed by offices and cubicles, through hallways and subhallways. The most important desks were closer to the front. Most managers were male, and white, and middle-aged. During one holiday party, some analysts put on a skit in which they impersonated their managers, wearing little paper circles on their heads to represent all the bald spots. The managers did not think the skit was especially funny.

Cindy wended her way through the warren until she reached, in the back, her assigned spot as a military analyst for Afghanistan, in a space she and two colleagues referred to as "the ghetto." The three-person Afghan account was what one might call NESA's "hole."

THE YEAR CINDY ARRIVED, 1989, happened to be the year her often overlooked patch of real estate would assume a global import. Ten years earlier, in 1979, the Soviet Army had engineered a Communist revolution in this mountainous, tribal part of South Asia, then invaded and occupied the country. A proxy war ensued in which President Carter ordered the CIA to assist Afghan fighters resisting the Soviet occupation. By the time Cindy arrived, the agency had spent a decade essentially running the Afghan war. For five years, the struggle had been a mostly losing game in which Afghan resistance fighters managed to kill Soviets and Afghan Communists, but took tremendous casualties, while the civilian population suffered human rights abuses at the hands of the Soviet occupiers.

In 1986, the Reagan administration decided that rather than wound the Soviets, it might be possible to push them out.

"We changed the rules," as Milt Bearden, a CIA station chief, put it.

That rule change came courtesy of the Stinger missile. Bearden was present for the arrival of the first one hundred handheld Stingers and saw firsthand the effect the American hardware had on a flight of Soviet helicopters arriving from Jalalabad. As he later described it, the first Stinger misfired; the second struck a helicopter that exploded in midair and fell. Another fell, and another. By 1988, the Soviet Army was tired and broken, and so, as it happened, was the Soviet Union.

The Soviets signed a withdrawal treaty in Geneva. The Soviet withdrawal in February 1989—and the weakening it revealed—was followed by the ascent in Czechoslovakia of the playwright Václav Havel; the 1990 election of Solidarity leader Lech Wałesa in Poland; the execution of the Romanian dictator Nicolae Ceauşescu and his wife; revolutionary changes in Hungary; and, on November 9, 1989, the fall of the Berlin Wall. In December 1991, the Soviet Union collapsed.

People at Langley were unprepared for the speed at which the latter event unfolded; the collapse was a "discontinuity" if there ever was one. The central mission that animated the agency since its founding had vanished, virtually overnight. "When the Soviet Union fell apart, in my career it was the first time in anybody's career, anybody's modern career, that we didn't have one single threat, and we didn't know what to do, and our managers didn't know what to do," recalled Mia McCall, the operations officer who had been recruited by Sue McCloud.

CINDY STORER, HOWEVER, KNEW what to do. From her desk, she sought to master the shifting political landscape of postwar Afghanistan, the events taking place within it and new alliances that were forming. In 1992, she was promoted to the position of senior political military analyst. She now had a permanent slot as a bona fide all-source analyst, joining the lofty category of officers who exasperated her onetime colleagues at the NPIC.

It was a high-status role, but not exactly at a hot desk. People at Langley were eager to put the Afghan war behind them. "We walked away," CIA director William Webster would later admit, adding that it was a mistake to have done so. In greater Washington, "Afghanistanism" became a term to describe the weedy ravings of policy nerds who insisted on the importance of an obscure, inconsequential region. Cindy Storer was one of those who insisted. During the Afghan war, seven tribal factions had fought a common enemy, the Russians, even as they jockeyed against one another for the endgame. Now, as occupation gave way to civil war, the tribal factions were turning on each other in ways that, Cindy sensed, might have consequences that extended beyond the conflict. Each faction had its own aims and funders even as there existed hidden connections between them. Arms sent to one faction might end up with another. The US tried, and failed, to buy back all the Stingers. Some of Cindy's colleagues referred to the tribes as the "seven dwarves." This bothered Cindy; it struck her as dismissive and racist.

She studied land mine conventions, peace negotiations, the treatment of Soviet POWs. Sitting near her were analysts for Pakistan and India—they formed the "South Asia group"—and, with them, she looked at postwar relations between India and Pakistan, who had been on different sides of the Afghan war. It was a lot for their little band of three Afghan analysts to keep track of, and they did their best.

She had a great boss: a former Marine sharpshooter who assigned her to look through hundreds of paper files lining a wall of the vault to see which should be computerized. For an analyst, this was by no means scut work; more like a graduate course in the hidden history of her region. Happily browsing, Cindy came across a 1982 paper written by two of her predecessors describing "foreign fighters," a term for Arab men who traveled to Afghanistan from the Middle East, Africa, and Asia to help repel the Soviet occupiers. The fighters called themselves *mujahideen:* Islamic warriors pursuing jihad, or holy war, against non-Islamic nations. The paper predicted they'd become a problem after the war.

Cindy could see that they were right. As part of her work toward a master's degree, she had taken a course in insurgency, a military clash in which a small, mobile group of fighters, often outsiders, aspires to defeat a larger entrenched force. At her desk, she was reading reports from aid workers saying that the foreign fighters were violent, vehemently anti-Western, and growing in number. The conflict with the Soviets was over, but the foreign fighters weren't going home. Many couldn't, having committed crimes or otherwise become persona non grata in their home countries. Instead, they were fanning out. With the collapse of the Soviet Union, many Central Asian states, formerly under Soviet control, had become unstable, and the fighters began taking advantage of the chaos to cross borders, to join with Islamic groups and overthrow non-Islamic leaders. Some showed up in Chechnya, where Cindy started seeing reports of foreign fighters holding up banks and stealing cars to raise money for jihad. She read complaints from Soviets, about how Afghan veterans were setting off bombs in Chechnya and Bosnia.

Who, she wondered, was behind what looked like coordinated actions? The reports mentioned a number of Islamic extremist leaders, among them a wealthy Saudi named Osama bin Laden.

Cindy and her colleagues on the Afghan desk already knew a little bit about Osama bin Laden. The eighteenth son of a wealthy engineer—one of fifty-five children in all—Osama bin Laden came from immense wealth, thanks to his father's construction company, the Saudi Binladin Group, and the oil money that financed its contracts. Bin Laden from an early age was drawn to solitary religiosity, and the death of his father in 1967 in a plane crash drove him further toward fundamentalist Islam. Like many young Arabs, he was deeply affected by Israel's Six-Day War against Egypt, Jordan, and Syria, in June of that same year, which struck many Arabs as a true "civilizational defeat" by Westernized powers and proved, for bin Laden, an impetus for radicalization. He joined the jihad in Afghanistan against Soviet infidels, where a mortar shell, falling unexploded at his feet, convinced him that God wanted him to continue the fight even after the war ended. Bin Laden and his Egyptian commanders decided to start an organization devoted to prolonging jihad.

More than a fighter, bin Laden was a money man. During the Afghan war, he had served as a conduit for countries, like Saudi Arabia, that were secretly supporting certain tribal factions. In some ways, the emerging fighters network was like a Silicon Valley startup, and bin Laden was like a venture capitalist, leveraging his initial investment to attract other funders.

By the time Cindy Storer started paying close attention, bin Laden had relocated to Sudan, where the government in Khartoum welcomed his help resisting Christian separatists in the south. His whereabouts were not secret, though many of his contacts were. He was in touch with extremist Islamic leaders, some of whom were running training camps for new fighters. But there was no central organization that Cindy could make out. There was no stated name for the network; no board of directors; no personnel list.

Something was forming—but what? At NPIC, Cindy had been trained to study an indistinct shape until she made out what it was. She began sifting through "bits of information" in the form of phone calls, radio reports, State Department dispatches, and articles by some brave Arab language reporters who ventured into the training camps to do interviews. An Arab language magazine, *Al-Jihad,* published articles about jihad. Cindy had them translated. Ads told where to donate money, providing clues about the identities of jihad funders. Some were nongovernmental organizations—charities that proliferated during the Afghan war, drawing on the Muslim sense of obligation to the *umma*, the worldwide Muslim community. These charitable organizations raised money for humanitarian efforts, including refugee camps for displaced Afghans. Some, however, were secretly diverting the donations they collected, to pay for arms and travel for the fighters. Other funders included rich people and radical clerics. Cindy set out to track which fighters were being influenced by which countries, people, and groups.

And she sought to keep Afghanistan—where the Taliban had come to power after the withdrawal, imposing their own extreme ideology of Shariah law on the country—part of the greater Washington conversation. Every morning, she and her colleagues met to propose topics for the President's Daily Brief—the PDB. Among the many kinds of papers the Directorate of Intelligence published, the PDB was the most precious piece of intellectual real estate and the most hard-fought. Also known as the "book," the PDB consisted of a leather binder containing short articles of five hundred words or so, printed on heavy paper, containing the most urgent intelligence of the day. The book was presented to the president every morning, delivered by a briefer who fielded questions, coming in early to read it.

Writing a single five-hundred-word PDB item took a full day, spent not just researching and writing but walking or running all over headquarters. Every word had to be agreed upon by any analyst with a stake in the topic. Cindy kept a pair of sneakers at her desk. She might visit the same office three or four times. The item then went to the PDB editorial staff, whose editors might send it back for revisions, or spike it on the grounds that it had been OBE—overtaken by events—or was BT, below the threshold of risk. If a PDB did get slated for publication, Cindy would sit waiting for editors to call with questions, then field more from the White House briefers.

Cindy began experimenting with ways to describe what she was seeing in post-Soviet Afghanistan and beyond. Thanks to the women who converted paper files to computer records, the DI now had a rich data bank of all the items once kept on microfiche in central reference: cables and photos and signals intelligence and open-source material.

Cindy taught herself how to design Boolean searches, creating search profiles that fished up any item with the phrase "foreign fighters" or "Afghan Arabs." Boolean searches were refined by quotation marks, question marks, asterisks, and parentheses, so what she was doing was a kind of elementary coding. The DI database regularly scoured its holdings, dumping fresh items to her inbox as new material arrived. Mornings, she'd come in and turn on her computer. While it warmed up, she'd fetch coffee and return to see what was new. Some days, her inbox held ten items; some days, one hundred. The profiles gave her a view of a growing network of violent operatives. It was like trying to get her head around SPECTRE in James Bond.

And so Cindy did what she'd done all her life. She made a map. This one consisted of slides, tracking where the fighters were moving and using symbols to denote what they did. Activities might include: Establish an office. Set up a training camp. Make a bank deposit. Blow something up. She dated each one. She ended up with a slide deck that depicted how "I have an office" led, inevitably, to "I blew something up." She had to conjecture how many fighters were involved, based on past estimates and her own gut instinct. In intelligence analysis, this is jokingly known as a SWAG—a scientific wild-ass guess. Flipping fast through the slides, she could show the thing she was tracking— whatever it was—expanding. Training camps appearing. Offices being set up. Networks forming. The graphic was powerful, Cindy felt. Persuasive. Something was happening, all over the world, and Cindy's map proved it. But for as much as she waved her hands, and circulated her map, Cindy was unable to get attention in the building. Afghanistan was over, as far as most colleagues were concerned, and so were the fighters emanating from its regions.

"Nobody wanted to hear about it."

CHAPTER 15

YOU DON'T BELONG HERE

Mid-1990s

NOBODY, THAT IS, BUT A SMALL GROUP OF WOMEN WHO WERE becoming as addicted as Cindy herself, noodling around in a field that hardly anybody had heard of, keenly intrigued by the transit and doings of jihad fighters. In the warren of cubicles that comprised NESA, Cindy crossed paths with one of them: an analyst who looked at regional issues all over the Near East and South Asia, with an expansive portfolio and a seniority that placed her higher in the pecking order than Cindy. The analyst was another woman, seasoned, exquisitely well educated, more than ten years older than she was. Her name was Barbara Sude. She had bangs and glasses and an immaculately trimmed pageboy. When Cindy got up the nerve to send her a message, Sude turned out to be good-humored and down-to-earth. An expert in medieval Islamic thought, Barbara Sude also knew how to follow a trail of illicit financial transactions. Her mandate included governments and charities—or so-called charities—and their spending habits. Cindy's message suggested to Barbara that she add Islamic extremists to her portfolio.

Like Cindy, Barbara Sude had begun her career in an agency backwater, despite a staggering array of credentials every bit the equal of the men who sat in the executive dining room wearing neckties from Yale or Stanford. Barbara had grown up in Port Washington, Long Island, a community of public servants and first responders where her family had lived for six generations. Her mother, a professional typist, served during World War II as one of the first female Marines. As a girl, Barbara was as fascinated by history as Cindy Storer was by maps; a children's book about a traveling minstrel, *Adam of the Road,* inspired an obsession with English history. In high school she discovered her facility for languages and took Latin, French, and Spanish. A paper about the influence of Arabic words on the Spanish language led to an interest in the Muslim presence in Spain, which sparked an interest in medieval Islam and the centuries-old conflicts between the Christian West and the Arab world. In a class called "Third World Studies," her peers wrote about modern Palestine while Barbara Sude wrote about the first Crusade.

Barbara had entered Georgetown University in the mid-1960s, majoring in Arabic studies. In grad school—at the University of Pennsylvania and then Princeton University—she specialized in Islamic intellectual history, and she wrote her PhD dissertation on Ibn al-Haytham, an Islamic mathematician who advanced understanding of optics and vision. When she earned her PhD, in 1974, there were few Arabic studies scholars and few institutions interested in hiring them. A male peer with less credentials—she spoke Persian; he did not—got a job at Yale, but Barbara, shy and reluctant to put herself forward or tout her linguistic skills, got mostly rejections. A friend suggested they both apply to the CIA; Barbara did some reading about the agency and its history and thought *Why not?*

The CIA's New York application office was located below Canal Street, in Chinatown, where the smell of oil and brass and frying food reminded her of Cairo. Barbara took the test with the pink cover and answered questions like: *If you took a position overseas, how long could you go without soap?* Upon being hired, Barbara, boasting a PhD from one of the top universities in the world, was an obvious candidate to become an all-source analyst. Instead, she was routed to the Foreign Broadcast Information Service, an outpost located in Rosslyn, Virginia, the same suburb where Heidi August had been set to work folding maps.

FBIS was a support unit, albeit one with a storied history that pre-dated the CIA. Just before America entered World War II, during Roosevelt's early efforts to build a spy service, an array of foreign language speakers—housewives, businessmen, bricklayers—were engaged to listen to foreign broadcasts and write reports, employing "propaganda analysis" to discern the lies of foreign leaders and determine their intent and impact. Three decades after the war ended, FBIS was still the agency's open-source analytic operation—analyzing foreign media, both print and broadcast—and remained little changed, down to the manual typewriters its staffers used to peck out their reports. When a few IBM Selectrics arrived, cheering broke out. The service—ironically, given its sparse technical resources—belonged to the whiz-bang Directorate of Science & Technology, whose Christmas parties were renowned for dazzling lasers and light shows. It was an arrangement left over from the war and the need to intercept long-range radio broadcasts.

The FBIS workforce tended to be more diverse than at headquarters, with bilingual Americans poring over newspapers that arrived weeks after being printed. Granted, diversity had its limits. Subbing for her boss at a managers' meeting, Barbara counted twenty-seven male managers, and two women. In other ways, the office was a breath of fresh air. Desks were shoved up against each other; having been immersed for years in solitary study of medieval manuscripts, she enjoyed the chatter and "reading the news day in and day out." Display ads conveyed what people were buying in supermarkets. Even typefaces and ink were evocative.

Barbara read the Arab world's take on crises that consumed the work of ops officers like Heidi August. The 1979 Iranian hostage crisis; the 1981 assassination of Egyptian president Anwar Sadat; the riots and rock-throwing protests, known as intifada, waged by Palestinians against Israel's twenty-year occupation of the West Bank and Gaza. For a scholar of the Middle East, terrorism was always present in the background. On a grad-school trip to Cairo, Barbara had made a plane connection in Athens airport just days before terrorists shot up people in line at the reservations counter. On her return, she could see bullet holes pockmarking the windows.

To everything taking place, Barbara brought her own deep understanding of the history of Islam. She knew that for Muslims, the Qur'an is the infallible word of God. She also knew that as with all great religions, there existed many schools of thought. The Sufis were a nonviolent sect that took a mystical approach, permitting individuals to make life decisions based on direct communication with God. Contrasted to them were Salafi-Jihadists, strict constructionists who wanted to go back to the early days of Islam, emulating what they believed the Prophet Muhammad wanted. Fundamentalist clerics were advancing the idea that to the five pillars of Islam—the creed, prayer, fasting, alms giving, and the hajj, the pilgrimage to Mecca—a sixth should be added: fighting. One interpretation of "fighting" meant struggling to improve one's own nature: improving yourself to make yourself a better Muslim, a better person, the struggle against sin.

But as a conservative form of Islam came to the fore in the 1980s, leaders emerged who called for literal combat.

They were the jihadists. Propagandists—fundamentalist clerics— fanned this idea and politicized it. Only a small number of Muslims accepted this approach, but the whole point of propaganda is to make something that is not socially acceptable, socially acceptable, through repetition and amplification. The jihadists, Barbara knew, could not be written off as crazy. They believed that by fighting they would save themselves from eternal damnation. It was Barbara's view that they could not be unpersuaded. It might be possible, though, to defeat their plans.

Barbara also noted Arab women's experience of the rising wave of fundamentalist thinking. Radical clerics, like the Taliban in Afghanistan and Ayatollah Khomeini in Iran, cherished a merciless conviction that women were subordinate to men, and that the lives, minds, and sexuality of girls and women must be severely constrained. In Afghanistan, the Talib mullahs worked to ensure that women remained sequestered and unschooled. In Iran, women were compelled to wear hijab—head coverings that once had been voluntary—and beaten for showing an ankle. A "morality police" enforced the edicts.

Gender was a core issue, not a sideline. The foreign fighters, and the leaders who exhorted them, were preoccupied with female sexuality.

The fighters were often recruited with the promise of virgins waiting in the afterlife, as well as bootlegged pornography to enjoy in the here and now. The jihad movement was a fight against everything Barbara and Cindy represented: women becoming educated, women contributing to public life, women living lives equal to men. Barbara also took note of opposition to the new strictures. She kept a cartoon from a Lebanese magazine that showed a full chador: a headscarf and a wrap-around cloak. In the cartoon, there was no head under the head covering; instead, there were sheets tied together coming out of the opening, with footprints walking down the block and away, suggesting a woman had escaped.

Another cartoon depicted an executive asking a secretary to make a call, and she says, "Well, it's a little hard with the veil between my teeth."

And, Barbara kept evidence that the strictures were not historically valid, whatever the fundamentalists might argue. Also taped in her workspace was a copy of an illustration from a fourteenth-century manuscript, showing a woman at a medieval university in what is now Iraq, lecturing men on Islamic law.

BARBARA SUDE WAS A half generation older than Cindy, and it had taken her more than a decade to win a spot at Langley. One incentive—for her—was irritation. During her time at FBIS, all-source analysts visiting from headquarters adopted such a condescending attitude that even a person of her even temperament found it galling. One told her to "run down the hall" to find somebody; others implied FBIS was not part of the CIA. When she began to put out job feelers, the Directorate of Operations offered her a job that paid less than she was making, so she said no thanks. When she applied to the analytic directorate, they suggested she hadn't learned the sacred "DI methodology" of considering a problem from many sides.

"Isn't there some lawsuit for discrimination against women?" she inquired. The Category B lawsuit was making its way through the operations directorate and didn't directly affect the corps of analysts, but she figured it wouldn't hurt to bring it up.

Her persistence paid off. When one of her Georgetown professors, a woman, came to give a talk, spotted Barbara, and hugged her, Barbara's profile was elevated. She was recruited to the DI's Africa office and then to NESA, where she began looking at charities and their spending. When Cindy Storer contacted her, the two women began getting together and attending informal meetings with colleagues at other federal agencies.

And that's how it came to be that among the first people in Washington with a deep knowledge of a growing threat—a man named Osama bin Laden, and a terrorist group called al-Qaeda—happened to be a trio of women.

THEY MET IN BORROWED spaces around the city, offices reserved for an hour or so, at different agencies, every couple of months, beginning in the early 1990s. Attending was a shifting handful of intelligence and national security officers, most of them young, many of them female, not yet eminent, not yet locked in careers, junior people who did not have a stake in the old Cold War alliances and enmities and felt attuned to a new kind of threat. The group included people from the FBI, the NSA, and the Federal Aviation Administration. The nature of the work was friendly and collaborative; if one of them couldn't get a piece of writing published, they'd pass it to somebody who could. The organizing force was the third member of what would become a power trio: a twentysomething State Department officer named Gina Bennett.

Like Cindy Storer, Gina Bennett had grown up in eastern Virginia—in her case, Virginia Beach. Her father was a naval officer. She graduated in 1988 from the University of Virginia, with a double major in economics and foreign policy and a minor in religion. During her student years, Gina would ride her bike to the Miller Center—UVA's political affairs think tank, a half mile from the main campus—and sit, bike lying on the gravel beside her, gazing at the building.

"Someday I'm going to be in there," she told herself. "And I am going to give a speech on breakthrough Middle East foreign policy."

Gina applied to the CIA but did not get an interview. Anxious not to return home after graduation, she answered a classified ad for a clerk-typist at the State Department. She took tests in typing and alphabetizing—for which she was required to wear a skirt—and got a three-month temporary position. A fast typist, Gina was taken aback when, after handling the out-processing of Secretary of State George Shultz, "typing along as he answered questions," she was called to the personnel office. "You don't belong here," the head of human resources told her.

She assumed she was being fired and rose to collect her things.

Instead, the officer told her she didn't belong in the secretarial pool; she belonged on a career track.

At twenty-two, her talent having announced itself, Gina Bennett was promoted to the State Department's Bureau of Intelligence and Research, known as the INR. The smallest of Washington's (now) eighteen intelligence organizations, INR exists to produce intelligence tailored to US diplomats. Gina became a junior analyst pulling eight-hour shifts in the "terrorism watch office," which operated twenty-four hours a day, receiving cables about explosions and threats. It was a Foggy Bottom backwater, but Gina had found her place. From her own desk on Twenty-third Street, she, too, observed the outflow of foreign fighters. She watched them going into Chechnya, Kashmir, the Philippines; surfacing in Algeria, Tunisia, Egypt, Burma. She relished the detective work of divining their movements, even as she felt alarmed by the violence they evangelized.

Gina Bennett was clear-eyed, even empathetic, as she observed the forces that propelled this coalescing army. With her own grounding in Middle East politics and global religions, Gina perceived that what she was seeing, in many extremist Islamic movements, was people fighting the legacy of colonialization by seeking to purge elitist, very white European-centric political structures that aimed to keep the elites in power, the same structures that produced cozy arrangements between Western governments (and oil companies) and puppets like King Idris of Libya. The American Revolution, in its way, had been the same thing: a rejection of colonial power. Many countries where terrorists were active were struggling to find an authentic form of self-government—Arab nationalism, nonalignment—but no new system was really working. The countries were experiencing an existential crisis, which often breeds violence.

Gina also felt being female gave her extra insight. She well knew what it felt like to be treated as second-class. She identified with Arab countries that had suffered poverty, exploitation, being conquered and reconquered and told what to do. "We could understand the abyss of grievance that was completely legitimate," she said. "We could understand living with that resentment, that anger, the injustice of it, the unfairness of it, year after year. And you can understand how much of a toll that takes."

But, as she grew more conversant with terrorist movements— European Marxist-Leninist groups were among the first she studied— Gina perceived something else. She saw that all terrorist groups commit the same first crime: the crime of theft. "They steal a legitimate griev-ance, and appropriate it, and say they're championing it," Gina reflected. "Legitimate grievance suffers for it. The people—the massive popula-tion that is suffering under that legitimate grievance—now has a ter-rorist organization coming that it doesn't necessarily want."

And terrorists were unfazed by deaths of civilians, including chil-dren. Six months into her new job, on December 21, 1988, Pam Am flight 103 exploded over Lockerbie, Scotland. Nearly three hundred people died in a bombing funded by Libya. Thirty-five of the dead were students at Syracuse University, a year or two younger than Gina. She was called to assist their bereaved parents. Reading the passenger man-ifest, she saw that whole families had died, including at least one infant.

She also knew this: The new movements were being fueled by vio-lent men taught to construct a hypermasculine identity that saw women as temptresses, and legitimate targets for violence including rape and sex slavery. As the national security expert Tom Nichols would later write: For jihadists, becoming radicalized involved joining groups that proffered "forbidden Western delights, such as music, alcohol, drugs, and pornography" even as they fulminated against immorality. These Western pleasures were sought, secretly parceled out, used for recruit-ment; and at the same time, reviled. "For these men, terrorism may be, among other things, some sort of self-purification," Nichols wrote, "a way to deny their illicit desires by destroying the places and people that supposedly coax them toward perdition."

Subjugating women, while desiring them, was a feature of the move-ment. As many mass shootings attest, and studies have proved: Mass violence often starts with domestic violence at home, against a parent, grandparent, wife, or partner.

Sexual violence was something with which Gina Bennett was personally familiar. As a girl of five and six, she had been molested, repeatedly, by an older family member. This was in an era when sexual abuse was widespread at many institutions, in the United States and worldwide, including schools and the Catholic Church, but had not yet been acknowledged, much less addressed. Vulnerable victims often had no one to turn to. When Gina Bennett told her mother what was occurring, her mother didn't believe her. She said Gina had dreamed it. She seemed unable to cope with the enormity of the transgression. Gina could never bring herself to tell her father; she later conjectured that "if he said it didn't happen, I would be broken."

Her childhood suffering affected Gina Bennett on a number of levels. She felt that the ability to disassociate—the coping mechanism she developed while being molested—made her perform better at work. "I never panicked whenever anything was crisis-oriented," she reflected. Instead, she stayed "calm and stoic." When people in Washington seemed uninterested in her insights, the experience of not being listened to felt somehow familiar. When the women ran into roadblocks—and they often did—as they tried to call attention to their findings, Cindy Storer, in Gina's view, had an "appropriate, visceral and emotional response," displaying a frustration and even anger that Gina saw as "healthy." For her part, when Gina couldn't get buy-in, she didn't get mad. Her response was "go find more research"—to keep pushing.

This pushing is what led to the ad hoc group that met in "warning sessions" to discuss the foreign fighters. Trading notes, Gina admired the colleagues who found their way to her meetings. Barbara Sude "was brilliant" and careful—"our touchstone," Gina called her—and Cindy Storer, with her gift for visualization, was a vital addition. The group sought to understand the mindset of the jihadist: his childhood, his schooling, the way of thinking in which he was guided. The group members were nerds, as Gina put it, developing a kind of obsessive expertise the outside world did not share. There were "so few of us, we were the only ones reading what we were reading in the context of what we were reading," Gina said.

"We had each other's backs," is how Cindy Storer put it. "We had to. Nobody else did."

AMONG THE THREE OF THEM, the core group had Cindy, a trained imagery analyst with expertise in the fighters' network; Gina, a natural connector of people and details; and Barbara, an expert in Islamic thought who knew how to follow a money trail. They were a formidable group, but up against a huge challenge. In 1992, one year after the Soviet Union collapsed, a gregarious Southerner named Bill Clinton won the US presidency on a platform of peace and economic prosperity. Unlike his predecessor—President George H. W. Bush, a former CIA director—the new president was not a close friend of the intelligence community. In trade parlance, he was not an avid "customer." His director, James Woolsey, began giving a "snakes and dragon" speech making the point that America had slain the dragon but set free a nest of snakes. While Woolsey wasn't wrong, he was not an effective messenger, and nobody much wanted to listen. In the absence of a bipolar competition, people wanted to enjoy a respite. Congress sought to claw back money spent on defense and national security.

Washington, and the West, welcomed a breather from fear of existential destruction. Nuclear war had been averted. America was "high on this peace dividend," as Gina put it.

But it was clear to the women that a new group of bad guys was gathering strength and momentum, chasing money and power even as funding dried up in the intelligence business, where, as Gina put it, "your whole meaning of life is warning." Many people assumed the hard work of promoting a democratic way of life had been accomplished, and the arc of justice would bend toward democratic freedoms. "And in so many ways, we stopped propagandizing democracy as a solution. It looked like democracy was breaking out all over the world," Gina said. "But underneath it, you could see that wasn't the case." Drug lords, arms dealers, and terrorists started taking advantage of a newfound freedom of movement.

Gina felt an increasing "sense of dread without being able to articulate it in a compelling way."

THE WOMEN WEREN'T JUST coping with a new world order; they were coping with a new kind of intelligence stream. During the Cold War, intelligence arrived at least partly digested, in the form of photos, open-source articles, cables, scientific papers, the constitutions of new countries with which the agency might want to fiddle. That kind of intel wasn't easy to obtain, nor was making sense of it easy; but the product, the thing itself, arrived in words and complete sentences. Ideas were spelled out; plans were laid.

Terrorist collection was chaos. It consisted of fragments: bank transactions, plane tickets, incorporation documents, snatches of intercepted conversations. Even translated, the transcriptions were bewildering. In a place like the Office of Soviet Analysis, with its conventional targets, an analyst usually knew the real name of the politician, general, or scientist in whom she was interested. By contrast, a terrorism analyst had to figure out every code name and whether the same fighter had lots of code names or whether the same code name had lots of fighters using it. Many jihadists chose Abu Mohammed as a nom de guerre, and the fighters themselves became confused. Gina and her working group read transcripts of jihadists saying things like "Are you the Abu Mohammed who is the cousin of so-and-so?"

While pregnant with her first child, Gina Bennett began working on a memo to lay out what she and her colleagues were seeing. At the State Department, the Bureau of Intelligence and Research published a daily classified bulletin, much like the PDB. In the early winter of 1993, Gina was putting the finishing touches on a draft when, sitting at her desk, her water broke four weeks early and she went into labor. Then the contractions began, intensely painful. She called her husband— her college sweetheart; they'd married soon after graduation—and two female colleagues helped her get up from her desk. At the elevator, they pushed the Down button and waited; the office was on the sixth floor. When the door opened, standing in the elevator was UN ambassador Madeleine Albright, who had been visiting Secretary of State Warren Christopher on the seventh floor and was, like them, going down.

Gina hobbled on. "Just breathe," her friends kept telling her, holding her upright. The elevator stopped on each floor, and more people got on. It would have been hard not to notice that one member of the crowd was a woman in active labor. When they reached the ground floor, Madeleine Albright pushed her way out. "How rude! She is *in labor!*" her friend called to the departing ambassador. Outside, Gina's husband was waiting in the car to pick her up. Twenty-four difficult hours later, she underwent an emergency C-section, delivering a healthy son.

Three days after Gina gave birth, an attack occurred less than 250 miles north of the Arlington hospital where she was recovering. On February 26, 1993, a terrorist drove a van packed with explosives down a ramp and into the underground parking garage of New York's World Trade Center in Lower Manhattan. The car bomb exploded, killing six people and injuring more than a thousand. The planner, Ramzi Yousef, was a nephew of Khalid Sheikh Mohammed, a known terrorist with ties to the foreign fighters. The phone rang beside Gina's bed. "Your people did this!" the voice at the other end shouted. It was her supervisor—crediting her, in an abrupt way, with having had her eyes on the right suspects. Foggy with painkillers, she took a few minutes to grasp what had occurred. Several INR colleagues drove to the hospital and gathered at her bedside. Gina was back to work within weeks of giving birth.

Gina's finished memo ran in the August 21–22, 1993, weekend edition of the INR's bulletin. In a five-page article, Gina laid out the global context in which the New York explosion had occurred. Her analysis, "The Wandering Mujahidin: Armed and Dangerous," pointed out that during the ten-year Afghan war against the Soviets, "eager Arab youths" had joined a jihad against what they saw as an infidel nation—the Soviet Union. Four years after the war ended, the network that had "funneled money, supplies, and manpower to supplement the Afghan mujahidin is now contributing experienced fighters to military Islamic groups worldwide."

As a result, "new bases and waystations" were sheltering a cohort of mujahidin. This network, funded by many donors, was "fluid enough to withstand most government crackdowns." Victory over the Soviets had inspired jihadists to take the fight to "other infidels, including the US,

Israel, and more secular Middle East regimes." Displaying a fine an-
tenna for relationships, she noted that militant groups—the Islamic
Gama'at in Egypt; splinter factions of Algeria's Islamic Salvation Front;
Yemen's Islamic Jihad—were welcoming the fighters and benefiting
from their "wartime expertise and religious zeal." The Afghan fighters
were hailed as conquering heroes—"victorious Muslim fighters of a
successful jihad against a superpower"—and had won the respect of
many people, Arab and non-Arab.

Gina gave the fighters their due, pointing out that they excelled at
guerrilla warfare; were trained in small arms, explosives, and other
weapons; had fake passports, visas, and identity papers; could travel easily; understood communications and logistics; and possessed a "wide
range of technological knowledge" about computers, faxes, and other
equipment that enabled them to share propaganda and strategies with
Islamic opposition groups in other countries. They were a highly net-
worked mobile force. They didn't need infrastructure like parliament
buildings or legislatures or voting machines. They were lean, confident,
and respected. They were on a roll, and the roll was headed in America's
direction.

"The perception that the US has an anti-Islamic foreign policy
agenda raises the likelihood that US interests increasingly will become
targets for violence from the former mujahidin," she warned.

The article also demonstrated how alliances get made, pointing out
that the fighters enjoyed a "close working relationship" and "circle of
mutual admiration" with groups in Egypt, Yemen, and Sudan. Personal
ties mattered, including marital ones, as in medieval Europe. "Familial
bonds intensify through intermarriages," she observed, relating a piece
of salient gossip. "The sister of Afghan Prime Minister Gulbuddin
Hekmatyar is married to Algerian militant figure Boudjemaa Bounaoa,"
and bonds like this led to "safehavens, bases, and logistical support."

Among the leading private donors, one stood out: a rich Saudi,
Osama bin Laden, "famous for his religious zeal and financial largesse."
Describing him as a "Saudi businessman living in Khartoum," Gina
noted that joint ventures with Sudanese businessmen provide "front
companies for his exploits" and that his "money has enabled hundreds
of Arab veterans to return to safe havens and bases in Yemen and

Sudan," where fighters were being trained. The jihadists were creating problems for North African nations like Algeria, where "returning mujahidin have been responsible for some of the most violent attacks" against security services. Even Qaddafi, in Libya, feared "and has lashed out publicly against them." Beyond South Asia and the Middle East, they were forming alliances and "taking up causes from Somalia to the Philippines."

The World Trade Center attack, Gina warned, was just a warm-up. The Afghan veterans could "surprise the US with violence in unexpected locales." A sidebar pointed out that many of the WTC bombing suspects—and those arrested in June, for a second plot to bomb the United Nations—"had been involved in fundraising and recruitment for the Afghan war." The jihadists were also recruiting in the United States. The Al Kifah Refugee Center in Jersey City was supporting the mujahideen. She published the memo hoping it would end up on the desk of the secretary of state, even the president, and find its way into the Washington conversation. A week later, she published another memo. The financier, she noted, had "established an organization called Al-Qa'ida in the late 1980s," she wrote, and he was funding and training fighters. (The name was the Arabic word for "the base," which referred to the base of fighters bin Laden had established during the Afghan war, in the mountains of eastern Afghanistan.)

Gina's memo described what was occurring, and other members of the group did what they could to help raise awareness. One of Gina's State Department colleagues, intelligence analyst Lyndsay Howard, was also following these developments. Howard's own focus was Central Asia, a region that borders Afghanistan and provided a launching point for the Soviet war in the 1980s. On a trip to Tajikistan, a former Soviet republic, Howard saw that boys orphaned during the Afghan war were being educated in madrassas—religious schools that indoctrinated young male minds with the teachings of jihad. She was acutely aware that denizens of Afghan refugee war camps along the border, desperate and entrapped, "provided easy cannon fodder for Islamist causes." Howard stayed up late, smoking cigars to stay awake, writing cables to Gina, who sat smoking cigars in another time zone.

Lyndsay Howard also admired Cindy Storer's work. "Cindy was

central to tracking the change, locations, and personalities who were driving the dramatically more dangerous evolutions in the Afghan veterans network," she said. When it came to data and statistics, Cindy "always had the goods." Howard set out to reinforce Gina's memo by inviting Cindy—a "hero to many of us"—to make a presentation about what she'd divined.

Around late 1993 or early 1994, Howard organized a State Department briefing in which Cindy and two colleagues, including an official from the Pentagon, could raise awareness about the foreign fighters. Howard went door-to-door to leading bureaus—political affairs, economics, Near East/South Asian, the deputy secretary of state—and begged them to send somebody senior. She didn't want anybody to be able to say they hadn't been warned. They met in a secure conference room in INR's operations center, where Gina had begun her career on the terrorism watch desk. Cindy "was the star of the show," Howard recollected. "She was brilliant." The group listened, asked questions, and, when the session ended, walked into the hallway. Howard followed.

What she heard stunned and dismayed her. Two or three people walked down the corridor—laughing. They seemed to think Cindy was exaggerating, ginning up a new enemy to justify the CIA's continued existence, and, of course, continued appropriations.

Yet back at Langley, Cindy could hardly get the threat acknowledged. The agency was slow to shift its focus or its resources. In the analytic division, no powerful office chief was giving up slots, not without screaming and bloodshed. In February 1993, Cindy had sent an item about the foreign fighters to the editors of the President's Daily Brief. The authors were two of her colleagues. The editors declined to publish, saying the president had not requested the item. After the WTC bomb exploded, the head editor called, and Cindy happened to answer the phone. The editor asked what her office knew about "Afghan Arabs." She suggested he read the PDB item that had been sitting in the drawer for two weeks.

"The entire time, we always look like we're behind," she said. "When in fact our analysis is way ahead—but we can't push it out the door."

CHAPTER 16

A BRIGHT AND ATTRACTIVE REDHEAD

WASHINGTON, DC

January 1993

H EIDI AUGUST'S LATEST CAR WAS A MERCEDES. IT WAS WHITE with a tan interior—a fitting answer to the day nearly a quarter-century earlier, when, as a clerk preparing for her first overseas tour, she'd ridden with Tom Twetten to the CIA's preferred furniture shop in Georgetown. At the time, she had admired Twetten's car, which, he confided, he'd had custom-made in Germany, and his reserved parking space at headquarters. Now Heidi's own car was just as nice—maybe nicer—and she had a parking space of her own.

Heidi's old friend Tom Twetten had done well, rising in 1991 to become deputy director of operations, the formal title for the head of the clandestine service. In part, this was thanks to a key counterterrorism win. In the late 1980s, the CIA had succeeded in bringing about the demise of the Abu Nidal organization, the terrorist group responsible for the Malta hijacking. This was accomplished by means of a psychological operation that exploited the leader's paranoia. With help from both Israel and the PLO, the agency approached Abu Nidal members, feigning an effort to recruit them, not so much in order to really do so, but to convince the leader his own men were betraying him. It worked; Abu Nidal had henchmen executed and the group imploded, bringing a measure of justice to the memory of Scarlett Rogenkamp, who was awarded a posthumous Purple Heart.

Heidi August had done well, too. After opening two stations—in the Mediterranean and Dublin—and serving in the Middle East, Heidi had been posted overseas during the first Gulf War, where Iraqi missiles flew over her roof, and she hosted "Scuds and Suds" parties at her home. But she couldn't stay in the field forever, stimulating though the field might be. To qualify for the Senior Intelligence Service, the elite corps of top officers, she needed an "out of body experience"—a rotation outside the agency—so she went to the US Naval War College in Newport, Rhode Island. Assigned to headquarters after that, she was put in charge of the clandestine service's South Asia operations. Now Heidi was the one wielding a seven-thousand-mile screwdriver.

Heidi hated headquarters and didn't see why anybody wanted to work there. Each meeting felt like pushing a boulder up a hill. Some initiative would get teed up, the meeting would commence, hours would go by, and nothing would change. In the peace dividend era, the CIA was shrinking and people were told to do more with less. The boulder always rolled back down, and she had to get it started back up. She looked forward to her next posting, to India.

AROUND EIGHT O'CLOCK ON January 25, 1993—first thing on a Monday morning—Heidi was in her comfortable Mercedes, headed west on Route 123, a sleepy stretch of suburbia with fields, Dutch colonials, split-rail fences, and the occasional grazing horse. Her westerly direction meant she was on the same side of the road as CIA headquarters. As she slowed to make the right turn toward the guard gate, she happened to notice a brown Datsun, traveling on the opposite, eastbound side of the highway, pull over onto the shoulder and park. That seemed a little strange, she reflected. What was stranger—surreal, actually—was when a man emerged from the Datsun holding an AK-47 assault rifle. He began walking along the cars that were stopped at a red light, heading eastward, in the opposite lane of traffic, facing Heidi. Like her, they were CIA employees, arriving on time to start their workday, waiting to turn left in headquarters. As Heidi watched, the man opened fire, cold-bloodedly shooting into one of the cars and then moving on to another, peppering the trapped commuters with a stream of gunfire that pop-popped-popped in the cold morning air.

"Holy crap!" Heidi exclaimed, pushing the gas pedal as a security officer emerged from the grassy area around the entrance and began waving cars in her line of traffic to get inside the compound. "Active shooter!" the officer shouted at Heidi as she steered toward the guard gate. "I know, I just saw him!" she shouted back. The security officers feared the gunman might make it onto CIA property. Instead, during the confusion, the shooter got back into his car and drove east on 123, unpursued.

As Heidi badged into headquarters, it emerged that two CIA officers were dead. The gunman had shot Frank Darling, a twenty-eight-year-old communications expert, while he was sitting with his wife in his Volkswagen. The shooter continued walking, firing more than seventy rounds and also killing sixty-six-year-old analyst Lansing Bennett. He wounded three others, two of them agency employees.

The shooting soon made the news; an FBI agent sent to the crime scene, Brad Garrett, found it like a movie set, with broken windshield glass everywhere. A gun shop owner in Chantilly, Virginia, saw an FBI composite sketch and went through his records. Within days, the shooter was identified as Mir Aimal Kansi, a Pakistani immigrant. That made him, as Heidi put it, "my problem." Kansi by then had boarded a flight to JFK and then on to Karachi, Pakistan. Finding him became an obsession at Langley. The agency would try "every trick in the book" to find Kansi. "We had all kinds of crazy things, like dropping matchbooks from airplanes with reward things on it. I mean, we did everything known to man."

THE 123 SHOOTING SENT a frisson of anxiety through drivers throughout the Washington region. Agency employees, feeling newly vulnerable, began reflexively leaving three car lengths between themselves and the next car at stoplights, to be able to get away. What wasn't clear was whether there was any connection between the 123 shooting and the

World Trade Center bombing, which occurred a month later. Together with her boss, the analyst Cindy Storer gave a briefing on the topic to a congressional aide. Cindy didn't see an apparent connection—Kansi's motives and background were obscure—but she did happen to make a remark about unrest in Pakistan that led the staffer to remark that the CIA was fabricating new threats to justify its continued existence. Cindy wanted to "jump across the table and throttle him." She was getting used to the accusation. But that didn't make it easier to put up with.

OKAY, SO THERE HAD just been two homeland attacks, by foreign actors. Cindy Storer wanted to probe the patterns and continue along the trail she had started down. People in the Near East South Asia office were encouraged to take rotations every three years, to get to know a new topic or region. Her supervisor wanted to send her to a unit that dealt with narcotics trafficking, but Cindy chose to rotate to the counterterrorist center, a unit that no CIA officer with ambition wanted to enter. Occupying a space in old headquarters, the CTC was in its own way a kind of hole.

When Cindy walked into the vault that housed her new office, she could see maybe sixty, maybe eighty bent heads: less than 1 percent of the Agency's workforce of twenty thousand. It was a small unit with a mandate that embraced every worldwide group, old and new, that aspired to kill people in large numbers. Sri Lanka's Tamil Tigers; Peru's Sendero Luminoso; the Japanese doomsday cult Aum Shinrikyo. Remnants of left-wing European groups like the Red Army Brigade and the Red Army Faction. FARC, in Colombia. The Armed Islamic Group, in Algeria. Egyptian Islamic Jihad and the Islamic Group, in Egypt, which together had just tried to assassinate President Hosni Mubarak as part of a campaign against the Egyptian government. Anarchists. Bosnians. Groups in South Asia, India, Pakistan, the Philippines, Greece. State sponsors like Iran, Iraq, and Sudan. The Israeli-Palestinian conflict and groups such as the PLO, Hamas, and Hezbollah, the Shi'ite Muslim political party and militant group responsible for the kidnapping and death under torture of William Buckley, CIA station chief in Beirut. The counterterrorist center amounted to one-stop shopping for tracking every group with mass homicidal intent. Ferrying her things to her desk, Cindy could sense hoarding and competition, the kind of jostling for status that occurs in a workplace suffering from insecurity and underestimation. People would rip things off the printer, or snatch documents from the pneumatic tube, and keep them. Cindy described the mindset as "information is power, I hide my information for myself."

She also noted that, for the first time in her career, the team she'd be working with consisted almost entirely of women.

THE COUNTERTERRORIST CENTER WAS the brainchild of one of the more notorious personalities of the clandestine service: Duane "Dewey" Clarridge, the baron who had been at the other end of the phone line in 1985 when Heidi August was trying to prevent an Egyptair plane from burning up on the tarmac in Malta. Clarridge was a charter member of the agency's old-boys network—a founding member, in fact. An alumnus of Brown University, he joined the CIA in 1955, eight years after the agency was created. The antithesis of the ideal spy—a proverbial "gray man" envisioned by William Colby—Clarridge did much to call attention to himself, favoring linen suits, colorful pocket squares, and preposterous cover names like Mr. Maroney. He cultivated an if-only-you-knew-what-I-know air of belligerent self-justification in an era when the agency's 1980s covert operations and illegal arms deals began coming to light. During the CIA's forays into Central America, it was Clarridge who proposed the infamous tactic of placing underwater mines in Nicaraguan harbors, to damage the economy and discredit the Sandinista regime. A Spanish-speaking reports officer, Amy Tozzi, warned director Bill Casey not to do it. Casey wouldn't listen. Called to testify before Congress about the Iran-Contra scandal, Clarridge was indicted on a charge of perjury and received a presidential pardon. He had the pardon framed and hung in the front hallway of his home.

Like many ops men of his generation, Dewey Clarridge was incapable of mentioning women without noting whether their appearance pleased him. In his 1997 autobiography, *A Spy for All Seasons*, women are "attractive," "pretty," "gorgeous," "very attractive," and in the case of the CIA lawyer Kathleen McGinn, who attempted to guide him through the thickets of a hostile Congress, "a bright and attractive redhead." But he also recognized women's value in undercover work. As chief of the Latin America division, Clarridge led the CIA's role in the invasion of Grenada, and he called out praise for Linda Flohr, a case officer who had monitored the airstrip unnoticed.

Clarridge also served as station chief in Rome, where he experienced firsthand the grim drumbeat of hijackings and bombings in Europe and the Middle East. Many attacks targeted Americans, among them the 1983 bombing in Beirut that killed 241 US service members, mostly Marines; the April 5, 1986, explosion at La Belle discotheque in West Berlin, which was popular with US servicemen; and the hijacking Heidi August handled in Malta, where American and Israeli passengers were called to the front and shot.

Clarridge grasped that stopping these attacks called for fresh tactics. Terrorists didn't work for embassies or mingle at black-tie functions where they could be cultivated over champagne or invited to a quiet get-to-know-each-other dinner. Most didn't drink. They behaved, often, like gangs. They dealt with illicit banks and arms dealers; recruited trusted family members; maintained discreet cells whose plans were unknown to other cells; and often made new members commit a heinous act—a felony or even a murder—to bind them to the group. It was hard for the CIA to seed an asset if murder was the ticket for entry.

In 1985, Clarridge approached Casey, who gave him an office on the seventh floor and invited him to come up with a new approach. Perceiving that the agency's geographic divisions presented a real problem—"An Arab terrorist group may be based in Libya or Syria, but its operations are likely to take place in Rome or London or Athens"—Clarridge also understood that tracking plotters is a "business of minutiae" involving "bits and pieces of data on people, events, places."

Clarridge proposed that CIA analysts and operations people work together—side by side—in a way that had never occurred. The agency's two main directorates were truly oil and water. The line of demarcation was sacred, a firewall erected to protect the sources and methods of the clandestine side, and the objectivity of the analytic one. The firewall was so thick that in the Office of Leadership Analysis, one analyst worked for months on a biographical paper, only to find, as she was about to publish, that her subject was an asset of the DO and that articles he had "written" had been composed on the other side of the building. A colleague tipped her off.

The counterterrorist center opened shop in 1986, with Clarridge as its first director. It was one of three new "fusion" centers—the other two focused on counterintelligence and counternarcotics—representing the first real attempt to take on the "snakes" Woolsey later spoke of. A key tactic was "extraction": finding terrorists responsible for American deaths and bringing them to the US for trial. These were elaborate operations involving the FBI, other US law enforcement agencies, and foreign intelligence services. The practice was enabled by a 1986 law passed in response to the hijackings and attacks.

It was known as "rendition."

CIA OFFICERS DID NOT flock to join the new endeavors, however. All of the new centers were low-visibility projects. All three involved tracking people—drug lords, traitors, terrorists—rather than classic intelligence collection. And, while the idea was that operations people and analysts would cooperate on manhunting operations, in each center, a single directorate was given the lead. In the counterterrorist center, this was the Directorate of Operations, which set the rules and controlled the budget. Analysts had to accept a secondary status, working as handmaidens to operations rather than proud and separate peers. The setup didn't sit well with the thinkers, but the doers didn't like it, either. The job of extracting terrorists, while creative and even lurid—one hijacker, Fawaz Younis, was entertained with CIA-paid prostitutes, lured aboard a CIA-rented yacht, drugged by a CIA-employed doctor, and arrested by the FBI—felt like police work, not spying.

"Obstructionism was rampant," Clarridge complained in his memoir. The barons "let it be known they were not behind the CTC."

Headquarters, having created the centers, was obliged to assemble them from scraps, like a pie made from shards of leftover dough. The money did not exist to do the job all-out nor the bureaucratic will. Staffers came on loan from other places. Around the building, offices were expected to pony up a certain number of people, and managers did not want to pony up their best officers. Being loaned to the center could hurt a person's career, and likely would, since promotions depended on having your achievements known to your actual boss. The CTC thus became known as a place where managers sent people they wanted to get rid of. Being off-loaded to the counterterrorism effort was akin to being sent to teach at the Farm. You were perceived as having been warehoused, in the words of one staff operations officer, Jeanne Newell, because "you weren't smart enough to do something else."

It was also a radical experiment. Never had CIA analysts had their data-gathering skills harnessed for operations. Doing so was anathema to how the CIA had been designed. Normally information flowed from the operatives who collected it, to the analysts who processed it, not vice versa. For the first time, the point of an analyst's work was to give the ops people the information that would make something *happen*. Something concrete and drastic. In some other part of the world, a man would have a bag put over his head, or get rolled up in a carpet and exfiltrated to a waiting US jet. It was scary and, for many of the thinkers, disconcerting.

For some, though, the excitement was the allure. As an inspector general's report found, some analysts were attracted to the new center because they liked the idea of "nontraditional analysis" that entailed "support to operations."

While "dumping ground" represented the hall-file take on the CTC, it wasn't the whole truth. There were good reasons why a CIA officer might want to find her way to this godforsaken cubicle farm. An analyst might want to work terrorism because, like Cindy Storer, she wanted to pursue malefactors, trace connections, and protect innocent lives. Or she might have run into career roadblocks and hope that this new, kind of weird office might be a place she could find her way forward. The creation of the center opened intriguing fissures in the CIA infrastructure. There was something novel happening at its core. Nobody on the seventh floor was paying much attention. The usual guardrails were down. People could make up their own rules. Another major upside, for an analyst, was full access to the operational database. Elsewhere, analysts never got to see the DO's database and had no way to know which sources seemed reliable. Here, Cindy could see everything, or almost. She could talk to the operations people and benefit from a free flow of information.

For all its cacophony, the center did have a structure and a mission. Namely, to stop attacks by disrupting terrorist operations. The goal was to make an arrest, ideally before an attack could occur; or pressure foreign allies to disrupt the cell. It was, however, a tiny operation focused on an overwhelmingly diverse array of bad guys. There was no playbook, no instruction manual, no rules to speak of. People were building the car as they drove it, and fighting for control of the wheel.

The whole place was confusing. Responsibilities blended. If an attack occurred, it might not be clear which branch should handle it, since jurisdictions overlapped. It was hard to know what people did and who they worked for. Only about ten people in the entire place served as conventional analysts, like Cindy, writing papers to inform and predict. All the other analysts were serving operations.

Cindy's own destination was an obscure branch led by an obscure branch chief named Michael Scheuer, who, like her, was absorbed by Osama bin Laden and the fighters he seemed to be commanding.

IN AN AGENCY OF mission-driven people with intense work ethics, Mike Scheuer stood out, getting to work as early as four or five A.M. Arriving in morning darkness enabled him to beat traffic—and answer cables with hardly anybody present to interfere. In his mid-forties, with a beard, spectacles, and salt-and-pepper hair that accentuated his bookish aura, Scheuer could often be found sitting in semidarkness, his desk lit only by a green-shaded banker's lamp. In the dimness he looked like a Victorian sleuth or a Victorian villain—or, rather, both, half Sherlock Holmes, half Professor Moriarty.

When Cindy arrived, Scheuer was assembling material that, in addition to informing their own work, would later appear in a book, something that at the time was considered unusual and a perhaps unwise career move. When published—anonymously, at first—in 2002, the book, *Through Our Enemies' Eyes,* was dense with learned references to the likes of Thomas Paine, Gertrude Himmelfarb, Theodore Roosevelt, Bernard Lewis, the Arab historian Osamah Ibn Munqidh, and the great Arab fighters of the Crusades. A conservative Catholic educated at a Jesuit high school in New York, Mike Scheuer had a PhD in NATO and European history. He had a deep interest in the American Civil War, including the violence of the abolitionist John Brown and the scorched-earth tactics of General William Tecumseh Sherman, who had laid waste to Atlanta and whose willingness to torch infrastructure and kill civilians Scheuer saw echoed in the jihadist approach. Scheuer read everything Osama bin Laden ever said or wrote, and came to understand bin Laden as someone steeped in the killing ethos of the two world wars of the twentieth century. As Western powers moved away from a concept of warfare that accepted mass civilian deaths, terrorists, he argued, were just now coming to it.

People at CIA headquarters had lots of opinions about Mike Scheuer. Some thought him brilliant. Well before almost anybody else, Scheuer grasped the magnitude of bin Laden's success in strong-arming and cajoling other extremist leaders—themselves plenty influential and strong-armed—to come together in a multiethnic effort: Algerians working with Tunisians and Egyptians to kill Americans and drive the United States out of the Middle East. "When he was at his peak, he was committed, he was passionate, in command of his material," said one CIA briefer. But he also was a difficult person, thin-skinned and aggrieved—more comfortable immersed in the ancient enmities of the Crusades than in the office politics of the here and now.

He was not someone who functioned well in a bureaucracy, nor a political establishment for which he had a lively contempt. He had scholarly insight and the appropriate sense of urgency, but nursed a suspicion of lawyers, lawmakers, law-enforcement agencies, and anyone who did not share his zeal. His hall file was not good. According to one officer, he would "attack you viciously" if you disagreed with him. He felt the seventh floor was cautious and his FBI partners were leakers and credit-stealers. During the Afghan war, colleagues were unnerved by the satisfaction he took in the deaths of Soviet soldiers, and he brought the same approach to the fight against bin Laden and his network. "If I was just sweetness and light and just tugged my forelock every time they said, 'No, we don't want to kill him today,' I would've just become one of them," he said, in an interview for this book. "And that's nothing I wanted to be."

But he was a hard worker. If you called the CTC at any time, day or night, Mike Scheuer would likely answer. People on the seventh floor liked that kind of availability. "He was a nut, but he was our nut," as one officer put it. Others noticed that he would say three normal-sounding things, and then a fourth that was off the wall. "Mike is certifiably crazy," said Mike Sulick, a later head of the clandestine service who had a PhD himself, with a degree in comparative literature and a dissertation on *Hamlet* in translation to Russian and French.

"He was a pain in the ass" is how Heidi August put it. Barbara Sude was struck by Scheuer's urge to "project" himself in the space. "Mike's a wonderful guy, but sometimes he sort of jumps off the building," said John Rizzo, an agency lawyer.

It didn't help that Mike Scheuer was a cerebral male analyst in an office dominated by the macho men of operations, in a small office with barely breathing space between desks. Jeanne Newell, a staff operations officer, found him honest and direct, but "he was a DI analyst in an ops job," with a very different personality from the rugged cowboy types who set the norms. In the hair-trigger mano a mano competition that underlay so many CIA relationships, male analysts were seen by their ops counterparts as less masculine—as, in the words of one amused female analyst, "womanlike people." His writings suggest self-awareness in this regard. "I am not . . . a field intelligence officer," he admitted in a 2004 book, *Imperial Hubris*. "I have traveled some but am by training and temperament a career-long 'headquarters officer.'"

Nearly everybody else on Scheuer's team was female. As a regular analyst, Cindy reported up a different management chain than they did; unlike his team members, she was working *with* Scheuer, but not *for* him. The women on Scheuer's team were analysts, too, but they were supporting operations. They were young women, mostly in their mid-thirties. Their hall-file nickname would become "the Manson Family." Others called them "the coven." Mike Scheuer authorized a lot of over-time pay, and the women liked to shop. They were fans of *Buffy the Vampire Slayer* and made jokes about being Buffy. Like Cindy, they were obsessed with Osama bin Laden. They were also obsessed with Mike Scheuer, for whom they provided a kind of insulating layer.

In the "fusion" environment of the CTC, there was much saber rattling between the men of thought and the men of action. "Most of my closest colleagues are type-A individuals who won't back down from anyone or anything. We accept the fact that we live in a hard world and deal with that reality. It's dangerous work," asserted Gary Berntsen, a case officer who served in the CTC in the late 1990s and, in his book *Jawbreaker*, gave voice to the contempt that men of operations had for men of analysis. "What the hell's the matter with you guys sending a DI type to Nairobi?" he asked one DO officer, when he found out an analyst had been put in charge of a station in Africa. During the tenure of Deutch, Berntsen complained, analysts were put through a shortened field course and sent overseas to run stations. He felt that this "undermined" the mission.

For a pugnacious, scholarly analyst like Mike Scheuer, fusion meant dealing with this kind of ribbing and bluster from the ops guys. A team of women provided a buffer from the rhetorical towel-snapping. "He didn't have to deal with that male ego bullshit," ventured DeNeige Watson, an analyst, observing that the women on his team were "serious workhorses with great big brains." Scheuer said he would gladly have hung out a sign saying no men need apply. "I had enormous respect for the women who worked for me," he said in an interview, describing them as "diligent" and "able to make patterns out of things that I think a lot of men or a lot of other women probably also would miss. They were just experts at minutiae, putting pieces of information together or thinking, 'hey, two months ago I read something about this,' and they'd go back and find it. They didn't spend much time at all around the watercooler telling war stories. And I found the men, when I did have them, or several of them—sometimes it was, you had to get a second watercooler in, because one was always taken." The group he assembled was, in effect, a new kind of backroom operation, a niche unit staffed by officers who weren't prominent, or paid attention to, but who possessed the ferocity, suspicion, and steel-trap memories for which vault women were known.

But having a female team made it harder for him to get buy-in from the ops guys. "People were saying, 'What's his staff? It's all female.' It was just widely discussed at the time that it was a bunch of chicks," said ops officer Glenn Carle. "The perspective was frankly condescending and dismissive."

This was the mid-1990s, remember: precisely when the Category B class action suit was exposing the legacy of discrimination and misogyny in the Directorate of Operations. That attitude was apparent at the CTC, dominated as it was by the ethos of operations. Ops officers saw Scheuer's team as junior varsity, or maybe just the pep squad. "Junior analysts in tennis shoes" was a phrase used again and again. And yet the team was remarkable, even revolutionary, in that it amounted to an end run around how the Central Intelligence Agency had always done things. The women were creating jobs and taking them over, and—as time went on—driving operations without operational training. No training existed for the work they were engaged in. It was too new.

The team had a vault-woman mentality and vault-woman tactics, guarding their secrets. Most people didn't understand what they did, and many had reason to resent them. The ops directorate disliked being told what to do by "a bunch of female officers," as one officer put it. The analytic directorate had little use for them, because they weren't writing papers for the president. But nobody else wanted to do what they did. No self-respecting case officer wanted to work out of an unimportant headquarters office. The women surrounding Mike Scheuer were there because they wanted to be. They adored the man they worked for. "The whole thing was bizarre," said ops officer Mia McCall, noting that they got away with it because the stakes seemed small. "The rest of the DO figured [Scheuer] couldn't do much harm on bin Laden."

AND, AS THE HISTORY of backroom operations attests, it was by no means unusual for a branch chief to avail himself of female loyalists. Allen Dulles had the multilingual Mary Bancroft. CIA director John Deutch hired a woman, Nora Slatkin, as his own number two. Slatkin effectively ran the agency while Deutch, who had wanted to be secretary of defense, chose to focus on the director's role overseeing the greater intelligence community. And there were other male leaders known for assembling female teams. Paul Redmond, the irascible Bostonian who led the sleuths tracking Aldrich Ames, was one. The advantages were obvious. Female teams dug in, worked hard, and often consisted of brilliant, resilient women, like Jeanne Vertefeuille, who had, as they say, persisted. In some ways, these females functioned like a team of research assistants doing the work for a tenured professor. Women often expected little recognition, felt loyal to a man who helped them, built expertise their boss could harness, and acted as a Praetorian Guard.

In return, the male leader would lend them his protection, and his clout, if he had it. "Women who glom" is how one analyst described this setup, which she considered more helpful to the male leader than to his entourage, whose credibility rose or fell along with that of the boss. Mike Scheuer elevated the women on his team, but he also imparted his taint.

When Cindy arrived in 1995, Scheuer was putting together a branch called "Terrorist Financial Links." The goal was to follow the money trail and see how influential Osama bin Laden really was. According to Scheuer, they began by scouring the agency's own records: cables that mentioned bin Laden or his family, and soon had "something like seventeen or eighteen volumes of material." They found themselves running "across bin Laden in a lot of different places," he recollected. "Not personally but in terms of his influence, either through rhetoric, through audiotapes, through passports, through money—he seemed to turn up everywhere." Scheuer concluded he was "much more of a threat than I thought."

What started as a branch then became something more ambitious. In 1996, Deutch—who sought to impose changes to make the agency more like the corporate sector—proposed creating "virtual stations." It was not clear what "virtual" meant. "No one really knew," says Scheuer, "and in the end, it was impossible to do. So we had to run it as a conventional station within [headquarters]." But there was nothing conventional about the team he developed. As the third or fourth pick for the job of chief—earlier choices, he said, didn't "want to be on the bad side of the bureaucracy"—he assembled a staff consisting of a male deputy from the DO, a logistics officer, and a half-dozen women who moved over from a prior branch he'd been running. The proportion of women would grow, over the next couple of years, to nineteen out of two dozen total officers.

Around that time, the team was renamed Bin Laden Issue Station, the only CIA station focused on a lone individual. People referred to it as Alec Station, after Scheuer's young son. It was not part of a geographic division, had no traditional case officers, no discernable presence as far as most people could tell. The team moved around, housed mostly at headquarters, but briefly in a suburban office building in Tysons Corner. That relocation enabled Scheuer to get out from under the bureaucracy but contributed to Alec's reputation of being isolated and obscure, a backroom so secret that, for many, even in the counterterrorist center, it could hardly be said to exist.

BUT EXIST IT DID. In addition to the agency's own records, the Alec team studied open sources, including journals and foreign media. This research would inform Scheuer's book, which laid out the background of bin Laden, his intentions, and the disparate army he was assembling. *Through Our Enemies' Eyes* cites interviews and speeches from venues including the *Jakarta Post, Republika, Time, Al-Mustaquilla, The Jordan Times,* "A 1998 letter published by the AP," "Pakistani journalist Hamid Mir in 1997," *Middle East Policy, Frontline, Al-Hayat, Jane's Intelligence Review, Foreign Policy, Jeune Afrique, Al-Sharq Al-Awsat, Al-Arabiya,* and *Daily Jang,* Pakistan's biggest daily, to name a few. It amounted to a big nose-thumb at the men of operations, since every source was open, not clandestinely collected. Laying out bin Laden's ambition, Scheuer explains how bin Laden ably stoked the Arab world's memory of Catholic violence during the Crusades, and how he promoted the idea that the United States was determined to conquer the Arab world, as other powers had done in the past. The book showed how bin Laden created a "unique, multiethnic organization that includes not just Arabs but Muslims from the world over" with the aim of attacking the West.

Scheuer perceived that, unlike with Hezbollah or Abu Nidal, there was no evidence that bin Laden and his network depended on a state for "essential material or logistics support." Clearly, some nations turned a "blind eye" to "transiting fighters as a quid pro quo for not having attacks occur on their territory," but this new group was unprecedented in that it was funded by what we might now call crowdsourcing. Bin Laden tapped his own fortune; his family and other wealthy people; mosques and NGOs; and got "an undefined cut from the huge profits" of trafficking heroin in South Asia. Scheuer's writing also reveals an attunement to gender dynamics, as when he notes "the male-dominated Afghan culture infused with the attitude of settling differences man-to-man."

Like their boss, the women on Scheuer's team believed bin Laden's network posed a gathering threat; like their boss, they burrowed deep into bin Laden's whereabouts and allies. The team included two veteran reports officers who worked smoothly with counterparts around the agency; at the CIA, reports officers had their own "sisterhood," and explicitly used that term. The Alec reports officers knew how to work these in-house contacts; Scheuer described them as "geniuses" who could extract information "without causing any ruffled feathers."

Another team member, Jennifer Matthews, was heading up the station's nascent targeting operation, building its ability to trace connections, communications, and movements. Matthews, like Cindy Storer, had started out as an imagery analyst; she was one of the four friends who had arrived together on the bus to NPIC back in 1989. "She was talking to us about this Middle Eastern guy who was going to be a nightmare," her friend Kristin Wood said, recalling the day Matthews told them she'd be leaving for the CTC. "We all thought she was nuts." The friends did not lose touch; the bus-riding foursome gathered once a year for high tea at the Willard Hotel. Jennifer Matthews, now in her early thirties, had a sly sense of humor, blunt and fun and wisecracking, but fundamentally serious-minded. Like her boss, she was devout and approached fighting Islamic extremism from the perspective of an active, believing Christian. "Jen was always driven, she was a true believer," said analyst Diana Bolsinger. "She came out of the evangelical, reinvent-the-world struggle."

Another team member, Alfreda Bikowsky, was more vivid and kinetic; voluble and flirtatious; anxious and ambitious and mile a minute and usually away from her desk, off talking to somebody or doing something somewhere. Raised in very-small-town Pennsylvania, Freda, as people called her, had been the first in her family to go to college—the University of Pennsylvania, where she took a political science seminar from David Eisenhower, grandson of the president, who suggested she consider the CIA. What the heck, thought Freda; if she was going to aim high, she might as well aim for the nation's capital.

Like Gina Bennett, Freda Bikowsky had been deeply disturbed by the Lockerbie bombing and surge of terrorism in the 1980s. Clearly, the world was changing: Soviet soldiers "weren't coming across the Fulda Gap any time soon," she recalled in an interview, while terrorists meant business. Bikowsky also was struck by a comment made by a visiting Israeli professor. Talking about the rare women who became terrorists or active shooters, he theorized that when the motherly instinct is aroused, "something changes" and female terrorists could be "much more vicious than men." The phenomenon struck Bikowsky as "curious" and she would come to see a corollary in the hot resolve of women working against that very threat.

Doing graduate work at Tufts University's Fletcher School of Diplomacy, Bikowsky had focused on "low-intensity conflicts"—terrorism, insurgency—and the question of what is an appropriate use of force. Should terrorism be treated as all-out war—a posture that admits the prospect of collateral damage—or a series of crimes to be dealt with one by one by one? This was precisely the dilemma that America would struggle to answer for the next two decades; indeed, it would become a defining question of the early-twenty-first century.

At Tufts, Bikowsky read about the CIA counterterrorist center. A professor put her in touch with Dewey Clarridge himself. In a phone conversation, Bikowsky, starstruck, told the famous spy she believed in "things that go bump in the night" and that evil could prevail if good people didn't step up to stop it. Clarridge invited her to intern at CTC, and she did, working Hezbollah in the summers of 1988 and 1989. Rather than write a dissertation, Bikowsky jumped at the chance to take a job at the agency, and was offended, rather than gratified, when told that her testing and psych evaluations pointed her toward operations. "You're not hiring people, you're *casting* them," she protested.

At Langley, she felt the old-boy network was in full force and even the women who mentored her were trying too hard to be like the men. Signing on with the analytic directorate, she soon realized her mistake—"I was not cut out to be a traditional analyst," she acknowledges; "I really can't sit in a corner by myself"—and felt that her natural home was in CTC, where something betwixt-and-between was being birthed. After a stint as a briefer, she approached the operations directorate and offered her services to the emerging discipline of targeting.

Bikowsky, when she came to Alec Station in the late 1990s, would arrive as chief of operations. With Matthews and others, she would set about expanding the definition of what "operations" could mean. It didn't necessarily mean recruiting assets or planting propaganda. In the center, it meant "figuring out who it is that we should be looking for, who they're connected to, and what exactly we're going to do about it." It meant working with foreign partners to locate terrorists and run them to ground. "I'm never going to be the one to do a dead drop in Moscow," she acknowledged. "What I got good at was a very new tradecraft that no one really had done much of before that time. It was manhunting. Networking building." Bikowsky understood that she was, in many ways, a successor to the vault women who kept track of adversaries and assets.

Part of their job was figuring out what Congress and the White House would permit, both before and after a terrorist was located. The agency couldn't simply go after a group of fighters; it needed permission, it needed authority. The women were getting in at the ground level at a time when no one—literally no one—knew what was okay. It was a daunting question; an exciting question; a space that was open.

Ops guys were leery of work the center was pioneering, and she understood that. Why should trained operatives "take on a new discipline with so much risk and so little reward?" In a sense, the women of Alec Station were like the women of the computing industry, who pioneered software back in the 1950s, at a time when writing code was seen as little more than glorified typing. Here, women could join an important mission without having to surmount "every barrier in the world." Moreover, she contended, the women were acting out of a sense of justice, even outrage. "Those of us who signed up for this mission were really fixated on the idea that this is not okay with us," she said.

In the center, "operations" meant sparring with the FBI; with the Justice Department; and with ops officers in the field, insisting to case officers that she wasn't going to tell them how to make a dead drop, but that "you can put money on it: If I tell you this is the guy and this is the network and this is the steps to do, then this is what we do."

It meant pushing to figure out: Once you locate a terrorist, what can—should—you do with him? What is okay? How far is too far? Are we at war? Against one terrorist? All terrorists? "Are we out at war with al-Qaeda? Are we out to destroy them?" To this question, the women of Alec would often turn out to be more aggressive than the men who tried to boss them, including CIA directors and US presidents. They would retain a two-fisted demeanor, along with a chip on their shoulder when it came to training and certification. During her active career, when she was undercover, Bikowsky was often described in print as a "red-haired officer," as if hair color was her core defining trait. She and her team were at war with the enemy and, in a different way, with the agency they served. Told, repeatedly, to cool it, they refused. When it came to fighting al-Qaeda, she argued, "Everyone else was looking for an easier way to do it."

Cindy Storer, meanwhile, was in a distinct adjacent position: as a conventional analyst, it was her job to take the team's collection and use it, writing papers and trying to make sense of what was occurring. As such, Cindy was the lone bin Laden analyst charged with trying to get buy-in and persuade people at headquarters—and around Washington, including the White House—to pay attention. She was the unit's communications office, their PR squad, and their town crier, all in one.

WHEN CINDY BEGAN HER job at the CTC, Mike Scheuer had arranged to stand up a listening post—a wiretap—in a safe house in Peshawar, Pakistan. The house, used to run fighters in and out during the Afghan war, was now serving as a meeting venue for jihad leaders, who gathered to discuss how plots were commanded and fighters funneled. Reading transcripts, Cindy noted that the leaders were careful not to talk about actions they had planned. But they did go into numbing administrative detail. They were "moving money from one line item in

Contrary to popular belief, female spies throughout history have traded not on their sexuality, but on their perceived insignificance. In the nineteenth century, Kate Warne talked her way into a job at the Pinkerton Detective Agency. As part of her undercover work, Warne got wind of a plot to assassinate Abraham Lincoln and helped smuggle the president by train to Washington, posing as the humble caregiving sister of a tall, bearded invalid.

Harriet Tubman (left; shown here at her New York home, surrounded by family, friends, and neighbors) was a spymistress and logistical genius. She ran an extraordinary exfiltration operation, routing enslaved Americans to freedom under the noses of southern law enforcement, thwarting one of the most ruthless detection networks the world had ever known.

After the surprise attack at Pearl Harbor, the US government scrambled to prevent another intelligence failure. As tens of thousands of young men shipped off to war, America's first civilian spy service, the Office of Strategic Services, competed with other agencies, and with the US military, for female talent.

WOMAN'S PLACE IN WAR
The Army of the United States
has 239 kinds of jobs for women
THE WOMEN'S ARMY CORPS

Cora Du Bois, a renowned anthropologist, led the Southeast Asia research and analysis branch of the OSS, working with missionaries, travelers, and local assets to create an "unexcelled map service" that enabled Allied invasions and landings in the Pacific. After the war, a climate of intolerance set in; gays and lesbians were barred from federal jobs; and she and her lifelong companion, the artist and mapmaker Jeanne Taylor, were witch-hunted out of public service.

Among Cora Du Bois's OSS shipmates on her wartime voyage from San Francisco to Bombay was a young alumna of Smith College, the high-spirited Julia McWilliams. "Tall Julia"—as Du Bois fondly called her—later became known to the world as Julia Child.

The American entertainer Josephine Baker, shown here running her Parisian bar in 1928, smuggled sheet music out of Paris to Lisbon, using invisible ink to carry messages to Allied fighters planning the north Africa campaign.

Allen Dulles served as OSS station chief in Bern, Switzerland, where his success led to his role as foundational director of the CIA. But his top wartime asset, Nazi officer Hans Bernd Gisevius, was mostly handled by Dulles's right-hand woman, the multilingual Mary Bancroft (right). Bancroft is shown here with Dulles's long-suffering and oft-betrayed wife, Clover.

After the war, women were urged to depart government jobs and make room for returning GIs. Among those who stayed was Eloise Page, a highborn Virginian who started as a secretary, learned her bosses' secrets, and rose to become the first female overseas CIA station chief. Page was notoriously unhelpful to younger female colleagues, who saw her as aloof. She was, however, nice to her own secretary, Joanne Rich-creek (left), for whom she would leave cheery notes in shorthand.

During the war and for a decade afterward, the nation's civilian spy service operated out of a headquarters at 2430 E Street NW. Thousands of women kept the place running and built one of the world's most valuable sets of top secret intelligence records. Known as "vault women" or "sneaker ladies," the intimidating record keepers fiercely guarded their archive of 3 x 5 cards.

The CIA's Cold War operations depended to a surprising degree upon the energy, social savvy, and navigational skills of CIA wives. Among the best was Shirley Sulick, who relished driving elaborate routes that enabled her to shake off KGB tails in Moscow so her husband, Mike, could jump out of the car undetected.

Martha Peterson, a CIA wife whose husband, John, had been killed in Laos, became the first woman operative sent to Moscow. She posed as a visa processor and forged a cover identity as "Party Marti," a carefree single gal, while secretly handling a top asset code-named TRIGON. In 1977, when the asset was exposed by a traitor, Peterson (shown here under interrogation by the KGB) was arrested and detained in Lubyanka prison before being expelled.

Barbara Colby—the warm, witty spouse of CIA director Bill Colby—was, by many accounts, "the most loyal CIA wife ever." But this loyal wife forced a major reckoning when she used her Capitol Hill connections, and her forthright charm, to help engineer a new law ensuring that wives who helped their husbands overseas, only to be divorced later, were entitled to a portion of their ex-husbands' pensions.

In the 1990s, as the agency sought to find the mole responsible for the deaths of KBG officers working for the CIA, Aldrich Ames was unmasked by a mostly female team of implacable counter-intelligence officers, led by the gimlet-eyed Jeanne Vertefeuille.

Lisa Manfull's spy training commenced in her childhood, when she traveled with her diplomat father, Melvin Manfull, to Paris, in the 1950s.

Like other Ivy League universities, Brown was a rich recruiting ground for the OSS and, later, the CIA. Upon her graduation in 1966, Lisa Manfull was avidly recruited by emissaries from Langley, even as some of her classmates were starting to view government service with suspicion.

Upon graduation from Brown University, Lisa Manfull went to visit her parents in Brussels, where she was pressed into service representing the United States at an international debutante ball. Her peers had no idea that the white-gowned, deep-curtseying ingenue had been accepted by the CIA.

Embarking on clandestine training at "the Farm," the CIA's training facility in eastern Virginia, Lisa Manfull was dismayed to learn that women recruits were steered toward desk jobs. It took Lisa (center, in the wig and floppy white bow) ten years to work her way back to the full Farm course, during which recruits learned the dark arts of spotting, recruiting, and—as shown here—wearing disguises.

Recruits also received paramilitary training, along with standard tradecraft like "dead drops" and "brush passes." Lisa Manfull (now Harper) collaborated with the other women—and some men—to make sure everybody succeeded. She finished first in her class.

Lisa Harper developed a feminine approach to espionage, using empathy and emotional intelligence to win trust and elicit secrets. Defying many efforts to undermine her—an enduring specialty of the spy service—she rose to become the first female division chief, or "baroness."

As an eleven-year-old girl growing up in Tucson in the 1950s, Heidi August wrote to the CIA inquiring about careers and received in reply a brochure about how to become a clerk-secretary. Ten years later, in 1968, as a college senior at the University of Boulder, she approached a CIA recruiter and was handed . . . the same brochure.

Accepting a clerk's job, Heidi was posted to Libya, where she witnessed an uprising led by a little-known Libyan officer, Muammar Qaddafi. She moved on to European stations including Finland, where she cross-country skied with US ambassador David Mark. Her European postings also included Bonn, Germany, a spy setting out of a John le Carré novel. But work in the big station was more tedious than exotic; stuck in the typing pool, Heidi dated a Marine and worked for a boss the secretaries called Mr. Peepers.

Heidi's logistical skills impressed the men she worked for, particularly David Whipple, who became her mentor. Like many Cold War station chiefs, Whipple was eccentric, larger than life, and a drinker. He taught her cable writing by wadding up her drafts and throwing them at her; gave her advice over family dinners; and invited her as his right-hand woman to a posting in Cambodia. As the Khmer Rouge closed in, she evacuated on the last US helicopter out of Phnom Penh.

In 1978, Heidi joined the ranks of the men she worked for, graduating first in her class at the Farm with the aid of quiet advice from Lisa Manfull Harper. In her initial case officer posting, in Geneva, Heidi tapped into a wave of rising female discontent, targeting women assets, including one who was seeking revenge against her own exploitative bosses. Here, as part of her cover job, she escorts the diplomat and former child actress Shirley Temple Black.

Following a remarkable success obtaining communications technology in Geneva, Heidi was appointed station chief in the Mediterranean, followed by postings in the Middle East, Ireland, and India (shown here). Among the first CIA officers sent to Baghdad after the 2003 invasion of Iraq, she felt initially enthusiastic about liberating the country from Saddam Hussein but quickly realized the invasion had been a mistake.

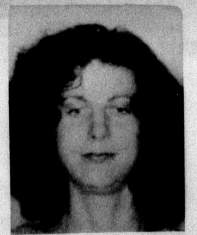

The turning point in Heidi August's career came in 1985, when she found herself on the island of Malta when a bullet-riddled Egyptair jet landed at Luqa airport after being hijacked by the terrorist group Abu Nidal. Among the scores of passengers killed was an American woman, Scarlett Rogenkamp, shot point-blank by one of the hijackers as Heidi watched from a control tower. Heidi felt a bond with the dead woman, and, in an era when fighting Communism was still the CIA's central mission, vowed to devote her career to fighting terrorism.

In the 1980s, a new generation of women entered on duty. The Title IX women showed up fresh-faced, well educated, self-confident, and eager. But even in the analytic corps, women often were marginalized and channeled into niche fields—like counterterrorism—where, as it happened, they were perfectly positioned to spot a rising menace. In 1995, the analyst Cindy Storer was among the first CIA officers tracking a stateless group of Arab fighters who had helped drive the Soviets from Afghanistan.

In 1996, Storer began working with the mostly female team of "Alec Station," a unit led by the analyst Michael Scheuer, which sought to divine the intentions of a wealthy Saudi-born businessman-turned-jihadist named Osama bin Laden.

But not until 1998, with the simultaneous horrific bombings of the US embassies in Kenya (shown here) and Tanzania, did most others at Langley start paying attention to the murderous intentions—and capabilities—of an obscure group called al-Qaeda.

The analyst Barbara Sude, equipped with a PhD from Princeton and a keen nose for a money trail, authored the famous August 6, 2001, President's Daily Brief warning that al-Qaeda wanted to mount a strike on US soil.

Gina Bennett, as early as 1993, had written the first published warning about the "wandering mujahidin" and she continued to write prescient warnings based on her strategic instincts, even as she and fellow terrorism "nerds" went ignored by others in the agency.

The women worked in a windowless basement unit of the CIA's headquarters, whose workforce had first sensed its own vulnerability in 1993, when a gunman opened fire on the route of their commute. The team struggled to raise awareness even as threats—and explosions—mounted with a 2000 suicide attack on the USS *Cole*, a US Navy ship refueling in Yemen.

On September 11, 2001, the world woke up to the reality of what the analysts had been predicting when two hijacked jets slammed into the twin towers of the World Trade Center in Manhattan, another crashed into the Pentagon, and a fourth was brought down by passengers in a field in Pennsylvania. The traumatized analysts stayed at their posts as the rest of the CIA evacuated. Later, these same analysts would be blamed by a Bush administration official for a "failure of imagination."

Among the other buildings destroyed when the towers collapsed was World Trade Center 7, a nearby office building that housed the CIA station in New York. Officers there had been close enough to see bodies falling. The chief of station, Mary Margaret Graham, evacuated staff safely and ensured that no classified documents were compromised.

Tom Brokaw
NBC TV
30 Rockefeller Plaza
New York NY 10112

Letter to Tom Brokaw

In the days after 9/11, threats—real and fake—multiplied. Among them were letters sent to US senators and the news media containing spores of deadly anthrax, which, along with the smoking rubble of the Pentagon, contributed to an air of persistent fear.

4th Grade
Greendale School
Franklin Park NJ 08852

Senator Daschle
509 Hart Senate Office
Building
Washington D.C. 205

Letter to Senator Daschle

The events of 9/11 attracted a new wave of recruits, including Rosa Smothers (shown here with CIA director Michael Hayden), a computer expert who tracked—and hacked—terrorist use of the internet. The corps of analysts was divided as some participated in the agency's notorious "enhanced interrogation" program while many others refused or, like Smothers, did not know of its existence.

Among the efforts to target terrorist leaders—"putting warheads on foreheads," it was called—none was more high-stakes than the hunt for Osama bin Laden. Stymied for nearly a decade, the hunt was reenergized in 2010, when targeters, many of them women, began sifting through old clues, aided by new technologies that helped locate a white SUV used by the courier who ferried messages to an intriguing compound in Abbottabad, Pakistan.

Aerial surveillance revealed enough drying laundry to suggest that three families lived at the Abbottabad compound. One resident was a tall man they called "the Pacer." A detailed model of the compound was constructed to help with planning. When President Barack Obama and CIA director Leon Panetta asked top government and military officers how certain they were that the Pacer was bin Laden, the analysts were the most confident group, at 95 percent. This time, the officials listened.

After 9/11 transformed the world she grew up in, Molly Chambers joined a third generation of female clandestine officers. Molly and her female colleagues called themselves "lady case officers" and texted to cheer one another on amid the loneliness and anxiety of overseas postings in isolated and dangerous regions.

In the twenty-first century, a case officer's arsenal of tools included the usual surreal mix of cash, IDs, passports, quick-change license plates, maps, and a handbag containing a "shark fin" that enabled her to vacuum up cellphone numbers at a cocktail party.

In Nigeria, Chambers performed targeting of a humanitarian sort, seeking the Chibok school girls kidnapped by the terrorist group Boko Haram. Some returned Chibok girls are shown here.

the budget to another," talking about salaries, travel costs, and other expenses. She also became aware of a legal case in London over who owned the safe house. Two Saudis were having a real estate dispute in open court, and Cindy got those documents as well. "It was awesome."

The women on Scheuer's team were pulling together this kind of data. A major disadvantage afflicting Alec Station was that it did not have its own case officers to run operations or collect intelligence. If the women wanted to ask questions of an overseas asset, they had to ask the clandestine services' regional stations—in Rome, say, or Peshawar—to do so. The team was always sending cables to the field, suggesting leads, begging, exhorting, saying person X was doing Y and Z, and could the station's case officers include the following questions on their next meeting with an asset.

Whether this got done depended on whether the overseas station felt like putting its own case officers at risk for the benefit of some new-fangled "virtual station." Near East division tended to balk; Africa division tended to help. Stations, in the peace-dividend era, were themselves short-staffed and busy. "We would get cables once in a while" from "this station named Alec," said Paula Doyle, a case officer in the Levant. To her own overworked station, Alec seemed little more than an amorphous cable site; she didn't know anybody who worked there, and "we were so busy with Hezbollah and other regional conflicts" that the attitude was "Oh, we'll get to that whenever."

"I think I was not alone in not really understanding al-Qaeda or why they established a station," said Doyle, who came to realize that "the centers did exceptionally important work."

The station, like its target, remained a backroom mystery to almost everyone. In the mid-1990s, operations officer Mia McCall was in her first management job in what was now the Central Eurasin division, which had been created to focus on the former Soviet republics. Her boss, Robert Baer, asked her to meet with a former Soviet linguist on Scheuer's team. He warned that she might seem a little odd, a little sneaker-ladyish. McCall took the meeting. "Her hair was on fire about this guy named UBL—Usama bin Laden—and I'm like, 'Who's that?'"

CHAPTER 17

STRESS AND
A GRAY ROOM

MCLEAN, VIRGINIA

1995

THE QUESTION THEN BECAME, FOR CINDY STORER: IF BIN LADEN
was as critical as he appeared to be, what was the nature of this web
of fighters he seemed, like a spider, to be at the center of? What held
them together? What were they called? To help determine this, the
women of Alec Station began consulting other countries' spy agencies—
what is known as liaison work. Though not as flashy as spy recruitment,
liaison work was and remains critical to stopping attacks. After all, it
was mostly other countries, in Africa and the Middle East, losing innocent lives to the anti-Western jihad when hijackings occurred or
bombs went off in their midst. Many foreign services were eager to
share what they knew and even run operations under CIA guidance.
Cindy Storer noticed that many liaison teams included a lot of women.
The Israelis, even the Saudis—they all had female intelligence officers
behind the scenes. Women, Cindy concluded, "will do the thing that's
not sexy."

Working with foreign counterparts, the Alec women amassed a
great deal of open-source material: "gray literature" such as police records, financial filings, the kind of papers that were publicly available but
more easily obtained by foreign nationals than Westerners. Cindy tried,
once, on an overseas tour, and had doors slammed in her face. "They

went out to all liaison services all over the world and said, 'We're working on this, what do you know?' And brought back troves of information. Troves."

Cindy began to grasp that the fighters weren't a loose federation. They seemed, in fact, unexpectedly bureaucratic. "We actually got their incorporation documents and saw that they were all about being a worldwide Jihadi group. It was right there," said Cindy, who found herself reading mission statements, signed covenants, onboarding papers. "This is who we are, this is what we do, this is what we want to do, here are the qualifications to be a leader, here's how the organization is structured. Here's our philosophy, our ideology." She noticed that the group was meticulously recording its spending. "They're accounting for every little desk chair."

She began creating Microsoft Word files, using the search function to keep track of who was talking to whom. She ended up with more than a hundred files. "I don't know anything about this guy. Let me look at my database for the phone number. All these other people come up. I'll put that on my Word sheet. Okay. Who's he associated with? Write their names. What places are they associated with?" She was drilling down, making linkages, identifying gaps and trying to fill them.

Yet in the counterterrorism center itself, other branches remained skeptical that a scattered bunch of traveling Abu Mohammeds could pose a serious threat on the level of Hezbollah or Hamas. People regarded the fighters as "ragheads who lived in a cave," Cindy said, when in truth, many of them were "doctors and lawyers and military officers who knew their shit."

It fell to Cindy—the lone analyst writing up what Alec Station collected—to win over all of Langley. "That's when I started getting serious stress and depression," she recalled.

But Cindy plunged in and did her best. "We had piles and piles of documents . . . and just started assembling all this stuff to make a picture." Having taken a graduate class in organizational science, she decided to ask the right question of the data. She put names in boxes, drew lines, and links began to form. "Oh, that guy, he's the finance guy. And he talks to this guy and that guy does this over here. And this guy has the passports. And I just started laying out the network and it fell right into a hierarchy." Cindy saw how money was moving between members of the group to fund purchases.

"Who does that?" she thought.

In 1995, she had begun her formal labors; after a year and a half, she had an epiphany moment. "I'm like, Holy crap, it's a terrorist *organization.*"

MORE PIECES FELL INTO place in May 1996, when a walk-in named Jamal Ahmed al-Fadl appeared at a US embassy in Eritrea. The number three person in bin Laden's organization, al-Fadl had served as a business agent to bin Laden during the Afghan war. He had spent time in the United States and was recruited at a mosque in Brooklyn. Now he was in big trouble. He had embezzled more than $100,000 from the group, and needed an escape plan. The CIA station chief was on leave, but the chief of administration, a woman, stepped up and debriefed him, listening as he talked about this fighter network that wanted to go to war against the United States. She quickly cabled headquarters that she had a "guy here talking about bin Laden."

Al-Fadl soon found himself relocated to a pleasant hotel suite in New Jersey, where, for more than a year, he hosted visits from the FBI as well as the women of Alec. He was charismatic and flirtatious, and the women called him Junior. They relayed their findings to Cindy, who stayed at headquarters to preserve her objectivity, uninfluenced by personal contact with the asset. Her findings were so in sync with his reporting that it was as if "we lived in each other's pockets."

Junior shared new information about operations, as well as membership numbers. "I'm like, 'Oh my God I know exactly what he's talking about,'" said Cindy. She began plugging more names into her org chart, mapping alliances, trying "to figure out what was going on in all these different threads of activity all over the world. And I was figuring, 'Oh, these guys in the Philippines are doing X and these guys are here doing Y.'"

Bin Laden's group was a bureaucracy complete with a payroll and franchises. But what was it called? Now that the name al-Qaeda is famous—infamous, rather—it's hard to remember that there was a time when people, even experts, literally did not know its name. Over at State, Gina Bennett had referred to "Al Qai'da" in her own 1993 memo, but at the agency, people were cautious; managers had far more say over what was written; analysts could not publish under their own names; and Cindy was required to coordinate every assertion—every word, even——before she could publish. To say Osama bin Laden was a terrorist financier was one thing; to say that his network not only was real, but had a real name, provoked much argumentation. "We couldn't call it anything. We were still referring to him as a financier, having internal debates," Cindy remembers. To her, the name seemed perfectly clear. Al-Qaeda was "what they have on their letterhead."

Cindy's own branch chief, the person above her responsible for her analytic product, meanwhile evinced little interest. Managers were beleaguered, and a new group was just one more thing to deal with. But Cindy could be hard-headed. Around 1997, she brushed aside other assignments and set out to write a long piece that named and fully described al-Qaeda. It would be a definitive background paper with, as she put it, "everything you wanted to know about bin Laden and al-Qaeda: This is a terrorist group, it's organized, this is how they recruit and train, here's their motive and intent, here's all the attacks they've probably already been involved in, one way or another, even messing around with trying to get nuclear material." The draft ran to seventy pages. But the topics touched on the mandates of so many other branches, "I couldn't get other desks to agree," she later recollected. She needed buy-in from "anybody with any stake at all," the "regional desks, some technical officers—talking about WMD— anybody who has anything to do with arms trafficking." Her branch chief told her nobody would read a long paper. He wanted her to break it into small parts. The full version never got published. It was a long, agonizing snafu, and in some ways, recalled the rocket-motors-versus-discarded-tires argument from back at NPIC. What *was* this thing that she was seeing? How dangerous was it, really? People had doubts. Conventional wisdom held that Hezbollah was the world's most dangerous terrorist group, having killed the most Americans to date. Cindy kept arguing: No, you also must consider how many people a group *wants* to kill. You must consider its intent.

It felt to Cindy as though other branches in the center saw her as a competitor—for funding and slots—rather than an ally. There was no mechanism for funneling up a radically new insight—the reality of a stateless terrorist group. Colleagues argued that the group couldn't be that coordinated because "Arabs are not well educated, they're disorganized, they won't fight." To which her reply was: "What do you mean, I can't say it's that organized? We have documents, we have intercepts, we have everything."

Try as she did, Cindy could not find a mentor to take her findings and lend them credibility and heft. "Part of my job as a DI analyst is to convince people that this is a thing. And Mike was very frustrated with my management because I couldn't get stuff out," said Cindy, who became, in her own words, "a little grumpy."

"Mike was a patron to his people. I didn't have that," reflected Cindy. "I wasn't part of his group. I mean, he was good to me. There wasn't anything he could do for me. I needed help navigating, that's not a talent with me. I don't have the people skills. You just couldn't get any forward momentum."

A NEW TRUTH, MEANWHILE, began emerging in the counterterrorist center. Not only did terrorism require a different kind of analysis; it extracted a very different psychic cost. In November 1995, a car bomb exploded at a US military post in Riyadh, Saudi Arabia, killing seven people and injuring more than sixty. Saudis influenced by bin Laden were arrested. The next year, terrorists bombed a housing complex in Khobar, Saudi Arabia—Khobar Towers—where nineteen US Air Force personnel were killed and 498 others, of many nationalities, injured. One CTC analyst started giving a talk to newcomers about what it felt like to get a letter from an American mother who lost her only son in Khobar Towers. He would read the letter aloud, and cry every time, wondering if he could have spotted something that might have stopped it.

On top of this was the strain of working with other US agencies— or trying to. Part of the "fusion" approach involved bringing in emissaries from other agencies, and sending CIA representatives there in return. A "hostage swap," people called it. It made sense: An overseas rendition often required wiretapping from NSA and arrest by the FBI. But decades-old interagency rivalry—even mutual hatred—persisted. One reason why ambitious ops guys didn't want to be sent to the counterterrorist center was because nobody wanted to be "sent down there to sit around with those FBI guys," as one CIA officer, Robert Baer, put it.

The struggle between the agency and the bureau was epic, historical, and baked in. FBI likes to make arrests; CIA sometimes prefers to leave bad guys in place, "turning" them to use as assets in spy operations. The FBI are the cops—as the saying goes—and the CIA are the robbers. When a joint operation succeeded, the two agencies competed for credit: In 1994, after Aldrich Ames was arrested, FBI director Louis Freeh agreed to a joint press conference but then jumped the gun, holding a preemptive conference to steal credit from the CIA and its female sleuths. When an operation failed, both strove to shift the blame.

The FBI had a huge Washington building, but in many ways, what it really was, was a network of localized investigative field offices. It was set up so that a local field officer who began an investigation kept ownership of that investigation. During the successful investigation of the 1993 World Trade Center bombing, John O'Neill, in the New York office, spearheaded that operation and thus became the FBI's top counterterrorism official. A hard-boiled gumshoe out of central casting, O'Neill was all double-breasted suits and tough talk. He liked to dine at the see-and-be-seen restaurant Elaine's in New York and had a penchant for uttering Louis XIV–type proclamations like "I *am* the FBI." O'Neill, moreover, was in a major midlife crisis: Separated from his wife, he was conducting affairs with three women, telling each she was his only girlfriend. It's hard to imagine a worse matchup than the mobbed-up-looking John O'Neill and the rumpled but equally combative Mike Scheuer, who concedes that the relationship was "disastrous."

The women were caught in the crossfire and confusion. Lines of authority were vague, legal boundaries important but ill defined. The CIA had to be careful not to get involved in domestic operations, as history—and the Church committee hearings—made clear. Whatever

happened on US soil was the FBI's purview. Even in overseas operations, the FBI was the agency that made arrests. But during an investigation, the FBI often seized all sorts of documents and other evidence
that the CIA wanted to see. The CIA was able to look at it under some
circumstances but not others. Nobody, yet, had figured this out or nailed
it down. The rendition program was too new. Lawyers had to be called
in and even they sometimes could not agree. Often, the unhappy upshot was plain old dog-in-the-manger hoarding. "Fuck you. I've got it.
I'm keeping it. It's mine," O'Neill reportedly told staffers, refusing to
hand over a notebook retrieved from one al-Qaeda operative. Back at
Langley, Mike Scheuer complained about the FBI's unwillingness to
share. "I bet we sent 700 or 800 requests for information to the FBI,
and we never got an answer to any of them," he later told a reporter. But
Scheuer himself sometimes hoarded. "They won't do anything with it,"
a colleague at the CTC heard him mutter. In an interview for this book,
Scheuer said he was often reluctant to share because FBI officers talked
recklessly about classified information. He added that bureau officers
"stole documents by the boxes;" that O'Neill told him there wasn't any
point helping if the bureau didn't get credit; and a big part of the problem was that FBI director Freeh would not upgrade their outdated
communications equipment. "You fax it, and they say, 'Well, we can't
find the machine it went to.'"

After the Khobar bombing, Cindy was assigned to a joint task force
on the aftermath. She found herself riding a shuttle bus to FBI
headquarters—being sent "behind enemy lines," it was called. The bus
deposited her at the J. Edgar Hoover Building, whose bulk loomed
along an entire block of Pennsylvania Avenue. Cindy pinned a visitor's
badge on her shirt and found her way to an upper floor where the Khobar materials were kept in an old wooden file cabinet in a broom closet.
John O'Neill would not let her take notes or copy so much as a piece of
paper. He seemed to think she would go back to headquarters and trigger some action that would impede the investigation.

It seemed to Cindy an attack of this magnitude was bound to yield
something useful she and her colleagues could see. A single official—
luckily, the special agent in charge of the investigation—agreed. When

O'Neill was away, the staffer invited Cindy to copy every file. She did, standing at a Xerox machine and putting the copies into a secure bag that she lugged on the shuttle back to Langley. That was how two of the world's leading agencies were communicating in the mid-1990s. "We created our own black filing cabinet at the CIA from all the crap I copied and carried back."

In an ideal world, given the monumental pileup of snafus, the National Security Council—the president's top team of national security advisers—might have helped set a more cooperative tone, untangling warring policies and helping intense, committed, and belligerent personalities manage to get along. And the Clinton administration's NSC terrorism emissary, Richard Clarke, took terrorism seriously. But Clarke himself was cranky, mercurial, authoritarian, unilateral—"a madman," as one CIA analyst put it, while another called him "a truly painful individual to work with." Nobody in this group would ever be voted Mr. Congeniality. Mike Scheuer saw Clarke as "an interferer of the first level" and an "empire builder" who shot things down. Clarke accused Mike Scheuer of "throwing tantrums."

Scheuer also resented officials on the seventh floor of CIA headquarters, whom he saw as dismissive and sexist. "The overwhelming majority of officers who worked for me were women," he later told *Vanity Fair*. "And they don't care for that. They don't care for women, period, but they especially don't care for successful women."

AS THE WOMEN DUCKED fire between the Mikes, the Johns, and the Dicks, it is worth pointing out that they themselves—like real sisters—did not always get along. There were tensions between Cindy's job as an analyst, which was to be objective and unbiased, and the driven, active role of the women working for Mike Scheuer. In keeping with the spirit of backroom operations, the Alec women, or some of them, exhibited ferocity and suspicion, and regarded outsiders, even Cindy, as not necessarily entitled to know what they knew. The women were running operations, collecting information but also identifying leaders they wanted to see arrested. Cindy felt these tactics were "utilitarian." She worried that a toppled leader might create a vacuum that would be filled by somebody worse. "Mike liked them because they would just go off and get stuff done."

Cindy got along fine with some of the team members, but it struck her that Jennifer Matthews and Alfreda Bikowsky, in particular, were loath to have their thinking challenged. Consistently over the years, the sisterhood was divided between those who favored an aggressive approach to detainment and arrest, and those, like Cindy, who sometimes felt that a leader, left in place, was preferable to whatever chaos might follow. When it came to disrupting operations, at first all Alec could really do was flag a terrorist to the FBI, or to a cooperating liaison force, who might or might not act. Later on, the goal was more likely arrest and detainment. The calls were hard and so were the debates. Cindy felt that the pair "overdrew conclusions," that they "didn't really like to listen to other people and they thought they were better than everyone else analytically." Some of their operations struck her as "ill-advised," and she told them so. Cindy knew she could be stubborn, too, and paranoid. Office politics felt hard. There were times it wasn't clear whether the women of Alec were working with her, for her, or against her. She would make appointments to travel to New York to talk to the FBI, only to find that the meeting had been canceled.

After the Khobar bombings, National Security Advisor Sandy Berger went to Alec Station to meet with Scheuer and his team. Scheuer liked to give the women on his team a lead role in the briefings.

Berger then came to meet with Cindy and a few colleagues in the section of the CTC where analysts sat. The Alec women showed up as well—just materialized and sat down. Cindy felt they "came over to get attention."

AS A STUNNING NUMBER of jihadists—thousands upon thousands— cycled through training camps in Africa and South Asia in the mid-1990s, the sisterhood focused on their intentions remained tiny, growing by ones and twos. In May 1996, Osama bin Laden was expelled from Sudan, which aspired to normalize relations with the United States by showing it was no longer giving sanctuary to terrorists. Over at the

State Department, the analyst Gina Bennett suspected that bin Laden's departure from Sudan would make him more, not less, of a threat, as his whereabouts got harder to track. In an article published in the State Department's INR bulletin on July 18, 1996, she made a series of prescient observations. Gina pointed out that bin Laden had been sighted in the UK, Yemen, Somalia, Afghanistan, Pakistan, and Sudan, and that his "many passports—and private plane—allow him considerable freedom to travel with little fear of being intercepted or tracked." She noted that his interest in supporting radical Islamists "extends well beyond the Middle East."

Conjecturing about where bin Laden would likely end up, Gina predicted that he would "feel comfortable returning to Afghanistan," which had become "an even more desirable location for extremists" and "maybe even an ideal haven." Describing him as an "increasingly confident military leader," she pointed out that he and his associates remained suspects in the Khobar Towers attack, and that his willingness to speak to the press "suggests a man emboldened." She predicted that bin Laden's "prolonged stay in Afghanistan—where hundreds of 'Arab mujahidin' receive terrorist training and key extremist leaders often congregate—could prove more dangerous to US interests in the long run than his three-year liaison with Khartoum."

Many State Department colleagues thought Gina was going recklessly far with her predictions. Gina, like Cindy Storer, was seen as having gone out on a shaky limb. In some ways, she reflected later, it was true. "I wasn't biased by a belief that terrorism could only be a certain way. I was too young for that."

To win buy-in, Gina Bennett had built a symbiotic relationship with Mike Scheuer. At her desk in the State Department, she used the "little dribs and drabs" that Alec Station collected to inform her own writings, which included a thirty-page memo recommending diplomatic responses to the jihad threat. Scheuer would take Gina's published work and deploy it, bolstering his case to policymakers that "this was a threat that they really needed to take seriously." He would tell people that "analysts in Washington are saying this," when, in fact—she laughs—the "analysts" were she herself.

Gina Bennett felt championed by Scheuer and created the working group—the one Cindy and Barbara Sude had joined in the early 1990s—to give him backup. "I knew he would have more ammunition if it was an interagency body of analysts," she said. "Even though we were the one individual in each of our organizations saying this stuff, when you put us together, you couldn't ignore it as easily." But the idea that there was a new threat, so soon after the old one had been vanquished, "was impossible for people to believe."

In 1997, CNN analyst Peter Bergen secured a television interview with Osama bin Laden, riding with a camera crew to an undisclosed location where bin Laden surprised them, and the world, by declaring war on America on cable TV. On the seventh floor of the CIA, the new director, George Tenet, declared war on Osama bin Laden, but it was not clear how (and if) that war would be fought. That same year, Gina Bennett became a bona fide member of the CIA sisterhood when she left State to join Mike Scheuer's team. He had been after her to bring her expertise to Alec Station, which had moved out of its suburban quarters and back to headquarters and the CTC. The counterterrorist center, meanwhile, relocated to a bleak windowless room on the basement floor of the new headquarters, where the sun never shone and there was no respite, visual or otherwise, from the stream of threat. People working in cubicles could not escape the murmur of colleagues talking to babysitters, making doctor's appointments, arranging after-school pickups. The floor was concrete, covered by a wooden platform that hid electrical wires, topped by dingy carpet.

Gina Bennett took a spot in what people referred to as the "matrix," doing a hybrid job that was part analysis, part operations. It was her job to publish papers but also to assist with operations by writing "targeting profiles" to help locate terrorists and anticipate their movements. With a foot in each directorate, Gina was a thinker and a doer.

When she got there, Alec Station still was in the frustrating position of having to beg overseas stations to ask questions of sources. The team countered with stratagems of their own. "Everyone that we ever wanted to talk to was characterized as a 'senior bin Laden lieutenant,' because it was the only way we could get someone in the field to say, okay, we'll ask the set of questions," said Gina, who felt the gender makeup of the team was one reason the seventh floor wouldn't give them case officers. In her view, Alec Station still suffered from a sneaker-lady reputation. Senior leaders viewed the small group as a "backwater" with "not well-trained individuals—read women—who had been analysts." She imagined their thinking: "Do we really want to trust them with driving and telling people to go do this?"

Gina, who always felt cold, was given a desk below one of new headquarters' problematic vents, so she rigged a tent to deflect the fetid air. She sat companionably close to Cindy, sharing insights with Jennifer Matthews, admiring how the women of Alec asserted themselves and held their own. As mothers of young children, Gina and Jennifer bonded over challenges like finding a room to breast-pump. Gina liked Jennifer Matthews, finding her warm, witty, smart, kind, and "unapologetically herself"; she talked about breastfeeding in front of ops guys, "and just made me feel it was okay to be a woman in this business."

GINA BENNETT BEGAN WORKING with Jennifer Matthews to study the pipelines moving people and supplies from Peshawar into Afghanistan and to training camps. They sought to know: What method did the terrorists use to communicate with one another? When did they use radio? Satellite phones? Couriers? How did they talk to members who were deployed elsewhere? How did they talk to the Islamist extremist groups that they were courting, or that were seeking guidance from bin Laden? They traced the movements of "red crescent stickers," which are badges, like the red cross, used to signal a humanitarian purpose. The terrorists were putting red crescent stickers on storage units to transport weapons.

Since al-Qaeda wasn't a government and didn't have its own ministry of communications or transportation, it had to tap into outside systems. How did they get access? Did they hire people? Bribe people? Threaten people? What methods did they use to develop assets? If a bin Laden lieutenant travels to talk to an affiliated group that could help run an operation in, say, Mindanao, how does he get there? Who handles the travel? Who picks him up at the airport? Which hotels or guest houses does he stay in? Where does he eat? How often does he use that route? Whom does he meet with twice? Three times? Frequent meetings were key. The work took slogging and patience. The goal was to work fast enough to get a step ahead, notify liaison authorities, and have a team in place when a target showed up.

Sometimes what they tracked wasn't people but behavior. They looked for indicators of activities. These might include equipment moving, people converging, communications suggesting paramilitary activity, or evidence that a group was closing shop and dispersing, suggesting something was going down and it was time to close in.

What Scheuer had put together, in Gina's view, was a team with "the patience to understand a network" and a dose of obsessiveness, too: "It's just like a cop on the beat tracking a serial killer for thirty years."

The work was fantastically hard. Key pieces of information rarely arrived at the right time. Gina at one point worked with the center's renditions branch, whose members were trying to find Khalid Sheikh Mohammed, an indicted coconspirator for the 1993 World Trade Center attack. His nephew, Ramzi Yousef, had been tried as the mastermind of the explosion, but nobody believed Yousef was the real mastermind. Suspecting KSM, they hoped to get him to a country that had an extradition treaty with the United States. Gina helped look for connections in Peshawar but couldn't find any. There were a million other things to look at and they didn't realize he should be a high priority. That's because he was still a freelancer, a kind of contractor; his name wasn't on al-Qaeda membership rolls. Later, her biggest regret was that she didn't stick with trying to find KSM: "Obviously we didn't know who he was. But I wonder, if we had been able to render him, if there wouldn't have been a 9/11, you know?"

TOGETHER, THE WOMEN OF Alec Station also began to challenge the culture when it came to family life. As recently as the 1980s, a female analyst who had the temerity to marry was considered shocking—and often sidelined. The incompatibility of intelligence work and family responsibilities was taken as a given, for women. In 1975, *Parade* interviewed several women of the CIA, including the redoubtable Helene Boatner; Pat Taylor, an analyst in counterintelligence; Jenonne Walker, an aide to William Colby; and an unnamed fifty-four-year-old branch chief of Soviet Internal Affairs who was steeped in everything known about Communist Party boss Leonid Brezhnev. The author of the article, Connecticut Walker, saw fit to describe Colby's aide as "an attractive woman" and noted that none of the women was married.

Ray Cline, the World War II analyst who rose to be deputy director for intelligence, explained why: Women in responsible positions needed to be flexible, hence "Most of them are single."

Marriage was bad enough; childbirth, unthinkable. Into the 1980s, women were expected to surrender their security badges when they went into labor. "The presumption was that you weren't coming back," said Sue Gordon, a rising star in the technology directorate who had her first child in 1984. Gordon made hall-file history by refusing to give up her badge. "I just said no," she recalled. "I didn't want to allow the possibility that someone could, with my badge in hand, decide that I wasn't going to come back." Gordon had her baby and returned to her job. When Barbara Sude was pregnant in 1979, and then again in 1984, smoking was permitted in the office, so a friend put up a sign that said, FETAL GROWTH IN PROGRESS, NO SMOKING. Once, when Barbara went to the bathroom, a colleague joked that she'd returned so quickly that he "couldn't finish the cigarette." Lactating new mothers sat in a bathroom stall to use a hand pump.

As the culture changed, this led to generational clashes. When analyst DeNeige Watson was hired, she noticed that above her were "very impressive women leaders" who were "great role models" but that "none of them had families." When she married, and came up for a promotion, she remembered her female manager stopping her in the hallway and saying, "How dare you think you should be promoted? You made a choice and got married."

The women of Alec Station defied these constraints. But they also gravitated toward work with a slightly more forgiving timeline. Another reason why women tended to end up on the counterterrorism effort was because it was (marginally) more family-friendly: Everybody worked long hours, but writing targeting packages permitted a hard stop at the end of the day. Other analytic jobs bled into the evening hours, waiting for a PDB editor to weigh in. Working counterterrorism was harrowing, but most days had a more predictable conclusion.

Still, the pace was relentless, and nobody was making their lives easier, so the women improvised. When Gina Bennett delivered her second child in 1996, she had hoped to take a year's sabbatical. But her husband's nonprofit folded, so he became the parent who stayed home. Her third child was born in 1998; during one crisis period, she breastfed at her desk and then put the sleeping baby down so she could type up a cable. "I had her in my lap, shifting my legs back and forth and patting her," when her supervisor, a man, swooped in and took the baby to give her a break. She went upstairs to a meeting, then came down and hunted around till she found both her baby and her boss.

In the absence of institutional support—the federal workforce was not entitled to twelve weeks of paid parental leave until October 2020— it was not uncommon to see a child in a car seat in the office. Around the same time Gina was returning from her third maternity leave—the women were able to take six weeks, using sick leave, but often came back sooner—Jennifer Matthews was about to give birth to her second. Jennifer asked Gina to take her job while she was away, but Gina's boss didn't want to lose her, so Gina did both. Messy as it was, Gina saw advantages to a life where the "chaos and demands" of work gave way to the "chaos and demands" of home. "When I came home, I had to get somebody to baseball practice, somebody to ballet. That was very grounding."

Even so, the difficulty of getting the building to pay attention was harrowing. "From 1993 on, it was just a series of things, worse and worse and worse."

THEY DID GET HELP, however, from one of the few female supervisors in their workspace. In 1996, Heidi August joined the center as chief of operations—the number three job, known as "cops." Heidi had just come from three years in New Delhi, India, where she once again availed herself of nanny cover, living with a family and taking the children on trips to a pay phone. Every Saturday, she placed a call to a CIA asset who had been released after a quarter-century in prison, to ensure he got the cash reward to which he was entitled.

By now, nearly three decades into her CIA career, Heidi August had been awarded her spot in the elite Senior Intelligence Service—the equivalent of being an admiral in the Navy—where women had long been underrepresented. The cops job was an SIS position and fitted the mission to which she had devoted her career.

Dewey Clarridge had by then retired as CTC director; the new head of the center, Geoff O'Connell, was a quiet and funny man whom Heidi respected and liked. But it was impossible to ignore the woes afflicting the center, chief among them the fact that people arrived on loan from their home divisions. Heidi began pressing for a true career track, so officers could commit to the field, build expertise, and get promoted.

Heidi also helped women attain the family life she herself had been discouraged from pursuing. When one analyst, Diana Bolsinger, approached to say she was withdrawing from an overseas position because her boyfriend had asked her to marry him, and there wasn't a job overseas for him, Heidi—who controlled the job and had supported her candidacy for it—gave the younger woman a hard talking to, warning about the repercussions to her career. Then—formalities over—she proceeded to smile warmly and congratulate her. The repercussions ended up being negligible. "She never raised it again," Bolsinger said. "I can't think of a way she could have handled it better." Bolsinger remembers that Heidi "did her job superbly well" and held her own in a hectic center where Mike Scheuer was not the only contentious personality. Scheuer and another branch chief, who focused on Sunni extremists, "fought like cats and dogs." Heidi, she said, provided a welcome dose of normalcy and humanity, untangling snafus rather than creating them.

Heidi also pushed her own bosses to expand their thinking about the kinds of people who could occupy top jobs. In a conversation with O'Connell, she learned that the center needed someone to lead the unit that conducts surveillance during overseas operations. It was a rough and gritty job, critical to the safety of ops officers meeting with terrorists. The unit was in some disarray. Heidi suggested Ellie Duckett, a much-respected case officer who had been overlooked for most of her career, then promoted only to step back when she developed virulent breast cancer. Duckett had undergone a bone marrow transplant and was recovering at home. Heidi thought it would be good for Ellie to get back in the office.

O'Connell worried that her treatment might interfere with her ability to do the job. Heidi argued that medical issues should not disqualify her. O'Connell agreed to meet with Duckett at the McLean Family Restaurant, an agency hangout in a nearby strip mall. Heidi ate a Greek salad and listened as Duckett impressed the men with her intellect and low-key manner. Starting out part time, she turned out to be a natural leader, bringing order to the surveillance unit and going on to head the National Resources division, the network of stations the agency maintains in the United States, to debrief people returning from abroad. Duckett imposed a rule that half the domestic centers be run by women, half by men. Thanks to Heidi, Duckett had a second chance at achieving.

In Heidi's capacity managing the center's operations, she also oversaw Alec Station. The people working for Mike Scheuer reminded her very much of the backroom women who caught Aldrich Ames, except that they were more outspoken and in-your-face. Heidi watched them with bemusement and some alarm. "They had big personalities," she recollected. "Each one tried to be more of an expert than the other one. I could sense there was a lot of competition, probably for Mike's attention." Scheuer gave the team such a free rein that it almost seemed the women were running their boss. ("I got chewed on quite a bit by those ladies," acknowledged Scheuer, who saw it as being "for the good of the mission.") When Alec station moved to the off-campus location, their out-of-sight, out-of-mind status made Heidi nervous: She suspected Scheuer was pushing the FBI and NSA harder for information than he should. "Mike frequently got ahead of his skis," she said. "He made a lot of enemies."

CHAPTER 18

THE NICKED EARLOBE

O N FRIDAY, MAY 30, 1997, A YEAR INTO HER TENURE AT THE
CTC, Heidi was in her office when her secure phone rang. On the
line was Patricia Moynihan, a thirty-year-old operations officer serving
as chief of base in Karachi, Pakistan. Moynihan was calling to report a
walk-in at the consulate in Karachi. Two walk-ins: both men, one of
them a bureaucratic functionary, who claimed to know the whereabouts
of Mir Aimal Kansi, the Route 123 shooter.

Heidi listened with interest—and skepticism. In the four years since
she'd witnessed her colleagues gunned down in cold blood during their
morning commute, countless so-called informants had contacted the
agency claiming to know where Kansi was. This was not surprising,
given that the US government was proferring a $2 million reward,
through the State Department's Rewards for Justice program. The hunt
remained foremost on the minds at the CIA, which had mounted many
operations and attracted any number of bounty hunters. "Just give me
the money and then I'll tell you—this kind of stuff."

But the situation got more intriguing as Patricia Moynihan related
it to her. The walk-ins, who came from the region around Quetta,
claimed they had Kansi in custody and were prepared to surrender him.

Heidi began to think this really could come to something, but first they had to be sure the person in question was truly Mir Aimal Kansi.

At the CIA base in Karachi, a city of some 9 million in the southern part of the country, on the Arabian Sea, Patricia Moynihan was already at work on this question. Walk-ins can be huge liars, and one thing a case officer must do is sort fiction from fact. When the two men first materialized, they claimed they had Kansi "chained to a goat" so he couldn't get away. Patricia Moynihan had listened—"I'm like, what do you mean, chained to a *goat*?"—along with Scott Jessee, an FBI agent and former college ice hockey player based out of Islamabad, who happened to be in town. Moynihan, like Heidi, worked well with her counterparts at other agencies. She had to; in a dangerous place like Karachi, the compound was locked down and your NSA, FBI, and State colleagues were your social life. It was her birthday, and she and Jessee were supposed to go out to a Chinese restaurant to celebrate.

But walk-ins tended to have long, circuituous shaggy-dog stories. "You're just like, fuck me, you have to take each one seriously," Moynihan recalled. At the CIA, there are three key things that can get an operations officer fired: misusing money, misusing a weapon, and poorly handling a walk-in. Moynihan, who had graduated eight years earlier from Denison University, was on her second overseas posting. Her first had been to Moscow, where her cover job had been in the consulate stamping visas, a job that involved being spit on, literally, by Russians; the spittle would come through little holes in the glass. In the wake of the collapse of the Soviet Union, there'd been a lot of walk-ins and Moynihan had gotten a lot of practice. After that assignment she was supposed to go to India, and the base-chief posting at Karachi had been a last-minute change, with two weeks' notice. It was a tough assignment and officers weren't clamoring to take it.

At the main CIA station in Islamabad, chief Gary Schroen had suggested she let her State Department counterparts at the consulate know that she was eager to hear from Kansi-related walk-ins. So she spread the word. A State officer visiting Quetta had been approached by the walk-ins and contacted Patricia. And now here she was, listening to them talk. The goat story seemed weird—and turned out to be nonsense—but they did have what they claimed were Kansi's fingerprints from his driver's license application. Scott Jessee went upstairs, checked some prints, came down, and said they looked like a match. Moynihan couldn't believe it. The next thing to do was call Islamabad Station; Gary Schroen was away, and his deputy answered. Patricia talked; he listened. "This could be the real thing," he told her. That's when she called the counterterrorist center and got Heidi.

Moynihan never went out for her birthday dinner. Day turned into night. She worked for hours. Washington was nine hours behind. Heidi needed a photo, and the walk-ins had brought one, which Patricia tried to fax. Problem was, Karachi was a small base and didn't have enough bandwidth to fax, so she called New Delhi and asked that station to shut down their communications channel to free up bandwith. New Delhi effectively told her to fuck herself; they weren't shutting down for Karachi, run by a GS-12 female. So Moynihan called Islamabad Station, who called New Delhi Station. She watched her screen as New Delhi's system went down. Now she could fax a photo. The face in the photo was fleshier, now, and older.

Back in Washington, Heidi recalls standing at her own fax machine, having called FBI agent Brad Garrett, who had investigated the crime scene and worked the case for four years. They stood together watching the fax.

Kansi, they knew, had a nick on one of his earlobes. The thin fax paper started unspooling, and a face began emerging: the top of his head, his hair, his forehead, his nose. "And the thing was coming down and down, and we finally get to the ear. And sure enough there's this little indentation in his earlobe. And Brad said, 'Holy fuck.'"

When Heidi headed to see Dave Cohen, the head of operations, his secretary told them he was in a meeting. "I think you're going to want to interrupt him," Heidi remembers saying. She and her boss went into Cohen's office, "and I said, 'Okay, we got him. We found him. Or we know somebody now who can get him.'"

Cohen, she recalled, leapt out of his chair and headed to get George Tenet, who also talked to Moynihan during the inevitable financial negotiations; the tribesmen wanted $3.5 million, almost twice the advertised reward. Tenet said yes. Heidi enlisted her deputy and a few others, who obtained paperwork from the Justice Department and bearer's bonds to pay the informants. That took a couple of days. Garrett boarded a plane accompanied by Heidi's deputy. They were joined by officers from Islamabad Station.

On June 15, a little over two weeks after Patricia Moynihan called Heidi, Mir Aimal Kansi was staying at a guest house called the Shalimar Hotel. At four A.M., as he was preparing for prayers, a joint FBI-CIA team, aided by Pakistani intelligence officers, quietly approached the hotel, disguised in the loose garments known as shalwar kameez, with weapons underneath.

WHILE THE CAPTURE OPERATION was in process, Heidi drove her Mercedes to a Jewish deli in Maryland that DDO Dave Cohen liked, picking out an array of cold cuts and cheeses. She headed over the Potomac back to Langley, and made her way to the Global Response Center, a counterterrorism operations center on the sixth floor of headquarters, where she laid out the bounty. Tenet, Cohen, and other officers joined her, gathering around the "Kansi café." They knew it could be a long night.

Across the world, the arrest team had been told the hotel door would be unlocked, with no security guard. Instead, it was locked and a security guard let them in. His eyes widened when he saw them. The men ran upstairs, kicked down the door, wrestled a startled Mir Aimal Kansi to the floor, and handcuffed him. The radio to which Heidi and the others were intently listening came alive with the code phrase "Red Zulu!" People started high-fiving and backslapping. Tenet lit a "victory cigar," dropping so many ashes that a framed piece of burned carpet was later hung in the room.

Several days later, Heidi went to Dulles Airport, where she, Tenet, and others gathered in a building at the end of the runway. The plane carrying Kansi descended, rolled along the tarmac, and stopped, close enough so that they could see the door as it opened. "Brad got off with this guy in handcuffs," said Heidi, "and we high-fived and we had a party." Around headquarters, "wanted" posters with Kansi's face still hung. Overnight, the group had the printing office print up banners that said "Captured." They slapped the banners onto the posters. When the workforce arrived the next morning, the reaction was ecstatic. Tenet invited the FBI to a celebratory ceremony that concluded with Bruce Springsteen's "Born in the USA." Heidi felt the operation would not have succeeded without Patricia Moynihan's adept handling of things, working seamlessly and productively with the FBI and State. When Moynihan and Scott Jessee wrote cables to their respective headquarters, they worked side by side so there would be no daylight between them.

Mir Aimal Kansi was executed in prison in Jarratt, Virginia, on November 14, 2002. Capital punishment was not Heidi's preferred conclusion. The FBI saw the shooting as a crime; she saw it as terrorism. If he was working with confederates, she said, "we'll never know."

THE CELEBRATION WAS SHORT-LIVED. While a single murderer had been brought to justice, thousands more were amassing. For the entirety of 1998, Cindy Storer's analytic antennae had been quivering about another attack. In the spring of that year, Osama bin Laden published a fatwa in an Arab newspaper in London, announcing that "to kill Americans and their allies—civilian and military—is an individual duty for every Muslim." Alec Station noted in an internal report that this was "the first religious ruling sanctifying such attacks" and warned that sooner or later, he would "attack US interests."

Over the past two years, Cindy had seen plots forming around the world, some fomented by al-Qaeda and others by what they suspected were allied groups. A cell in Manila hatched a plot to bring down twelve US airplanes over the Pacific Ocean; another to attack the pope; another to fly a plane into CIA headquarters. Those plots failed, but they were deeply disturbing. Cindy could see that certain major figures—bin Laden, Khalid Sheikh Mohammed, and Ramzi Yousef—were all connected, but she still didn't understand how. In 1996, a senior member of bin Laden's organization was killed in a ferry accident in Africa, so they knew there must be a cell in that area.

Now the terrorists were sending the kinds of signals they needed to send before mounting another attack, using specific religious rhetoric that Cindy recognized.

In the late summer of 1998, Cindy wrote a memo arguing that bin Laden's organization had trained in multiple car bombings and had a pattern of staging simultaneous attacks. Once again, she could not get traction. In her prolonged frustration, Cindy had decided to rotate to a related project involving a Middle Eastern country. Talking to Barbara Sude, she suggested Barbara take her place as the bin Laden analyst. Barbara had joined the counterterrorism center the previous year, working Hezbollah.

Barbara said she would think it over.

ON FRIDAY, AUGUST 7, 1998, Barbara Sude drove to Charlottesville, Virginia, to pick up her son from camp at UVA. Her husband was gassing up the car and listening to the radio. He called to say major explosions had just occurred at two US embassies in East Africa. In Dar es Salaam, Tanzania, a white pickup had driven to the embassy and tried to enter a gated area just as a large water tanker was exiting. A passenger got out to demand admittance. The pickup exploded. The water truck absorbed much of the blast, but a guard was killed, and waiting visa applicants were killed or badly injured. Ten minutes later, a bomb went off near the US embassy in Nairobi, Kenya, in a congested urban area where drivers, pedestrians, and street vendors were hit by flying concrete, metal, and glass. Inside the embassy, most American officials were in a meeting on the other side of the building, so it was African embassy workers who took the brunt of the blasts. The bombs killed 224 people, including a dozen Americans, and injured more than five thousand, mostly Kenyans.

"I guess I'm working on bin Laden now," Barbara Sude told her boss when she came into work on Monday. Her boss looked at her as if he did not understand why she said that.

TO BE SURE, CONVENTIONAL wisdom at the CIA still pointed to other possible perpetrators, namely an established group like Hezbollah. This was the assumption of Gary Berntsen, a CIA case officer detailed to the unit focused on the terrorist arm of Hezbollah, who

traveled to Tanzania to track down perpetrators of the embassy bombings. With him was one of the women from Alec Station, whom he
refers to by the pseudonym Donna in his book *Jawbreaker*. Meeting
with an African law enforcement contact, he asked for a list of suspected terrorists in the region. Assuming Hezbollah was behind the
twin bombings—who else would be capable of such a well-timed, con-
certed effort?—he scanned the list looking for Lebanese and Jordanian
names.

Donna opened his eyes to another possibility. "Say it's not Hezbollah," she suggested. "Say we're looking at Sunni extremists like Osama
bin Laden." She explained that al-Qaeda was using NGOs—charities
created to build hospitals and feed children—to "transfer money, build
and transport bombs and move personnel," and suggested he ask for
lists of NGOs. Sure enough, when a personal secretary to bin Laden,
Wadih El Hage, was arrested a few days later, it emerged that he'd
planned the bombings under cover of an NGO called Help Africa People. Mohammed Sadiq Odeh, a perpetrator of the Nairobi bombing,
had been immediately arrested in Karachi for using a false passport;
flown back to Kenya, he shared "everything he knew about Osama bin
Laden and al-Qaeda."

The embassy attacks were conclusively linked to al-Qaeda. Alec Station's Donna, Berntsen realized, "was correct." To him, this was a "profound" revelation in that it put bin Laden in the company of Hezbollah
in terms of being able to conduct "large scale bombings of US targets."
Within weeks, two perpetrators were rendered to the United States and
later convicted, in 2001. More followed. In November, bin Laden and
several members of his network were named in an indictment. Also
indicted was a terrorist named Ayman Al-Zawahiri. When Cindy
Storer wrote an item for the PDB, she was—for the first time—allowed
to use the term "al-Qaeda." It had taken five years.

"Nobody was taking it seriously until after the Africa bombings, and
even then it was hard to get through," said Barbara Sude. Cindy, she
noted, was the first to try to put things together, with her paper that
never got published, and even now Barbara ran into some of the same
problems. In 1999, Barbara was asked to contribute an item to an annual unclassified compendium of patterns of global terrorism, pub-

lished by the State Department for the greater government community. She wanted to write an item presenting bin Laden as a "major terrorist leader of this big terrorist organization," but her manager suggested she was making bin Laden too much of a big shot. At the agency, resources had not shifted, and she sensed her manager was overwhelmed. "It's all a matter of who gets the money," recalled Barbara, musing that this is speculation, of course, but "speculation based on the history of bureaucracy."

AS BARBARA SUDE SETTLED in as the new bin Laden analyst, she perceived that the counterterrorist center was still underresourced and low priority, despite the growing scope and ferocity of overseas attacks. Case officers still saw it as a backwater. Within Washington, the twin Africa bombings did unleash a new understanding of the threat the US was facing, and a wave of disagreement over how to respond. For all the public impression that the CIA can do what it wants, where it wants, the truth was that the agency was legally constrained by a law forbidding foreign assassinations. So—what could be done about Osama bin Laden, short of killing him deliberately?

Gender factored into this quandary, in a complex way that reflected President Bill Clinton's problematic relationship to women. When Clinton took office in 1993, one of his much-touted goals was appointing the first female attorney general. While welcome to many, Clinton's efforts to promote women had the flavor of a medieval sinner purchasing indulgences from the Catholic Church, in that his so-called feminism also aimed to persuade women's groups to overlook serial marital infidelities. The AG pick turned out to be harder than expected. His first nominee, Zoë Baird, was disqualified for having employed illegal immigrants, as a babysitter and driver, and not paid their Social Security taxes. A second pick, Kimba Wood, had also employed an illegal alien as nanny. Clinton landed on Janet Reno, a former Florida state attorney general who had the (in this case) advantage of being unmarried and childless. Reno was six feet one inch tall, short-haired, and matter-of-fact about fashion; she wore near-identical blue dresses ordered from the same catalog. Naturally, she was made fun of by late-night comics, whose ribbing was tinged with speculation about whether she might be, you know, a lesbian. The actor Will Ferrell played Reno on *Saturday Night Live;* the comedian Jay Leno joked about Reno having to choose between "boxers or briefs." When one member of Congress referred to her as "General" Reno, she affably informed him that "general," in the title "attorney general," functioned as an adjective, not a noun.

One of the first challenges Reno faced was a religious cult, the Branch Davidians, holed up in a bunker in Waco, Texas, under the leadership of a madman named David Koresh. Koresh declared himself a messiah and children born to him as sacred. He "married" several women in his congregation, fathered more than a dozen children with different women, and amassed a cache of illegal arms. In late February 1993—the same month of the first WTC attack—the Bureau of Alcohol, Tobacco, and Firearms served arrest warrants on the compound. An epically botched fifty-one-day standoff followed, in which the FBI tried everything from loud music to Abrams tanks to bring the cult members out. Nearly nine hundred law enforcement officials joined the siege. On April 19, the FBI raided the compound; a fire broke out, cult members were trapped, and seventy-six people, including children, died.

The Waco incident fresh on her mind, Janet Reno approached every operation involving bin Laden with one question: How many women and children are at risk?

The answer often amounted to: (1) quite a few but (2) they didn't know exactly how many. Bin Laden—a polygamist like Koresh—secured his own safety by surrounding himself with a phalanx of wives and the children they bore for him. The problem arose over and over, as Alec Station floated plans to get bin Laden apprehended. In Scheuer's view, bin Laden's move to Afghanistan was a "godsend" in that the CIA could reawaken old networks from its days running the Afghan war. They had assets and knew the terrain. In late 1997 and early 1998, Alec Station had devised a plan to capture bin Laden and bring him to the United States to stand trial. Bin Laden's whereabouts were no longer open, but he was by no means impossible to find. Tribal assets provided what Tenet called "some very good tracking data" revealing that bin

Laden was living in a compound called Tarnak Farms, from which he commuted to the city of Kandahar, twelve miles away, to do business.

Alec Station devised a plan for the tribesmen to enter the compound and overpower guards. They'd capture bin Laden, roll him up in a carpet, and hide him until the United States could exfiltrate him to stand trial. The agency ran four rehearsals in late 1997 and early 1998. "No capture plan before 9/11 ever again attained the same level of detail and preparation," the 9/11 Commission Report would later point out.

But CIA officials felt the chances of success were low. The seventh floor worried that it would look too much like the CIA assassinations of old. Sandy Berger worried that bin Laden might be acquitted. Janet Reno worried about the wives and the children. Heidi August felt as if she were watching a ping-pong match between Mike Scheuer and Geoff O'Connell and the FBI and Janet Reno. In the end, Tenet accepted the opinion of senior officers who felt "the chances of killing innocent women and children were too high."

The Alec team could not forgive him. After the 1998 embassy bombing, Tenet paid a visit to Alec Station, where one of the female members approached him and, "quivering with emotion, confronted me about my Tarnak Farms decision. 'If you had allowed us to go ahead with our operation,' she said, 'those people might still be alive.'" Tenet, in his memoir, said it was a "tough moment" and "of course I had some self-doubt" but that "given the emotion of the moment, I let the analyst vent and just walked away."

When Tenet's memoir was published, many female CIA officers noticed the phrase "quivering with emotion" and resented its implication that the women on the team were emotional and weak. If anybody was weak, in the minds of the Alec women, it was the people at the top, who seemed to find it "impossible to comprehend, to appreciate the gravity of this," said Alfreda Bikowsky, who felt that US officials kept hoping "some other country will do something." To her mind, top officials persisted in dismissing bin Laden's declarations as propaganda; they seemed unaccustomed to a leader who did not prevaricate or hedge his intentions. To the contrary, he was making his intentions all too clear. "It was strange," she thinks, "to be Americans and hear a leader say what he means and mean what he says," she said. "I don't think they

believed it." In response to the 1998 embassy attacks, the Clinton administration ordered missile strikes on a training camp in Khost, Afghanistan, and a pharmaceutical factory in Khartoum that was suspected
of producing nerve gas. People died, but bin Laden was not among
them.

THE OPERATIONAL WOMEN OF Alec Station continued looking for
opportunities. "You guys are going to be out of the job because we're
going to get him," one told Barbara Sude. (Barbara thought of the operational women of Alec as the "arm twisters.") Toward the end of 1998,
Alec Station proposed a missile attack on a house in Kandahar where
bin Laden was known to be staying. But the administration was reluctant to conduct air strikes. The president's personal problems continued
to influence events: During the entirety of 1998, the sordid sex scandal
unfolded in which the world learned Clinton had embarked on an affair in early 1995 with White House intern Monica Lewinsky. Newspaper columnists conjectured that Clinton might resort to the scenario
depicted in *Wag the Dog*, a 1997 movie in which a president initiates a
military strike to distract from private problems. This consideration
might or might not have factored into any decision, but either way, senior officials nixed the strike, and Scheuer was "so upset he was unable
to sleep."

In early 1999, Alec Station had evidence that bin Laden would stay
at a hunting camp near Kandahar on February 11. Officials from the
United Arab Emirates were nearby, however, so the administration vac-
illated. By February 12, he was gone. Scheuer later estimated that the
women of Alec had given the US government ten chances to capture or
kill bin Laden. Richard Clarke disagreed, saying Alec Station "never
penetrated al-Qaeda" and could not provide pinpointed information.
Scheuer and Clarke both blamed Tenet, who wrote that the agency was
not in the business of assassinations; others blamed the Pentagon.

Operations officer Gary Berntsen ran into Mike Scheuer and noted
Scheuer's clear disgust at the failure to bomb the hunting camp. They
commiserated about how President Clinton was averse to military action and felt the same way about George Tenet. "It was a frustrating

time," said Berntsen. At headquarters, conversation began about changing the approach—disruption, arrests, and rendering—to something more aggressive.

BARBARA SUDE SET ABOUT working with the files Cindy Storer had left when she departed the bin Laden desk. Barbara assembled a schema of top al-Qaeda leadership and tried to fill in gaps. There was still much the analysts didn't know: Who was bin Laden's number two? The terrorist Ayman al-Zawahiri ran a group called Egyptian Islamic Jihad, but they didn't know whether, or how, his group was connected to al-Qaeda. Each arrest yielded more documents, more transcripts. Hazy facts would become concrete—but not always the facts they needed, and not always at the right time. Incoming intelligence also included false information.

The volume was enormous, the counterterrorism center's analytic unit tiny. It consisted of just thirty—count them, thirty—analysts writing about all terrorists, everywhere. The unit focused on bin Laden and al-Qaeda had two dedicated analysts writing PDBs and longer papers. These were Barbara and a male colleague, with help from Gina Bennett. Each day, when Barbara came to work, there would be five hundred new emails, six hundred new messages, a thousand left over from the day before. When she was writing a PDB—and she usually was—she didn't have a chance to read anything apart from messages that helped her update the item. Scanning her inbox, she might note a new item—"Oh, that looks scary"—and never have the chance to look back at it.

Software in the CTC routinely crashed, and they had no good way of filing things electronically. She put important emails in a special folder, but was always getting internal messages saying storage was limited and inboxes must be pruned. Barbara began printing out hard copies of key papers; she was the office laughingstock with big piles on her small desk. Barbara put painstaking work into a wiring diagram to depict the hierarchy of al-Qaeda, but the chart didn't look like anything the managers were used to seeing, and she couldn't gin up interest. She stored it, and when new people came in—specialists, say, dealing with personalities—then she would show them: *Here's a copy of my chart. It's got my sources in it. So go ahead and use it.*

The problem was obvious to Susan Hasler, a new branch chief who arrived in the summer of 2000 to supervise publication of the work of all analysts in the entire CTC. Hasler was a wry, funny, ironic woman who grew up in a conservative, Mennonite-dominated community in Virginia's Shenandoah Valley, where, under the influence of Bella Abzug and Simone de Beauvoir, she conceived ambitions out of sync with the culture. She was a top student at a public school where it was a given that boys would take the best prizes and get the best jobs. Her schoolmates thought it was hilarious to refer to "women's lib" as "women's lip."

Like Gina Bennett, Susan Hasler had been the victim of sexual predation. As a girl, she was molested by a preacher who came by their home when her parents weren't there. In the absence of anyone to turn to—her mother had not even warned her about menstruation—she decided, as she put it, not to let men profess to teach her religion. For much of her agency career, Hasler worked in the Office of Soviet Analysis, where the volume of material was smaller even during crises. During the coup that installed Boris Yeltsin, she got perhaps a couple hundred items in her inbox per day.

With terrorism, it could be a few thousand.

Hasler also saw that analysts here were not only swamped but disrespected. The seventh floor had them pegged as "a culture of people who tracked stuff." Yet nothing, she realized, could be further from the truth. Cindy, Gina, and Barbara struck her as enormously impressive. Immersed in a wholly new kind of data stream, the analysts, not the managers, were the people innovating an "entirely different type of analysis." Susan had worked all around the building, and the CTC "relied on collaboration more than any other place." There was a mass of information. Everybody saw a different part. "If Analyst A sees one piece and analyst B sees the other, it's meaningless unless B knows what A needs to know." For terrorism, she saw, you need big databases, you need information where it can be discovered by others.

The seventh floor didn't understand how capable the center's analysts were—far more knowledgeable, often, than the midlevel managers directly above them. Prevailing was "an attitude that managers knew best," Susan Hasler later reflected. In the basement vault, she said, what the analysts walked into, every day, was "just stress and a gray room."

With few people at the top to look out for them, the women looked out for each other. Gina Bennett admired Barbara Sude, seeing her intellectual caution as a valuable corrective. "She's very academic, very by the book, very objective," said Gina. "She's always been that way—never prone to exaggeration or hyperbole. If someone says 'always,' she says, 'let's be careful, it's not always.'" Barbara had an encyclopedic memory and hyperrational approach. "When it comes to the tradecraft of what we do, keeping that objectivity and removing the emotion and the bias, she was extremely good at that."

Gina's own ability to disassociate, owing to her own childhood trauma, enabled her to take a philosophical approach to policymakers' failure to react in a coherent way. She understood that the American people were relieved by the retreat of the nuclear threat, and slow to acknowledge a new one. "That is the downside of being a decent analyst. Anybody can be an analyst. It's hard to be a decent analyst. If you are a decent analyst, you're able to forecast things that are going to happen. And people can't believe them. You have to wait ten years."

ONE DAY, AS AMERICA anticipated the approach of a new millennium, CIA general counsel John Rizzo found himself standing in a hallway talking to the new head of the clandestine service. As George Tenet endeavored to reinvigorate an agency that was somewhat flailing, he brought out of retirement a square-jawed, Harvard-educated former Marine named Jack Downing to direct operations. Chatting with Rizzo, Downing was gossiping about Mike Scheuer. "I can't believe this guy Scheuer just hired—the only people who work for him are girls," said Downing. It was a small moment, but significant enough that Rizzo never forgot the term the director of operations used about the women of Alec Station. "I remember him saying 'girls,'" Rizzo recalled in an interview for this book, before his death in 2021. "He wanted to, you know, get rid of Mike, and put some—get some hardball guys in there."

There now ensued much talk, in the halls, of who had *cojones* and who did not. "I was urging Tenet to get somebody to run the CTC who had balls," the NSC's Richard Clarke later told a reporter. In 1999, to move the needle, Tenet also installed a new head of the counterterrorism center: Cofer Black, an operations officer who had made his name with the capture of the assassin Carlos the Jackal. "People said he had 'brass balls,' and he spent a lot of time talking about 'body bags,'" said Richard Clarke, describing the hall-file conversation around Cofer Black. Tenet said he didn't know Black personally, "but by all reports he's got big *cojones*." Under his leadership, the approach would be more forward-leaning, entailing going into Afghanistan and working with Ahmad Massoud, the head of the Northern Alliance—the chief opposition to the Taliban—to capture bin Laden.

Mike Scheuer was deposed and exiled to a vague position working in the CIA library. In his place, Tenet assigned a veteran operations officer, Rich Blee, to head Alec Station. Asked to describe Blee, one female operations officer gave it some thought and said, "Well, he was—normal." Scheuer angrily reflected that he was the victim of what amounted to gender discrimination: "We'll get rid of these little DI people and women."

THE WOMEN OF ALEC were also angry about their boss's defenestration, but they themselves survived it. They retained their jobs and—in an environment where genitalia now occupied so much conversation—their demeanors. It was around this time that Alfreda Bikowsky formally joined the unit as chief of operations, and the result, at first, was a bit of an internal standoff; Jennifer Matthews "came right over to my desk," Bikowsky later recalled, and said she had one question: "Are you just going to take all of my cases?" Happy that somebody—anybody—had come over to greet her, Bikowsky replied that she didn't plan to, whereupon Matthews, who was known as a bulldog, "just laughed and said, 'All right, okay, just setting the tone here.'" The two women became close and Bikowsky found her friend "refreshingly candid." But outsiders, especially female ones, didn't always get a warm welcome: In 1999, a first-time case officer who remains undercover—I'll call her "Mallory"—

paid a courtesy call to Alec Station before her overseas assignment to Peshawar. Mallory was surprised when Bikowsky and Matthews turned out to be "extremely mean." Their manner seemed counterproductive, given that Mallory, overseas, would be able to collect information on their behalf.

Along with her on the courtesy call was another first-timer, a male case officer en route to Islamabad. "They were super nice to him and then extremely rude and condescending to me," Mallory remembered. "Even the case officer, when we left, was like, 'What was that?' And I was like, 'I don't know.'"

Thinking about it later, she felt she understood why they acted as they did. "No one cared about al-Qaeda at that time. And they were females and honest to God, females were treated like crap." Plus, Mallory had a credential—full operational training—which the women of Alec lacked. There was always tension between people who attended the Farm and those who had not. Still. "I'm like, 'Look, lady, you've never done it. Why are you being a bitch to me?'"

Their pugnacity also came through in written communications. In Peshawar, Mallory noticed that whenever a reports officer changed any wording while transmitting a request from Alec Station, the women "would get very mad at that. They had a, like how dare you?" She sensed that the chip on their shoulders was owing in part to old-fashioned CIA turf wars. "They were resentful of Near East, because we owned Earth. They owned the target."

LIKE HEIDI AUGUST AND Lisa Harper before her, Mallory found that being female often worked to her advantage. A lot of Arab men had not spent much time with women outside their homes and felt curious to meet her. "They never think you're a threat. They look at us like they look at their own women, right? So, they look at us as like, what could she possibly know? And if she did, what is she going to do with it?" After a first encounter, she found "it was extremely easy for me to get a second date"—that is, a next meeting with a potential asset. She and her female colleagues called it "operational dating," behaving as a woman might in the early, rosy dating stages. "We are like the perfect girlfriend," she said. "Fantasy football, how awesome! We listen to everything. We never let the crazy out."

On plane rides, she'd prep by reading tabloids. Some of the people she dealt with were kings; some were national security advisers; everybody enjoyed hearing about Jennifer Aniston or Michael Jackson. She tried to take a light-hearted approach to elicitation. "When you treat it like gossip, the people don't think it's betraying their country. You're just talking, and everybody knows gossiping is a little bit wrong, but it's awesome."

But the atmosphere was ominous and sometimes terrifying. Driving around Pakistan in 1999, Mallory could see Taliban soldiers on street corners, wearing the short skirts that marked them as Salafis, as jihadi. The Taliban were ruthless; they took their enemies out into the desert, in crates, and left them to broil alive. Mallory sensed the rising threat of an attack by al-Qaeda. "We were collecting information the entire time about them wanting to and preparing to," she said. "We knew they were a danger. I don't think I knew it was as imminent, because it's almost like you get inured to it. You're in the middle of being threatened every day for two years. And you kind of can't be on that heightened level the whole time." The work was so tough that "you don't realize how stressed you are until you're out of it. Every time I would go on R and R I would get extremely sick."

She, too, wished the Clinton administration had been more aggressive in its approach to bin Laden. "We had all kinds of chances to take him out."

CHAPTER 19

"I'VE GOT A TARGET ON MY BACK"

SUMMER OF 2000

Rockville, Maryland

LISA MANFULL HARPER'S FIRST THOUGHT, WHEN RICHARD BLEE called and asked to meet with her—then materialized at her front door, all six feet and more of him filling her living room with his presence—was that he had shown up to seduce her. But no, not at all. Blee had come to seek her help. Lisa, intrigued, sat down and listened.

After stepping down as the first female division chief in CIA history, Lisa Harper had spent a full year following her doctor's regimen to repair the damage from the brain injury that felled her. It was the first time in a thirty-year career that Lisa had slowed down to see to her own well-being. By the summer of 2000, she was recovered, but no longer on a career track. Now in her mid-fifties, she was living in Rockville, Maryland, trying to decide what to do with the rest of her life.

Lisa's ex-husband had by now remarried. He'd gone on to have children and sometimes sent her photos. Thumbing through his family pictures made Lisa a little sad—he hadn't wanted children when they married, and by the time they'd started trying, it was too late—but she was glad to see such beautiful kids. He was a brilliant, handsome man, and she wondered what his life would have been like if he'd married a different woman from the get-go. As Lisa grew into her own gifts, he used to ask, "Where is the sweet little girl I married?"

Lisa regretted being compelled to retire from the CIA, especially at such a senior rank. She told herself she'd fought the good fight. She still had a few years before she qualified for a full pension, however, so she'd gotten certified to teach at a CIA training facility not far away. But when she took a tour there, she sensed the same old "sexist garbage." The men who made her work life so difficult were now retiring and, like her, coming back as annuitants—retirees on contract. Many annuitant jobs involved duties like paperwork and declassification, whereas teaching was fun and paid well. She heard so many muttered remarks that she thought, "I can't do this. The old boys really don't want me in here." She'd been approached by a private company—the kind of lucrative government contractor where lots of retired intelligence officers end up. The CEO called her an "opportunist," as if that were a good thing. He sought Lisa's ability to spot targets and reel them in. His approach turned her off, so she cast about for a way to employ her talents.

She was surprised when the phone rang that summer. On the other end was Blee, an operations officer who, like Lisa, had served in Francophone Africa. Rich's voice was urgent, and he asked if he could talk to her. Lisa said yes. Now here he was. A big terrorist attack was coming and it was his job to stop it, he told her. "I've got a target on my back," is how he put it. He wanted Lisa to come out of retirement and join Alec Station.

Lisa wasn't done with headquarters after all.

HER NEW BOSS, RICH BLEE, was a veteran ops guy—the son of David Blee, he had a legacy CIA pedigree. Rich was straightforward and experienced and Lisa, who'd crossed paths with him in Africa, liked him. Rich knew of Lisa and understood her to be "the real thing."

Rich Blee also understood the peace-dividend constraints CIA director George Tenet was facing in the summer of 2000. Before taking over as head of Alec Station, Blee had gotten a taste of the dynamics of the seventh floor while serving as an executive assistant for Tenet. Executive assistant is a high-level but thankless staff job that entails trailing the principal and making things happen—teeing up meetings, writing down action items, handling logistics. But working on the seventh floor had given Blee a sense of the situation with which he would be dealing.

George Tenet—Clinton's third CIA director—had been appointed in 1997, after serving as deputy to the much-disliked John Deutch. A former Capitol Hill staffer, Tenet was eyed with suspicion, at first, as an outsider and a glad-handing creature of Capitol Hill. Every director faces an institutional learning curve: When Tenet ascended to director, someone in his entourage felt he needed décor worthy of the station. According to one administrative staffer, a monumental door, complete with sconces, was installed at the entrance to the director's office. The agency likes to consider itself an egalitarian place and people thought Tenet's grandiose door was hilarious. It became a "laughingstock in minutes," as the staffer put it, and people would stop by just to gaze upon it. Tenet had the sense to ask people what they thought of the door. Before long, it vanished, replaced by a normal one.

Tenet was personable and endearing, and more popular than Deutch. But everybody who knew him agreed he did not like making hard choices about money—decisions where one person won and another lost. By the time Rich Blee was staffing up Alec Station, resources at the agency had been cut by a third. The workforce was being cannibalized; managers were stealing each other's staff. Funding a new initiative meant taking funds from an existing one. Tenet didn't like to do that. "You would tee something up, you would say, okay, George, you want to give more to the—fill in the blank, terrorism—here are five places where you could find a million dollars to take it from," said one staffer. "And we would leave the meeting with no money because, well, we can't cut that."

Tenet was a guy's guy; his memoir, *At the Center of the Storm*, published in 2007, is prefaced by a list of "Principal Characters" he worked with. Of the thirty-two names, some well known, some less so— Lt. Gen. John "Soup" Campbell, "Doc" O'Connor, chief of his security detail—just three were female. One was Jami Miscik, head of the analytic directorate at the time. The others were his two assistants. He liked cigars and maintained an open-door policy that the men knew how to take advantage of. In the scramble for funds, barons would back-channel him, saying, *George, you can't believe what I'm doing this program on!* The barons knew all the games: If you get a freebie one year—if Congress gives you a supplemental appropriation—and you don't get it the next year, you buttonhole George and sputter that you've suffered a 25 percent budget cut. The old boys would do this, and Tenet would go: *Jesus Christ!* The director's own description of the female analyst at Alec Station "quivering with emotion" seems ironic given the histrionics among the men in Tenet's orbit. There was shouting and door slamming, much of which flowed from the director and his big personality. "It was all this macho crap from the DO, and it mattered a lot where you sat," said one female analytic officer, meaning that it mattered where, at the table, a person sat during a meeting. Tenet "liked having his group of guys" was her impression. There was a certain fraternity atmosphere. "They acted like guys. They could play basketball at lunchtime."

For his part, Richard Blee appreciated the extent of the terrorist threat. As chief of station in Algiers, he had witnessed firsthand the bloody consequences of Islamic extremism, watching Algeria go from a peaceful country to one engaged in a civil war where tens of thousands died. It was Blee's sense that a "large number" of his seventh-floor colleagues "thought the al-Qaeda threat was not real; that it was being blown out of proportion," and that they worked to protect Tenet from hearing too much about it. Blee did some back-channeling of his own, warning Tenet that if he wasn't careful, terrorism would "bite you in the ass." Upon replacing Scheuer as head of Alec Station, Blee set out to steer the battleship differently by, among other things, improving relations with the FBI.

Alec Station by then consisted of maybe two dozen people. About 80 percent were women, mostly analysts, some running operations. Blee saw the setup as good in that the analysts were fearless and creative; bad, in that their operational guidance was not always drawn from knowledge of what worked. In the subterranean counterterrorism center, it felt like the nation was already at war, and Blee was trying to build an army. It was easier to hire an annuitant than lure officers from other divisions or hire from the outside. Blee knew that the early women case officers had to be tough and smart. He also knew Lisa Harper was "a real Mata Hari spy" who was "brilliant and underemployed."

AND SO LISA MANFULL Harper also joined the sisterhood of Alec Station, badging back into headquarters just a few years after badging out. When she punched in the vault code and opened the door to the counterterrorism center, Lisa liked what she saw. For ten years, the CIA had been uncertain what to focus on. Here, now, was something like the Cold War. Here was a worthy adversary. The office environment was dingy, but she had worked in worse places.

Far from feeling demoted, Lisa Harper felt freed. After occupying the ranks of top CIA management, it did not seem odd to come back on a lower level. To the contrary: She was back in her wheelhouse. Working in a bare-bones operation alongside overworked comrades, she felt like a young case officer again. She didn't have to manage people or worry about being sabotaged by colleagues. As much as she had believed in defeating Communism, she believed in this mission. All the indicators were that al-Qaeda was preparing something big.

Lisa, with her fluent French and regional expertise, was assigned to focus on terrorist cells in Africa. Her role was to find leads and guide collection. She, too, was now helping define and refine the new field of targeting, which had begun in the mid-1990s as a way of fighting nuclear proliferation; targeters helped with the excruciatingly tough job of studying hard-target countries such as Iran; sussing the very few potential assets who travelled in and out, maybe attending an annual conference in another country, who might know nuclear secrets. This kind of intense focus on figures of interest was what vault women had done in the past; but what was different, now, was that targeters also told ops officers how to make an approach. The field was gaining currency, nowhere more than in the counterterrorist center. Much work thwarting terrorists comes down to understanding—and tracking—relationships among people. That's what al-Qaeda was. It wasn't a country or a government; it was *people*, globally dispersed, in relationships with one another, who had to find ways to communicate or meet. Locating a person often required finding the people who knew that person.

Targeting amounts to contact tracing of criminals engaged in clandestine plotting. It requires figuring out who was talking to whom—

and how often—and whom those two people were also talking to. Every time Lisa read a cable or intercept suggesting person X talked to person Y, who then talked to person Z, she and colleagues could start building that into the contact tracing. If person X talked to Y another twenty times, the line connecting them became darker. If Z, X, and Y were talking a lot, and if X was a known bomb maker, they could watch a plot develop as the lines thickened. Then the Alec team would start trying to figure out how to penetrate the network.

Exciting as the work was, the atmosphere felt oppressive. In most operations, there was no imminent threat to American lives. Lisa well knew how hard a terrorist group is to penetrate. Terrorist groups are not states, but they do maintain counterintelligence units; if a member were to disappear briefly—say, to meet a CIA case officer—the counterintelligence arm of al-Qaeda would take note.

And unlike, say, a Russian asset, most terrorists couldn't be recruited by dangling a Western lifestyle. They didn't want a Western lifestyle. They wanted a fundamentalist way of life. Al-Qaeda populated its ranks with men who were troubled or outcasts, men who would be true believers. She was reading all the time, looking for that rare recruitable person. Somebody with access, who wasn't a member but had dealings with them. Despite having recovered her health, Lisa felt sick to her stomach. There were so many targets. You could only watch so many places. Lisa had never seen people working so long, so late. People brought food. George Tenet came down to visit. Lisa liked Tenet. He was talking to the analysts, talking to case officers.

The center had a casual, nonhierarchical feel; someone would call out, asking who wanted to go overseas, and hands would go up. The place was in constant need of people. Scanning a list of annuitants, Lisa spotted the name of her colleague who'd had the affair at the Farm, lo these many years ago, and called her. "I'm a pariah," the woman protested. It didn't matter, Lisa assured her. "You're a good officer."

WHEN LISA ARRIVED, the counterterrorist center had just emerged from a hectic period and the pace was reaching a new pitch. As 1999 gave way to 2000, Americans had braced for a "Y2K" disaster, when, it was feared, digital clocks would roll over and the last two zeros of "2000" would make computers think it was 1900. It wasn't clear what would happen then—Fires? Alarm bells? Financial meltdown? In the end, nothing much did. The millennium was ushered in with a rather wan fireworks display over the National Mall, and life proceeded.

Within the center, however, millennium-related anxiety was more acute and specific. Islamic extremists knew the year 2000 had significance for the West, but the traffic Alec Station was reading suggested al-Qaeda thought the import was spiritual rather than digital—that the millennium, two thousand years after the birth of Christ, had great religious meaning for a largely Christian nation. It stood to reason that the adversary would attack then.

As Tenet noted in his memoir, by the end of 1999, the threat situation was "bad" and getting worse. The agency had responded with a "quiet but effective sweep" of Hezbollah in East Asia and a "disruption" campaign against the Iranian intelligence service that supported Hezbollah. Disruption entails harassment, sometimes comically basic. John Brennan, station chief in Saudi Arabia, knocked on the car window of the local head of the Iranian intelligence unit, knowing even this glancing contact could put his adversary under suspicion of being a CIA asset. In December, Jordanians arrested a team planning an attack in the country. All those efforts were against targets other than al-Qaeda. But Tenet wrote that "we told President Clinton that Usama Bin Ladin was planning between five and fifteen attacks around the world during the millennium and that some of these might be inside the United States." The agency launched operations "in fifty-five countries against thirty-eight targets."

Diana Bolsinger, an analyst in the counterterrorist center, remembered the months before and after January 1, 2000, as harrowing and impressive. Gone, for the time being, were the days of a "hard stop" and family balance. People were sleeping in the office. "It was a whole government just getting together and throwing everything we had. We were there Christmas, New Year's, and January, February." Plots were foiled and "we were preempting operations." One that became public was the attempted bombing of Los Angeles International Airport:

When a terrorist named Ahmed Ressam tried to cross into the United States from Canada, an alert US Customs official searched his car. In it were nitroglycerine and timing devices. Tenet admitted that "looking back, much more should have been made about the significance" of his attempted entry, because it "signaled al-Qaida was coming here." (He might also have noted that the attempt was thwarted by customs, not the CIA.) He felt the government-wide response was "managed haphazardly": Borders were not hardened, nor airplane cockpits.

But in the chaos, it emerged later, what also happened is that a key piece of intelligence got bottled up. Two suspected al-Qaeda members, Nawaf al-Hazmi and Khalid al-Mihdhar, attended an al-Qaeda summit meeting in Malaysia on January 5, 2000. The CIA was tracking them but failed to "watch-list" them with the State Department. The two flew into Los Angeles on January 15, and the CIA also failed to alert the FBI. According to a report by the inspector general, some "fifty to sixty" CIA officers read a cable in January, showing the two men coming to the US, and yet two CIA officials refused to let the FBI representative pass it on. The reason the cable never got sent would be much debated. Some said it did get sent, and the FBI lost track. The NSC's Richard Clarke speculated that Alec Station wanted to recruit the terrorists rather than hand them over. What the evidence does confirm is that many people assumed the next big attack would likely occur overseas.

BUT THERE WAS ANOTHER incident in which the analysts got it right—so right that it created new problems for them. During December 1999 and into January 2000, Gina Bennett and colleagues pieced together a plot hatched by top al-Qaeda officials in Afghanistan. The analysts knew bin Laden had been criticized for killing fellow Muslims in the 1998 embassy bombings, and their detective work suggested he intended to make up for it by hitting a hardened US military target. The analysts concluded that al-Qaeda planned to bomb the USS *The Sullivans*, a naval destroyer named after the five brothers who died when their ship was sunk in the Battle of Guadalcanal in World War II. The ship was moored in the port of Aden, in Yemen, the ancestral home of the bin Ladens.

The attack was set to occur on January 3, 2000, and the team spread the word. "We had an understanding of that chain of command and how it worked," said Gina. "We were warning and warning. A lot of people thought we were nuts."

January 3 came and went, and nothing happened.

Gina was glad the ship remained safe, of course. But the blowback was mortifying. "We got laughed at—ridiculed by our own colleagues, by the people we tried to protect, certainly by foreign liaison services. They all thought we had gone over the top."

In fact, the analysts were correct. Al-Qaeda had tried to bomb the USS *The Sullivans*. But the suicide bombers failed to get the shaped charge properly fitted into the hull of the attack boat and sank their own ship before it could reach the destroyer. Only years later, after the attacks of 9/11, did the details of the attempted attack become known. "After raiding camps and getting materials, when we started capturing people and materials, we were able to find out," she said. The news was "vindicating" but came "too late." For Gina, December 1999 had been "the worst Christmas."

It was worse than painful; the attack that never happened damaged the analysts' reputation, as did the apparent calm after such a big drumroll of anxious anticipation. "The fact that no attack took place during the millennium hurt us later," Gina reflected. "We went around to a lot of government and liaison services and put pressure on them to do what they could to disrupt al-Qaeda people in their country and traveling through. And when nothing happens, that's when we got a bad reputation for exaggerating, embellishing the threat."

An analyst's reputation has bearing on her ability to get buy-in. And if she can't get buy-in, she can't publish. Analysts working on a "functional" topic like terrorism couldn't publish an item in the PDB unless the regional office agreed to chop on its contents. It didn't work the other way: Regional analysts did not have to seek permission from Gina and her colleagues. It sounds like a bureaucratic distinction, but it mattered. "It was a lot of trying to persuade a lot of people just to get things out the door."

AFTER THE MISHAP WITH the USS *The Sullivans*, it took al-Qaeda nine months to rebuild and obtain more plastic explosives. In October 2000, an inflatable Zodiac-type speedboat—a suicide vessel loaded with five hundred pounds of explosives—blew a hole in the side of the USS *Cole*, a naval destroyer refueling in Yemen. Seventeen US service members were killed. The attack occurred weeks before the US presidential election. "The *Cole* attack was very disturbing to us," said Barbara Sude, who was shocked by the lack of policymaker reaction to an assault that amounted, in her view, to an act of war. "It was sickening," said Alfreda Bikowsky. "You're al-Qaeda. What do you think? Like: Oh my God, we just slaughtered [seventeen] sailors, and they're not going to do anything. They're going to do exactly nothing." By 2000, as operations officer Gary Berntsen points out, "al-Qaeda had established terrorist cells in as many as sixty countries around the world and had attracted thousands of young jihadists to its terrorist training camps and bases in eastern Afghanistan." Arrayed against them were a couple hundred CIA officers.

From Richard Blee's vantage point, it seemed likely the Clinton administration was trying to get through the November contest between Al Gore and George W. Bush before retaliating for the USS *Cole* incident in any potentially controversial way. But then the 2000 election deadlocked, owing in part to voter confusion over printed ballots in Florida—the nation was transfixed by the televised spectacle of manual vote counting and "hanging chads," little pieces of paper that made it hard to know which hole voters had intended to punch—and dragged into December. By the time the US Supreme Court ruled for Bush, the USS *Cole* felt like ancient history and the Clinton team no longer saw retaliation as its problem. The change of administration "had the greatest impact, in my estimation, on the war on terror," Tenet wrote. At "the top tier, there was a loss of urgency."

The advent of George Bush should have been an advantage for the CIA. As Tenet notes, his meetings with Bill Clinton had been "interesting" but sporadic. In contrast, the incoming president was the son of a former CIA director, and made it clear he wanted Tenet present at

PDB briefings. But the Bush administration was dominated by hard-line neoconservatives fixated on adversary states like Iraq and Iran—Vice President Dick Cheney; Secretary of Defense Donald Rumsfeld; Deputy Secretary of Defense Paul Wolfowitz—and these men could not accept that a network of fighters, commanded by men working from caves and obscure safe houses, a group with no army, no uniforms, no fighter jets, no advanced military hardware, had the ability to kill thousands at once. Their resistance amounted to yet another level of pushback, from NFL-quality push-backers. Tenet also had a hard time connecting with the lone woman on Bush's main national security team: National Security Advisor Condoleezza Rice, a Soviet expert, who, unlike her predecessor Sandy Berger, was not a back-slapper. Tenet found Rice "remote," pointing out that "she knew the president's mind well but tended to stay out of policy fights that Sandy would have come brawling into."

By March 2001, though, Tenet had visited the CTC often enough that his hair was on fire. He asked the president's team for authorization for CIA or its partners to "plan and carry out operations to kill UBL without first trying to capture him." Rice and her staff asked him to table the request for a few months. In February 2001, Tenet told the Senate that bin Laden was "capable of planning multiple attacks with little or no warning." Later that spring, he told Congress, "I consider it likely that over the next year or so that there will be an attempted terrorist attack against US interests," but he was frustrated that the CIA couldn't figure out when, where, or how.

TENET, WHO MANAGED DEEP into the building, was trying to drive change by bringing in a cluster of new people to the counterterrorism center. In 1999, Heidi August departed as scheduled for Stuttgart, Germany, as CIA's liaison to the US European command, working as the agency's liaison with all US military units in Europe. Replacing Heidi was Hank Crumpton, an operations officer who took over as "cops." Tenet also sought to replace the head of the analytic unit—the CTC official supervising the center's band of analysts, which still had not grown or not much. He chose Pattie Kindsvater, a veteran officer who became the only woman at, or even near, the top of the CTC.

PRIOR TO TAKING OVER the analytic unit, Pattie Kindsvater had built a successful career thanks to a gift for organization, a willingness to speak forthrightly, and an ability to make hard choices other people avoided. A native of Florida—her great-grandparents ran a turpentine still—she was the oldest of four children, put in charge at an early age. She majored in political science at Vanderbilt University, focusing on Soviet studies, and joined the CIA in 1978. Assigned to an office on the north side of the building, she shivered through the mid-Atlantic winter; Jimmy Carter not only turned the heat down in federal buildings but turned the hot water off in the bathrooms. Starting out as an indexer in the Office of Central Reference, she was fascinated by the materials coming across her desk: State Department cables, photos of what might be a missile silo, news of a food shortage after a hard winter. When a branch chief peered over the cubicle to point out the coffee-maker had run out of coffee, she and a colleague showed him how to make his own.

The OCR consisted mostly of mediocre older men when Pattie started out, but a young Black personnel manager, a high school graduate named Dottie Thorns, took it upon herself to upgrade the staff with sharp college grads like Pattie, which meant older men who could not make their own coffee were replaced, gradually, by young women, which meant Dottie Thorns was one of the unsung people who influenced how the workforce developed. Thorns urged Pattie to apply for a team leader post in the classified library, where documents were turned into microfiche. Pattie got the job over more senior applicants, becoming a supervisor of supervisors, with people reporting to her who had people reporting to them. She then moved to a leadership role in the unit computerizing the records, a job she didn't want—but one at which she succeeded beyond her wildest dreams.

Along the way, she got a master's degree in Soviet studies and became a team chief in the unit's USSR division—her real love—tracking scientists and other figures of interest. When leadership analysis was created, she worked Soviet issues there. She married a fellow officer in 1989, went overseas with her husband, and upon her return, the Soviet Union having collapsed, rose to be deputy chief of the Europe division, a big-time break. When that unit was reorganized, she became director of "plans" for the analytic directorate, a job that was important but required forcing barons to focus on things like office square footage that bored them.

In the 1990s, the glass ceiling study had prompted every all-male promotion panel to realize it needed a female member. Pattie and other top-level women became what one called "rent-a-skirts," called to sit on panel after panel. Most recently, she had been senior executive assistant for General John Gordon, Tenet's deputy, giving her, too, a taste of life on the seventh floor. She was deeply knowledgeable about Europe and the Soviet Union. What she did not have, and she was acutely aware of this, was experience in terrorism analysis.

Pattie Kindsvater knew that the hall-file take on CTC analysts was that the unit didn't produce "strategic analysis"—that is, long-range written products. The view existed in part because Charlie Allen, the reigning terrorism expert whose career dated to the plane hijackings of the 1980s, said so and continued to say so. "You could have done five hundred papers of a hundred pages plus, and he wouldn't have changed his mind," she later realized. Allen was a good old boy who'd had Bill Casey's ear and now had George Tenet's. He liked to address the director familiarly as "George John," after the Greek tradition of using both first names. His view was that CTC analysis was tactical, not high-end or long-range; "a bomb went off yesterday, more to come."

In the fall of 2000, Pattie was called in and told that the CTC analytic unit needed retooling. It seemed to her they were appointing her because she was tough and because she was a senior woman without another obvious place to go. Her areas of expertise were crowded. Pattie took the real message to be: She wasn't an old boy, didn't quite fit into the seventh-floor culture, and "we really would like to get rid of her." They were not hiring a person with terrorism knowledge; they were hiring a person who knew how to run something. The head of Alec Station was new; the cops was new; Pattie was new. "All of us were thrown down there" with a mandate to "get the place in order."

Not long after, she found herself in a small office in the basement of new headquarters, where one ops officer leaned on her desk and asked what terrorism books he should be reading. Pattie hadn't had a chance to read any herself. It may be that he genuinely wanted to know, but what she heard was: Well, Miss Smarty-Pants Analyst. Welcome!

Here, as on the seventh floor, norms were set by operations, which had a more hierarchical office culture. Once, at a meeting, a senior ops officer was speaking, and Pattie made the mistake of . . . weighing in. She suggested considering the topic from another angle. To Pattie, it was a routine exchange, banal by DI standards. But several women back-benching the meeting—reports officers, exec assistants—audibly gasped.

What she saw in the counterterrorism center astonished her, however. In addition to having access to the operational database, analysts had access to the operations officers and to the policies being set. On the downside, apart from senior analysts like Barbara, Gina, and Cindy, most people in her very-small band were newcomers in their early twenties. Personnel officials in the Directorate of Intelligence feared that if they sent seasoned analysts to the center, they'd lose them out the back door to operations.

Here in the gray zone of "fusion," the ops guys were world-class poachers. Shrewd case officers would woo analysts over to support operations, promising they could do exciting work with real impact. Targeting studies didn't require getting colleagues to chop. If an analyst moved over to work with ops, Pattie couldn't replace them. She already lacked 25 percent of her allotted staff.

The scarcity of experienced staff was one problem; another was "discoverability." After the attack on the USS *Cole*, the FBI had investigative responsibility to prove who did it. Pattie's group wrote papers on the topic, as they should do. She fielded angry calls from Justice Department officials, warning her not to write anything discoverable. "We would try to write things and they'd be like, 'No, this is going to go to a US court. You can't comment because it would be discoverable.'"

A discoverable document might enable defense to say that, while the FBI accused a certain individual of a crime, the analytic group said there were two other people who might be the culprit.

Pattie was used to hard work and did not shrink from conflict, but terrorism work took this to a new level. Twice a week, Pattie or somebody in her unit had to attend a teleconference with the National Security Council's terrorism office. In those meetings, every threat was seen as equal. In the Philippines, a group called ASG was causing horrific local problems but clearly not coming to the United States. The administration had trouble prioritizing, and so did Tenet.

In the center, resources flowed through the DO. In the analytic directorate, Pattie would have had a budget of her own. Here she had to beg the ops guys for money to, say, send a staffer on an overseas trip or bring in an outside expert. As the only woman in the top ranks, Pattie realized she, too, had a hall file. When she started, she was an SIS-2. When she got her promotion to SIS-3, jaws dropped. The ops guys couldn't believe she—woman, analyst—was an SIS at all.

Pattie Kindsvater did not immediately become part of the sisterhood. The analysts at first did not know how to regard her. Some worried she had been fed the line that they were not top-tier. When she took over, though, Gina Bennett was struck that when Pattie introduced herself, she said words to the effect of: *I'm not a warm and fuzzy person. It doesn't mean that I don't care.* To Gina, this felt plenty warm. One night, a couple of years later, intelligence arrived that needed to go into the PDB book right away. The analyst responsible had left for the day, so Gina said she'd handle it. The next morning, she had a handwritten thank-you note from Pattie. It was the first work-related thank-you note Gina Bennett had ever gotten.

IN OCTOBER 2000, CINDY STORER returned to the analytic unit, after spending two years on rotation. Her friend Susan Hasler noticed eye rolling among colleagues. Cindy, like many prophets, had a reputation for being cranky and hard to deal with. For her part, Cindy sensed a new mood and a new pace. The atmosphere felt crazed. Nobody walked.

They trotted or ran. Cindy was part of a "strategic analysis" group created in response to Charlie Allen's insistence that none existed.

Managers tasked Cindy to look back at the Malaysia summit to understand what had gone wrong. She was also reading terrorist communications, including intercepts coming out of Afghanistan. The mujahideen were using terms like "Olympic-sized" and "Armageddon," talking about how people should come to Afghanistan for the big whatever. They were using Islamic eschatology, talking about the end of the world. Cindy had been arguing for years that al-Qaeda tended to plot multiple simultaneous attacks and could pull them off. Every other terrorist group in the world looked at al-Qaeda and was like: Damn! The summer of 2001 got worse and worse. People thought the big attack could happen in June and then there were warnings and canceled holidays; they worked through the Fourth of July. Cindy felt scared, and she felt an enormous sense of responsibility: This is your watch.

This is going to happen on your watch.

IN HIS MEMOIR, GEORGE TENET names some of the threats with which the CIA was confronted during the second half of 2001. These included: Yemeni terrorists planning an attack in Jordan. Pakistanis planning to bomb a US community in Jeddah. FARC, in Colombia, planning to car-bomb the US embassy in Bogotá. Hezbollah active in Southeast Asia. An attack against the US embassy in Yemen by "an extremist group." Four Saudi nationals planning to attack US interests in Kuwait. Algerian terrorists planning to attack the Vatican, or the US embassy in Rome. The AQ operatives who bombed the USS *Cole* planning "new attacks against the United States."

And on it went. In June, Osama bin Laden gave an interview to the Arab satellite channel MBC, saying there would be a "big surprise" in coming weeks. The chatter was overwhelming, and so were the warning signs. AQ operatives were leaving Saudi Arabia to return to Afghanistan, where Arabs were "anticipating as many as eight celebrations." A key Chechen Islamic leader had promised "very big news" to his troops. Islamic extremists were traveling to Afghanistan "in greater numbers."

A top bin Laden lieutenant, Abu Zubaydah, was planning attacks; the primary target appeared to be Israel, but "other US assets around the world were at risk." Ahmed Ressam, the LAX bomber, told the FBI "Zubaydah was considering attacks in several US cities." Ayman al-Zawahiri, bin Laden's number two, was omnipresent in threat reporting, preparing operations. "A key Afghan camp commander was reportedly weeping with joy because he believed he could see his trainees in heaven." Important operatives were disappearing or preparing for martyrdom. By late June the CIA had launched "disruption efforts in nearly two dozen countries." Liaison and unilateral teams abroad were urged to beef up collection, US embassies were closed, Navy ships left Middle East ports and headed out to sea. There was a lot of obtaining of warrants, to surveil suspected foreign agents in the US.

On July 5, 2001, CTC officers briefed US attorney general John Ashcroft and told him a significant attack was imminent. "We continued to believe, however, that an attack was more likely to be conducted overseas," Tenet later wrote.

And that was the great question. Where would the attack occur? Up to now, most had occurred abroad. In July, Cofer Black gave Tenet a briefing that "literally made my hair stand on end." Along with Black and Blee, Tenet hurried to a meeting with Rice and Richard Clarke and Rice's number two, Steve Hadley. "There will be a significant terrorist attack in the coming weeks or months," Blee told them. Bush officials wanted to know when; they explained that bin Laden wasn't "beholden to attacks on specific dates."

Blee told Rice that the attack would be "spectacular" and occur with little or no warning. Tenet begged for a "proactive" approach. They wanted to "take the battle to UBL in Afghanistan": that is, take advantage of Afghan armed opposition and fatigue with Taliban rule. "This country needs to go on a war footing now," said Black. The men urged her to ask Bush to grant the authority he had asked for in March, to let them kill or capture bin Laden, saying the president needed to "align his policy with the new reality." Tenet wrote that "she assured me this would happen." Some Bush officials wondered if all the chatter amounted to "misinformation." Tenet assured them it did not. "The whole world seemed on the edge of eruption." The Predator drone had been under development, and the NSC authorized them to begin deploying it on September 1, armed or unarmed, which he took as a positive sign. A principals' meeting was needed to thrash out the policy, but the NSC "decided to put it off until after Labor Day."

During all this frantic back-and-forth, there had been a moment in late July when Rich Blee said, "They're coming here." According to Tenet, silence followed.

THERE ARE MULTIPLE VERSIONS of how it came to be that the CTC analytic staff wrote a paper predicting that bin Laden did intend to attack inside the United States. According to Tenet's memoir, whenever a PDB mentioned a possible al-Qaeda attack, the president would ask CIA briefer Mike Morell what the chances were it would occur in the United States. In August, Tenet said, Morell asked analysts to "prepare a piece that would try to address that question."

But Pattie Kindsvater's team was considering the same key issue, and she remembers the idea also coming about when her unit was brainstorming pieces for August publication. She sometimes half joked that if al-Qaeda knew about the habits of US working parents, they'd attack on Thanksgiving, or during the two weeks before Labor Day. Daycare centers were closed; people went on vacation. Knowing how thin-staffed things would get later in the summer, her approach in July was to look for pieces to write that could run in August—pieces that weren't based on urgent intel but that they wanted to get in front of policymakers. Pattie's deputy ran a brainstorming session for analysts, asking: What is the question everybody is wondering about? The answer was obvious. Would the big attack occur on the US mainland? Her deputy presented the results, and Pattie said: We'll write that.

Barbara Sude was tasked with writing up the item. She remembers her boss coming over and saying words to the effect of, "They are looking for a piece on bin Laden and the US." It was from this loose instruction that she fashioned what would become one of the most famous warnings in US history.

Barbara, as it happened, was getting a "vibe." A vibe is akin to an epiphany: It's what happens in an analyst's brain after months—years—

of intense focus. In June 2000, a video showed an agreement between bin Laden and the terrorist leader Zawahiri to merge al-Qaeda and the Egyptian Islamic Jihad. In September 2000, bin Laden appeared on a video for the first time in more than a year. That video showed a meeting of bin Laden and other confederates, including the son of the Blind Sheikh, the radical cleric jailed after the first World Trade Center bombing. The men were talking about hijacking a plane to free the Blind Sheikh. In June 2001, another video was released, a documentary that started with a Palestinian boy hiding behind a piece of concrete from Israeli troops. The boy was shot and killed, right next to his father. In June, a reporter from Middle East Broadcasting interviewed bin Laden. A deputy could be heard off camera saying the coming weeks would hold certain surprises that would target American and Israeli interests in the world.

All these developments had been written up for the policymakers. Barbara Sude and a few colleagues wrote nearly forty items from January to August 2001. They wrote "Bin Ladin Planning Multiple Operations" on April 20; "Bin Ladin Network's Plans Advancing" on May 26; "Bin Ladin Threats are Real" on June 30; "Threat of Impending al-Qaeda Plans Delayed but Not Abandoned" on July 13. Sometimes she worried they were warning too much.

By the time Barbara was assigned as principal author on a memo about a homeland attack, she had a pile of papers two feet high on the corner of her desk. In the stack was a paper by the FAA about hijackings. She had another piece from 1998 talking about a potential hijacking to free the Blind Sheikh. In 2001, they had gotten a report that al-Qaeda might sponsor people to hijack aircraft or storm US embassies. She proceeded methodically to refine the topic of the item. So, she asked herself, what *about* bin Laden and the US? Well, bin Laden hated the US and wanted to hit it. So: He had the intent. What about the capability? Yes. And if he hadn't succeeded before, he'd try again. Okay, so what were they doing about it? So she resolved to lay it out.

Before writing anything, though, Barbara pointed out that she had to talk to the FBI. The homeland was the bureau's responsibility. CIA analysts were reminded of that fact often. "We've been brought up— every year, we had the Executive Order 12333, compulsory to re-read every year, that CIA has certain restrictions on it, and we only do foreign."

So, from the counterterrorist center's in-house FBI contact, she got the name of an analyst at the bureau and placed a call. "I've been asked to write something about bin Laden and the US," she recalled saying. "Are you seeing anything?" The analyst listened, then, still on the phone, turned to a colleague and said, "Aren't you looking at hijackings?" The answer was yes. Barbara replied, "I'm thinking the same thing."

Once she started writing what would become known as the August 6 memo, Barbara was scrupulously careful. She noted that bin Laden, since as early as 1997, had made it clear he wanted to conduct attacks in the United States. He implied in TV interviews that he wanted to follow the example of the 1993 World Trade Center bomber and "bring the fighting to America," in the words of Ramzi Yousef. The paper pointed out that after the 1998 missile strikes on his base in Afghanistan, he said he wanted to retaliate in Washington. The would-be LAX bombing may have been part of his "first serious attempt" to strike in America. The 1998 embassy bombings, which he'd started planning in 1993, showed al-Qaeda was "not deterred by setbacks." Al-Qaeda members "have resided in or traveled to the US for years," she noted, and could support an operation inside the country. There had been threat reporting that bin Laden wanted to hijack a US aircraft, and that the FBI had noted patterns of activity suggesting "preparations for hijackings or other types of attacks."

She confirmed the memo with the FBI, faxing a copy over. She sent it up to the PDB editors, who gave it a title she liked: "Bin Ladin Determined to Strike in US." But the editors also sent the piece back to her for an addition, asking for more statistics from the FBI. So she called the bureau again. This time, she learned that the bureau was conducting seventy full "field investigations" around the country, looking into "bin Ladin–related" activity in the United States. Barbara added that to the item. Seventy separate investigations—that's a lot. She called the FBI back and read them the sentence she added. Later, she said, bureau officials sought deniability, apparently unhappy that a staffer had revealed just how much activity was being looked into. "They said they never heard of it; where the hell did we get that from."

THE ITEM WAS PUT in the book on August 6, and the president was briefed.

Barbara Sude would always wonder: When George W. Bush was briefed on the existence of more than seventy FBI investigations into bin Laden activities within the United States, did the commander in chief wonder? Did the president ever call the FBI director and ask him what was going on? She'd think it would be something a president might do. The president later told congressional investigators that, rather than feel alarmed, he felt "it was heartening" to learn of so many investigations. He took it to mean things were under control.

Condoleezza Rice would object that the CIA had not told them the exact day the attack was going to happen. But after the August 6 PDB ran, it would be four weeks—September 4, 2001—before the Bush administration had its first cabinet-level meeting about the threat posed by al-Qaeda. Barbara and her unit had been warning for months. They had been warning all year.

AS THE SUMMER HAD worn on, Pattie Kindsvater felt beleaguered from all sides. There were ops guys poaching her staffers; PDB editors claiming their warnings were repetitive; Charlie Allen saying no strategic analysis was being done. There was the military calling to ask if she had counterterrorist analysts she could lend out. And then one day, she was walking in the hallway, and she saw George Tenet. As she recalled it, Tenet stopped her, and started going on about how there was no strategic analysis coming from her unit. Pattie snapped. *George, you have no freaking idea what the situation is,* she said. He invited her to brief him.

So she did. She went back to her desk and ran the numbers. She had 25 percent fewer staff than allotted. The ones she did have were ten years younger, on average, than the DI average. She measured advanced degrees, language capability, overseas experience, time as an analyst. In every case, her unit was measurably below the DI average. What she had were smart young people who knew little about terrorism. To do a good job, she needed to tap external expertise. She needed money for training. She needed travel. She needed analysts with language expertise. You find a safe house, and suddenly you have a huge trove of documents. They were working themselves to death.

The morning of the briefing, the printer malfunctioned, and they barely had the charts printed out in time. But they got there. Pattie recalled Tenet saying words to the effect of: "Oh my God, I never knew." "And I said, 'Well, George, here we are. You know. This is what I have to work with.'" Tenet listened. He sent her to brief the executive director, Buzzy Krongard. The CFO came as well. Word got passed to the DI, and the front office committed to fully staffing Pattie's analytic group. Most were experienced officers looking for a new challenge. She didn't get an increased allocation. She just got her empty slots filled.

The reinforcements arrived on September 10, 2001.

CHAPTER 20

SEPTEMBER 11, 2001

A T SEVEN O'CLOCK ON THE MORNING OF TUESDAY, SEPTEMBER 11, 2001, Pattie Kindsvater, chief of analysis in the counterterrorist center, and Ben Bonk, deputy chief of the CTC, met to discuss a sexual affair taking place between people in the office, which had spilled over to create problems in the workplace. It was a routine HR mess—not a threat to the nation—but had to be dealt with. They got to it early, before the regular business of the day.

Pattie Kindsvater's second meeting, around eight or eight-fifteen, took place in her office. Attending was the chief of analysis in the counternarcotics center, who wanted Pattie to help fund a joint effort on al-Qaeda's role in the drug trade. Pattie's secretary came in just after 8:46 A.M. and said: *Turn on the TV.*

Pattie's office was small, with just enough room for a desk and chairs and a television fixed to the side wall. She turned on CNN. Moments earlier, anchors had been talking about the usual late-summer concerns: hurricanes in Florida, the start of the trading day on the New York Stock Exchange. Now the network had switched to footage of the skyline of Lower Manhattan. In the center was the World Trade Center, the twin towers with their narrow wales reaching skyward. One tower showed a jagged hole, like a wound, three-quarters of the way up. A producer was on the line reporting that a "large commercial passenger jet" had flown into the North Tower, which had a plume of dark-gray smoke billowing above it. The producer, who happened to be in the vicinity, said that before it hit, the jet had been "teetering back and forth wingtip to wingtip."

The anchors began asking questions, incredulous. "Does it appear to you that the plane is still inside the World Trade Center?" one asked. Addressing viewers, the anchor said, "You're looking at a live picture of the World Trade Center" where a passenger jet "appears to be still embedded inside the building."

On the line came an eyewitness who lived in Battery Park City and reported that her TV had gone out, she heard a sonic boom, and the "side of the World Trade Center exploded." Debris was fluttering down "like leaflets." The anchors observed that the North Tower was the one with the observatory and viewing deck. People, they pointed out, might be trapped above the point of impact. This was true. At 8:30, the Risk Waters Group had begun a conference on the 106th floor of the North Tower, where seventy-two restaurant staff had arrived. Of course, what was taking place inside the building was not visible on the screen.

What was visible, at 9:03 A.M., was a Boeing 767 streaking from the right side of the television screen and plunging into the South Tower, around the eightieth floor. Flames erupted, and now twin gray plumes merged and twisted upward. Moments after the second tower was hit, the counternarcotics chief stood up, said she realized Pattie had other things to do, and left. After the strike on the first tower, it had been possible to think they were seeing a freak accident, but the second plane made it clear that this was an act of terrorism.

Pattie's first concrete thought was procedural. They were going to have to formally address who did it. Of course. But that led to a second thought: "Am I going to screw up the FBI's legal brief?"

There was no television camera to capture the impact when, at 9:37, American Airlines Flight 77 flew low over Crystal City, a suburban cluster of office buildings in Arlington, Virginia. About twenty minutes before, Barbara Olson, a passenger aboard Flight 77, which had departed from Dulles Airport in Virginia, had called her husband, Solicitor General Ted Olson, to say the plane had been hijacked and passengers herded to the rear. Inside the Pentagon, personnel were on telephones talking to friends and family about the New York attack. Phones went dead as the plane smashed through three of the Pentagon's five concentric rings, killing 53 passengers, 6 crew, and 125 military and civilian personnel.

Pattie began to manage response in the main counterterrorism center.

Elsewhere, CTC head Cofer Black had a hasty videoconference with Richard Clarke, the National Security Council's terrorism expert. On the sixth floor of headquarters, the CTC maintained a global crisis center, which received a report of another commercial jet unaccounted for. People started receiving other reports: the State Department had been hit; the White House was on fire. Those weren't official accounts—just rumors, most false, somebody rushing in and saying, "My friend at State says . . ." The Soviet Union had not had crises of this nature. Even coups unfolded slowly in comparison. What kind of writing should the analysts produce? How to organize twenty-four-hour coverage?

The analysts who arrived the day before did not yet have computer access. Wanting to be helpful, one new manager came into Pattie Kindsvater's office and pointed out that the cafeteria was closing and would likely stay closed. She offered to fetch pizzas and bring them back. Daycare centers began shutting down and people were calling spouses to pick up kids. Pattie called her analysts together and told them this was their moment; whatever else was happening at the CIA, they would stay.

George Tenet had been breakfasting at the St. Regis Hotel on Sixteenth Street, two blocks from the White House, with former Oklahoma senator David Boren. His security officer, Tim Ward, looking "urgent," interrupted to tell him about the first plane strike. Tenet raced to his car, calling ahead on a secure line to instruct his senior staff and some CTC officials to gather in the conference room beside his office. Gridlock seized the capital: People in downtown Washington began walking home to suburban Virginia and Maryland, a stream of workers pouring over the Key and Memorial bridges, seeking children and spouses. As Tenet was driven over the Potomac, the CIA director experienced a "communications blackout," unable to get through until he reached headquarters and made his way to the seventh floor. His office had a view of the Potomac, which was used by pilots for navigation heading into National Airport. Here was the brain trust of the CIA, congregated in the adjacent conference room.

The chief of Tenet's security detail moved the group to a ground-floor office, then spirited Tenet to the nearby printing plant, a makeshift bunker where communications options were "rudimentary." The White House and US Capitol were evacuated, and for the first time in US history, a "continuity of government plan" put in place. The decision was made to evacuate the CIA. But Cofer Black, like Pattie Kindsvater, felt the counterterrorism center should remain, including the half dozen people staffing the center's sixth-floor Global Reaction Center, which had sent out an alert to stations to intensify collection. When Tenet pointed out that the people on the sixth floor could die, Black said, "Well, sir, then they're just going to have to die." At ten o'clock a message went out instructing the agency's workforce to evacuate, except for the CTC.

Tenet, cut off from most computer access, was scrambling to get phones operational. His staff called Pattie for an update, so she sent an analyst to brief him. Tenet told the analyst to stay. Presently they called for another update, so she sent another analyst over. Then another. Pattie had half the world calling her wanting to know what was going on. The head of the al-Qaeda team was now with Tenet. She had to call over and ask for her analysts to be sent back.

Cable traffic started pouring in. Pattie's team of analysts had to process all that and keep Tenet informed. Her staffing ranks remained so thin that a few days later, when Winston Wiley, the head of the intelligence directorate, called asking her to send somebody to brief him, Pattie was obliged to send one of her newest analysts, a young man named Mark. He walked to original headquarters and got on the elevator, nervously shuffling papers. A man in the elevator asked what was wrong. Mark confessed he had to brief the DDI and had no idea what he was doing. He was talking to the DDI, Winston Wiley, a kind man who invited him into his office. When Mark returned to the center, he stood pounding his head against the wall.

On the morning of the attacks, President George W. Bush had been reading to schoolchildren in Florida when Andrew Card, his chief of staff, hurried over and whispered in his ear. The second plane had struck. Video footage would show the president looking frozen. He later said he didn't jump up right away because he didn't want to alarm the children. After making brief remarks—calling the attacks an "evil, despicable act of terror"—the president was hurried aboard Air Force One. At 9:55 A.M., the plane headed west, looking for a safe place to land so the president could address the American people. Air Force One landed at 11:45 at Barksdale Air Force in Louisiana, where the president taped an address. Then it took off again, for Offutt Air Force Base in Nebraska. President Bush would not return to Washington until the evening.

Michael Morell, the president's briefer, called Pattie a few times. She worried about talking over an open line, but then thought: Wait a minute, the world's ending, so she did. There were lulls when she did not hear from Morell. Somebody asked: Where's the president? They didn't know. That was a low moment. For her, that was the worst part of the day.

SUSAN HASLER HAD AN office next to Pattie's, and around 8:50 A.M. she saw a middle-aged male analyst running toward Pattie's office. The secretary stopped him and went in to get Pattie. Susan and other analysts crowded around, watching the TV through the glass. Susan felt no doubt about who was behind the attacks. She and her colleagues had known an attack could happen. But watching people die—it was real. It was really taking place. At 9:59, the South Tower collapsed. The North Tower followed a half hour later. Among the nearly three thousand dead was John O'Neill, the FBI's former chief counterterrorism expert, who had started a new job as chief of security for the trade center. People in Lower Manhattan were taking video footage. A man, running from a debris cloud, ducked behind a car, saying, "I hope I live. I hope I live." A news anchor said, "Good lord. There are no words."

Susan Hasler's husband worked as an analyst in the CIA's Soviet division. His office was on the east side of the original headquarters, one floor below Tenet's. If a plane hit Langley, it would strike that side.

Her husband had a doctor's appointment later that morning. Before the evacuation order, Susan called and urged him to go. New headquarters was less vulnerable—though flimsier. Logistics officers began taking up the floor, installing wiring and putting in more computers, snatched from closets and hallways, and creating a crisis center. Susan wondered: If a plane did hit, how would they escape with all these cables and holes? From a basement?

LISA HARPER WAS ALSO in CIA headquarters on the morning of 9/11, also in a meeting. A foreign delegation was paying a call. The delegation had information to share, and had traveled to the United States to talk to the State Department, the FBI, and the CIA. The meeting had just begun. Lisa was undercover, posing as a translator. All at once, a security official burst in and said, *You've got to get out of here.* There were reports of another plane in the air, also hijacked, likely headed for Washington. It later turned out to be United Flight 93, which crash-landed in Shanksville, Pennsylvania, at 10:02, after passengers rushed the hijackers. Lisa herded the delegation out of the building and into several cars.

Lisa got in with them. The delegation made its way onto Route 123, proceeding to a nearby hotel booked for the group. The hotel was on lockdown. Lisa had a huge group on her hands, including high-ranking officials. She couldn't leave them on the sidewalk, so she slipped around the side of the hotel and used her tradecraft to enter from the back. She might have blown her cover a bit, but what could she do? Their other appointments were canceled, which seemed too bad; they might know something useful. Nothing was flying. Secretary of Defense Donald Rumsfeld directed the military to DEFCON3, and all nonemergency civilian aircraft were grounded. Civilian airspace did not reopen until September 13, after which the DCI arranged for a plane to take them to their home country.

Lisa's first thought was: They had worked so hard—all the people in the windowless basement—and hadn't been able to get there. They'd kept waiting for the missing piece to fall into place; that one report narrowing down the possibilities. The day it happened was like the day John F. Kennedy died: "It's just one of those days that changes your life."

CINDY STORER AND GINA Bennett had carpooled to work. The two women, longtime colleagues who could finish each other's sentences, chatted about an ominous development. On September 9, suicide bombers had assassinated Ahmad Shah Massoud, leader of Afghanistan's Northern Alliance faction, which provided the Taliban's main opposition. Massoud, a legendary commander, was known as the Lion of the Panjshir. His assassination was a gift from bin Laden to his Taliban hosts. Al-Qaeda tricked Massoud by sending two so-called journalists who were actually terrorists wearing suicide vests. Cindy felt the agency could have prevented the hit. She'd seen a plot developing between some Egyptians, who were getting material and press passes. One wanted to be a martyr. She'd been going back and forth with CIA operations officers, trying to get the warning to Massoud. But they'd had less than a day and it hadn't been enough time. Massoud's death, the women knew, was a prelude.

Cindy headed to her desk and settled in. She felt desolate and frustrated. *We're not going to figure it out,* she told a senior analyst who had just joined the center. *What you need to understand,* she said, *is we're all going to die, and here's why. Because of the disconnect with the FBI. Because of management never listening. We're not going to figure it out.*

Somebody in the sea of cubicles announced that a plane had flown into the World Trade Center. Cindy clambered onto her desk. The analyst on the other side of her partition had a RealPlayer insert, a tiny video box in the corner of his screen, streaming CNN. Peering at the footage, Cindy thought they might be talking about the World Trade Center in Kuala Lumpur, Malaysia, a low, peaked building in a country much on her mind. But then she saw it was New York. People around her were murmuring with analytic caution: *It's a small plane. Don't panic. You don't want to go straight to . . .* Then she saw the second plane hit. The first thing she said was, *Oh my God.* The second thing was: *Activate your call lists, because we're going to war.* By this, she meant people should call the people in their lives, who would call everybody else to do what was needed: Watch their kids. Walk their dogs. They were in for a long haul. There was no question in Cindy's mind what the US reaction would be: Pound the shit out of the people who did this, and anybody who helped them.

Cindy knew that in 1995, al-Qaeda had developed the plot to fly a plane into CIA headquarters. She went to the front office and suggested her office should leave the building, pointing out: *Look, if they fly a plane into Langley, it will be like Pearl Harbor, where nearly the entire US Pacific fleet was moored in one place. All the terrorism expertise is here.* But the directive had been issued for the center to stay. She called her preacher, who called her friends and neighbors.

Cindy volunteered to take night shifts, knowing Barbara Sude would have to take the day shift, to answer calls and write. The two women knew the most about al-Qaeda. The night shift ushered the PDB through the editing process, and Cindy could talk to the briefers at four in the morning. She slept on cots for weeks.

A few days in, Pattie Kindsvater came over to Cindy. Pattie was tall, reserved, and typically nonemotive. *I'm freaking out. Are you freaking out?* she confided. It was a moment of transformation. Cindy sensed that their boss was now one of them.

Welcome to counterterrorism, she said. *We're all freaking out together. Have a seat.*

A few weeks in, Cindy went to choir practice at her Arlington church, seeking solace and respite. One choir member began telling stories about being on the side of the Pentagon where the plane hit and crawling out of the rubble. He started explaining who Osama bin Laden was. Nobody looked at Cindy. Once again she had this feeling of invisibility. She had been warning so long, she had seen it coming, and now it felt like she didn't exist. "I'm just sitting in the background going 'What the fuck.'"

BARBARA SUDE WAS AT her desk when someone called out about a plane hitting the trade center. For an instant, she, too, allowed herself to hope it was a small plane that had lost its way; but the second strike told her all she needed to know. Aware that her back faced the wall, Barbara could feel fear creeping up her spine. She was assigned to write talking points for the director. Flashing across her computer screen was the cable instructing counterterrorism people to remain in place.

Barbara resigned herself to whatever was going to happen. Her children were safe and her husband worked at home. Before she got started on the talking points, she told her boss she wanted to go to the restroom, in case she got caught in the rubble. If Armageddon was coming to the CIA building, she wanted to face it with an empty bladder. In early afternoon, analysts got passenger manifests from the hijacked airplanes. On the list were Nawaf al-Hazmi and Khalid al-Mihdhar, the two al-Qaeda members living in California. Their names had been rediscovered in CIA records in August, and the FBI, informed, had been hunting them ever since. Before August, Barbara's analytic unit had not known anything about those two being in the United States. The manifests were rushed to Tenet. It was al-Qaeda, for sure.

In the days and nights that followed, Barbara had to work late writing PDBs. Often the only one left, late at night, she would start thinking: "I want to get out of here." It felt creepy. If she went to the restroom, she would have to lock the vault door behind her. Often she'd just sit there and hold it. If she hadn't had a chance to get dinner and was starving, she'd end up searching desks. Candy? Pretzels? Anything?

Barbara's manager predicted things would blow over now that the big attack happened. Barbara thought to herself: This is not going to blow over. As the casualty reports began arriving, Barbara learned there were many cars in the commuter parking lot near her childhood home, in Long Island, whose owners did not come to claim them at the end of the day.

"MALLORY," THE UNDERCOVER CASE officer who had returned from Pakistan, after splashing the Salafis with her jeep, was taking French language training prior to a tour in Algeria. She had come to headquarters for a meeting on the sixth floor. She walked in to see people staring at the TV. The first plane had just hit. A man in the office, a former Marine Corps pilot, declared it couldn't be an accident. Planes don't fly

in that part of Manhattan. His name was Bob and he had long advo-
cated that the 1993 World Trade Center bombing was a prelude to
something worse. They failed the first time; they're going to try again.
He got so obsessed that people avoided him. They were all standing
there, listening to Bob, when they saw the second plane hit.

Silence settled over the office. People looked at each other. Presently,
they all sat down at their desks. "Like, what do you do? It's our job,"
Mallory remembered thinking. "We're supposed to stop this. We're
supposed to do something. So now what? So, everybody was kind of
sitting there, waiting for direction. Who do we trace? What do we do?
What do you need from us? We'll go wherever." A security officer came
in and told people the director was sending everybody home. Get your
things, they were instructed: Make an orderly process.

Everybody started to leave. They were all talking, grabbing purses.
Nobody seemed to be in a hurry. "And he comes running back in and
I'll never forget this because he was gray, he looked like he was going to
throw up. And he was like, 'there's a plane coming, get out of this building right now. We don't know where it's going, get out of this building.
You have to go.' He's like, 'Leave your stuff, get out.' And he was like,
one of these former action guys, and he was shaking and scared."

They all tried to leave at once. People headed for the stairways only
to confront a backup. "So, we're standing there, and I remember the
stairs were silent. Nobody was talking. It was just the creepiest thing.
And it took about thirty minutes, frankly, to get down six floors. People
were carrying older people and wheelchairs." Once the workforce
reached the parking lots, they sat in traffic on the CIA compound. "And
it was just the most terrifying thing," she recalled. "And I'd been in Peshawar. Which was the weirdest thing. It was more terrifying."

Mallory could not escape her sense of failure. Congress would begin
looking into why the attacks occurred and why they had come as a surprise. She knew such an investigation was needed. But the inevitable
report felt like a personal attack. "For two years of my life, I was trying
to do the right thing, and people died, and you felt like it was your fault.
And then people were saying, it *was* your fault. And it really, it affected
us a lot. . . . We have to be right a hundred percent of the time. They
only have to be right once. . . . It was really hard."

And she felt guilty. "So of course, everything anyone says—like, 'Why didn't you know?' You're like, 'I don't know. Why didn't I know? Did I not ask the right question? Should I have gone out on that weekend, when I stayed home?'"

KRISTIN WOOD WAS ALSO working in headquarters on September 11. After starting her career as an imagery analyst, she had risen to become a briefer for Scooter Libby, Dick Cheney's chief of staff. Briefing was a punishing job that required getting to headquarters at two A.M., reading the PDB, absorbing updates, then going downtown to deliver the day's intelligence. That morning, she'd briefed Libby, and they'd discussed the murder of Massoud and what it portended. She'd come back to headquarters and was on the seventh floor, typing up her notes in the little closet-sized room that serves as a briefer's office. A colleague came in to tell her to watch the communal TV, and she knew it was bad "from the look on his face."

She saw the second plane hit. She knew who it was. Her husband worked twenty yards from her own desk. They knew the building might be a target. They had young children, and agreed that in an emergency, one of them would leave to ensure one parent survived. Her husband supported a principal, so Kristin turned off her computer without taking the time to log off; she just left, walking down the stairs alongside colleagues. Many were crying.

They had missed it. "We failed." It was her only thought. "We couldn't have done worse." There was no way around it. Those three thousand people had died, and short of bringing them back to life, there was no way to make it better. No way to make it okay. It was a huge failure of the intelligence community. Later, she would feel grateful that at least she could serve. The only thing to do was to work harder. "How do we make sure this never happens again?"

IN NEW YORK, THE CIA'S clandestine station was operating out of World Trade Center Building 7, a smaller office tower in the trade center complex. CIA officers were close enough to see, through the windows, the bodies of people jumping to escape the flames. An orderly evacuation was overseen by the station chief, Mary Margaret Graham, who ensured that nobody was hurt and no classified material was compromised. Graham, a close friend of Heidi August, later said that her "first thought," upon seeing the second plane hit, was that she had joined the agency to protect the country, and after twenty-six years of a career, "I had failed." The station was destroyed when the twin towers collapsed.

THREE WEEKS AFTER THE ATTACKS, Heidi August returned to the United States from Europe. During an afternoon meeting in Stuttgart, she had watched the towers fall on CNN. One of the first things she did was call Mary Margaret's father to make sure her friend was okay. Upon Heidi's return to the United States, everybody at CIA headquarters was talking about bin Laden and where a next attack might come from. She visited New York; Manhattan smelled charred. On the Upper East Side, there were American flags posted in windows. "I could tell that things had really changed in the United States. It was a different country when I came back."

Part Three

GETTING THEIR GUYS

I've lived twenty-five
years of my life abroad,
and wherever you go, your
level of failure is
directly proportional to
the lack of involvement
of women in the thing.

—MILT BEARDEN,
CIA STATION CHIEF,
ORAL HISTORY INTERVIEW,
NATIONAL SEPTEMBER 11
MEMORIAL & MUSEUM,
2009

THE THREAT MATRIX

September 2001

GETTING READY FOR BED, GINA BENNETT REALIZED SHE HADN'T felt the baby move in days. A few months into her fourth pregnancy when the attacks occurred, Gina hadn't yet told her co-workers she was pregnant. Working fourteen- and sixteen-hour shifts in the counterterrorist center in the days and weeks after September 11, she forgot to take breaks or stop for a drink of water. Padding into her kitchen in the darkness of the quiet house, she opened the refrigerator, took out a carton of orange juice, poured a glass, drank it, and waited twenty minutes for the sugar to do its work. She felt no movement.

Gina called her doctor's emergency number, which connected her to the labor and delivery unit at Arlington Hospital, who told her to come in to be checked. She woke her husband and told him she was driving to the hospital. Doctors determined that Gina's amniotic fluid was low, likely owing to dehydration, and that she had a urinary tract infection. The nurses inserted an IV line, pumped her full of saline solution, and put her on antibiotics. By ten o'clock they had confirmed no long-term damage to the fetus. Gina left the hospital and headed to work.

That's what life was like in the weeks after September 11. In the counterterrorist center, there were not nearly enough hours to do what they needed to. Each analyst received as many as a thousand emails a day: threat reporting, papers, cables, news articles, more threat reporting. They had every reason to believe there would be follow-on operations. They felt the ticking clock, the pressure to find the next plot in time to destroy it. At the CTC, a sign went up that would remain in place for years: "Today is September 12, 2001."

PATTIE KINDSVATER, CHIEF OF analysis in the counterterrorist center, often woke in the dark and scribbled notes. Her team of analysts worked nonstop. Some lived close enough to go home to sleep, while others slept at headquarters. Pattie got in each morning about five o'clock and left nineteen hours later, after signing off on the threat matrix. One Sunday not long after the attacks, one of the officers started babbling during an exchange. He hadn't slept in three days. Another, stepping into an elevator in the US Capitol, started thinking about how United Flight 93 had been headed for Washington and had a full-blown panic attack.

"Whenever I walked down the corridor and saw someone rushed, distracted, and looking like shit, I could be fairly sure they worked in CTC," Susan Hasler wrote in an unpublished memoir she could never bring herself to finish; the emotions it summoned remained too raw.

The women would discuss their recurrent dreams. Barbara Sude's entailed being the last person in the vault at night. Susan's went like this: She was trapped in an M. C. Escheresque version of headquarters. A plane had struck, and the workforce was trying to escape down staircases that spiraled into a void. Susan, who suffered from a family tendency toward depression, began feeling a compulsion to check the stove and other appliances before leaving the house. She was so busy she had trouble keeping doctor's appointments or tending to a dairy farm she and her husband owned in the Shenandoah Valley. Sensing a depressive episode pending, she began seeing an agency-approved psychiatrist. Lexapro helped, somewhat. She could deliver clearer, less emotional briefings. But sometimes she would watch visitors clock in and out of headquarters and fantasize about handing in her badge.

CIA director George Tenet observed that he talked often with his deputy John McLaughlin, Jim Pavitt, the director of operations, and Cofer Black "about the emotional toll the attacks were taking on our employees." They fully expected "an emotional response" from the counterterrorist center, but "it never came."

At least not audibly. The women were grief-stricken and traumatized. They internalized their anguish and kept going.

TENET INAUGURATED A DAILY "threat matrix" meeting to review every threat that came in. Pattie Kindsvater and her analysts were told not to leave anything off, no matter how unlikely. New threats had begun the day of the attacks, when French liaison shared intelligence suggesting another group of terrorists within US borders, planning a second wave. Not all the threats had to do with explosions, and many were all too real. In mid-September, envelopes containing anthrax spores were sent to Tom Brokaw of NBC News and to the *New York Post*; three weeks later, similar letters arrived in the offices of US senators Tom Daschle and Patrick Leahy. Five people died of anthrax poisoning, and nearly twenty more fell ill. President Bush and Vice President Cheney floated the idea that al-Qaeda was behind the anthrax attacks. Years later, the perpetrator was found to be an aggrieved government microbiologist.

The threat matrix meeting took place each afternoon at five, in Tenet's conference room, at a big wooden table. Pattie Kindsvater or her deputy would roll out a chart, fresh off the center's huge printer, showing networks of phone numbers, maps, and charts. There was, as Tenet put it, "a palpable fear in the room that the United States was about to be hit again." The matrix remained a fluid document until one in the morning, when it would be printed and included in the president's briefing. Tenet in his memoir summarized the threats that confronted them on a single day in November. These included a report from the Persian Gulf by a source claiming to know of imminent strikes, and the same prediction posted on a website by a Jordanian who had also posted on September 10 saying "zero hour" was closing in. An al-Qaeda associate predicted big events in November; an official at the Egyptian embassy in Saudi Arabia, with ties to Egyptian Islamic Jihad, had faxed in his resignation and disappeared. A senior bin Laden operative had shared the name of an AQ person planning a suicide operation. And on and on. Most days, the list went on for pages. The director gathered people to envision hit lists within the United States: movie studios, amusement parks, sports stadiums, airports, harbors, bridges. The Washington Monument, the Statue of Liberty, Mount Rushmore.

The counterterrorist center was "the hub around which all of our efforts revolved," Tenet noted. Everybody assumed the 9/11 attacks were "simply the first wave." Plenty of evidence emerged to support the likelihood of a second wave. On December 22, 2001, a passenger named Richard Reid was subdued on board an American Airlines flight from Paris to Miami while trying to set off a shoe bomb. The following weeks, months, and years would see attacks around the world by al-Qaeda and affiliated groups. On October 12, 2002, an Indonesian group called Jemaah Islamiyah detonated a car bomb outside a nightclub in Bali. Chechen terrorists raided a Moscow theater and held more than eight hundred people hostage.

And Cindy Storer's prediction came true: The United States intended to go after everybody. At 8:30 P.M. on September 11, President Bush gave a speech saying the perpetrators would be brought to justice, and "we will make no distinction between the terrorists who committed these acts and those who harbor them." Two days later, Tenet presented the president with a plan for the CIA to take the lead in the upcoming war. His plan called for covert action to carry the fight to Afghanistan and worldwide. Tenet argued that the war should be driven by intelligence, saying the challenge was to "find the enemy," after which, "defeating him would be easy." Cofer Black predicted that the United States could defeat the Taliban and al-Qaeda in "a matter of weeks." On September 15, Tenet briefed the war cabinet at Camp David, saying the agency would seal off Afghanistan and needed to detain operatives around the world. Tenet, who did not want the war to fall "under Pentagon control," argued that they needed to cripple terrorist leaders, facilitators, planners, financiers. He returned to DC and on September 16 "fired off a memo" to top officials, titled "We're at war." On September 17, Bush signed a covert action Memorandum of Notification granting the CIA authority to covertly capture and detain individuals "posing a continuing, serious threat of violence or death to US persons and interests or planning terrorist activities."

The counterterrorist center added a special operations branch and
sent officers in to work with the Northern Alliance. By September 27,
the CIA inserted its first covert team into Afghanistan: ninety paramilitary officers, plus special forces and Afghan militia. They engaged
the Taliban and killed or captured one-fourth of bin Laden's top lieutenants, including Mohammed Atef, a key player in the attacks. Rich
Blee left Alec Station for the war theater, and Hank Crumpton became
head of special operations, assigned to win the cooperation of fickle
warlords. He needed saddles, horse feed, millions of dollars. When one
Taliban intelligence official declined to help, the ops guys rolled him up
in a carpet and spirited him to US-controlled territory for questioning.
On October 7, US and UK air forces bombed Taliban bases in Afghanistan, starting the US-led invasion. The first casualty was an agency
officer, Mike Spann, murdered on November 25 by Taliban prisoners,
leaving behind a wife and young child.

Al-Qaeda was not defeated within weeks. Osama bin Laden fled
toward Tora Bora. Although thirty of bin Laden's bodyguards were
captured hiking through Pakistan, bin Laden was not with them, nor
was his second in command, Ayman al-Zawahiri. In January the agency
informed the president that High Value Target #1 had probably fought
at Tora Bora and survived. Bin Laden had escaped. HVT #2 was alive
as well.

Two decades of war in Afghanistan were just beginning, and the
geographic challenges would spread further.

"Once you dislodge al-Qaeda from Afghanistan, poof, they go off
into the world, and then you've got to find them all over again," said
Gina Bennett.

DAYS AFTER THE ATTACK, the head of the intelligence directorate,
Winston Wiley, decided to enlarge the center's analytic corps, and with
that, the sisterhood grew. He created an Office of Terrorism Analysis,
expanding the number of counterterrorism analysts tenfold. Even as
she was dealing with daily threats, Pattie Kindsvater—who had spent
more than a year begging for a single person—was told to draw up a
diagram of what such an office should look like: names, units, descrip-

tions. She completed it in a weekend. Headquarters signed off and decided she'd be second in command to the new director, Bruce Pease. With the creation of OTA, the agency had, at last, a fully staffed unit of counterterrorist analysts—hundreds of them.

People now were thrown at them right and left. The front office relocated whole units—analysts and bosses, like moving entire houses—over to counterterrorism. Russian specialists arrived and dug in. A team of monetary specialists showed up, pencils sharpened. Military analysts started calling: Baltic analysts left over from the Yugoslav conflict, bored and fired up and eager. People couldn't apply; they had to be assigned. Some managers used the mandate to off-load people who seemed to them less crucial. One office decided it could do without several branches of leadership analysts—subgroups of about fifteen people—so they dumped them en masse on the new office.

Many newcomers rose to the challenge. A whole branch of leadership analysts did nothing but monitor threats. And Barbara Sude quickly appreciated what leadership analysts could bring to the table. "They could squeeze blood out of a stone," she noticed. They had a special skill set and "were pretty clever at it." If Barbara had a part of a name, they "would figure out who it was, and have a whole biography. They were fabulous researchers. We had never had that before," she said, "and it was really useful."

Sometime around Christmas, the Office of Terrorism Analysis had a holiday party—sober, with Cokes—during which Pease informed Kindsvater that he was moving to the front office and she was the new director of OTA. Merry Christmas! Kindsvater now had people she could throw at any problem. Her team had money. It had the attention of the customer. Nobody on the PDB staff was going to say *We're not running that piece because we don't think there's going to be a terrorist attack tomorrow.*

Now they could tackle hard things and get them done.

ANOTHER CONSEQUENCE OF THE influx of resources was that women who until then had been marginalized now found themselves in lead positions. Cindy Storer was everywhere, bending over desks, giving lessons. Soon the basement vault could no longer contain people working what had become the agency's central mission. Office space was found and members of the original sisterhood struggled to stay together. Susan Hasler was working an overnight shift when summoned by Pattie Kindsvater, who spread out the bedsheet-sized chart. Susan thought it was a terrorist wiring diagram, then realized it depicted her and her colleagues. Kindsvater asked what office she'd like to head. Susan chose to work as a senior analyst alongside Barbara Sude and Cindy Storer.

Among the arrivals were young couples—analysts married to each other—and at least one couple had a new baby. Everybody's life was chaos. At one town hall, George Tenet told them: For the next three months, you don't have a life outside Langley. The thing was, people did. They had small children, elderly relatives. The institution provided little help. At the town hall, Cindy noticed Tenet's hands were shaking. He had lost friends in the attacks: Michele Heidenberger, a flight attendant on Flight 77, which hit the Pentagon; and a high school friend, Bob Speisman, on the same plane. The director had to stop talking and ask for Excedrin.

Meticulous work and long hours meant many other things got put on hold in the months that followed. Marriages. Sex. Childcare. One counterterrorism analyst felt bad about taking time off when her husband, their child's primary caregiver, died of a ruptured hernia.

Then again, the work was addictive. Stopping attacks and getting terrorists caught provided instant gratification. Cindy Storer was appointed to a working group led by the Treasury Department, representing the CIA as the expert on terrorism finance. Having a lead role was a novel experience. Under John Deutch, the only people who talked to senior managers were other senior managers. Nobody but senior management talked to the National Security Council. Cindy felt this rigid approach had been at the root of a lot of the agency's pre-9/11 problems; the analysts' views had been stifled. Now Cindy was told: *You go downtown and take care of it.* Other offices began to complain that terrorism analysts were getting promoted faster. Envious colleagues would say: *We are doing groundbreaking work and you're doing transactional work. And you are getting rewarded.*

Terrorism analysis, people doing it began saying, was a blast.

SUSAN HASLER'S HUSBAND WAS one of many Soviet analysts reassigned to the counterterrorism beat. He was tasked with finding proof that Mohammed Atta, one of the 9/11 hijackers, had met with Iraqi intelligence in Prague. This was a pet theory put forth by the Bush administration, which was bent on finding a link between al-Qaeda and Iraq and fully prepared to outflank, steamroll, bully, and ignore the CIA, in its zeal to justify a war with Iraq, even as a renewed war on terror was just getting started. Hasler's husband wrote PDB after PDB showing such a meeting never occurred. On nights her husband had to stay late, Susan would wait for him on a bench and indulge in her fantasy about resigning.

Susan Hasler's anxiety worsened when she learned of a new entity called the "red cell": a team of senior analysts empowered to overrule her and her colleagues. The red cell had been conceived around midnight on September 12, when Tenet, in a manic moment, proposed creating a team to "think contrarian thoughts" and go "outside the box" so far that "they would be in a different zip code." One of the first names on the list was Paul Frandano, whom Tenet described as "a Harvard-trained senior analyst with a goatee and a liking for colorful bow ties." The point was to "free some of our best people" to "think unconventionally." The upshot was reports with names like "How Usama Might Try to Sink the U.S. Economy" and "The View from Usama's Cave." Susan Hasler was appalled. Speculative reports were exactly what she and her colleagues were not permitted to write. The women had been thinking outside the box for nearly a decade. It seemed to Susan the red cell was stacked with white men, mostly former Soviet experts, who were getting "a level of visibility and a level of respect and a level of autonomy that Barbara and Cindy never got."

Barbara Sude felt the same way. Some incoming analysts acted like they were the cavalry, coming to save the day. "We're treated like we never knew anything, we screwed up," said Barbara, one of the world's leading experts on al-Qaeda, who found herself "training all these new people," many of whom treated her like a B-teamer. The analysts also were tasked with providing material to congressional investigators. "We knew we were in trouble," said Barbara, who soon found herself called in and interviewed by staff members of a joint congressional inquiry. The analysts, of course, knew accountability was important. But the questions from the joint inquiry staffer struck Barbara as aggressive and contemptuous, from people with a "half-assed knowledge" of what the analysts did. The experience was "horrible." Next came the full-blown 9/11 Commission investigation. Before that report was published, the original small team of thirty-odd CTC analysts were gathered at a table and told what it would say about them. The FBI would be called to task for errors such as failing to pay attention to reports from a Minnesota flight school that an adult student, Zacarias Moussaoui, wanted to learn to fly a Boeing 747, but not take off or land. The CIA analysts would be criticized for three perceived failures. The first was the failure to be compelling. The second was the failure to connect the dots. The third was a failure of imagination. The last phrase would never leave them. The criticism "really hurt," said Gina Bennett, who remembers even-tempered Barbara taking great exception. "That's the only time I ever saw her break down in tears." Barbara thinks she may have suppressed a memory of that meeting. They had to cope somehow.

The commission also noted that "the intelligence community did not describe the organization [al-Qaeda,] at least in documents we have seen, until 1999." Cindy Storer, who had tried so hard to publish a long paper describing al-Qaeda, back in 1997, felt she had been written out of American history. She felt invisible.

On October 8, 2001, her birthday, Cindy Storer arrived at the Pentagon to brief Deputy Secretary of Defense Paul Wolfowitz. Suffering from a broken knee—she'd been walking her dog in a hurry—Cindy hoisted herself up five flights of stairs to talk Wolfowitz out of his idea that it was Iraq that had orchestrated the 1993 World Trade Center attack. Wolfowitz was genial, listening as Cindy tried to show him the theory was "bollocks." Knowing she failed, she limped down and made her way around the compound, past unsympathetic Marine guards and barred exits.

The analytic sisterhood felt the full force of the heavyweight neoconservatives within the Bush administration, even as they were dealing with threats and tracking down dispersed members of al-Qaeda.

The day after the attacks, George Tenet walked into the West Wing of the White House and saw Richard Perle, a Reagan-era neoconservative now advising Donald Rumsfeld, emerging. "Iraq has to pay a price for what happened yesterday," Perle told Tenet, who was "stunned but said nothing." To Tenet, the exchange showed how quickly the Bush administration set out to produce a rationale for invading Iraq.

A week after the attack, Cindy and Gina were presented with a list of questions from the White House, inquiring about the possibility that Iran, Iraq, or another nation had colluded in the 9/11 attacks. The analysts wrote a twenty-page point-by-point reply refuting the idea. "It just seemed to me that people could not believe that this ragtag group in Afghanistan could do this without state support, even though for ten years we had been warning them that they could," said Gina. Around September 22, Gina was called in and told she would become the agency's analyst looking at Iraq's ties to terrorism. Up to now, there had not been one. Gina was told it was her job to "restore our credibility with the vice president," who felt the analysts were not taking the Iraq angle seriously.

Gina knew she was taking one for the team. She accepted, so that her colleagues could work on the correct target: al-Qaeda. She recalls saying she would follow the facts where they led, "if by 'restore credibility,' you mean I'll look under every rock, scrutinize every possible thing left and right, and we will give exactly what we found, nothing more, nothing less." She remained the sole Iraq analyst until February, when Gina's father died and she went on a bereavement leave, followed by a brief maternity leave in March. By the time she returned, the team had expanded. Pattie Kindsvater had been told to assign more analysts to investigate the Iraq connection. Pattie made it clear to her own supervisor that if called to testify before a congressional committee, she would say that diverting analysts to Iraq meant taking analysts away from al-Qaeda.

By spring 2002, the pressure to find an Iraq connection had not abated. Jami Miscik, the agency's number two analyst, complained to Tenet about a "drumbeat of repetitive queries on Iraq and al-Qa'ida" and told him policymakers "never seemed satisfied with our answers." The Bush team had wanted to oust Saddam Hussein for years and "seized on the emotional impact of 9/11 and created a psychological connection," as Tenet put it. There was "never a serious debate" within the administration about whether Iraq presented an imminent threat. At the Camp David war meeting, Wolfowitz was "fixated on the question of including Saddam in any US response."

The agency devoted "extraordinary effort" to the "Atta in Prague" theory—the one Susan Hasler's husband was assigned to dive into—but, Tenet said, "could never find any convincing evidence that the visit had happened." It's hard to prove a negative, so "we kept being asked to investigate the matter."

As the administration pressed the war case, CIA director George Tenet learned the hard way that analysts—not managers—knew the details and, hence, were the best people to bring to briefings. In his memoir he recalls a meeting in September 2002 in which Vice President Dick Cheney, Scooter Libby, and Paul Wolfowitz descended upon his conference room. Tenet had invited a manager to answer their questions ("always a mistake," Gina Bennett remarked) and the manager proved no match for Libby and Cheney, who had such detailed "knowledge on people, sources, and timelines that the senior CIA analytic manager doing the briefing that day simply could not compete." The briefing, Tenet admitted, was a "disaster." Scooter Libby was a top-dollar litigator, trained in asking questions and piling one hypothetical on top of another. "It was bad," said Kristin Wood, who was present as an observer. "Really bad."

Thus began the sisterhood's elevated role in high-level briefings. From then on, Tenet insisted that subject-matter analysts—"people who knew a lot about a narrow range of topics"—be brought in to briefings. Some of the briefers were newish and junior. To ensure they didn't end up as lambs led to slaughter, Kristin Wood, head of the team assigned to look for an Iraq–al-Qaeda connection, created "murder boards." These were role-playing exercises in which she trained the newcomers in the art of self-defense and offense, blustering and berating them in the persona of a not-taking-no-for-an-answer neocon. She preferred that junior officers freak out in a dress rehearsal, so as to handle the briefing calmly at game time. Some of the trainees complained. Kristin reminded them that the institution was trusting their brainpower, and suggested they regard this as an honor. The stakes were war. The pressure, Kristin Wood said, was like being in a "constant state of alert—like a frequency, a vibration."

In January 2003, her team published a paper saying that the agency found no link between Saddam Hussein and the events of 9/11, and no Iraqi authority, direction, or control over al-Qaeda.

"We held our line that al-Qaeda and Iraq did not have an operational relationship. We held that," said Gina Bennett. "And then they went off on WMD."

THE QUESTION, REALLY, WAS not whether the United States would go to war in Iraq, but when. On August 26, 2002, the vice president gave a speech to the Veterans of Foreign Wars 103rd National Convention, saying "there is no doubt that Saddam Hussein now has weapons of mass destruction" and planned to use them against the United States and its friends and allies. Cheney did not clear the speech with the CIA, Tenet said. It went far beyond what analysts could support, and surprised even Tenet. But the agency eventually bent under the pressure. In early 2001, Iraq had been caught trying to import sixty thousand aluminum tubes that, if modified, were capable of being used to produce a nuclear weapon. A German-run source, "Curveball," reported that the country had mobile production trailers. The agency bought the line. The flawed analysis went into a speech by Secretary of State Colin Powell to the United Nations on February 5, 2003. The bad intelligence got through in part owing to confirmation bias—the tendency to see only evidence that confirms a hypothesis—and because the very officers employed to prevent such bias were told to stand down.

"It was obvious Rumsfeld and Cheney were determined to go to war against Iraq," said Jeanne Newell, a staff operations officer who saw that the reports officer in her unit was furious upon being told to let intelligence through without the usual standards of vetting. "She was told the threshold was lower. The White House wanted *everything*." Reports officers, the original sisterhood of the CIA, since 1947 had served as the conscience of the ops directorate, truth-squadding intelligence to ensure assets were credible. But, Newell said, word came down that "you can put out more marginal reporting," even as walk-ins around the world got the message that America was paying cash for evidence of a connection. "Knowing people are interested—that Uncle Sam is interested in information—they'll tell you anything."

CINDY STORER EARLY ON saw that policymakers were bent on war, and nothing she, as an analyst, said mattered. The administration was peopled by men with ideas. Ideas drive actions, and the idea they nurtured was that Saddam Hussein would be deposed, America would be greeted as liberators, and democracy would blossom in the Middle East. Cindy could not convince them otherwise, so she refused to join the Iraq analysis team. "I said, 'I've been through this rodeo too many times. You didn't do what we told you needed to be done, and I am not cleaning up the mess.'"

But Cindy did see it as her job to shape the context in which the administration would make decisions—to light the policymaker's path into the world that existed rather than the one it wanted to believe in. She set out to demonstrate how ordinary people become radicalized. Working with Susan Hasler, she produced a compelling paper, which they referred to as "The Ziggurat of Zealotry," using her visual skills to depict a terrorist's journey from obscurity to mass homicide.

The paper featured an illustration of a ziggurat, a pyramid-like stepped tower. The ground floor included the *umma*, the entire Muslim community, to which everyone feels a sense of obligation. Most Muslims had no interest in jihad and no sympathy for terrorists, and people on this level were not actively recruited by groups like al-Qaeda. However, when leaders spread the message that "the *umma* is under attack," susceptible individuals could be induced to donate to collection boxes in mosques, or provide housing to fellow Muslims, with no questions asked. A few might move to the second level of the ziggurat, activated by "call" organizations and making a "critical transition" toward active service. Fewer still might proceed to level three, where they were told of a "*collective duty* to defend the faith through jihad," induced by the "perceived occupation of Muslim lands" and the "ability of international organizations and networks to transport and train Jihadist fighters." On level four, the clear message became that the *umma* was under attack and each Muslim "has an *individual duty* to defend it" through jihad. On level five was al-Qaeda, preaching that Muslims "will not be safe until the entire nation-state system is abolished." The enemy was "sharply defined as the Jewish-Crusader alliance"—the United States and Israel, with America as the head of the snake. The diagram showed how the rhetoric a person uses can identify what level of the ziggurat that person exists on, and how entities like NGOs served as "elevators," pulling people up toward a full commitment to jihad.

CINDY'S RADICALIZATION MODEL STRUCK her colleagues as brilliant, with insights other analysts would think about for years. The paper, completed in 2004, did not, however, deter the neocons or inform how events unfolded. The administration invaded Iraq on March 20, 2003, throwing tens of thousands of Iraqis out of jobs and making the country more lawless and unstable. By creating a void into which a new group—ISIS—rushed, the administration did the opposite of what Cindy suggested. It accelerated jihad rather than curbing it.

"Daily, I watched the Bush Administration towing a high-capacity seed spreader across the globe, sowing terrorism. Was there a point to anything I was doing?" Susan Hasler wrote in her memoir. "Some days I would get a claustrophobic panic and have to run down to the basement to walk the continuous loop of corridors under Old and New Headquarters Building."

People in Jeanne Newell's office watched the Iraq invasion—launched just over one month after Powell's speech—with dismay. "It was a stupid decision. Not only was it stupid but they did it incorrectly, by disbanding the police and the army." The coalition forces fired Iraqis who belonged to the Ba'ath Party. Under Saddam Hussein, everybody who wanted a job had had to join the Ba'ath Party. So "you lost all your experts on electricity, dams, everything else." The Iraq war would draw off CIA resources, analysts, case officers, and targeting personnel for years.

The aluminum tubes, she said, ended up as desk toys in Langley, grim reminders of the administration's folly and the agency's culpability by acquiescing.

And the pressure would continue even after the invasion began; in June of 2003, Kristin Wood's team was told that a trove of newly uncovered Iraqi documents really did prove Mohammed Atta, the hijacker, had gotten training in Baghdad. Kristin felt instantly skeptical, and her team went "all out" to analyze this so-called discovery. Scrutinizing the contents of one letter, the team spotted problems with salutations and hierarchy. Dates didn't match, nor relationships. They partnered with the Secret Service's counterfeiting department, whose paper-and-ink experts reported that the paper was newer than the purported date. It was a forgery—disinformation. Kristin Wood had to break the news to Dick Cheney and Scooter Libby. Kristin kept thinking somebody else would inform them, somebody senior, a "grown-up in the room." Then she realized that the "somebody more senior," the grown-up, was now her.

CHAPTER 22

THE NEW GIRLS

LAKELAND, FLORIDA

September 2001

N 1981, A NEW COMPUTER CALLED THE COMMODORE VIC-20 HIT the market—the first low-cost PC aimed at a general public, perfect for gaming and learning to program. Clunky, beige, ugly, and affordable, the Commodore was marketed to teenaged boys and helped establish men's dominance of the computer industry as it expanded. Rosa Smothers bought hers in the mid-1980s, used and already outdated. Smothers wasn't a boy, but she loved systems and set about buying more as she could afford them. Graduating from a Florida community college, she found her way into information management and got used to being the only woman at a party of tech aficionados.

On September 11, 2001, Rosa, now twenty-eight, was installing software at a client's site in Lakeland, Florida, when she overheard people saying a plane hit the World Trade Center. There wasn't a TV nearby, so she kept her head down and continued working, picturing a small twin-engine, like a crop duster. It was only during her drive home, listening to the radio, that she realized all hell was breaking loose in Washington and New York. But she didn't grasp the scope until she got back to her apartment and turned on her own TV.

Up until then, events in the Middle East and South Asia had seemed to Rosa Smothers not unimportant—exactly—but not relevant to her daily life. Now, her awakened curiosity felt boundless. An avid reader, she wanted to understand Osama bin Laden's background and everything else about him; his family, children, wives. Why would a man from great wealth give it all up to live in a cave and kill thousands? Why would he risk the inevitable retribution? She checked out library books and went online. She studied everything bin Laden said in public, including his declaration of war against the United States.

The more she read, the more Rosa Smothers felt one emotion: the urge for revenge. She moved to Tallahassee and enrolled at Florida State University, graduating with a bachelor's degree in information studies. At a job fair, she talked to a recruiter for the Defense Intelligence Agency, who asked for her contact information. A job offer quickly followed.

Rosa by then had accumulated about twenty computers. She loaded them all in her truck, gave them away to friends, said goodbye to her parents, drove north on I-95, and rented a studio apartment in downtown Washington, DC. Her first day at work, office conditions dismayed her; it took three months to get a computer, even though she'd been hired to study terrorists' use of the internet. Her analyses soon found their way to the CIA, who hired her away and had her account set up the day she arrived. In a matter of just a few years, Smothers had transformed herself from an IT technician to a CIA terrorism analyst.

The internet in the early 2000s was still a mystery to many users, and Rosa watched al-Qaeda's facility with digital technology evolve. When she started, terrorists were not using computers with "as much of a sense of healthy paranoia as they could have been," as she put it. Osama bin Laden was an engineer, and his number two, Ayman al-Zawahiri, a surgeon. Neither career required understanding computers per se. The terrorists were often more focused on getting a message to its end point than on vulnerabilities along the way. There were, she was pleased to find, hackable gaps.

Smothers also knew that computers are like any other consumer product; how you use them depends on your gender, age, society, upbringing, and location. How terrorists used technology in Afghanistan or Pakistan differed from how they used it in Southeast Asia. All these things changed over time. Years before YouTube and Dropbox existed, terrorists found ways to produce jihadist videos and put them in hidden directories where recruits could view them. They uploaded artsy-looking "banners"—de facto ads for jihad. As social media emerged, terrorists got better at video production and at using the internet for radicalization.

Smothers also learned that a passion for technology transcended language, culture, and even gender barriers. Participating in one debriefing session with a Middle Eastern asset well versed in terrorist use of the internet, she was assigned the lead role when it became clear that the asset enjoyed her questions more than those of her supervisor. "We were," she discovered, "both just inherently nerds."

LIKE THOUSANDS OF AMERICANS, Rosa Smothers joined the counterterrorism effort at a time of upheaval and expansion in the American intelligence community, when resources began flooding in—and with them, a new generation of women. Some, like her, broke away from existing careers in fields like disaster management, law, and technology. Some came straight from college. It was not yet possible for women to occupy a frontline combat role, and spy work offered a way to defend the homeland. "Women wanted to be in the fight, and this is how you do it," Cindy Storer observed. "You're not going to be on the front lines with a gun—not then. After, but not then. But you could sure as hell get the fuckers."

Counterterrorism became the high-vis job. "We got such a surge of people," said Mallory, the case officer, who plunged into a fight spreading around the globe as terrorist groups splintered and multiplied. In Algeria, where terrorists were trying to kill her chief of station, officers tracked leaders of "Al-Qaeda in the Maghreb." Smaller groups opened al-Qaeda franchises. It was much like buying a Subway franchise; the group would pay what amounted to an al-Qaeda central office to avail itself of social media, videography, and other resources. Among the plots Mallory worked to prevent was one to put ricin, a poison, into Nivea hand cream. The pressure on operations officers became more intense. Prior to 9/11, asset recruiting had been high-level and strategic. In Pakistan, case officers had confined their recruiting to the inner circle of President Pervez Musharraf. "We wanted his bodyguards. We wanted the military. We wanted the nuke thing. We didn't care about the low-level economic things." But "once a lot of people came in and 9/11 happened and all our failings were put out there, we were told, why aren't you collecting on oil infrastructure? Why aren't you collecting on all this different stuff that you frankly didn't have time for?"

The attacks served as a shot of growth hormone in CIA ranks. The discriminatory ban on gay and lesbian officers had been lifted in 1995, when President Bill Clinton signed an executive order saying security clearances could not be denied based on sexual orientation. Gay men and lesbians joined the effort against a retrograde adversary opposed to the acceptance that Western society, however slowly, was beginning to exhibit toward same-sex couples. On September 11, Holly Bond had just come back from a trip to Ireland, to visit a woman she had met. Holly had intended to find work in Ireland and see what developed between them. After the attacks, Bond changed her mind. A onetime military intelligence officer, she decided to finish her college degree, to qualify for a job at the CIA. After graduating from American University, Bond enrolled in the CIA unit tasked with defusing improvised explosive devices—IEDs—and training liaison partners.

She had done bomb-squad work in the military, taking a grueling course that "was like nothing I had ever done, or had to do since." A day of training might consist of nine hours of learning about ten kinds of land mines, absorbing instruction about weapons and ammunition—American, Russian, Italian, German, Japanese—followed by chow, followed by study hall from six to ten. Instructors would test them by throwing out ordnance for defusion. She went to Iraq to train people and help CIA case officers vet sources. If an asset claimed to be part of a bomb-making group, Holly could help gauge whether that was true.

Holly then joined the "physical access group"—the agency's team of experts at breaking and entering. Even there, she found divisions by sex. When she joined the domain most intriguing to her—machine locks— she was puzzled to learn that locks had been an all-male preserve. After all, a pair of women standing at a hotel room door, late at night, making a clandestine entry, look far less suspicious than two men. They could be prostitutes, escorts, girlfriends. But for anybody, physical access was high-risk work and the consequences of being caught were dire. The teams were exquisitely well prepared. She found the CIA's logistics and technical abilities extraordinary. Physical access work was a dream job. Bond remembered thinking: "You're telling me I'm the first woman who did this?"

Women's roles also expanded at headquarters, as the agency began shuttering old units and opening new ones. Obscure jobs became high-profile ones. These often were in fields toward which women had been steered. Hunting terrorists required skills now understood to matter, in a way they had not mattered before. For all the meetings, white papers, studies, rent-a-skirt efforts, glass ceiling commissions, offsite training sessions, televised apologies, EEOC complaints, sex discrimination lawsuits, and focus groups conducted over decades, what it took to advance women at the CIA turned out to be large-scale disaster.

One reason women rose was because analysts like Gina Bennett, Barbara Sude, Kristin Wood, and Cindy Storer had reached points of maturity in their own careers and could exert more influence. Another was because techniques such as targeting had matured and become, in this arena, as important as old-fashioned street-level human recruitment. The vault women's long, unsung tenure writing biographical profiles and computerizing 3 x 5 cards emerged as the skill set needed to "find the enemy," as Tenet had put it, where he resided. As targeting gained respectability and became a bona fide career track, drafted into it (some might say thrown into it) were officers from two obvious categories. The first were leadership analysts; the second were staff operations officers, or SOOs, the so-called sneaker ladies whose duties included fielding cable traffic and who thus were well positioned to track a single person as he traveled: a Tajik, say, en route to Kampala. Both disciplines were largely female, because, up to now, both had been seen as secondary.

The intensity of the work took a toll on these women, their lives and relationships, just as the life of an overseas station chief—stress, alcoholism, overwork—had taken a toll on men. "Counterterrorism in general just ate people up with their passion for it," observed Sue Gordon, a former top CIA officer who from 2017 to 2019 served as Principal

Deputy Director of National Intelligence, a mouthful of a title for an exalted role familiarly called P-Diddy. "To understand CT, you have to understand that the intelligence community and the CIA in particular felt like we'd failed the nation. The idea of the 9/11 attacks was an assault on our responsibility. Counterterrorism consumed everyone who participated in it, because we needed to do it because we had failed."

Mike Sulick, whose wife, Shirley, had been such an asset to his own career in Moscow and other places, became head of the clandestine service in 2007. He, too, was struck by the elevated presence of targeting analysts. Fighting terrorism requires a different skill set from fighting Communism. "It's easy for a guy to walk out in Peru and go to a party, and you know, he doesn't even have to read a book. All he has to do is like, 'Look at me. You want me to offer you a drink? Vodka? I could pound it back with you, Ivan.'" But when it came to finding Osama bin Laden, "It takes patience and work."

At Tenet's five o'clock meetings, top-level officials brought targeters with them so as not to be caught flat-footed. The CIA director would be "firing questions at them, and they'd remember everything that happened here, and this is the connection to it. They were just so grounded, immersed."

Sulick added, "I would probably stop being a terrorist if I met those women and knew what they knew about me and my ilk."

BUT WOMEN'S RISING PROMINENCE occurred at a dark moment, too, when intelligence work bent to include harrowing operations of a kind the agency had never engaged in. Before 9/11, many "kinetic" operations were governed by the concept known as "find, fix, and finish," which meant finding a terrorist and persuading the FBI or a cooperative liaison service to disrupt his ability to do business. After 9/11, "find, fix, and finish" took on a more clearly lethal scope. It could mean locating a human being to arrest or kidnap him to be taken to a secret prison. Initially, the main goal, after locating a terrorist, was to detain him and find out what he knew. Eventually, in the era of drone strikes, it would also come to mean killing him. By helping put the X on the head of a human being, analysts and targeters were morally implicated in the finish. "We put warheads on foreheads" became a form of gallows humor among the analytic corps.

It was not the first time in US history, however, that behind-the-scenes intelligence work led to the deaths of faraway combatants, nor the first time that women were involved. During World War II, thousands of women came to Washington, DC, to break the coded messages used by Japanese supply ships in the Pacific Ocean and German U-boats in the Atlantic. Their work enabled US submarine commanders to sink enemy ships, causing the loss of tens of thousands of Axis lives. Those women understood this. They were at war. In April 1943, cheering erupted—the women joining in—in a Washington, DC, compound after the US military shot down the plane carrying Admiral Yamamoto, the commander of the Japanese Navy and mastermind of the Pearl Harbor attacks, using code-breaking intelligence. The Yamamoto shootdown provided some of the legal justification for authorized killing after the 9/11 attacks.

For analysts in the twenty-first century, the enemy's work was remote—but no longer unseen. The women entered at an awful time when even the most deskbound officer was compelled to behold the most unspeakable atrocities. In 2002, the *Wall Street Journal* reporter Daniel Pearl was abducted in Karachi and beheaded, his murder filmed on a camcorder, and videotapes distributed. On May 7, 2004, Nicholas Berg, a twenty-six-year-old American freelance radio technician, was beheaded in Iraq, by Islamist fighters who posted it on the internet. The executioner, Abu Musab al-Zarqawi, ushered in a wave of mass murder in Iraq. The analysts had to not only watch the videos but study them. "Those of us that have worked counterterrorism targets have seen horrendous things," said Rosa Smothers, the Floridian who loaded up her truck to help with the effort. "Beheading someone doesn't take five seconds. It takes several minutes of cutting." Returning from Iraq, she would find herself walking in circles around her parents' kitchen, unable to talk or sleep.

The change in tenor was felt throughout the intelligence community. Mathematicians and analysts at the National Security Agency in Fort Meade, Maryland, had to reckon with knowing that their work was being used to fix coordinates for drone attacks on terrorists and possibly on women and children traveling with them. Some quit. "A lot of NSA analysts didn't want to do that," said Linda Millis, a historian of intelligence who teaches at Marymount University in Virginia and who worked at both the CIA and the NSA during the Cold War. As part of her own work, she spied on scientists to see what nuclear weapons they were developing. That seemed different from saying "I'm going to give you the coordinates so that you can drop a bomb on somebody and kill them."

"The pre-9/11 CIA versus post-9/11 CIA is drastic," said Millis. The 9/11 attacks attracted officers with a more military approach, more right-wing, even as the agency was seeking to diversify. This created a clash of cultures.

The visible presence of women at the CIA, more than a half century after its founding, proved one of the biggest cultural shifts. "If you want to be really karmic about it, about how the universe aligned," consider what the world would have looked like without women playing a lead role after the attacks, suggests Sue Gordon. "If 9/11 and the hunt for UBL had happened, say, early in my days when [the targeting] discipline hadn't really issued forth, when you didn't have as many women," it's not clear that the hunt for Osama bin Laden would have succeeded, nor the wider war on terrorism. The gender makeup of the team tracking bin Laden—not just targeters, but case officers and drone pilots— was so noticeable that it struck Nicholas Dujmovic, an agency historian, to wonder what bin Laden might have thought had he known who was coming after him.

PUTTING WARHEADS ON FOREHEADS

LOCATIONS OVERSEAS

2003

N THE MONTHS AFTER THE SEPTEMBER 11 ATTACKS, CINDY STORER found herself consulting with an ops team headed to Afghanistan, pursuing a terrorist cell she happened to know a lot about. She was sharing what she knew, when one ops officer started talking about finding "an offshore ship" to take a rendered terrorist. Cindy was enough of a student of history to know what that likely meant: They were taking him to a place where international law did not apply, so that coercive measures, possibly torture, could be used. Her suspicion was right: As the fight escalated, the agency began employing physical and psychological abuse to try to make people divulge information. "I made the decision right then and there, I wanted nothing to do with it," she said later. "I told my management. I said, 'I will have nothing to do with this, and you can't make me.'" Instead, she devoted her time to analyzing overseas attacks in Madrid and London and Bali, "just a constant stream of terrorist attacks for the first three years."

The years 2002 and 2003 inaugurated a deeply complex time, as the sisterhood coped with guilt, blame, grief, and the need to quickly decide how far they were willing to go, to access information to do their job. The women had to examine their own motives for not only staying in the fight but escalating it to the point of becoming aggressors. To vary-ing degrees, every woman, like every man, had to assess whether she was willing to be part of an effort that included methods many consid-ered torture—or whether to refuse, like Cindy, or even resign. The women's feelings about their own complicity would evolve over time, and their responses to this moral inventory varied.

THE AGENCY'S "ENHANCED INTERROGATION" program began, amid haste and chaos, in March 2002, when Pakistani officials raided several safe houses in Faisalabad and arrested more than two dozen al-Qaeda members. Among these was Abu Zubaydah, a logistics expert who ran a training camp believed to have ties to bin Laden. Abu Zubaydah was shot and wounded during his capture, and the CIA found itself in the peculiar position of trying to keep a terrorist alive, to find out what he knew. Lawyers were brought in, and the decision was made to hold "High Value Detainees" for questioning.

What sort of techniques could be used against him? US law forbade torture, as did the Geneva Conventions. Lawyers for the Bush admin-istration came up with a rationale that (1) certain physical methods weren't torture per se, and (2) even if they were, it was okay if the abuse occurred in a country that permitted it. The so-called torture memos were drafted by Justice Department lawyers in August 2002, the first of these being penned by Deputy Assistant Attorney John Yoo. They gave the president the power to order enhanced interrogation of cap-tured terrorists and protected the interrogators from liability. Among other things, the memo outlined that tactics such as waterboarding and confining suspects to a small box did not violate the torture statute. Ac-cording to Tenet, the "most aggressive" techniques were reserved for "a handful of the worst terrorists on the planet." Legal or not, even many CIA officials who knew or learned about them, deemed them, as one put it, "morally indefensible."

The interrogations were conducted in countries whose cooperation first had to be secured. Struggling to find a place to transport Abu Zubaydah, the agency sent him to a secret prison in Thailand, where he recovered from injuries, then, in August 2002, was interrogated for two weeks on a "near 24-hour-per-day basis," according to an exhaustive report released by the Senate Intelligence Committee at the behest of its chairman, California Democratic senator Dianne Feinstein. The techniques included waterboarding, a method in which an interrogator puts a cloth over the detainee's mouth and another pours water over it to simulate the sensation of drowning, with a limit of ten seconds. Zubaydah, according to one CIA source, was waterboarded eighty-three times, subjected to sleep deprivation, and locked in a coffin-sized box for eleven days. The officers employing these methods were trained by a pair of psychologists, Air Force veterans working as contractors, James Elmer Mitchell and John Bruce Jessen, who also applied the techniques.

The spectacle of Zubaydah's waterboarding was so disturbing that CIA officers present were "visually and psychologically very uncomfortable," according to a Senate report that said witnessing an early session "had a profound effect on all staff members present." Officers were choking up, and threatening to transfer. Upon being waterboarded, Zubaydah became "completely unresponsive, with bubbles rising through his open, full mouth."

The Senate report would also find that Abu Zubaydah's importance had been exaggerated. He had been "miscast" as a "senior al-Qaeda lieutenant," and the camp he ran was not tied to bin Laden. He did identify Khalid Sheikh Mohammed from a photo, however, and revealed KSM's central role in plotting the September 11 attacks. Jennifer Matthews, one of the founding members of Alec Station, was deeply knowledgeable about the Afghan-Pakistan border region and had been instrumental in Abu Zubaydah's capture. Matthews traveled to Thailand and was present during his interrogations. She relayed the information back to headquarters, where Gina Bennett had to absorb the hard news about KSM's key role, having tracked him in the 1990s but given up.

On March 1, 2003, CIA and Pakistani officers captured Khalid Sheikh Mohammed himself, with the help of an asset who hid in a bathroom and texted his location at a safe house in Rawalpindi, Pakistan. The CIA took the architect of 9/11 to a secret prison in Poland, where, over a period of weeks, the al-Qaeda propagandist was subjected to slaps, walling—being slammed against a wall—and waterboarding, as CIA officers sought to find out what new operations might be planned. "I want to know what he knows, and I want to know it fast," operations director Jim Pavitt said. KSM, according to Tenet, would confess to involvement in the September 11 attacks; the Richard Reid attempted shoe bombing; the 1993 WTC attacks; and the beheading of Daniel Pearl.

Among those who participated in KSM's enhanced interrogation was Alfreda Bikowsky, the voluble former grad student who had told Dewey Clarridge she wanted to combat evil, now serving as deputy chief of Alec Station. Factors in her ascent included her capacious knowledge and urgent, whip-smart manner at briefings. Tenet was known to like dramatic briefers who brought clarity and passion to the conference table, and Bikowsky was among the most articulate and vivid. At one meeting, Tenet was so disappointed in one briefer—serious, careful, monotone— that he called a break and summoned Bikowsky as a replacement.

Freda—as people called her—played a role not only in waterboarding sessions but in shaping the strategy used to defend them. In 2004, two years after the program commenced, the CIA inspector general's office began to investigate potential abuses. "Let's be foward [sic] leaning" in defending the program, she urged colleagues. Techniques like waterboarding, sleep deprivation, and stress positions—she argued in cables—were "key to unlocking" intelligence to save American lives. She wrote an email in 2004 saying the information from KSM and others had saved "several hundred, perhaps thousands, of lives." Other high-level CIA officials made the same argument to Congress, often using her memos for backup. These included Jose Rodriguez, who succeeded Cofer Black as the head of the CTC; and Tenet's successor, CIA director Michael Hayden.

The Senate report, released in 2014, and running to more than five hundred pages in just its public, redacted version, debunked these claims of effectiveness. The report concluded that coercive techniques were useless or counterproductive. Footnotes suggest some of Bikowsky's cables provoked eye rolling among colleagues. One described Abu Zubaydah as being defiant and declaring America weak. "Everything I have read indicated he used a nondeifiant [sic] resistance strategy," a colleague wrote. Another replied that the tale was "probably a combo" of Alfreda Bikowsky and another officer and "I'll leave it at that."

The language in the cables sometimes veers toward a kind of hard-boiled elation. In 2003, Bikowsky suggested she was looking forward to asking KSM about one detainee's assertion that a group of African American Muslim converts were enrolled in al-Qaeda training camps. She wrote that she was "loving" the story of black Muslims and that "Mukie," as she called KSM, "is going to be hatin' life on this one." But, according to the report, she had made a mistake; misconstruing the first detainee's report, she thought the trainees were already in the United States. KSM, who regularly fed his interrogators false information, asserted this and later retracted it. The purported converts were a fiction, and the error led to a wild-goose chase for black Muslims in, of all places, Montana.

Bikowsky, the report concluded, also was part of an operation that resulted in the kidnapping of at least one innocent person. A German citizen, Khalid El-Masri, was arrested while traveling on a bus in Macedonia and handed over to the CIA. Flown to Afghanistan, he was interrogated and released nearly five months later, after the agency realized he wasn't a member of al-Qaeda; his name resembled that of an associate of a 9/11 hijacker. One former intel officer told NBC that her errors and obfuscations were such that "she should be put on trial and put in jail for what she has done."

The Senate report argued that a technique called "rapport building" produced better intelligence, pointing out that KSM and others responded to "creature comforts and sense of importance." A key piece of intelligence—that bin Laden was often seen with a courier named Abu Ahmed al-Kuwaiti—was shared by one detainee in a relaxed setting. The detainee, Hassan Ghul, was in a safe house, "literally having tea," according to Nada Bakos, a targeter in Iraq. "He wasn't handcuffed to anything. He was having a free-flowing conversation" during which he talked about leaders, their locations, movement, operational security, and training.

———

AS THE COERCION PROGRAM continued, and became public, outcry and discomfort ensued. The accumulation of detainees, and the treatment they received, emerged as one of the lowest moments of post-9/11 America. Public revulsion was exacerbated by the revelations of torture, sexual abuse, and other atrocities committed in the US military prison at Abu Ghraib, accounts of which emerged in 2004. In November 2007, the agency conducted its last enhanced interrogation, and in 2009, the secret prisons closed. But some prisoners sent to Guantánamo Bay would remain there for—at present count—seventeen years. Bikowsky's identity was protected in the Senate report, and, as terrorism spread and changed form, Alec Station was rebranded as Global Jihad and she became its chief. Some colleagues were shocked she had been "entrusted with such power," according to an NBC investigation. But one former CIA officer, John Maguire, told NBC that while the Senate report was mostly accurate—in stating, for instance, that torture did not work—Alfreda Bikowsky, whose identity was still shielded, was an "extraordinarily capable analyst."

"She has a caustic personality, but she is frighteningly intelligent and knows more about al-Qaeda than virtually anyone else at the CIA. She's hard to manage but brings a lot to the table," he said. "She wasn't afraid to make mistakes." Another top CTC official, interviewed for this book, said that she had a huge number of groups to track; her hyperactive manner enabled her ably to do so; she wasn't nice, but her "knowledge was encyclopedic."

Bikowsky broke her own cover after retiring from the agency in 2021. In an interview for this book, she expressed no regrets about the role she played in the enhanced interrogation program. She described the program as "a job that I think no one wanted to ever see happen," stressing that she served as a "subject matter expert" and not an interrogator. She jumped at the ability to get information "from the horse's mouth" and felt it was "absolutely necessary" and that key intelligence was obtained. Acknowledging that "reasonable people can disagree" on the program's morality, Bikowsky contended that the CIA's action "had 100 percent legal authority" and that "I can say without any equivocation that I was never, ever asked to do anything that I believed was immoral or illegal, nor did I ever, ever witness that."

She felt the authors of the Senate report had the benefit of hindsight, while "we were piecing it together in real time." She recalled the urgency she felt in the days after 9/11, remembering sitting in Rich Blee's office within days of the attacks, and hearing talk of a tactical nuclear weapon in New York City. "It was pandemonium. It was just crazy." She objected to pieces written about her while under cover, often mentioning her hair and lipstick color—"as if they were painting a picture of Cruella de Vil."

By the time of her own retirement, Bikowsky had married Mike Scheuer, the former head of Alec Station, and reinvented herself as a life coach. At one point, according to Reuters, she had an online beauty site, YBeU Beauty, focused on helping women "look good, feel good, and do good." On the site, she said her career required her to leave her "comfort zone," leading teams of women in can't-fail missions, and "I loved every minute of it." In my conversation with her, she said that she devoted her entire career to the global fight against terrorism and felt "blessed" to be able to live her purpose. "I was offered jobs to throttle back a bit, reconstitute, and I just never wanted to. I made a commitment to finish it, and I feel like I did."

Darrell Blocker, a clandestine officer who served as deputy director of CTC from 2012 to 2013, said that "she and her team are heroes" for what they contributed to a counterterrorism effort that went on for decades, long after the EIT program was ended. Of enhanced interrogation, however, he says: "How we ended up in that is still kind of shocking to me."

AND ONE PARTICIPANT DID publicly repent. That person was future CIA director Gina Haspel, who oversaw a secret prison in Thailand in 2002, including while a suspect was being waterboarded. As deputy to CTC director Jose Rodriguez, she also aided in destroying tapes of Abu Zubaydah's interrogation sessions. More than a decade later, nominated to become the first female CIA director, Haspel vowed to the Senate Select Committee on Intelligence that the program would never be reinstated and said she regretted it had occurred. "I'm not going to sit here, with the benefit of hindsight, and judge the very good people who made hard decisions, who were running the agency in very extraordinary circumstances," she said. She offered another rationale for why it should never be repeated: It exacted too high a cost on officers administering it. Arizona Republican John McCain, a former prisoner of war who chaired the Armed Services Committee, said "her refusal to acknowledge torture's immorality is disqualifying" and urged his colleagues to vote against her. She was confirmed by a vote of 54 to 45.

DURING THE TIME WHEN the enhanced interrogation program was under way, many analysts had no idea it was going on. Others found themselves brought in to vet assertions and suggest questions. Others availed themselves of the intelligence even if they didn't take part. After all, they told themselves, lawyers said it was okay. Some now wish they had resigned or switched jobs; but others still defend the techniques to which the agency resorted, in a time of extreme fear and prolonged peril. "I'm fine with the dirty side of clandestine tradecraft," said Gina Bennett, in an interview for this book. "I have no problem with tormenting or torturing Khalid Sheikh Mohammed. I don't care if they suffered at all."

The women had to read communications, including the diary of Abu Zubaydah and "what he wanted to do with women," as Tenet put it in his memoir (he did not reveal details). Reading the terrorist's words had an impact. "Having read the personal communications with each other and understanding the amount of pain and agony and death and destruction they wanted and did cause," Gina reflected, "I just don't feel like any kind of enhanced interrogation technique we used was ever disproportionate to the crime, not anywhere near." She accepts that studies show torture doesn't provide good information. But she counters that analysts spent years fearing an attack would happen again, and every morsel of information factored in.

"One thing I really don't think people understand or can appreciate is how little we knew about the organization of al-Qaeda," she said. "How little we knew about who was who, how they operated, where they operated in the world, where they were sending everything. You have no idea how hard it is to penetrate a clandestine intelligence organization in a country where we don't have a presence, that has for years been building up their ability." In her view, every revelation helped bring the picture into focus. "It might not have pointed to a bomb about to go off in New York, but the things we did get were things that we did not have. And if you're a targeter, you have to put those tiny little things together, to get things that you didn't otherwise have. How critical all that information is, at a time when you don't have years to penetrate an organization."

Gina Bennett does agree it's worth seeking a world where the greatest democracy on earth doesn't engage in torture or methods close to it. She cites a quote by Cicero to the effect that there are things so despicable or wicked that a man shouldn't be asked to do them on behalf of his country, nor should his country ask them of him. "You can protect it all, but if you turn around and look back and what you see is no longer America, then what was it for?"

"I have never known a single day at work where the Constitution didn't come up," she reflected. "Well, maybe a little bit probably in the post-9/11 period."

BUT THE PROGRAM HAD another impact: As the excesses of the war on terror became known, and women's roles were highlighted in films like *Zero Dark Thirty* (2012), a strain of feminism developed, arguing that while counterterrorism did bring women front and center in intelligence, it amounted to a racist display of white women trying to emulate white men by abusing men of color. This argument reflects a Hollywood-inflected view of women's involvement in the counterterrorism effort, which was somewhat more diverse, in terms of race and gender, than that movie suggested, but it raises an important point.

Because it's true, the dynamics of the enhanced interrogation program created more problems for an agency that has always had trouble attracting Black officers and those from other communities of color. In part, this dates back to the covert action programs of the 1960s and 1970s, and the efforts to infiltrate civil-rights groups as well as students.

The revelations of the Church and Pike committee hearings created a lingering stigma that affected the agency's ability to recruit from minority communities, for decades going forward. "Didn't the CIA kill Martin Luther King?" a Black officer, Nicole Ash, remembers thinking as a twenty-year-old college student back in 1991, when a white college professor urged her to apply to the CIA. When she hesitated, he dropped the application in front of her at the lunch table, so she applied, to appease him. The agency didn't kill King; that was her impression back then, and it was understandable. It was the FBI that harassed Dr. King, and even wrote him a letter urging him to commit suicide; the agency, however, did spy on civil rights groups. During the serial exposés of the 1970s, the doings of both agencies got tangled together, conflated. And then there were the agency's efforts at killing and unseating democratically elected leaders in Africa and Latin America. These two threads—domestic mucking around in the civil-rights community; bad dealings in countries whose citizens were mostly Black and brown—embedded themselves in the public mind in a way that has been hard to dispel. Nicole Ash did apply, as it happened; given her choice of four positions, she worked for a white male boss who became a powerful sponsor of her and was proud when she rose higher than he did. She overcame more than one racist supervisor, worked to improve the conversation around these issues, and had a brilliant career in the field of open-source intelligence.

But the post-9/11 spectacle of targeting Arab men would be an enduring problem for the agency.

CHAPTER 24

ESPIONAGE IS ESPIONAGE

LISA HARPER, NEARING SIXTY, WAS ANOTHER MEMBER OF ALEC Station who refused to have anything to do with the coerced interrogation program. To Lisa, any technique that smacked of torture violated her personal code of conduct. So much dirty business is possible, working undercover, that every officer must find the place to draw the line, and Lisa knew hers. Being of the "catch more flies with honey than vinegar" school of elicitation, Lisa felt torture was wrong and immoral and that it amounted to bad tradecraft. But she could tell that some younger officers thought coerced interrogation seemed awesome. "Oh, yes," she said; some were eager to go "running around the world with a private jet and capturing these people and interrogating them."

Lisa understood their motives. Bin Laden had gone to ground, and targeters, who lived every move he'd made for years, could neither find him nor get the information they needed. "They thought that the end justified the means. They were frustrated at not being able to get ahead any other way." But Lisa "told all my young friends that were eagerly" raising their hands, especially Arabic speakers being asked to translate detainee debriefings, to "be very, very careful. It's going to bite you." The Agency, she warned them, will be the fall guy.

With her long decades of experience, Lisa also didn't suffer as much guilt for not having prevented the attacks as some of these younger colleagues did. It seemed to Lisa the enemy was not being given enough credit. The CIA, she felt, had done a good job, but on that single day in September, terrorists had done a better one. "Al-Qaeda was an excellent organization," Lisa reflected. "It was a well-run organization that changed its tactics. They find out that phone communications are being intercepted—well, they go back to couriers. They were flexible, they were well funded because they had all their friends in the Middle East who were secretly funding them."

Raised with a belief in American exceptionalism, Lisa Harper remained convinced her country could offer a moral example. Counterterrorism appealed to her for this reason. "I was a Cold War girl and now I had a new mission." America had brought down the Berlin Wall and defeated the Soviet Union. The same kind of victory, she believed, could be achieved now.

In the months and years after 9/11, Lisa traveled frequently—departing for a tour of duty, coming back to file a report, raising her hand for another. She was an operational pinch hitter, an elite consultant. It was the kind of work she'd joined the agency to do, back in 1968. Her skills, she was pleased to find, had not diminished; she knew to trust her instincts and to validate them. As theories emerged about new attack scenarios, she was among those sent to test them. Around 2004, George Tenet noted that a stream of reporting "told us of al-Qai'da plans to smuggle operatives through Mexico to conduct suicide operations inside the United States." Lisa was among a group of four retirees—Cold Warriors all—sent to check out the possibility of another homeland attack, via the country's southern border.

The retirees flew in, met in a Mexican airport, and descended upon the local CIA station. Their biggest challenge, at first, seemed to be their own colleagues: younger officers threatened by their experience and suspicious of their motives. The youngsters saw the arriving annuitants as geezers and boomers, maybe even spies sent to report back to headquarters. Lisa pointed out that her own active career was over; she wasn't gunning for a promotion, and only wanted to help them. Having taken refresher computer courses, she dived into the station's database, to identify targets and suggest ways to gain access. Together they proved the sneaking-over-the-southern-border theory was a red herring. The station did a good job, she said, but "I think that we were a force multiplier."

Lisa also worked to shore up the safety of US embassies in Africa, always so vulnerable, as evidenced in Nairobi and Dar es Salaam—and, later, Benghazi. It was critical work but also tended to inflame interagency rivalries, since embassies were State Department by definition. Dispatched to one African city, Lisa saw that local officials had put a roadblock on a certain road but were still admitting ambulances. A terrorist could repurpose an ambulance to get close to the embassy and bomb it. When she delivered her analysis, the embassy's security officer bristled, and the deputy chief of mission was reluctant to ruffle feathers with a demarche asking local officials to close the road to ambulance traffic. The DCM tried to persuade his boss, the ambassador, that Lisa was a flighty middle-aged woman—a "menopausal Minnie," as Lisa put it.

It may or may not have helped that the ambassador was also a middle-aged woman. She bought into the propaganda war until, at one diplomatic reception, she heard Lisa conversing in immaculate French. "She started thinking, well maybe there's something to it," recalled Lisa, who knew this because the two middle-aged women became friends. The demarche was made and complied with. Alec Station stopped hearing chatter about a hit. They never knew whether foiling one plot caused the perpetrators to relocate to an easier target. But after every attack, successful or foiled, they learned something new about the adversary's methodology.

Lisa felt she was able to take her Cold War skill set and apply it to al-Qaeda in a one-to-one transfer of methods. She was aiming to dismantle a system as well as an ideology—not Communism this time, but the idea of a caliphate or religious state. She was once more fighting an organized body, a group whose philosophy and tactics opposed American values.

And there are only so many ways to fight an organized body. These included working with the US embassy and with foreign officials, whose willingness to help the CIA never ceased to amaze her. "You don't do anything without the local government's permission. You really need them, because they're the ones who are going to know which mosques harbor transients. They're going to know how the money travels." In one operation, a local intelligence officer met with an al-Qaeda member who was furious after bin Laden left his sister behind at Tora Bora, and she died. The officer happened to be from the same ethnic minority as the disaffected terrorist, who handed over a phone number for an al-Qaeda call center. The liaison passed it on to Alec Station. "That's what you work for, is when you get this one little tip and boom!"

Lisa also did deradicalization training, teaching local people to dissuade their friends, relatives, and neighbors from joining jihad. African citizens didn't want bombs going off in their streets and shopping malls. Lisa's French proved a key asset, and her caretaking instincts served her well. Training adult students who arrived after a long bus trip and, unlike her, did not receive a lavish per diem, she realized they were hungry—literally hungry—and used her funds to buy them food.

She trained them in how to recruit terrorists and their confederates as assets; how to dangle inducements like money or resettlement; how to shatter a belief system; how to identify somebody doing reconnaissance; how, after an attack, to find the ways the perpetrators exposed themselves. She couldn't divulge high-level tradecraft, but the basic methods sufficed. "You'd be surprised; it's not rocket science. You can teach people very fast how to do this."

And she taught trainees to counter false propaganda about Islam. Lisa, as it happened, was now happily remarried. Her husband, Charlie, was a Sunni Muslim who had lived in the States for years. They'd met while Lisa was doing a stint as a freelance interpreter, work that was well paying and pleasant. Charlie, like her, was worldly and well traveled. His family came from a town in northern Morocco—Ouazzane—with great spiritual significance. The town was home to an ancient Sufi brotherhood of which his father, a descendant of the founder, was the titular head. The Sufis are a nonviolent, contemplative sect of Islam. Charlie knew a lot about Sufism and Lisa was an eager learner. She reread the Qur'an and did her own research, learning to speak about the merciful, peaceful nature of the Islamic faith. She had to study what the Qur'an said women could and couldn't do. She dressed modestly, working overseas, but did not wear a hijab. If someone was insulted, she would explain that the hijab is not in the Qur'an; it's part of the Hadith, the interpretations that came down later. If someone wanted to know why she, a married woman, was not home with her husband, she would point out that one of the Prophet's wives was a businesswoman and a powerhouse.

She also had to validate herself as someone worth paying attention to. Lisa knew she was up against a "testosterone-driven" adversary whose leaders saw women as child-bearers and chattel. Women, in their view, could be beaten, silenced, used as human shields. Leadership in these groups put forth the notion that there was no justification in the Qur'an for female equality—that women exist only to be helpmates to men, and that if a woman is raped it's her own fault because the burden is on the woman not to incite lewd thoughts in men.

So Lisa would tell assets she had been specially selected. Precisely because she was a woman—she'd point out—people would never think she was spying. When talking to a male asset, she'd assure him that being sent a woman was added protection for him.

Once, she went to Lebanon to sub for a case officer, handling assets while he was away. One asset complained she was asking too many questions. The next time they met, Lisa retorted: "Do you know how many reports you get with fewer questions? You get one." She had fired off three, she told him, and Washington was delighted. "All of a sudden, I'm not just a little woman who was foisted on them because their male officer was gone. I was somebody worth knowing," she said. After that, he always asked for the question lady.

When one asset tried to rest his hand on her knee, Lisa gave him a friendly caution. "I said, 'You know what we do with our assets that harass women? The boys come and kill them.'" Lisa never reported advances. She dealt with them. It felt like the same work she had been doing all her life: turning the tables, matching wits. "You really have to know your Qur'an and you have to be able to argue and to get into the 'Thou shalt not kill,' and what does 'jihad' really mean. You're challenging a belief system. Which is pretty much the same as Communism.

"At the end of the day," she concluded, "espionage is espionage."

CHAPTER 25

I MADE BAD PEOPLE HAVE BAD DAYS

Early 2002

THE PORSCHE FACTORY WAS LUXURIOUS, THE SALESMAN CON-genial. After Heidi August enjoyed a meal in the factory's elegant dining room, he insisted she visit the seamstresses who sewed the car upholstery, to select a color for the contrast stitching on the navy blue seats of her custom-made Porsche. The Porsche itself would be silver, so Heidi chose silver thread. The seamstress took three shades from a cabinet of spools, and they went outside to see which ones glittered best in sunlight.

Heidi loved the new Porsche—the best kind of European car, she'd decided—and had it shipped back after her tour in Germany ended in 2002. But she couldn't enjoy it long. In early 2003, Heidi was sent to Iraq. She volunteered for the mission. She'd been detailed to the NSA in the interim and felt she had useful skills that might be helpful. She worked well with the military and had always found war zones exciting. Both her parents were gone, now, and could not worry about her. She had to present an up-to-date will to prove her own affairs were in order, in case she didn't return. She garaged the Porsche and packed her things.

As the coalition invasion of Iraq commenced in March 2003, Heidi waited in the Kuwait Hilton, with other civilian officials. Not long after

US Marines pulled down the giant statue of Saddam Hussein in Baghdad, she joined a group of officials making the long drive to the Iraqi capital: one hundred people traveling four to a car, in twenty-five brand-new sport utility vehicles. Her SUV pulled up at what had been Hussein's main palace. The infrastructure had been mostly destroyed and things were not yet up and running. US soldiers were still eating MREs and barbecuing hot dogs on grills. She slept in a sleeping bag the first couple of nights.

Exploring the palace, Heidi found a side kitchen on an upper floor. The room had a refrigerator and a sink with running water. She approached workers at a little communications center and persuaded them to run an internet connection to the kitchen, which she turned into a command center and bedroom. A generator provided electricity to plug in her laptop. Driving around, she noticed a street vendor selling air conditioners. She bought one and had a carpenter fit it into her window. To discourage visitors, she hung a sign that said, "Women Only." The air conditioner masked sounds, and she slept fine. Before long, she and other officials were relocated to the Al Rasheed Hotel, where there was no electricity or running water. Heidi missed her snug palace setup.

Heidi's job was to restore the city's cellphone service, a tasking that earned her the nickname "Ma Bell of Baghdad." Coalition bombing had destroyed switching stations and there was no playbook for how to get the phone system up and running. It was just the kind of challenge Heidi liked. She knew nothing about telecommunications, but she knew how to find people who did. She had a sign put up outside one empty building: telecommunications engineers wanted. Applicants showed up—Iraqi men wearing ties, Iraqi women wearing high heels and looking polished. The women were engineers with PhDs in communications. They'd had good jobs under the Hussein regime and lost them with the invasion.

The project required a lot of new antennae, which meant she needed access to a lot of roofs. She hit upon the strategy of giving cellphones not only to high-level officials but to lower-level workers, like janitors. Here: Call your cousin in Canada. Call anybody you want. The janitors provided access and looked after the hardware. She got Baghdad back in service, which was fun, sort of. She could also make calls. Heidi would be driving around and call Mary Margaret Graham. "Guess where I am," she would say.

After about two weeks, Iraq stopped being fun. People started getting kidnapped and shot. It very quickly became clear to her that the invasion and subsequent occupation were not going well. "This is going to turn into another Beirut," she predicted to her friend Barbara McNamara, a top official at NSA. McNamara asked if she could quote Heidi. Depends on who you're quoting me to, she replied. Not long after, Heidi drove out to the airport, where, in the VIP lounge, she ran into George Tenet. *This is not going to be another Beirut,* the CIA director snapped. Heidi frankly told him that might be his opinion, but she had a different take.

A local telecommunications expert gave her a tour of the city, and during their drive, Heidi opened an MRE and introduced him to peanut butter and saltines. He liked it, so she gave him peanut butter to take to his kids. He reciprocated by inviting her for dinner. The evening was pleasant, except that his wife kept blaming Heidi for the war. She kept asking: Why are you occupying our country? Why are you ruining our country?

The thing was, Heidi did not like the mission. She hated it. Everybody did.

GINA BENNETT HAD JUST delivered her fourth baby when coalition forces invaded Iraq. When she returned from a brief maternity leave, George Tenet asked Gina to compile a soup-to-nuts biographical study on Abu Musab al-Zarqawi, the terrorist leader who was partnering with al-Qaeda. Gina was all too familiar with Zarqawi. She'd tracked him in the mid-1990s, when he was blamed for a string of attacks against Jordanian cinemas showing Western movies. He'd returned to the Afghanistan/Pakistan region, where his Palestinian roots endeared him to local extremists, who admired Palestinians for, as Gina put it, "their determination and never giving up creating their own country."

At the time, bin Laden had been a much bigger problem, and she'd lost track of Zarqawi. Now Gina wrote an extensive targeting profile to help the administration understand who they were dealing with. Where'd he come from? What does he aspire to be? How is he different, if at all, from bin Laden?

Gina arrived in Baghdad in the fall of 2003, at a time when it was clear that Operation Iraqi Freedom was turning into a disaster. In May, President Bush had landed on an aircraft carrier to proclaim "mission accomplished," claiming that major combat operations had ended. But the insurgency was accelerating, not ending; the invasion would develop into an eight-year sectarian war, with far more Americans killed than had been killed on 9/11. The Iraqi civil service and security forces had been disbanded; weapons depots were left unguarded, the border insecure. To get a sense of what they were dealing with, Gina and agency colleagues took a tour outside the Green Zone, traveling by helicopter and truck to explore the areas beyond where American officials were living and working. Afterward, one of her companions said he was surprised at how normal things looked; there were people on the streets and in the markets.

Gina, the only woman in the group, was stunned. What *she'd* noticed was that there had not been a single woman or a single child. "I don't know what you guys are seeing," she said. "But I don't see normal." In an elevator with a senior US official, she urged him not to think al-Qaeda was done. None of it was done; not al-Qaeda, not jihad. To think al-Qaeda was on its last legs was wishful thinking of the highest order.

It seemed clear to Gina a new chapter of jihad was just beginning. For years, Osama bin Laden had been propagandizing that America was out to conquer and control the Muslim world, like so many colonizers before it. "And that's what we did. We set foot in some of the holiest places in Islam, the center of one of the most important caliphates. I was like: You have no idea what we've done, we have turned his propaganda and prophecy into reality. It's just—I don't know, I just thought they were nuts." The Iraq war drove some women, like Gina's colleague Susan Hasler, to quit the agency for good. Susan realized the fantasy of handing in her badge, and gave notice in 2003, taking retirement and embarking on a new career as a novelist.

OTHERS, HOWEVER, WERE PULLED into work that grew more and more central to the agency's mission. As America embarked on a global war on terrorism—GWOT, it was called—the discipline of targeting came into its own as a way to follow terrorists, their financiers and suppliers. Leadership analysts became targeters; regular analysts became targeters; staff operations officers became targeters. Now, more than ever, in Iraq and around the world, a major part of the mission entailed finding people, plain and simple. The Defense Intelligence Agency famously produced a set of "most wanted" playing cards, to depict Saddam Hussein, his sons and henchmen. FREs—"former regime elements"—had to be located before they could be dealt with. So did jihadists. So did people who knew or worked with them. Even veteran analysts got drawn into targeting work; during a tour in the Middle East, Cindy Storer found the best way to learn targeting was from other targeters. Consultants were useless. The field was too new. Younger targeters referred to veteran analysts—Cindy, Gina, Barbara—as "the goddesses."

Some targeters wrote profiles of terrorist leaders. Others hit the streets, moving block by block, accompanying paramilitary teams to ensure they kicked down the right doors. The number of targets multiplied when Abu Musab al-Zarqawi joined his network to al-Qaeda's and created al-Qaeda in Iraq, which then became the Islamic State—later known as ISIS or Daesh. The targeters had to reckon with the furies Zarqawi unleashed as he turned an insurgency against the United States into a war against the country's entire Shi'ite population, resorting to beheadings, suicide bombings, hostage execution, and wholesale slaughter.

For some women, it was not the work they had expected when they joined the CIA. A native Montanan named Nada Bakos had answered an ad for a job in human resources and now found herself on the streets of Baghdad, where she could not help but notice Iraqi women becoming more fearful and less friendly. As abductions and sexual assaults rose, the lawlessness and danger were—she felt—a key reason US troops weren't welcomed with the enthusiasm planners expected. Terrorists began using rape as a recruiting tool, attracting an even more violent cadre of recruits and providing "a real indicator of whom, exactly, the coalition was up against." Each month saw hundreds of attacks against coalition forces; in a ten-day period, Zarqawi oversaw the killing of 125 people. The sight of children in detention camps was traumatizing and inescapable.

The escalation of the war meant—as war often does—that women, like men, were pushed into leadership roles before they felt ready. Nada Bakos found herself managing a group of cybersleuths who maintained a six-by-six-foot wall map of Iraq and photos of Zarqawi's operations team. Debriefing detainees, she found many were discomfited by a woman interviewer. Some were startled out of stock answers, while others assumed she'd "fall back on some innate motherly instinct and take pity on them." Bakos had no problem putting an X on the heads in the photos. Some terrorists "just need killing," and she "looked forward" to granting Zarqawi "that honor."

AS WARS IN BOTH countries ground on, targeting remained key to arrests and detainments, and, eventually, to killings and drone strikes. But it also continued to serve as a way to enhance a case officer's chance of success in recruiting assets. In, say, a country like Sudan, a CIA case officer might seek an asset in the National Congress Party with ties to the president, vice president, and their inner circle. A targeter could make that happen by considering the candidates, picking one who seemed plausible and studying that person's friends, contacts, interests, and social media presence. The resulting targeting package—he loves Celine Dion; his wife does this; his kids go to school here; he used to be the Sudanese ambassador in DC; he went to school in California; he hangs out in casinos when he travels—helped the case officer make a bump and be well prepared.

Targeters also arrived from the private sector, attracted by work that felt operational and active. One, Lisa Rager, joined in 2005 after prospering in the tech sector and getting a master's in national security at Georgetown. She felt put off by the "insane competitiveness" of work as a case officer, but didn't relish the analytic culture of recreational argumentation. Single at the time, with no kids and no spouse, she volunteered to go to Iraq where she targeted for classic intelligence collection.

Targeting turned out to be the "most fun" she'd ever had. She liked writing cables that got read quickly; liked producing intelligence that got acted upon; liked helping case officers succeed. She had "incredible access to Iraqi cellular information," millions of lines of metadata. The data could locate people—if someone's phone started pinging, targeters could alert ops forces who could instantly find him—or help case officers set up encounters. If GPS reports showed a certain cellphone moved in and out of the Green Zone on a regular basis, that suggested its owner had a Green Zone pass, and "we could meet with him super easily."

She used concentric mathematical models to spot people who sat in central nodes. On the counterterrorism side, this technique could reveal whose detainment or arrest would "make the most impact on this network," or, for intelligence gathering, suggested who knew the most about any given set of people. It also indicated who were the most dangerous people in a certain place.

During the surge in January 2007, the Bush administration sent twenty thousand more combat forces into Iraq. To defeat radical Sunnism, the US military aimed to harness the Shia majority, enlisting tribal leaders to buttress American forces. Southern Iraq was basically all Shia, but it was also rural, and the United States hadn't spent time engaging with nonurban populations. As quite a few leaders in southern Iraq vied to be considered most influential, Rager set out to create "an objective measure of influence and prominence." She collected email addresses, dropped them into her modeler, looked at contacts one and two levels out, and from this could tell who was super-connected and who wasn't. She created an ingenious way to evaluate puissance.

Case officers had neither the tools nor the time that she did; they were always out, spotting and recruiting. She could also help them figure out how to use the intelligence they gathered. In one country, an asset brought a list of families with children at an American school. The targeters plugged names into databases to figure out who was worth approaching. A PTA list became a targeting list. "I always felt like I had magic," said Rager, who, when I interviewed her, was retired from the

CIA—a suburban mother of two, living in the San Francisco Bay area and working for Tesla.

Rager made three trips to Iraq between November 2005 and February 2009. She was there on June 7, 2006, when a bomb was dropped on a safe house harboring Abu Musab al-Zarqawi. It was hard not to notice that the targeting team that took him off the map was entirely female.

JUST AS IT INVOLVED a middle ground between operations and analysis, targeting sometimes occupied an ethical no-man's-land between nonlethal and lethal actions. "You track 'em," the ops guys liked to say, "we whack 'em." Targeters had to figure out how they felt about residing somewhere in a chain of command that led to something bad happening to a bad person somewhere.

Angie Lewis learned to live reasonably comfortably in that gray zone. Joining the agency in 2002, she, like Lisa Rager, felt herself drawn toward work that had a concrete outcome. She liked diving deep into data, liked throwing leads in people's laps. Working in one Middle Eastern country, she identified a terrorist she felt should be arrested. A case officer brought her to a meeting with senior liaison officers from the country's intelligence service; there, as in many places, the CIA played an "advisory" role—wink, wink—wrapping its own operations in local forces. She floated the man's name and location but lacked the authority to order the arrest. "What do you want us to do?" the liaison team asked. "I think you should do whatever you deem appropriate, given the threat he may pose," she carefully suggested. Twenty-four hours later, they arrested him, which was exciting—to know she had provided the intelligence to take an adversary out of action.

Back in DC, she was driving past CIA headquarters and saw protesters wearing orange jumpsuits and standing in the grassy median of Route 123. One carried a small model of a predator drone. Angie's daughter, who was around seven or eight, asked what a plane like that did. "It makes bad guys go away," Angie told her.

Motherhood led to tough conversations, but motherhood was also why she did the work. During training, an instructor asked if she would be okay learning to shoot a gun. Her first thought was: no. Then she reflected that if her daughter were in danger, the answer would be yes. When her daughter was a baby, she'd had to take a seven-month separated tour. To get through their time apart, she reminded herself she was helping improve the world her daughter would grow up in. She wanted to show it's possible to take on hard things and get them done. As a targeter, she "definitely helped get a few bad guys taken off the playing field" and felt proud she did.

When we spoke, Lewis was working as head of global security for Disney. We chatted in sunny Burbank while her fourteen-year-old daughter played tennis nearby, preparing to try out for the high school team, and she reflected on what her targeting work boiled down to. "I made bad people have bad days. That was my job. Point zero zero percent of the time, it was like *Zero Dark Thirty*."

CHAPTER 26

ANYTHING
TO FIT IN

LANGLEY, VIRGINIA

December 2009

TWENTY-TWO-YEAR-OLD MOLLY CHAMBERS WAS WORKING AS a professional trainee on the Jordan desk at headquarters on December 30, 2009, when her branch chief asked her to find a phone number for the wife of Darren LaBonte, a case officer based in Amman. He didn't say why.

Molly belonged to the generation of female intelligence officers who entered on duty not only after 9/11, but well after. She was fourteen years old when, as she saw it, "nineteen men changed the course of history and changed the trajectory of where the US went." Coming of age in Southern California, Molly was a self-described "fat, angry kid" who, by the time she was in high school, was "obsessed with history and military history and a little bit with the agency." Her freshman year at UC Davis, Molly discovered she had "an interesting ability to manipulate people without them knowing it was happening, which is a weird thing to realize about yourself at age eighteen." She thought she might be good in sales. An "unremarkable student," she started out as a comparative economics major and was flunking out when her dad told her she had one quarter to get her grades up. She began studying Arabic and by her junior year "could speak Arabic like a three-year-old." She was also, by now, a young adult who was outgoing, alert, funny, and game.

Working part time in the career services office, Molly Chambers got to know an FBI recruiter who knew a CIA recruiter. One day, hanging out in the Kappa Alpha Theta sorority house, she got a call. *I understand you're interested in us,* said the caller, who claimed to be from the CIA. Molly assumed it was a prank. "Absolutely," she replied, playing along. What unfurled next was the "tinfoil hat" interview—a baseline test for normalcy, to make sure "I wasn't in a basement somewhere speaking to aliens." She kept taking calls, kept doing well. That someone thought she could be a spy surprised her. Toward the end of her junior year, the agency flew Molly to Washington, where she was offered an internship with the National Clandestine Service, as the operations directorate had been renamed. She'd have to take off her fall quarter. An intern was required to work for six consecutive months.

Molly said okay. At twenty-one, she rented a one-bedroom in Centreville, Virginia, and began interning for Near East division's Iraq Operations Group, triaging intelligence from the overseas unit focused on Jaysh al-Madhi, a terrorist group that was attacking US personnel and installations in Baghdad's Green Zone. She found that if you were a functional warm body, the CIA was good at finding work you could do. She handled communications, fielded requests for name traces and encryption. She showed up every day wearing loafers from JC Penney and business casual from Old Navy—intimidated, afraid to make a mistake, awed by ops officers who had started in Baghdad in 2003 or 2004 and were by now legends.

At the end of six months, the internship director told her that once she got her degree, Molly could join a class headed for the Farm. The idea that the CIA wanted her was an ego boost that would sustain her through many hard days. She returned to UC Davis, where her sorority sisters wondered where she'd been all fall. Some assumed she'd disappeared to have a baby. She took double the usual credits, graduated in May 2009, and joined the CIA two weeks later.

Waiting for her Farm stint, Molly Chambers was on what was known as her "interims" that day in December when her branch officer pulled her aside. He first asked her to find a phone number for the mother of the Amman chief of station. The COS happened to be on a trip with his mom, and they couldn't get hold of him using his own number. Molly was the cable database person and knew how to find the mother's contact information. Next, he instructed Molly to find a contact for Darren LaBonte's wife, who was in Rome on R&R with her baby and in-laws. Then he needed her to go to the Staybridge Suites in McLean, Virginia, book three hotel rooms, and get on the phone and book a car. This time, he used a different noun for the woman married to LaBonte. The word he used was "widow." As in: "We're picking up his widow tonight."

That's how Molly Chambers became one of the first people to know that something awful had happened at a base in Khost, Afghanistan. Seven people working for the CIA were dead—five officers, two contractors. One was Jennifer Lynne Matthews.

JENNIFER MATTHEWS WAS A founding member of the sisterhood of Alec Station. In the 1990s, she had been one of the first people to perceive and confront the danger posed by bin Laden and al-Qaeda. By 2009, Matthews was serving as chief of the CIA base established on the grounds of Forward Operating Base Camp Chapman, an Army base in Khost where intelligence officers provided targeting information for drone strikes in Pakistan. Matthews helped grow the targeting field and develop it. A targeting colleague, Sandy Tveit, described her as "one of the best targeters I ever knew, the best of the best, so full of life and personality." She had devoted fifteen years of her life to tracking bin Laden—before 9/11 and after. Prior to going to Afghanistan, she spent four years in London, working with British liaison officers. Her husband and children accompanied her for the London assignment. She traveled without her family to Khost.

That December, a radicalized doctor, Humam Khalil Abu-Mulal al-Balawi, had been interrogated by Jordanian intelligence officers, who had a close liaison relationship with American counterparts. Between them, the Jordanian team and CIA colleagues believed they could convince the doctor to work as a double agent, penetrating al-Qaeda, reporting back, and leading them to bin Laden.

Nearly eight years had passed since bin Laden had escaped at Tora

Bora. Even as the Iraq war drew off resources, the determination to find him remained urgent; there were parts of the CIA that still felt as intense as the entire country had felt right after 9/11. Matthews arranged for Balawi to cross the border from Pakistan and visit the CIA base. The doctor was said to be nervous, and Matthews wanted to make him comfortable, so when he arrived in a car with an Afghan driver, he was waved through three security checkpoints without an inspection. Emerging from the vehicle, he was greeted by fourteen people, including Matthews, who was holding a cake in honor of his recent birthday. Before heading out, she'd messaged one of her oldest friends and colleagues, from the days of imagery analysis, saying she had to go meet someone.

Shortly after stepping out, the doctor triggered a bomb sewn into his vest. He was instantly killed. Jennifer Matthews, mortally wounded, ran several steps before collapsing, and was taken to the hospital, where she died. Also killed were a thirty-year-old targeter named Elizabeth Hanson, an economics major from Colby College who had joined the agency at twenty-six; CIA officers Scott Roberson, Harold Brown, Jr., and Darren LaBonte; two contractors, Dane Clark Paresi and Jeremy Wise; the Afghan driver, Arghawan; and the Jordanian liaison officer, Captain Sharif Ali bin Zeid. Six other CIA officers were seriously wounded. It was the deadliest single day at the agency since the US embassy bombing in Beirut in 1983. The bodies were flown back to the United States, and top officials went out to meet them. For Mike Sulick, head of the clandestine service, it was the hardest day of his career, worse than 9/11.

The death of seven CIA workers shocked the world and the agency workforce. It had a profound effect on female CIA officers, many of whom reacted not only to Matthews's death but to how she was treated in death. In February 2010, with a thick snow falling, a memorial service for the fallen officers took place in the bubble. President Barack Obama spoke, as did the new CIA director, Leon Panetta. To a newcomer like Molly Chambers, the event seemed surreal to the point of being unbelievable. "Like, I'm at a funeral at work?" It was so bad she didn't yet grasp how bad it was. The seven officers, all of whom had been working undercover, became seven chiseled stars on the wall.

So many CIA officers wanted to attend that not everybody could fit in the bubble's auditorium. Gina Bennett watched on video feed. Gina called Cindy Storer to let her know about Jennifer's death. Cindy had taken early retirement in 2007, worn out by regret, guilt, grief, and exhaustion. She had been unemployed for a year, living with her parents at Myrtle Beach in South Carolina. Cindy was astonished at how deeply she felt affected by Jennifer Matthews's death. As young analysts, the two women had worked together without really getting along. But ten years had gone by and "I'm sure she learned a lot in all those years, just like the rest of us, all of us did." Cindy felt stung that nobody else had reached out to her. "They always told you, this is a family, we take care of each other, and that was not my experience."

Following the Khost explosion, it felt to many women that the old boys' PR machine was up to its old tricks, planting news tidbits to manipulate the media and shift the blame. News accounts focused on Matthews's role and suggested she was inexperienced—dwelling on the decision to admit the doctor without a security search while glossing over the fact that her superiors, still undercover, were involved in planning the operation. The birthday cake was brought up, with the implication that it had been a silly, girly thing to offer. Jennifer Matthews's uncle, a retired case officer, told reporters he tried to dissuade her from going to Khost; he didn't think she, an analyst, was qualified, but she was determined.

The only woman in the decision-making chain that designed the operation, Jennifer Matthews got "crushed with blame," in the view of Kristin Wood, her friend and colleague, who felt disgusted with "leadership lack of accountability" and, like many, felt people would never have denigrated a fallen male comrade. When she got the news by phone, Kristin dropped to the floor. "He got her," she said. Meaning bin Laden. "She had been after him since 1994, and he got her."

People blamed Matthews for leaving her children to go to Khost, in a way they had not blamed Mike Spann, who died in Afghanistan, for leaving behind a wife and child. The reality of counterterrorism work was that many people had to leave families to follow the fight. Jennifer Matthews was a twenty-year veteran who was being treated as a junior analyst in tennis shoes. When Kristin and the other former imagery analysts next met for high tea—this time at the Ritz-Carlton in Pentagon City—the now-threesome of friends asked for a table for four, and left one chair empty.

BUT SOME WOMEN DID wonder whether Khost was the right place for a targeting analyst to be put in charge. When Diana Bolsinger's husband asked if she had heard of Jennifer Matthews, Diana's first wave of surprise, along with grief, was that Jennifer had been base chief at Khost. It did not seem a usual career path.

And it wasn't, or not exactly. Ops officers know that it's a cardinal rule to meet with assets one-on-one, never in a group. For all her targeting experience, Matthews—multiple sources agree—had been given a "short course" of operational training, not nearly as extensive as the full twenty-two-week Farm course. Authorities, however, considered her training sufficient; if it wasn't sufficient, the fault lay with the people who sent her. "We all took it pretty hard," said targeter Sandy Tveit. "This group of female targeters, who had struggled for a long time, after 9/11, we all did things we thought we'd never be asked to do, we took risks we never expected we'd have to do. We all did it. We all felt just a little invincible, until Khost, and I think that brought us all up short." The loss of their friend, and so many others, was unimaginable. "I don't know if any of us have ever recovered from it."

HEIDI AUGUST HAD RETIRED as well. Early in her tour in Iraq, she received an offer from MCI, the telecommunications company, which was doing some of the restoration work in Iraq. The pay was twice what she had been making. As a single woman, a salary increase like that mattered. She returned to Langley and filled out her retirement papers. By then, Heidi was an SIS-2 and received the Career Intelligence Medal. "You served your country for thirty-five-plus years, and you did it with great distinction," read a handwritten note from Jim Pavitt. On her last day, December 3, 2003, she received a flag that had flown over headquarters, in a glass case. She felt proud of her service even as she did not like what she saw in Iraq and thought it a mistake for the agency to create its own private army, at enormous taxpayer expense, and assume such a major paramilitary role. In her view, you should know where your agency's duty stops, and another's begins.

Learning of the Khost tragedy through the tight network of retired officers, Heidi, shocked and saddened, found herself reflecting on how she would have handled the operation. First, she would have made sure the doctor got polygraphed. People being held in prison, as he initially was, will say anything to get out. Rather than meet at a base, Heidi would have fabricated an excuse to get him on a plane to a neutral location. Maybe say he needed to visit family who were sick. She would have met him, alone, on a layover in an airport lounge where weapons were checked by airport security.

Lisa Harper reacted much as Heidi did, reflecting that in a place like Khost, full operational training and experience were called for. Because it's not just instinct that kicks in; it's the attunement born of years on the street. She conjectured that heading a base in a war zone would have been a way for an analyst to set herself apart. If you want to get promoted, chief of base in a war zone is where you want to be.

PRESENT AT JENNIFER MATTHEWS's funeral was a cadre of younger targeting analysts who were tough, obstinate, seasoned, and effective. One was a striking woman who wore expensive high heels and dressed well but not sexily; eschewing the standard trench coat or classic pencil skirt and silk blouse, she had her own feminine self-presentation. She did not feel the need to make men in the office feel comfortable with her. Jennifer Matthews had mentored and trained her. She was driven, focused, abrasive, unafraid of conflict, and willing to make herself a priority. She wasn't the kind of person to "stand in line and say please and thank you," as another mentor, Kristin Wood, put it. As the women around her sobbed, the high-heeled targeter said: *I am going to find him. Don't worry, I am going to do this, you guys have taught me, I'm going to do this.*

That targeter provided the model for Maya, the bin Laden tracker in *Zero Dark Thirty*.

In that movie, Maya is haunted by the death of her mentor, Matthews, whose character is gossipy and a bit ditzy. The portrayal irritated some colleagues. Among them was general counsel John Rizzo, who told a reporter that Jennifer Matthews was much more competent and experienced than her character in the movie. She was, he added, "much more good-looking" than the actress who played her. Even in death, even in 2014, women officers were judged on their looks. In 2015, an anonymous CIA officer, an ops guy, was quoted in *U.S. News & World Report* saying, of the women of Alec Station, "They just worked in their office in tennis shoes."

THE KHOST MASSACRE ALSO impacted female officers—targeters especially—who hadn't personally known any of their fallen colleagues. Ellen Dickey, a targeter who worked in Saudi Arabia, Pakistan, and Syria, remembered that when she was hired in 2004, the women of Alec Station had become legends. "People talked about them with a lot of respect as targeters who could do amazing things." It did seem to her that Jennifer Matthews was unfairly blamed. "So many of those decisions are made outside of the base's control."

Another person affected was Molly Chambers, who found herself motivated by the tragedy, by the suicide bomber's hatred of America, and by the sexism directed at Jennifer Matthews. Take the absurd criticism about the birthday cake. Molly, in her own operational work, gave assets gifts of food all the time. All case officers did. She flew out from DC with a box of Georgetown Cupcakes in her lap, because an African asset saw the confections touted on a Food Network show. "That kind of stuff happens constantly. You get them small gifts. You demonstrate that you're thinking about them." One of her Nigerian assets loved American-style pizza; there was a Domino's in the city where she was stationed, but prices were high for locals. "So guess who got a Domino's pizza every time we met? That's normal. . . . That's part of our training. That's called rapport building."

For Molly, the loss of so many CIA officers, and the idea that someone could hate America enough to blow himself up, clarified her desire to do her part. She drove to Baltimore to attend Darren LaBonte's funeral. She didn't consider herself a superstar. Molly saw herself as part of a cadre of officers "who were not necessarily the best, but who were the ones that showed up to participate in that fight." This is what they were told during orientation in the bubble: Don't get arrogant ideas; you're here because you're the ones who showed up. US national security was up to people like her: people who showed up.

As her own career unfolded, Molly became a hunter, too, but this was a different kind of hunting. It was not a hunt to kill terrorists, or detain them, but rather, a hunt to reunite families, save lives, and rescue some of the most vulnerable terrorism victims on the planet: stolen children.

IN JULY 2011, MOLLY CHAMBERS found herself at the Farm for six months of immersion training. There were more female recruits than in the days of Heidi August and Lisa Harper, but certain behavioral aspects did linger. Sex remained rampant. Male and female trainees had sex and they had it with each other. Planning hookups was one way to practice tradecraft. Molly and one classmate put secret markings on a dorm door. There was a hotel not far away, the Hospitality House, that people nicknamed the Ho House. "We also had sex in cars a lot," Molly said. "You're each given a vehicle, and to ensure that a car pickup location is safe, you need to be able to stay there for a few minutes without anybody coming or going and seeing you. So what better way to test it?" The strange old intimacy of the job had not abated. Working with a male colleague meant studying his features, waiting for that gesture, that look, a turn of the head to signal the next move in an operation.

The use of pseudonyms gave a weird anonymous quality to interactions; communication with colleagues was like meeting a stranger on the internet, like encountering an avatar. You knew people by their pseudonyms; you didn't even know real names. In remote stations, people were bored and restless; in their off hours, there was little to do but play Jenga. Colleagues visiting on TDYs, or short tours, provided diversion. In Africa, one new chief of station was very interested, as she put it, in the "pussy around town."

"I was so young, I knew nothing else," reflected Molly, who was twenty-two when she was working as a desk officer. During her stint on the desk, she'd opened a drawer and found a seven-page list of "Rules for Being a Case Officer," an informal document some predecessor had composed. The list, printed in the agency's trademark courier font, included: Always have at least two meetings a day. Keep up to date with issues and news. Sharpen the sword. Have a nice suit or two for receptions. A few drinks are expected. Don't sleep with assets or domestic staff. Never pass up the chance to wear sunglasses. Be strategically aggressive but tactically patient. Some of it—the suits and the edict about no sex with staff—seemed more tailored to men, but overall, she took the advice to heart. Going on her first tour at twenty-five, "I was like a teenage bride. I had no other context, and I was desperate to be good at it. And I was good at it, but I would have done anything to remain cool and in the crowd."

The list was correct: Officers did wear sunglasses, and did not have sex with assets. But sex with colleagues and civilians, she thinks, bespoke an overall sense of living outside the law. "I think a sense of this plays into the mentality of case officers, both male and female, that rules do not apply in any way, shape, or form. Because our entire mission is to break the rules. I had a colleague who said the moment he steps foot into a new country, he thinks: Big mistake you guys, I'm going to ruin this place."

NOT MOLLY. HER OWN career unfolded in the wake of Khost, as terrorism spread globally, defining the climate in which she would maneuver. At the Farm, in response to the Khost tragedy, case officer training expanded to include a weeklong course on how to prepare for a "high threat meeting," using tools such as surveillance, possibly weapons or communications systems. By the time Molly was choosing which division she hoped to sign with, Africa, not Europe, was the coolest and most highly sought. To her surprise, she got a slot and "totally fell in love" with the mission.

Molly's first posting, in 2012, was to Uganda. Nine months prior, there had been a terrorist attack on a neighborhood, Kabalagala, while African citizens were peacefully watching a World Cup match. The area was not far from the US embassy, and the perpetrator, al-Shabaab, by then had surpassed al-Qaeda as the most brutal terrorist organization in the world. The menace could be felt everywhere. Visiting a col-league in Nairobi the following year, she ate lunch at the Westgate Mall just a few weeks before four masked gunmen opened fire there in an al-Shabaab attack that left sixty-seven dead and two hundred wounded. In Uganda, she worked with a small group of Ugandans known as a Counter-Terrorism Operational Platform—CTOP—training them to do "indigenous counterterrorism" and combat terrorism in their midst. She worked "internal targets": recruiting Ugandan intelligence officers to get them to share what they knew about al-Shabaab that they weren't sharing in an overt capacity.

The work was grinding and lonely and exhilarating. She had a half dozen burner phones, some for CT missions, some for operational ones. The best burner phones were Nokias; they were cheap and reli-able, and you could pop the SIM card out with a quick motion. She had quick-change license plates and a list of phone numbers in her bra; she kept them there thinking an adversary service would not undress her if she were apprehended. Arriving at any new station, her first task was to spend weeks driving, memorizing the city's layout. She had a paper map annotated with squares and X's signifying things like bars and restau-rants and no-go zones. She had to be able to re-create the map in her head, on the fly, in case she was being followed. On any meeting with an asset, she went "black," with no electronics, and had to know her way.

She had a fistful of passports and ID cards. "We can do a couple of poses," the nice woman in the badge office at headquarters had told her. From these, she picked out her favorite, so that if she got PNG'd—thrown out of the country as a persona non grata—and her photo went viral, at least it would be a good one. She was granted a thousand pounds of "consumables," purchased at Costco in Arlington's Pentagon City. Things like cereal, Twizzlers, black beans, Tampax. On a first post-ing, you learn that if you open a huge gallon jar of mayonnaise, you can't take it with you when you move around. For condiments, it's better to get smaller jars from Target or Safeway. People do "consumables give-aways" when leaving one station for another.

In Africa, Molly attended a number of black-tie events, which could have been fun, except that she was able to join only after working her cover job from seven-thirty A.M. to five P.M. and doing an op from five to nine. The epitome of overseas life for her was wearing a cocktail dress in the middle of nowhere to attend a wedding on Christmas Eve. To go with her sparkly sequined dress, she carried a purse containing a "shark fin," a device that vacuumed up nearby phone numbers. A couple of targets were expected at the wedding and she wanted to get their contact information and know who they were talking to.

In Uganda, one of her missions was helping find boys kidnapped by the Lord's Resistance Army, a terrorist group led by a self-described prophet, Joseph Kony, who trafficked in child sex slaves and recruited child soldiers to wage war on the government of Uganda. Dreaming up an operation that she hoped would be effective and creative, Molly wrote a song, "Come Home," calling for "defectors"—as the boys were called—to materialize at re-collection points in the Central African Republic and South Sudan. The message was that their parents were waiting, and they wouldn't be stigmatized. In a nightclub, she approached Jose Chameleone, Uganda's rap sensation, and asked him to record it. He agreed, and the song became a runaway hit. Some boys did come home, drifting in by themselves or in pairs. Finding lost boys wasn't the agency's central mission, but was "totally worth it," a perfect forward action campaign.

Khartoum, her second posting, was harder; the city's National Intelligence and Security Service building had a sign that said, translated, "If you are not on the side of Allah and Muhammad, you will be in the den of hell with losers." It was an unnerving motto, and when a team of surveillance cars began tailing her, she shook them off but became scared. She wasn't afraid for herself, physically, but for her reputation. She developed a crippling fear of being caught and PND'd. "I keep waiting for the other shoe to drop," she wrote in a journal, cryptically communicating how terrified she felt. Therapy was out of the question; you don't want to be seen as upset or unfit. If a Russian walk-in shows up, you want to be the one chosen to do the handling and debriefing.

Her third posting was to Nigeria, where in April 2014, 276 female students had been kidnapped from a Christian boarding school in Chibok by the Islamic terrorist group Boko Haram. Boko Haram at that time was an ad hoc and strident boys' club, a homegrown group of religious extremists opposed to literacy and schooling. The name Boko

Haram roughly translates as "Western education is forbidden." That's why the girls were stolen. Number one, they were girls; and number two, they were, by definition, getting schooled. In late 2016, Boko Haram franchised with ISIS, or one faction did, as far as their sourcing could tell. That faction ceased being Boko Haram and became Islamic State / West Africa, making it a legitimate target for a counterterrorism mission. The group was in a godforsaken section of north Nigeria; there was a single CIA case officer in the region, but he needed a team, and that's where Molly came in.

Molly was sent to a very poor region near Lake Chad, where residents subsisted on farming and fishing. Climate change was affecting fishing; the lake was shrinking and jobs were scarce, idle fifteen-year-olds an easy mark for recruitment into Boko Haram. The Chibok kidnapping had given the group publicity, which it liked, and terrorist financiers sent donations, which it also liked. Maiduguri, her destination, was a tiny city—mostly slums—near the Sambisa Forest. The area was unmapped, and she developed a cover as an outfit that was mapping the area to sell to NGOs. In case of emergency, nobody would be coming to help her. Molly had a Glock 19 and thirty rounds of ammunition: twenty-nine for the enemy, and one for her.

Her job was to set up a safe house, which meant finding a compound and outfitting it to make it habitable. The case officer did a one-day turnover, gave her a hundred thousand dollars and said, "Call me if you need me." She found a compound with a main house and a guest house; signed the lease, squared it away. There was no electricity, no running water, no computer system, no secure coms. Molly got one support officer, a woman, who helped set things up. Nobody took US dollars, so Molly had to find a money changer who wouldn't rip her off. She bought a generator, arranged for fuel deliveries. She made the house habitable. She bought a car, tinted the windows herself, smoothing the tinting plastic with a Starbucks gift card.

Having set up the safe house for the support staff who would join the operation, Molly next had to penetrate Boko Haram. She cultivated an asset who told her that Abubakar Shekau—the head of Boko Haram—attended a mosque that looked "like stairs." A team member from the National Geospatial-Intelligence Agency found a building with a stairstep-shaped footprint, using overhead imagery. Boko Haram used courier systems like bin Laden's, in which one courier brings a message to one of several other couriers, who burst out in different directions. She had her targeter—male, now that targeting was a career track—and a "SIGINT": a signals intelligence guy who listened to Boko and ISIS West Africa intercepts. Working with the British and French, they hoped to get all the girls in one fell swoop, but some had been married off to fighters and were reluctant or unable to leave their babies, at least not right away. But they did get thirty at one time, and others, in ones and twos, trickling, terrified, from the thick forest, clutching the offspring of the men they'd been given to.

THROUGHOUT HER AFRICA POSTINGS, Molly found that gender helped in ways that surprised her. In Islamic countries, she discovered the existence of a "third gender," a cultural category that was neither male nor female. As a white Western American woman working in a professional setting, she wasn't female as females were locally understood; nor was she a man, exactly. Instead, she occupied an in-between, almost nonbinary category, which meant she could socialize with women but also with men. At dinners, the women would go into one room and the men into another. Molly could float back and forth. She could talk to the men about politics and then hang out in the kitchen and be welcomed by the secretaries and wives. She could develop male assets as well as female ones, which was something her male colleagues often couldn't do. At a party, people didn't know whether she was present in an official capacity or as somebody's date. She could walk in anywhere. It was as if she didn't count—and not counting was a huge advantage.

She encountered little to no sexism from assets. From her colleagues, yes: One embassy security officer called her Sugar Tits and mockingly asked if she was going to complain about being afraid in the interrogation room. But what really aggravated her was that the agency refused to count her Nigeria service as "war zone credit," though men who came after her did get it—after Molly had set up their living quarters. She'd also been the one chosen to "babysit" the wife of Director Mike

Pompeo during his official visit—a duty that didn't go to the men. The unique opportunities and lingering slights led to tight camaraderie among Molly and her female colleagues. They called themselves "lady case officers."

In Africa, working counterterrorism intersected with working hard targets like Russia, China, North Korea, and Iran; the mix was about fifty-fifty. Working hard targets was what Molly had joined the agency to do. Now, as in the Cold War, major powers wanted to harvest Africa's natural resources and build ties and allies. The Chinese Communist Party was actively developing airports, and there were lots of Chinese Communists on the continent, which felt to Molly "like the last real CIA posting." In Africa, exactly as Lisa Harper had found, officials from hard targets were less supervised and more accessible.

In Kampala, Molly's station colleagues suspected that a medical clinic run by North Koreans was really a money-laundering operation to fund the regime. The station drafted Molly to visit the clinic twice a week for full body massages—complete with cupping. Under the guise of having been in a car accident, Molly lay naked as hot glasses were pressed against her skin, chatting with the masseur and thinking of ways to elicit that did not make him suspicious. This went on for six months. When he revealed that he was a Keanu Reeves fan, she showed up with a thumb drive of Keanu Reeves movies. Her gregarious nature served her well. "Anything you're interested in, I'm interested in. And like, 'Oh my God, there's nine seasons of *Lost*! Let's watch all of them!' It's a little bit of making your personality malleable to whoever you need to be. And you lose yourself a bit in that." (Actually, six seasons.) One asset "triggered" her—that is, called a meeting—on her birthday. An urgent matter had come up. He apologized for bothering her, gave her a birthday card addressed "To My Dear Love," and confided: "I didn't sign it, for operational reasons."

Molly's career-making recruitment was from a hard target. She and her asset had regular meetings, until one day he failed to show up: what's known as "breaking contact." They had a recontact plan, an alternate location she visited at predetermined days and times. She went back and back for months—worrying he'd been caught, imagining his family being tortured—until one day she saw him approach. The look of relief on his face matched her own. He'd had a visitor and it wasn't safe to meet. She assured him he'd done the right thing. "He looked at me and said, 'I knew you would be here.'" She knew she would be, as well. She would never fail him, something she could not necessarily say in any other aspect of her own life.

Being a CIA case officer was the single best thing she had done. It was also the hardest: living in countries under conditions so dangerous she couldn't leave the compound, couldn't take walks, could only talk long distance to an online wellness coach. It was 95 percent misery—feeling "fueled by nicotine, caffeine, and self-loathing"; getting rejected, rejected, rejected; finding someone who wanted to be a source but had nothing to offer—and 5 percent wild satisfaction. She was in nine car accidents in six years. She had to do one operational act per day—a call, a meeting, a diplomatic function, dropping a signal—which was exhausting. At no time was she off the clock; she never went in a grocery store without first circling the parking lot, looking for diplomatic license plates to see who she might bump in the yogurt aisle.

When she left that last posting, she had to say goodbye to her career-making asset. He had taught himself English by watching American daytime talk shows. He would return to his home country, go back inside, suffer under an authoritarian regime. But at least he could be a voice. When they said good-bye, they sat in a car and reviewed what they had meant to each other. Molly said they would probably never see each other again, and he said he knew that. She said somebody would be there for him always. "But it won't be you," he replied. It was raining, so she said that from then on, whenever it rained at night, that would be the two of them communicating. It felt cheesy but she meant it. Later, a desk officer told her they read a lot of cables, and that exchange touched them. When rain is coming down, she thinks of her asset.

She wanted her hall file to say she was a good colleague. A person who took the hard, unglamorous assignments. At the agency, people's favorite movie isn't *Zero Dark Thirty;* it's *Black Hawk Down.* That movie's essence is distilled in a scene in which the Delta Force team leader, Hoot, says he didn't do what he did out of infatuation with war. "It's about the men next to you." Molly never wanted to let her colleagues down, or her assets. "A lot of my assets were dirtbags. A lot of them were selling because they could: They had information, and yeah, they wanted the USG to have it, great," she reflected. "But a couple of them really believed in America, and really believed that they were helping. Because they were."

CHAPTER 27

LAUNDRY ON THE LINE

May 2, 2011

FRAN MOORE HAD JUST ARRIVED AT WORK EARLY ONE MORNING in the late summer of 2010, when a report hit her desk that stunned her. Fran Moore was deputy director of analysis—head of the analytic directorate—and the report had been compiled by the small team of analysts hunting Osama bin Laden. The report described the path of a white Suzuki jeep belonging to a courier known to carry messages to bin Laden. The jeep had been tracked to a large compound in Abbottabad, Pakistan. The report pointed out that the compound had unusually high walls. Fran read the report with "great interest" but saw that the title—along the lines of "best lead ever to bin Laden"—conveyed more certitude than did the report. The title suggested that there was proof it was Osama bin Laden living in the compound, but the details didn't support that level of certainty.

Fran called the team's manager and cautioned that drafts like this one "have a way of getting downtown." High-level people would surely see the paper. They could well be onto something they'd never seen and couldn't afford to oversell their findings. She sent it back for revision and said she would look at every paper before it was sent on, to make sure "we don't have this much daylight between a summary and the content again." The tradecraft, she urged, had to be impeccable.

Having delivered that caution, Fran Moore took a moment to herself. "And then I was like, 'Oh, but this is so exciting. I can't believe it.'"

THAT FRAN MOORE WAS sitting at the top analytic desk in 2010 was owing not only to her excellence but to her persistence during a career in which she encountered "brick walls" because of her decision to have children. It was also owing to a long chain of quiet gestures of support. At a key moment in her career, Fran had been elevated by Mary Margaret Graham, who urged her to take a high-vis job that scared her. Graham was known for mentoring younger women, setting up an old-girls network and calling meetings to say, "If you're here, consider that you've been tapped." She was a good friend of Heidi August, who owed her own career in part to Lisa Harper, who herself had been helped at a critical moment by Sue McCloud, who had engineered the hiring of Mia McCall and tried, in her own clandestine way, to winnow out men who sabotaged women.

In short, Fran Moore belonged to a sisterhood that in some ways was not fully aware of itself, a chain of solidarity and achievement both known and unsung. And she happened to be in place at a key moment when the hunt for bin Laden took a turn, the fruition of years of work in which many women participated. Some, operational targeters like "Maya," were out in the field. Some, like Jennifer Matthews, died in the course of duty. Others, like Fran and the team working for her, labored at desks and in meetings, going back to old clues, old databases, using new technologies to surface patterns not visible to the human brain, coming up with fresh strategies for hunting. Director Michael Hayden called them a "band of sisters."

Many men, to be sure, were involved in the hunt for Osama bin Laden. The closer you got to the top ranks, the more men there were. CIA director Leon Panetta, who jump-started the hunt when he took over in 2009; Admiral William McRaven, who commanded a team of Navy SEALs that would assault the compound; President Barack Obama, who gave the go-ahead for the raid. But the women had a special vantage point and motivation. They were mothers, many of them, and daughters. They had fought for careers in public service. They were up against a psychopath for whom women and children were little more than projections of his own narcissistic ego. Some stayed in place for a decade or more to get him.

FRAN MOORE'S OWN CIA career had begun in the staffing bump-up during the Bill Casey era of the 1980s. She grew up in northern New Jersey, in a midcentury new-immigrant household. Her father, born in Italy, was a promising student—valedictorian of his senior class—but his formal education would have ended there were it not for the US military, which enrolled him in an engineering program during his World War II service. His college degree led to a career building bridges and skyscrapers, structures signifying America's might and wealth and promise—exactly what bin Laden would target for destruction.

As Fran grew up, she was aware that her parents and grandparents had come to America seeking opportunity and had found it. It was understood that you should give back through public service. The caption to Fran's high school yearbook photo said she planned a career in the US government.

Her family was Catholic, with six children—three boys, three girls—and old-fashioned notions of gender. In the hierarchy of who mattered, their mother "felt boys were intrinsically more valuable," a bias she herself seemed unaware of. Money was tight, and Fran's older brother tried to talk their parents out of paying Fran's college tuition, arguing that she would just get married after graduation. Her father pointed out that Fran had the best grades of the siblings, and "if anyone deserves to go to college, it's your sister."

At Elmira College in New York, Fran tutored hockey players to earn spending money. She majored in international relations and political science and finished Phi Beta Kappa summa cum laude, one of the top students in her class. She graduated in 1982, straight into the worst recession the United States had seen. She took a job as a secretary on Wall Street. Then one day she got a call. An application she had sent to the State Department had found its way to the CIA. She went for a polygraph in June and a few weeks later drove to Washington, with a laundry basket of clothes in the backseat.

The agency overall was about 75 percent male, 25 percent female, and the analytic division was not much better. There were far more men than women, and the higher you got in the hierarchy, the more skewed the ratio became. Fran's boss happened to be looking for a smart generalist—somebody who could research, write, and put a story together. Within a year, Fran was the senior analyst for the Philippines, a high-vis region in a high-vis era, the tenure of Ferdinand Marcos.

But as she looked around, one thing became clear. "There were very few women in management role models and the ones that there were, were childless," Fran saw. This truth was "very explicitly brought home" when she moved to the North Korea desk. On her last day as a Philippines analyst, she was called in by the office director, who told her he "wanted to have a chat with you before you go off and get married." The director had some advice. "I'm sure you don't think I'm an expert on this, but trust me, when you've been married three times, you have a lot of experience." As Fran listened, "he starts to talk about how I shouldn't be in a hurry to have children because it would derail my promising trajectory." In a way, he was doing her a favor. "He was trying to make it clear to me what my choices were at the time."

The message came through loud and clear, but Fran chose not to heed it. Extremely close to her own family, she met her husband, an agency officer, playing volleyball, and wanted a life where she could have a family life of her own, working hard but doing fun things, spending downtime with her husband and children. Ignoring her former boss's advice, Fran set about starting a family, and had a "a lot of trouble." Pregnancy after pregnancy did not come to term.

At the same time, Fran was getting all the signs from management that she was a high performer: When her husband was posted overseas, they found her a position and continued to invest in her training, a gesture unusual at the time. While they were overseas, she and her husband decided to adopt. Then Fran got pregnant, for the eighth time, and delivered a baby. They went from zero children to two children quickly. When they returned, she was put on a North Korea task force that was "literally grueling." Getting to work as early as five in the morning, she found herself at her desk long after dark, talking to her son on the phone "and telling my husband don't put the baby to bed, so I can at least hold her."

Despite her gifts and commitment, Fran Moore hit a maternal wall. A new set of units was created, and a female colleague junior to her was asked to lead it. The colleague pointed out to their supervisors that Fran was the person everybody went to for help. Why were they not having Fran run it? The answer: *She's got two kids. Too much on her plate.*

No matter that Fran was routinely working until ten P.M., while managers went home around six. Supervisors, when she approached them, "were polite: We really value you. But look, you're a mom." They continued to take advantage of her work ethic and she continued to produce analysis. "But I never got the tap on the shoulder that men with two kids were getting."

And so it went: Fran worked the East Asia office for twelve years, getting in early and staying late. "Because I was capable, no matter what I did, I was always the first person they went to to write for tomorrow." She would rewrite PDBs for a military analyst three grades senior to her. She was trusted to get things done but not rewarded for doing them.

Along the way, she got signals to dial back aspects of her workplace persona. One immediate supervisor tried to downgrade her performance ratings; looking at her stellar score for briefing skills, he speculated that she couldn't be that good, and marked her down despite having never seen her brief. He flagged, as problematic, an argument she had with a male colleague, saying she was being insufficiently deferential. She went over his head and told the manager above both of them that she couldn't sign off on the appraisal. The manager—unmarried, smart, decent, empathetic—did something unusual: She overruled the supervisor. Fran's high scores remained intact. Even so, the manager pulled her in. "Your intellect intimidates men, and you really have to watch it," she told Fran. Otherwise, "This is going to happen to you all the time. And I may not be there to right the wrong."

To Fran it felt like one more admonition to second-guess herself. She had bumped up against the limits of what the analytic directorate was going to let her do, so she took a job in human resources. There, she became truly aware of how women at the agency had been channeled historically; how, in the 1980s, some of the best and brightest analysts had been steered into leadership analysis when regional offices wouldn't take them; how women in the clandestine service had been channeled as reports officers, meaning "there were some incredibly capable women who should have been out running assets who simply weren't hired to do that." It was interesting work, but when George Tenet took over, a lot of the data driving that his predecessor, Deutch, had wanted was abandoned.

Fran figured she had twenty more years to go in her career. She could stay in human resources and run payroll or contracts, or she could return to her true love—writing analysis for the president—and see if the institution would permit her to lead. It was hard to find her way back. She moved through a variety of jobs and then, as a newly minted SIS, was offered the post of strategic planner for the PDB. That was the big hard job Mary Margaret Graham urged her to take. In 2005, she took over as head of the Office of Terrorism Analysis, which Pattie Kindsvater had built from scratch, creating a program to train the young analysts hired after 9/11. Fran landed at OTA just when the hunt for Osama bin Laden had quietly taken an important step, thanks to a woman who had achieved an elusive goal: finding a way to balance the obligations of work and motherhood.

BY THAT TIME, 2005, the hunt for HVT #1 had been under way for four years, and many members of the early sisterhood remained part of it. After bin Laden disappeared at Tora Bora, Barbara Sude joined a task force to brainstorm new approaches. Barbara's main job was writing analysis to prevent and predict more attacks, so the hunt was something of a second job for her. The team reviewed people with whom bin Laden was connected. Taking a lesson from Israel's experience hunting Nazis, they knew family ties could be important. Adolf Eichmann was living in Argentina when his son bragged to his girlfriend's father about his dad's Nazi past. The father contacted a judge in Germany, and Mossad apprehended Eichmann. Other hunts had focused on people close to the target, such as bodyguards.

Outside experts talked to Barbara's group about patterns of life that fugitives like Eric Rudolph—a domestic terrorist who bombed the 1996 Summer Olympics in Atlanta—had followed. Fugitives, they said, don't necessarily change residences often. You might think they would stay on the run, but they don't always. Okay—the team discussed—let's say he was staying put. How would such a tall, gaunt, recognizable man disguise himself? Shave his beard? Wear a pinstripe suit? KSM had been captured in a city; maybe bin Laden had settled in a dense urban location. There were lots of those in South Asia.

It often fell to Barbara to analyze tapes in which bin Laden appeared. In September 2003, al-Qaeda released a statement celebrating the 9/11 attacks, with footage showing bin Laden walking through a mountainous region. In October 2004, bin Laden delivered a videotaped "Message to the American People." That created a sensation. The team scoured the background for clues, inviting outside experts to scrutinize rocks and bird sounds. But they couldn't place his whereabouts.

By 2005, the team realized there wasn't going to be a single detainee report, a piece of signals intelligence, or any other magic item that led to him. The Iraq war distracted everybody, and al-Qaeda, meanwhile, was resurgent and the vision of a caliphate was spreading.

The hunters did enjoy one advantage: Technology had advanced. Tools had come online allowing analysts to build—in minutes— networks that would take days to construct by hand. The six-page memos of the vault women, and the early PowerPoint efforts of people like Cindy Storer, now could be achieved using "link analysis." The ability to sift through old information, compare it to new information, and array it had been revolutionized. They had far more information available through data than they had five years earlier, and more software to deploy. Technical collection had exploded, yielding high-grade satellite imagery and signals intelligence, the ability to compare older voice tapes to new ones.

Shortly after coming to OTA, Fran Moore had been briefed on a new methodology in which a lead analyst—still undercover, so let's call her Jill—had proposed a key reframing, suggesting a systematic focus on the people he was likely in contact with, a group that numbered no more than two dozen. The analyst suggested four vectors. One was his family, with whom, they knew, bin Laden traveled. Maybe somebody would slip up and say something. Another vector was whoever served as a courier or messenger for bin Laden. He had to have some point of contact with the outside world, however well hidden he might be. The third was al-Qaeda leadership; maybe one of those guys would talk on an open line. The fourth were his communications with media: video and audio tapes and the clues they still hoped to find hidden within them.

Jill happened to be a mother who had worked part time for years. Back in the 1970s, simply having children would have been enough to get her kicked out of the analytic corps. Fran, with her background in HR, knew how significant it was that a part-timer had been allowed to remain on a high-profile team. Because of the urgency of the mission, the counterterrorism center had an expansive notion of who might do a good job. "The higher the flames on the burning platform, the more creative you are about getting people in place to do the work," Fran surmised. "If you were really smart and wanted to work interesting stuff and only wanted to work twenty hours a week," counterterrorism had "a place to use you."

Four years had brought other changes. The women were more seasoned and vocal. It was understood at the agency, even if not explicitly, that women had driven some of the most successful hunts: for terrorists, traitors, drug lords. In part, this was because women had been steered into targeting at a time, as Fran put it, "when other paths to advancement were more fraught." It wasn't so much that there were more women than men in the effort, so much as that the women who were there were standouts.

Fran had other challenges, such as keeping her people. To try to resolve the factionalism that dogged the effort prior to 9/11, Congress had created a National Counter-Terrorism Center, staffed by many agencies, and a Director of National Intelligence, which now had responsibility for the President's Daily Brief. The hunt remained the domain of the CIA, where "support to operations" became a priority. Fran had to make sure her best analysts weren't picked off by the national center. "That was hugely critical," she said, "because many of the people who factored into finding Osama bin Laden probably would have been the first picks for the folks at NCTC. Honestly, the people who are the best writers for the president tend to be the best thinkers to target also. It's all the same expertise and skill set."

So, thanks to Fran Moore's ability to hold her own in a bureaucracy, a cadre of analysts stayed put, refining their skills and mining the reservoir of material as new software enabled them to go back to old data. People stayed on the beat, immersed in a data set that had grown with each interview, each arrest, each thumb drive dropped into a net bag by a special operations officer making a sweep of a safe house. Analysts worked closely with targeters in the field, generating the strategy the ops people would run with. A certain amount of tough-mindedness had set in. The analysts knew what it was like to endure public criticism that they had failed and were still failing. They knew what it felt like to worry people will die if you don't come in on a Saturday; to know that five years from now, your work may come under investigation. You'll have to explain why you made certain decisions, why you gave the information you did. They knew the only solution to the anxiety this created was tradecraft.

It was the Khost tragedy that re-galvanized the hunt. Taking office in 2009, President Obama ordered the agency to redouble efforts to "destroy, defeat and dismantle" al-Qaeda, and he instructed CIA director Leon Panetta to make finding bin Laden his number one goal.

IN 2007, THE TEAM hunting bin Laden had seen another breakthrough thanks to an analyst who, like many, had been flung into counterterrorism after the September 11 attacks. The analyst is still undercover, so let's call her Rachel. She started out tracking various al-Qaeda leaders, but after a few years, realized the hierarchy could endlessly reconstitute itself, and nothing would change until they found bin Laden himself. Each year, they had better technical intelligence, but a key problem remained. Equipped with a dazzling array of advanced technology, they needed to use it to find a man who did not, himself, use technology. Bin Laden was not using cellphones, nor online communication. He had not met in person with other al-Qaeda members since 2003. Instead, the targeters theorized, he communicated by means of couriers who got messages and recorded videos to other al-Qaeda leaders, in the form of letters and memos, saved onto disks and thumb drives.

Detainees reported that their target was likely in northern Pakistan. "We had to think creatively," recalled Rachel. The key, she realized, was to find the person or people close to him who did use technology. Looking at it this way, "something shifted in my brain," and she proposed they focus on the courier or couriers. She and her team compiled a composite of likely attributes. The courier—surely a he—must have been trusted before 9/11; must speak Arabic; must be able to travel in Pakistan without attracting notice.

Rachel worked with the field to generate more collection. They found a partial pseudonym for a courier whose significance was becoming more apparent. In 2004, in northern Iraq, Kurdish forces had arrested an al-Qaeda member, Hassan Ghul, traveling with a notebook full of names and numbers. He told the Kurds that bin Laden was always seen with a bodyguard who also moved messages. Khalid Sheikh Mohammed, captured in 2003, had spoken of a courier going by the alias of Abu Ahmed Al-Kuwaiti, who had helped bin Laden escape after Tora Bora. This coincided with information provided from an intended twentieth hijacker, Mohammad Ahman al-Qahtani, who talked of a courier, "the Kuwaiti," one of a pair of brothers guarding bin Laden. Other detainees had mentioned this courier, who went by other aliases including common names like Mohammed Khan, Bara Khan, and Tariq Khan.

Rachel set out to find his true name. She sifted through the archives, going back to old information they could consider in a new light. She figured the name search could take a year. Within just a few months, they located it, contained in intelligence gathered at a time when analysts couldn't yet grasp its import. In 2002, the CIA had gotten a tip from a foreign government that the courier's real name was Habib Al-Rahman. That, as it turned out, was the name of his dead brother. In 2007, another liaison service reported that the person they were hunting—the courier—was actually named Ibrahim Saeed Ahmed.

In 2009, Obama demanded a detailed plan from Panetta, who told him the Kuwaiti was a possibility. The NSA had collected "voice cuts" of the Kuwaiti back in 2002 and matched these to newer voice samples. Geolocation enabled NSA to zero in on his cellphone. The analysts heard the Kuwaiti talking to a colleague somewhere else in the world, speaking in a very ambiguous way about working with some "former friends." But his own tradecraft was sharp; he didn't turn on the phone, or even insert the battery, until far from wherever he was living.

The next breakthrough came in August 2010, when the courier used his phone, and an on-the-ground Pakistani asset found his white Suzuki jeep. The agency was able to track it from Peshawar to an upscale neighborhood in Abbottabad, a small city in northern Pakistan. Analysts wrote several high-vis memos, arguing that the Kuwaiti was the key to finding OBL. The papers—"Closing in on Usama bin Ladin's Courier," and "Anatomy of a Lead"—promised the best clue to bin Laden's whereabouts in a decade.

Further surveillance indicated the Kuwaiti was living in a large, fortified compound with few windows; high walls topped with barbed wire; and a third-floor terrace with a privacy wall. It had no landline, no internet hookup. Satellite imagery showed nearby houses had regular garbage pickup, but the occupants of the walled-off structure burned all their trash. The CIA set up a safe house to build a pattern-of-life analysis. They determined there were two families in the compound: two courier-bodyguards plus wives and children. The house was registered in the bodyguards' names. There seemed to be a third family on the topmost floor. The quantity of items fluttering on clotheslines seemed significant. Careful counting, and noting sizes and items, suggested the third family comprised several adults and at least nine children. Aerial surveillance revealed a tall man who walked in circles in the garden, but never left the compound. Analysts called him "the Pacer."

This is when Fran Moore got the exciting report. She knew that they could not oversell the finding, nor could they trigger action prematurely. Foremost in the mind of everyone was George Tenet describing the WMD intelligence that paved the way for the invasion of Iraq as a "slam dunk." In briefing Fran, the analysts were explicit about what they knew and what they didn't. Unlike the situation with Mir Aimal Kansi, there was no photographic evidence, no DNA match to prove the pacer was bin Laden. It was a circumstantial case. They couldn't see inside the compound; a curtain blocked satellite spying. A key attribute of analytic tradecraft is establishing what is normal, to understand when something is abnormal. The compound occupants made sure there was no abnormal activity. But the team did have satellite imagery. They had the Kuwaiti's phone calls. They had worked terrorism long enough to know what it felt like to pull and pull and pull and have everything unravel. But that wasn't happening now. The threads were holding.

The analysts knew to beware of "confirmation bias"—the classic mistake that occurred in the run-up to Iraq. As they were pulling their circumstantial case together, Fran called in a separate group of analysts to go through the evidence and arrive at their own conclusion—a process known as red-teaming. They worried about Pakistan's reaction, al-Qaeda's reaction, the world's reaction to a mission to capture or kill bin Laden, which meant violating another country's sovereignty.

What followed were many high-level meetings. The one that stood out for Fran Moore took place in Director Leon Panetta's office toward the end of the year. As she recalled it later, officials were asked to state their confidence level that it was bin Laden. Fran was at 70 percent. Normally, she wouldn't go that high unless she saw a National Intelligence Estimate that relied on signals intelligence and high-quality human intel. She knew they couldn't give the policymaker facial recognition, or DNA, or a reliable human source. She later reflected that even at a 70 percent confidence level, there were plenty of life decisions where she'd choose to stand down. Some people had a lower confidence level than she did; estimates ranged from 55 to 95 percent. But the closer they got to the analysts doing the work, the higher the confidence level.

And this time—this time—the analysts were listened to. Attending one briefing, CIA ops officer Michael Vickers thought to himself, "Holy shit, we've got the bastard." Panetta admitted, "I think I may have thought that myself."

OSAMA BIN LADEN HAD settled in a place that imposed on his wives, and his many children, near-total isolation. Like David Koresh, he was in many ways nothing more than a garden-variety cult leader, a fanatical, uninteresting man who believed the women and children in his family existed to serve him. His own father, Mohammed, had had twenty wives and fifty-five children. Women, to his father, were disposable; he was constantly divorcing wives and taking new ones. Osama bin Laden followed a similar course, with five wives and twenty-four children. His last wife was sixteen when he married her. Two wives left him because of the conditions in which he forced them to exist. When he took four wives and fourteen children to Sudan in the early 1990s, he made his family live in the desert, with limited water and food. He made his sons dig a hole in the dirt to sleep in. When he left for Afghanistan in 1996, he took the group to Tora Bora and made them live in a cave. The family survived on a subsistence diet; the children were always hungry. He married off a twelve-year-old daughter to an al-Qaeda fighter in Afghanistan; she died in 2007 after giving birth on the run. His Afghan hosts, the Taliban, barred females from schools and jobs, made women wear full-length burqas, forbade them to leave home unless accompanied by a male relative.

In his own household, women had no role in public affairs. Girls were separated from boys beginning at age three. Women had to depart the room if a man appeared on TV. Bin Laden wouldn't look at the face of a female news anchor. He wanted women living as they had five hundred years earlier, covered with garments that showed only their eyes. He constricted their existence to a domain so narrow it would be unfathomable to most women on the planet, and one that put the women in constant danger. He was the opposite of a protector. It was the most perverted idea of family—and masculinity—and the most dismissive idea of women and their value that could be imagined.

In contrast, the people tracking bin Laden included Maya; included Fran; included Rachel; included Secretary of State Hillary Clinton; included Letitia Long, director of the National Geospatial-Intelligence Agency, who later pointed out that it was the presence of women that enabled them to use the laundry on the line as one measure of household occupants and their numbers. To be sure, men do laundry. But if you want to make the case for diversity, it's a pretty good one. It's not that women are better. It's that women bring something different to the table. It is not an exaggeration to say that the decision to be what we would now call "inclusive" is one reason the mission succeeded.

BY JANUARY 2011, the intelligence had reached a tipping point. Admiral William H. McRaven, of the Joint Special Operations Command, used it to work on a plan to raid the compound, of which a detailed model was constructed, a diorama complete with buildings and walls and trees and human figures. Other JSOC officers convened at Langley and participated in the plan's development. On March 14, 2011, President Barack Obama held a meeting with his national security advisers, to talk about the options. A raid was one, a drone strike another. At several key meetings, people were asked to give a confidence assessment. At no time was anybody at 100 percent. By spring of 2011, it was widely accepted that more than twenty people lived in the Abbottabad compound: family members, bodyguards, support staff. The tight group of decision-makers worried that the lead would leak, that bin Laden might realize he was being watched or randomly decide to move elsewhere. Doing nothing was another option. Waiting was another. At a Thursday night meeting of top officials the last week in April, President Obama asked everyone in the room whether they recommended not going, waiting, or acting. "I'll let you all know in the morning," he then told them.

The president decided to raid the compound, turning the mission over to McRaven and a team of Navy SEALs, who had received a mysterious summons to North Carolina and set about training for three weeks. The SEALs flew to Bagram Air Base; one of the team members, who would later write a book about the raid under the pseudonym "Mark Owen," took a seat on the plane next to the targeter on whom Maya is based. In his book, he calls her by the pseudonym "Jen." When he asked Jen what were the odds it was bin Laden, she replied, "One hundred percent." She sounded, he said, "almost defiant." She had been working this target for years, she told him, while he and his "boys' club" were "just showing up for the big game." He agreed.

From Bagram, the SEALs proceeded to Jalalabad airfield. What followed was a hold-your-breath moment for the CIA, as ownership of the operation went outside their immediate purview. For the president, the White House Correspondents' Association Dinner, the previous night, had provided a useful distraction. And now—a moonless night—two helicopters descended on the compound in Abbottabad, as people in the White House Situation Room waited tensely. The first Black Hawk, after departing Jalalabad, was supposed to drop a team of SEALs onto the roof of the compound. But high temperatures affected the air density; the helicopter descended fast; the SEALs could see the ground rushing toward them, and expected to die in a crash. The helicopter dropped into an animal pen, catching on a wall and suspended in the air. SEALs, adjusting to the surprise, dropped ladders and poured out. The second helicopter landed outside the compound.

While the helicopters descended, Rachel—the analyst who had found the true name of the courier, the key breakthrough—waited back in Washington. Much like Maya, she felt 95 percent certain bin Laden was living in the compound. The only time she had a "moment of doubt" was when the helicopters were touching down and she experienced "a moment of wondering, what if he wasn't there." But she knew she had worked hard to put together a convincing narrative, talking to NSA, to NGA, to everybody. They had been so careful, so cognizant of confirmation bias, so conscientious about red-teaming. Realizing they had a courier with a line to bin Laden, they had used sensitive technical methods to confirm and keep track. They had wrestled with so many questions—Is this an individual who works for bin Laden? How to geolocate him? How do we figure out where he is?—and much failure. There had been a lot of fighting, a lot of disappointments.

Rachel had worked on the Khost operation involving the suicide bomber. Back in 2009, she had thought the doctor might be unreliable, but she did not think he was a double agent. She did not think he would do something to cause the death of CIA officers. She had been wrong. "So there was some humility there. We were über-rigorous, on the heels of the death of so many analysts."

BIN LADEN HEARD THE Black Hawks. His wives and children, awakened by the sounds, gathered. On the ground floor, the SEALs shot the two bodyguards, entered, blew a charge in a metal door, and proceeded up the stairs. Maya had told them a twenty-three-year-old son, Khalid, was likely on the second floor. He appeared and the SEALs shot him. Maya had also warned that the wives might be wearing suicide vests. A SEAL saw two women, swept them into his arms, and pushed them against the back wall to absorb any blast. In his memoir, *No Easy Day,* the SEAL "Mark Owen" would marvel that the analysts had gotten correct the locations of everyone in the compound. "The two couriers were exactly where the CIA said they would be," and so were the wives and children. "When Jen had pronounced one hundred percent, I should have believed her." At the top bin Laden appeared, retreated, was shot multiple times. People in the White House Situation Room heard the code word—"Geronimo"—confirming it was bin Laden. The next word was "KIA"—killed in action.

The corpse was transported to Jalalabad, where Admiral McRaven waited. To confirm his identity, they had to measure the corpse. McRaven, who had not brought a tape measure, got a tall SEAL to lie beside him. They transported bin Laden's body by helicopter to an aircraft carrier, the USS *Carl Vinson,* waiting in the Arabian Sea. Muslim rites were administered, the body weighted and dumped over the side. Mark Owens saw Maya looking "pale and stressed under the bright lights of the hangar," and later sobbing from the release of years of pressure. "It was one hundred percent," he told her. Later, she hugged him before departing on a C-17 to the States. The analysts had lots of new electronic matter, taken from the compound, to sort through. "This hunt," he reflected, "had been her life."

THE CAMPUS OF THE CIA—the academic oasis envisioned by Allen Dulles—is tree-lined, and languid in summer. Original headquarters is a plain rectangular solid with tall, narrow windows, the verticality of the windows contrasting with the blocky horizontal aspect of the building. Visitors pass under the portico and ascend a flight of stairs. Inside, to the left, is the statue of William Donovan; to the right is the wall of stars. There are marble columns and, as you walk through the door, the seal on the floor in black and white and gray.

In the summer of 2022, I paid a visit to CIA headquarters to interview Rachel, who found the courier's true name, and two other female analysts who worked on the hunt. More than ten years had passed since the hunt concluded. HVT #2, Zawahiri, remained at large. But targeted assassinations had not subsided; to the contrary, they had achieved a level of normalcy. In 2020, the US military launched a drone strike that took out Qasem Soleimani, an Iranian major general, one of hundreds of enemy leaders killed in the post-9/11 world.

Rachel, people say, is easier to work with than Maya, her operational counterpart. Rachel was sharply dressed, with long blond-highlighted hair, her eyes tired and a little puffy. She said she loathes talking about her role in catching UBL and prefers to emphasize collaboration: "It's not like it's one amazing woman; there are so many others who helped." In this she provides a contrast to Maya, who, seeing a congratulatory email sent to the agency workforce, reportedly sent a Reply All saying she deserved the credit. Maya left the agency after she did not get promoted; the explanation was that "She didn't exhibit the range of skills that a GS-15 analyst needs," said Kristin Wood, who was incredulous when this occurred. "I lost my mind. I just lost my mind." Many people sympathize with Maya's decision to leave. This was the person who had led people to bin Laden. Maybe some rules might have been bent. Are men ever described as "sharp-elbowed," the adjective commonly applied to her? There are rumors she took a high-paying job in the private sector.

Also present during my 2022 visit to the CIA was Linda Weissgold, head of the analytic directorate; and an officer with the Directorate of Science and Technology, who worked with Rachel on key technical aspects of the hunt. The technical officer—let's call her Tracy—started as an intern. She was in college, studying to be a mechanical engineer, on 9/11. Heading to class, she realized nobody else was, and saw people gathered around the television. Up to then, she had thought she'd "work in the aerospace industry and live near the beach." Instead, counterterrorism and public service—she does tactical technical collection, with experience in Iraq and Afghanistan—have defined her career.

As we chatted, Rachel reflected that analysis is needed now more than ever. So much data means even more disinformation to reckon with. Advances in technology still call for old-fashioned human critical thinking skills. When she was focusing on bin Laden, she was constantly seeking to rethink and reframe. They knew he didn't use technology. They were always asking: Who around him does? It goes back to relationships; people talking to other people, and the human need to communicate.

The larger sisterhood of analysts learned a lot in ten years. Such as: to take care of one another. As the hunt was under way, people were bringing in meals. You could always tell how bad the workload was by whether people were bringing in breakfast, lunch, and dinner. People made sure to ask one another how they were doing. As the date drew near for the raid, Tracy had just gotten married. Her husband did not know why she was so intensely occupied, so eager to get up and go to work. He knew not to ask.

THE DAY OSAMA BIN LADEN's death was announced, Barbara Sude was retired and living in North Carolina. She stayed with the hunt until 2009, hoping they might get him while she was still there. She was home and got a phone call from a former colleague. "Turn on the TV," the colleague suggested. "It's been a good day at the office." She saw a press conference in progress. When President Obama appeared and announced that bin Laden was dead, she experienced mixed feelings. She'd been reading about bin Laden for so long, his words, his speeches, his writings. She knew the names of his children and wives. She knew that he was the core, the controller. It was right to remove him. But it didn't make her feel glad.

In her mind, Barbara still rewrites that August 6 PDB. Could she have written a single word differently? Changed a sentence? Would it have made a difference? How might events have unfolded?

GINA BENNETT WAS AT work when they got HVT #1. A younger targeter messaged words to the effect of "Hey, really bad day for al-Qaeda." Gina: "Yeah, I guess it's a pretty bad day." The colleague responded: "What are you talking about? He's dead."

"Well, it's not the worst day," Gina responded.

How could she mean that?

Gina asked whether the targeter had ever heard of the Baader-Meinhof gang, a far-left German group of Communist urban guerrillas who in the name of fighting fascism were responsible for shootings, bombings, and attacks in the 1970s. Her colleague, twenty-six, had never heard of Baader-Meinhof.

"Okay, well, someday when the CTC targeter asks another CTC targeter, 'Have you ever heard of Osama bin Laden or al-Qaeda?' and they say no, that's the worst day for al-Qaeda," said Gina, who holds that all terrorist leaders are narcissists, and what narcissists want most of all is to be known. Like Barbara, she felt neither happy nor sad.

After the hunt, it fell to Gina to pore through the extraordinary trove of thumb drives and computer disks retrieved from the Abbottabad compound: some 470,000 files, including letters, diaries, and a cache of porn. A model of the compound now sits as a key exhibit in the CIA museum on the ground floor of Langley, replacing old Cold War exhibits that showed people hiding in the trunks of cars escaping from Berlin and Moscow.

The hunt, and everything that led up to it, has become part of history.

MOLLY CHAMBERS WAS ALSO at her desk the morning after the raid. The agency uses a green screen to flash agency-wide messages, which usually say things like "The parking lot will be closed" or "Don't use the water on the third floor" or "We're doing repairs." This time, the message asked staff to please clean up the champagne bottles in the parking lot. The message went to offices and stations all over the world.

Molly felt extremely proud. To her, what the raid said was: *This is the CIA at its best. This is what we can do.* The fact that the raid on bin Laden's compound succeeded, that it came as a total surprise, that it was such a closely guarded secret that nobody knew, even within the building. That morning, somebody put a little votive candle in front of Tenet's portrait in the directors' portrait gallery. People walked by and knew.

EPILOGUE

Fall 2016

E LLIE DUCKETT WANTED TO DIP HER TOES INTO THE OCEAN one last time. Carried by volunteers and hospice workers to Carolina Beach, the sixty-seven-year-old—one of the early women CIA case officers—was dying of metastatic breast cancer. Helping her in her illness was her close friend Marti Peterson Shogi, the first woman spy the CIA deployed in Moscow. The two operations officers worked together at headquarters, stayed close, and ended up in the same area. Marti remarried, twice, after her first husband was killed in Southeast Asia. Ellie Duckett would die after amassing quite a few engagement rings without going through an actual wedding. There was a rumor of a bridal gown never worn. She loved her operational career too much to let marriage compromise her ability to follow its path.

For the women of the Cold War spy sisterhood, a culture that discouraged them from having families meant many had no husband, children, or grandchildren to take care of them once their careers of public service ended. So they took care of one another. Jeanne Vertefeuille, the cold-eyed hunter who brought down Aldrich Ames, also never married, and her colleague Sandy Grimes looked after her until the end.

When I interviewed Heidi August, she was in her mid-seventies, living on her own in a townhouse in sunny Santa Barbara, California.

Her latest car was a red Mini Cooper, and she was thinking about upgrading to an electric car. Sometimes, when she is driving on the 101 Freeway, she'll find herself running through, in her mind, the pseudonyms of all the men she worked for. As a clerk, long ago, she promised herself that someday she would get a dog. Moving around the world, she felt it would be unfair to have a pet. When she retired, she got a little Norfolk terrier, Button; when he died, she got another red Norfolk, named Cardigan.

During the long years of the Covid-19 pandemic, Heidi spent much time alone with Cardi. Normally, she gets a lot of visitors. Retired spooks stay in touch. People passing through, sharing opinions about events like the withdrawal from Afghanistan. During the pandemic, she survived a sidewalk fall and two surgeries. Moving to a place where she didn't know people, she had settled in with her usual resourcefulness, joining clubs and fundraising. Strangers think she's cool. One day, when she was selling a patio table, the frat boys who bought it were fascinated to learn she was a CIA case officer and offered to take her out for a beer. After her retirement, she went to a dinner for the association that provides support for the families of fallen CIA officers. There, she noticed George Tenet, who had been so irritated when she predicted Iraq would become another Beirut. She figured he wouldn't remember her, so she introduced herself. What he said was: "You were right."

In the upper hallway of her house is a framed piece of needlepoint, which her friend Mary Margaret taught her to take her mind off the pressure of a big operation. In a small room are her many awards, and the wanted photo of Kansi, with that odd nick on his earlobe.

Once, during a visit to MI6, the British spy service, in London, Heidi was walking through a room, and a light was turned on to signal an outsider was present. She ran into a man who looked familiar. "Heidi?" he said. It was the boyfriend who lived across from her in Libya—the one she suspected might be a British intelligence officer. She said his name, and they looked at each other, then moved on.

SUE MCCLOUD, WHEN I interviewed her, was living in a gorgeous house near the beach in Carmel, California. After her own retirement, she had run for mayor of Carmel. At one time, a career with the CIA would have been seen as a black mark for a politician, especially one who, like Sue McCloud, had served as a case officer during the notorious old days of infiltrating student groups. After 9/11, public sentiment was such that being a retired CIA officer helped her. She served five terms in all, stepping down in 2012.

ONE DAY IN 2016, Susan Hasler, Cindy Storer, and Barbara Sude met to stay together in a cabin at Wildacres, a writers' retreat in the Appalachian mountains of North Carolina, variously armed with hot curlers, research papers, some antidepressants, a lot of wine, and a thick stack of freshly published books. The books were authored by George Tenet, Michael Morell, and many other men, defending and explaining their roles in the run-up to 9/11 and the war against terror. They had grave and epic titles like *The Great War of Our Time* (Morell) and *At the Center of the Storm* (Tenet). The women had gathered for the purpose of drawing up notes for a group project. Intending to discuss their careers, they became, as Susan Hasler later wrote, distracted anew by "the sea of largely white, male faces; the power handshakes; and the Oval Office shots" in the pages of the books, which endeavored to control the narrative of the war on terror, ignoring that "down at the working-level, the lion's share of the analysts who had followed Bin Ladin and the Mujahideen movement were women" along with "a lot of women working the issue in other agencies and in other countries, too." The women had lived the war, but from the books, hardly anyone would know they had existed. Trading notes on their own careers, they could not help but reflect on the slights they had weathered, the job networks to which they had not been privy.

Rather than drafting their own book, the trio ended up drinking and reading passages aloud in pompous stentorian voices. They got so irritated by the self-righteous self-presentation of the men that they started yelling. Even Barbara, reserved, self-disciplined Barbara, yelled. Somebody from a nearby cabin heard them. The neighbor came over and they showed her one of the paragraphs of one of the books. "Well, he certainly took it out and whipped it around, didn't he?" the neighbor remarked. The weekend was cathartic. The trio of former analysts still thought they might write a book of their own; but they just couldn't get around to it.

Of the three, Cindy Storer has had the hardest time. Since retiring, she has moved around, from Myrtle Beach, to Atlanta, to Florida. In 2019, she started doing cybersecurity for an Atlanta bank and felt optimistic. But the guys gave her grief. They refused to believe she had anything to do with Osama bin Laden. They acted like she was bragging. She quit and sold her house. She now lives in Florida, teaching intelligence history, writing security analyses on a freelance basis, staying in touch with some of her analytic sisters. She feels envious of veterans with their military benefits. The CIA formed a clandestine army, which she served as a civilian adviser. She bears all the psychic scars of a twenty-year war. Studies show that counterterrorism intelligence work during the war on terror led to PTSD in many analysts as well as operatives. Tell Cindy about it.

GINA BENNETT STAYED ON the job for more than twenty years after 9/11. During that time, the agency got HVT #2, Ayman Al-Zawahiri, who was tracked, targeted, found, and eliminated in 2022, when he stepped outside on the balcony of his safe house and was, essentially, vaporized. Gina, when I first interviewed her, was in a dark place. Back in 1993, the same year she warned about bin Laden, she compared him to a charismatic, narcissistic real estate magnate and television star named Donald Trump. Now that same man had been elected president. After the election of a man who, among many other problematic qualities, bragged about sexually assaulting women, she had come to feel the true threat to America came not from without but from within.

"There are 1.6 billion Muslims in the world," she pointed out. "Statistically zero percent, less than zero percent, have joined al-Qaeda. Statistically, less than zero percent want a caliphate as their form of government." By 2020, radicalization and domestic terrorism had increased in America to the point where, not far away from where we were sitting, an armed man who subscribed to the QAnon conspiracy theories had entered a neighborhood pizza restaurant, believing that in the basement were baby-eating sex traffickers, operating under the satanic leadership of Hillary Clinton. By 2021, in protest of Donald Trump's loss in the 2020 presidential election to Joe Biden, American citizens had stormed the US Capitol, destroyed government property, assaulted police officers, killed fellow Americans. If somebody is going to destroy the country in the years ahead, Gina predicted, it's not going to be hijackers in planes.

As Gina saw it, foreign terrorists could kill Americans, and did, but they couldn't kill America or what it stood for. The real threat to national security are people willing—no, eager—to tear down the democratic system. Even Mike Scheuer, founder of Alec Station, had expressed admiration for QAnon; he maintained a blog on which he supported mob violence against Black Lives Matter protesters, described Kyle Rittenhouse, the vigilante who shot and killed two people during unrest in Wisconsin, as a "young hero," called for the killing of various journalists, academics, and Democratic politicians—Barack Obama, Hillary Clinton—and supported conspiracy theories of election fraud. When I interviewed him, his contempt for government had reached a point where he felt "civil war" was the likely solution. He said he hoped I'd say good things about the women who worked for him, a quarter century earlier, and that "I don't care what you say about me."

"He bears no resemblance to the man I knew," said Gina. She hadn't seen him since Jennifer Matthews's funeral. She thinks maybe he never got over it.

To her, the 9/11 attacks did not strike at our national security the way the election of Donald Trump did. She was also shaken by the #MeToo movement and by her own decades of exposure to misogyny at its worst.

Gina by now was divorced. The demands of the job, the hours and workload, put an untenable strain on her marriage. This was true of many women I interviewed. The work was hard and made people sick. Others resigned early because they wanted to raise children. Overseas operations work still provides a challenge.

It may be that female intelligence officers have different trajectories than the generation who served in the Cold War, that some won't stay with the work for their whole career. One of the lawmakers on Capitol

Hill during the January 6 uprising, Abigail Spanberger, a Democrat from Virginia, served as a CIA case officer for eight years. She liked the work. Her husband accompanied her to postings. Even with a supportive spouse, she left because being a case officer is so hard on households and children. Widely regarded as an effective lawmaker, Spanberger held on to a vulnerable seat in the 2022 elections.

HOLLY BOND, WHO SO enjoyed her breaking-and-entering work, also retired; now in a marriage with a wife and children, she feels the private sector is more conducive, but misses the excellence of the PAC team. The targeters who left were snapped up by the private sector: Palantir, Disney, Tesla.

The women who stayed had to contend with the Trump administration, who distrusted what he called "the deep state." Sue Gordon, who declined to hand in her badge when she had children, rose to become Principal Deputy Director of National Intelligence at the Office of the Director of National Intelligence from August 2017 to August 2019—and was widely expected to become the first female director of national intelligence, supported by Republican and Democratic senators. Trump refused to promote her, so she resigned. The intelligence community rallied around, giving her every award in the book. Gina Haspel, meanwhile, nominated as CIA director by Trump in 2018, secured a vow from CIA staff to resign if President Trump fired her. "Basically the entire [intelligence community] would walk with her if that happened," a former Trump aide told a congressional committee. Haspel was tarnished by the war on terror, but to run a "suicide pact" operation against the Trump administration suggested the extent to which she remained respected by her colleagues.

Mallory, the case officer in Peshawar, was also unsettled by the Trump era. After returning from overseas, she worked in domestic stations, assignments that took her to border camps where babies were kept in cages. The treatment of migrants shook her idea of America and what it stood for. She hated words like "illegal." Or acronyms like FRE and HVT. She saw so much of that in the wars—linguistic dehumanization. "When you meet the Sudanese, the Pakistanis, they're just people." In Texas, she did an operation where a Black case officer, a brilliant man who spoke Mandarin Chinese, needed to check into a hotel room using cash—headquarters had screwed up his reservation—and the clerk wouldn't admit him. Mallory had to show up, a white woman, and pay. "They rented it to me, no questions asked."

There is now a statue of Harriet Tubman outside CIA headquarters.

LISA HARPER HAS RETAINED faith that America, and the values it stands for, will prevail. Over our series of interviews, Lisa Harper was traveling the world, with her husband, as the pandemic permitted. During a lull in contagion they took a long trip to Morocco and visited wild parts to go birding. In between her trips, we met in my backyard in urban Washington, which she sized up as a good meeting place: walled, secluded, quiet. Multiple means of egress. Lots of side streets on which a person could park, blocks away, to elude surveillance. I felt weirdly flattered.

Lisa stayed at the agency until 2016, teaching new officers. This generation of female intelligence officers, she observed, is taller and stronger. They are more athletic. They have real muscles. They can hold heavy rifles, like the M-4, that were hard for her. They take care of their bodies. They know self-care. They have "relationships with men that we could only dream of." And "they are beauties."

"Of course, we were beauties too," she reflected. Now, she feels, she can pass for a schoolteacher, and that's also a good cover. She was upbeat about the future. She felt that a lot of issues were getting aired. And that radicalization would not prevail. And that democracy would stand.

Lisa belongs to a sisterhood of retired female intelligence officers. They have an online community, trading emails about this and that. A few years ago, she was also invited to join a group of male case officers who get together weekly to drink red wine. The group is coed now. What struck her: In 2018, when Gina Haspel was being considered for CIA director, the men in the red-wine group actively supported Haspel's nomination. They wrote letters on her behalf. They considered her one of them. Lisa saw this as progress.

She felt her career had been worthwhile. "If my country needed me, I'd be glad to come out of retirement," said Lisa, who is now in her late seventies. She contributed critical intelligence that found its way to the desk of the US president—many times—and obtained secrets nobody else could have gotten. She influenced American history.

When we finished talking, Lisa slipped down a set of side stairs leading out of the garden and disappeared. Going down to close the gate, I never could quite make out where, on the street, she parked. It was almost as if she had never been there.

ACKNOWLEDGMENTS

I T IS A PLEASURE TO THANK THE MANY PEOPLE WHO HELPED bring this book to fruition. I am grateful to all those intelligence officers who gave interviews for this book—those who are named in these pages, as well as those who spoke but did not wish their names to appear, and those who went to great lengths to recommend and contact others. I would particularly like to thank Heidi August and Lisa Harper, who overcame years of clandestine training to, as they say, put themselves out there. Thanks to Darrell Blocker, who put much effort into connecting me with a variety of women whose stories he felt were important; he did it, he said, because he wanted readers to know what things are really like. Among the people Darrell recommended was the late Shirley Sulick, with whom I was emailing right before she died. Before she went into treatment for lung cancer, she messaged that she was not afraid of what lay in store. I am so sorry I did not get to meet her. Her husband, Mike Sulick, kindly put me in touch with other important subjects. So did Alison Fields, and officers at the Association for Former Intelligence Officers. There's a sisterhood, for sure.

The person who started me down this path, Peter Bergen, needs no introduction; he is a journalist and colleague whose work is a model and inspiration. I thank Steve Coll and Glenn Frankel, whose work sets a gold standard, and who provided advice at key moments. More thanks go to friends and colleagues Jack Shafer, Kate Julian, Ann Hulbert, Mary Kostel, Kate Moore, Susan Coll, Carl Hoffman, Todd Purdum, Debbie Stokes, Jim Semivan, and Abbott Kahler. Thanks to Kristie

Miller, who helped more than she knows. To Nell Minow and Margaret Talbot, all I can say is I could never have done any of this without your conversation, judgment, and friendship. Thanks to Vince Houghton, formerly with the International Spy Museum in Washington, now curator of the National Cryptologic Museum, for chatting. At the cryptologic museum library, the irreplaceable Rob Simpson, as always, dug up anything I asked for about cryptologic machines. In 2020, I was a research fellow with the Center for Cryptologic History, and while that research didn't play into this book directly, I appreciated conversations with those historians. At the CIA, Sara Lichterman and Stacey Suyat facilitated interviews. Historians Nicholas Reynolds, Toni Hiley, Nicholas Dujmovic, Linda McCarthy, and Christopher Andrew answered questions at key times. No intelligence agency reviewed this book.

At the 9/11 Memorial & Museum, Amy Weinstein went to great lengths to provide the insightful oral histories she and others conducted. And I so enjoyed a wide-ranging, thought-provoking lunch with three historians and Spy Museum curators, Amanda Ohlke, Jacqueline Eyl, and Alexis Albion, which turned out to be my last restaurant lunch for a long time, as the pandemic quickly followed.

I could not have slept at night without the backup of Julie Tate, researcher, sleuth, and fact-checker extraordinaire. The photographic research of Jenny Pouech was brilliant and unflagging. Tara Olivero found valuable material in many places. I am grateful for the expert reads of the manuscript given by Linda Millis, a historian of intelligence whose students are lucky to have her; and foreign policy historian Elizabeth Cobbs, whose witty and laser-sharp book talks are something to hear. Any errors are my own.

This is the second book I have been fortunate to write under the editorship of Paul Whitlatch, whose listening skills, patience, deft pencil, and clear thinking helped me both broaden and focus my approach. He strengthened ideas, lifted up language, and went to bat. Facilitating was assistant editor Katie Berry, so prompt and responsive. Emily DeHuff provided copyediting that always improved the written word. Barbara Bachman, associate director of art and design, designed the wonderful interior pages; creative director Chris Brand, the smashing cover. The process kept running smoothly thanks to senior production manager Erich Schoeneweiss, executive production editor Nancy Delia, and executive managing editor Sally Franklin Asta, who was instrumental in keeping a workable production schedule. Thanks go to associate managing editor Allie Fox and vice president and associate general counsel Amelia Zalcman. Ensuring the book reaches readers are Melissa Esner, deputy director of marketing; Julie Cepler, vice president and director of marketing; Gwyneth Stansfield, associate director of publicity; Dyana Messina, vice president and director of marketing; and director of sales Todd Berman. I am so grateful for the robust support of senior vice president and deputy publisher Annsley Rosner and senior publishing manager Michelle Guiseffi. Champions from start to finish at Crown were publisher and editor in chief Gillian Blake, and president David Drake. My agent, Todd Shuster, has been my friend and guide for more than twenty years, and I thank him and his staff at Aevitas, including Jack Haug and Lauren Liebow.

So many family members were supportive during visits, vacations, and holidays, when I was often an antisocial grind. I thank my mother, Jean Arrington, and my late father, Marshall Mundy. My children, Anna and Robin Bradley, to whom this book is dedicated, are the lodestar and give me so much pleasure, pride, and hope for the future. Other family members who have provided needed moral support are Stephens and Leigh Mundy, Alex Mundy, Robert Mundy, Mars Mundy, Natalie Mundy, Monika Mundy, Savannah Barker, Ryhan Plaisance, Breck Arrington, and Dan Branch. As someone who was in the Washington, DC, area on September 11, 2001, I thank the many friends, neighbors, and family members who work in intelligence, national security, the military, and other public service.

To Bill, all I can say is you have my gratitude for all your kindness in every way. You have listened, given counsel, improved my workspace, weighed in, tolerated late nights and absences, motivated, and reassured. And brought light and joy. Thank you.

NOTES

AUTHOR'S NOTE

xi   **In 1971, when CIA director Richard Helms:** "Excerpts from Speech by Helms to Society of Newspaper Editors," *New York Times,* April 15, 1971, 30.

xi   **A later director, William Colby:** William Colby and Peter Forbath, *Honorable Men: My Life in the CIA* (New York: Simon and Schuster, 1978).

xi   **Helms's own biography:** Thomas Powers, *The Man Who Kept the Secrets: Richard Helms and the CIA* (New York: Alfred A. Knopf, 1979).

xi   **Ray Cline, who founded US intelligence analysis:** Ray S. Cline, *Secrets, Spies and Scholars* (Washington: Acropolis Books, 1976), xi.

xi   **William Stephenson, the British emissary:** William Stevenson, *A Man Called Intrepid: The Incredible True Story of the Master Spy Who Helped Win World War II* (New York: Skyhorse, 2014).

xi   **A long-serving agency lawyer:** John Rizzo, *Company Man* (New York: Scribner, 2014).

xi   **The journalist Evan Thomas:** Evan Thomas, *The Very Best Men: The Daring Early Years of the CIA* (New York: Simon and Schuster, 2006).

xii   **One fact about the CIA, as it developed:** Dewey Clarridge gives a sense of what "career planning" meant when he says that in the 1970s, "I was slated to replace Clair George as deputy division chief of South Asia when he left to become chief in Beirut in the spring of 1975" and explains that "George was the protégé of Dave Blee" and "of John Waller," the Near East division chief. He describes Alan Wolfe as "an acerbic New Yorker with a rapier wit" who was "constantly" measuring "Waller's chair for size" and recounts that in the spring of 1975, "the Clandestine Service merry-go-round started up again. Alan Wolfe, as expected, became Near East division chief. Clair George plucked a plum assignment as chief in Beirut. . . . I was slated to become deputy chief of South Asia, but at the last minute Dave Blee decided, probably with advice from Alan Wolfe, to make me deputy chief for Arab Operations." Duane R. Clarridge with Digby Diehl, *A Spy for All Seasons: My Life in the CIA* (New York: Scribner, 1997), 152–53, 167.

xiv   **One poignant reminder:** Personnel Record Folder for War Department Civilian Employee (201) File: "Weston, Carolyn Cable," National Personnel Records Center, National Archives, St. Louis, Mo.

PROLOGUE

The description of events in Malta is taken from personal interviews with Heidi August on August 5, 2020, September 17, 2020, October 6, 2020, November 17, 2020, March 12, 2021, July 16, 2021, and November 18, 2023, and conversations in between, as well as photographs she shared and writing she kept about her career. Readers may also be interested in the CNN documentary *Terror in the Sky,* in which she discussed the hijacking and subsequent investigation and manhunt.

CHAPTER ONE: STATION W

3   **In the uncertain winter of late 1944:** The description of the assessment process can be found in OSS Assessment Staff, *Assessment of Men: Selection of Personnel for the Office of Strategic Services* (New York: Rinehart, 1948). The building is described on page 23. The initial moments, expectations, testing, lunch, and observations can be found on pages 316–32. The creation of the assessment "stations" is also well described in Kermit Roosevelt, *War Report of the OSS* (New York: Walker, 1976), 238–43.

7   **President Franklin Roosevelt needed to know two things:** There are many accounts of Roosevelt's decision to send William J. Donovan to England, and of the UK's efforts to persuade the Americans to create a spy service. Ray S. Cline, in *Secrets, Spies and Scholars,* points out that Churchill and a group of British officials "desperately wanted to help the United States create an effective intelligence system" better than "the patchwork of bureaucratic bits and pieces that they observed with dismay in 1939 and 1940 as they sought to educate American officials about the crucial need to counter the German threat in Europe." They wanted to avoid "careless handling" and make sure the intelligence was presented objectively. Cline, *Secrets, Spies,* 21–26.

7   **To the first question:** Joseph Kennedy, the American ambassador, predicted "early British collapse or surrender." Ibid., 27.

7   **Roosevelt wanted a second opinion:** Cline points out that Donovan went to England as observer for the president in the summer of 1940. Coming back in early August 1940, Donovan reported to Roosevelt that "the morale of Great Britain under Churchill was high" and that it had enormous assets in its air force, radar defense net, code breaking, and SOE. Ibid., 27–28.

7   **Up to then, US intelligence:** "Espionage had never been seriously conducted in the United States except in time of war." Ibid., 13.

7   **The UK "ran an operation":** William Stephenson, aka "Intrepid," a Canadian, was the British MI6 station chief in the United States. He set up as "the British Passport Control Officer" in the International Building in Rockefeller Center. Seeing that the US effort so far was, in Cline's words, "inadequate and chaotic," he proposed a "central, coordinated intelligence system," which survived the war. Ibid., 29–30. Stephenson's clandestine campaign is also well captured in Nicholas Reynolds, *Need to Know: World War II and the Rise of American Intelligence* (New York: Mariner, 2022), 41–57.

7   **The British model was constructed:** Created in 1942, the OSS represented "a revolutionary new concept in what was still peacetime—a civilian, central coordinating intelligence system." Cline, *Secrets, Spies,* 21.

8   **Donovan embodied the kind of man:** William Donovan's prodigality has been oft noted. Cline says he "permitted the 'wildest,' loosest kind of administrative and procedural chaos to develop while he concentrated on recruiting talent wherever he could find it—in universities, businesses, law firms, in the armed services, at Georgetown cocktail parties" (39). Cline describes Donovan's "cult of romanticism," and says he left "humdrum business" to his subordinates (40). An excellent description of his background, personalities, and liaisons can be found in Reynolds, *Need to Know,* who says he and his wife, Ruth, started to "grow apart" after their marriage in 1914, partly because she was a homebody while Donovan was incorrigibly restless and engaged in "trysts" as well as "longer relationships" with other women. Reynolds describes him as a "near-compulsive philanderer" (16–27, 59).

8   **"Like Nature, he was prodigal":** *Assessment of Men,* 10.

9   **By late 1943, the OSS was "busily and somewhat hazardly":** Ibid., 40.

9   **At a time when the US government and private sector:** the cobbling-together is described in ibid., 26.

9   **The group had to agree on:** Ibid., 9, 457.

10   **Candidates were brought together:** Ibid., 3.

10   **The OSS employed:** Ibid., 60.

10   **"The Harvard connection":** Cline notes that "the search for manpower was already so intense that the Navy promised my wife a job as cryptanalyst too if I would come" to work as a code breaker in August 1942, and in June 1943, he reported to 2430 E Street. Cline, *Secrets, Spies,* 54, 55.

11   **For three days, recruits play-acted:** *Assessment of Men,* 94–99.

11   **In another situation, each recruit:** Ibid., 102–103.

12   **"To Station W were sent":** Ibid., 4.

CHAPTER TWO: GET THE FOOD, MARY

13   **At its peak, the office of Strategic:** Cline and others estimate that OSS reached a "total strength of about 13,000," though it's likely more served during the years; there are 24,000 personnel files at the National Archives. The numbers for women are taken from a paper on the OSS by the historian Michael Warner and the CIA History Staff in the Center for the Study of Intelligence, "The Office of Strategic Services: America's First Intelligence Agency," cia.gov/static/7851e16f9e100b6f9cc4ef002028c e2f/Office-of-Strategic-Services.pdf.

13   **Some rose to be top administrators:** Vera Atkins has been written about in William Stevenson, *Spymistress: The True Story of the Greatest Female Secret Agent of World War II* (New York: Arcade, 2011), and Sarah Helm, *A Life in Secrets: Vera Atkins and the Missing Agents of World War II* (New York: Anchor Books, 2007). Among the growing literature of the women of SOE and OSS are Kathryn J. Atwood, *Women Heroes of World War II: 26 Stories of Espionage, Sabotage, Resistance, and Rescue* (Chicago: Chicago Review Press, 2011); Gordon Thomas and Greg Lewis, *Shadow Warriors of World War II: The Daring Women of the SOE* (Chicago: Chicago Review Press, 2017); and Sarah Rose, *D-Day Girls: The Spies Who Armed the Resistance, Sabotaged the Nazis, and Helped Win World War II* (New York: Crown, 2020).

14   **One wartime officer:** Christopher Andrew, *Defend the Realm* (New York: Vintage Books, 2010), 220–21. Knight's admonitions are also well told in Owen Bowcott, "Women Make Better Spies—as Long as They Forget Sex," *The Guardian,* May 20, 2004, https://www.theguardian.com/uk/2004/may/21/artsandhumanities.higher education.

14   **These women were uniquely vulnerable:** Rose, 22.

15   **The first known female spy for England:** Christopher Andrew, *The Secret World: A History of Intelligence* (New Haven: Yale University Press, 2017), 235.

15   **On something like the same principle:** Kelly B. Gormly, "How Kate Warne, America's First Woman Detective, Foiled a Plot to Assassinate Abraham Lincoln," *Smithsonian,* March 29, 2022, smithsonianmag.com/history/how-kate-warne-americas-first -woman-detective-foiled-a-plot-to-assassinate-abraham-lincoln-180979829/.

15   **During the Civil War, Washington-area society women:** The story of four female Civil War spies is told in Karen Abbott's wonderful book *Liar, Temptress, Soldier, Spy: Four Women Undercover in the Civil War* (New York: HarperCollins, 2014).

15   **In Richmond, a Southern heiress:** Abbott discusses Van Lew's background, spy services, and postwar life (38–48, 75–83, 124–30, 227–33). She points out that though she was rewarded by Ulysses S. Grant with the job of postmistress, Van Lew was scorned and vilified by the citizens of Richmond, who, after her death in 1900, believed she haunted her home. In Boston, meanwhile, a group of abolitionists erected a memorial stone, saying "She risked everything that is dear to man" in order that "slavery might be abolished and the Union preserved" (428). Another excellent source is Michael J. Sulick, *Spying in America: Espionage from the Revolutionary War to the Dawn of the Cold War* (Washington, DC: Georgetown University Press, 2014), 99–105.

16 **After one of his London meetings:** Thomas and Lewis, *Shadow Warriors*, 27.

16 **"The highest incomes before 1940":** *Assessment of Men*, 501.

16 **To take part, applicants gathered:** Ibid., 322.

17 **So they designed a test "expressly for women":** Ibid., 326–27.

19 **The two women met long after the war:** The story of how the two former spies found each other, and the work they did, is told by Ian Shapira, "Decades After Duty in the OSS and CIA, 'Spy Girls' Find Each Other in Retirement," *Washington Post*, June 26, 2011, washingtonpost.com/local/decades-after-duty-in-the-oss-and-cia -spy-girls-find-each-other-in-retirement/2011/05/28/AG2xvZmH_story.html.

19 **She later wrote two books:** Elizabeth P. MacDonald, *Undercover Girl* (New York: Time Life Books, 1993); Elizabeth P. McIntosh, *Sisterhood of Spies: Women of the OSS* (Annapolis: Naval Institute Press, 1998), 11, 96. McIntosh's story is also told in Ann Todd, *OSS Operation Blackmail: One Woman's Covert War Against the Imperial Japanese Army* (Annapolis: Naval Institute Press, 2017).

20 **A group of highly educated women:** The story of the Six Triple Eight is told in articles, in print, and online, but it's also worth going to the source and reading the memoir of their commander: Lt. Col. Charity Adams Earley, *One Woman's Army: A Black Officer Remembers the WAC* (Texas A&M University Military History Series, #12, October 1, 1995).

20 **In Washington, a group of "military mapping maidens":** The history office of the National Geospatial-Intelligence Agency introduced me to these women on a tour of the facility's museum on October 21, 2021. https://www.nga.mil/innovators-leaders /Military_Mapping_Maidens_of_WWII.html.

20 **At the University of Pennsylvania:** The story of the ENIAC women is told in numerous books and articles including Kathy Kleiman, *Proving Ground: The Untold Story of the Six Women Who Programmed the World's First Modern Computer* (New York: Grand Central, 2022).

20 **The American entertainer Josephine Baker:** Baker's contributions as a spy are recounted in Meredith H. Hindley's *Destination Casablanca: Exile, Espionage, and the Battle for North Africa in World War II* (New York: Public Affairs, 2017).

20 **In Paris, a young Frenchwoman:** David Ignatius, "After Five Decades, a Spy Tells Her Tale," *Washington Post*, December 28, 1998, washingtonpost.com/archive/politics /1998/12/28/after-five-decades-a-spy-tells-her-tale/8bfa5aae-5527-4eb5-8e45 -878f1ec823fb/; and Liza Mundy, "Jeannie Rousseau de Clarens: The Glass-Ceiling-Breaking Spy," *Politico*, December 28, 2017, washingtonpost.com/archive/politics /1998/12/28/after-five-decades-a-spy-tells-her-tale/8bfa5aae-5527-4eb5-8e45 -878f1ec823fb/.

21 **Another Frenchwoman, Marie-Madeleine Fourcade:** Lynne Olson, *Madame Fourcade's Secret War: The Daring Young Woman Who Led France's Largest Spy Network Against Hitler* (New York: Random House, 2019).

21 **Few were better at it than Virginia Hall:** Hall's remarkable story is told in Sonia Purnell, *A Woman of No Importance: The Untold Story of the American Spy Who Helped Win World War II* (New York: Viking, 2019) and Judith L. Pearson, *The Wolves at the Door: The True Story of America's Greatest Female Spy* (Guilford, Conn.: Lyons Press, 2005).

21 **"The star of the show was unquestionably":** Cline, *Secrets, Spies*, 61.

21 **(Cline ran the office of analysis):** Ibid., 59.

22 **Dulles sent a stream of intel back:** Cline says that Dulles's reports on Gisevius showed what was going on inside Nazi Germany and German intelligence agencies "in remarkable depth" and was "magnificent stuff and brought great credit to Donovan and his men." Ibid., 61–62.

22 **"Both of these men would discuss with me":** Bancroft tells her life story in Mary Bancroft, *Autobiography of a Spy* (New York: William Morrow, 1983), 112.

22 **"There was plenty of experimenting":** Ibid., 54.

22   **A few years in, they divorced:** Rufenacht also hit her. "On our second evening home I
      told Jean that I thought it would be better if we didn't get married," Bancroft notes.
      "Jean hauled off and hit me such a blow with his fist that it knocked me out." Ibid., 68.

23   **His sister, Eleanor, estimated:** Stephen Kinzer, "When a CIA Director Had Scores of
      Affairs," *New York Times*, November 10, 2012, nytimes.com/2012/11/10/opinion/when
      -a-cia-director-had-scores-of-affairs.html.

23   **On their first meeting, engineered by a mutual contact:** Bancroft describes their early
      meetings and says that on their second, "I was appalled that Allen was contemplat-
      ing anything more than just having me work for him" and "pretended not to notice
      Allen's expression." Bancroft, *Autobiography of a Spy*, 126–37.

23   **He also expected Bancroft:** Ibid., 200.

24   **When he complained Hitler was getting many facts wrong:** Ibid., 109, 144.

24   **"What do these people actually do?":** Ibid., 132, 191.

24   **Her housekeeper, Maria:** Ibid., 177–80.

24   **As Dulles expected, Bancroft by now:** Ibid., 152.

25   **"By chance, the maid was out":** Ibid., 161.

25   **She referred to it as:** Ibid., 174.

25   **Dulles confided in Mary Bancroft:** Ibid., 134 and 243–44.

26   **His role as a double agent:** Ibid., 140 and 165–66.

26   **So voluble were his confidences:** Ibid., 162, and 192–95.

26   **He would go on to become:** Cline, *Secrets, Spies,* describes Dulles as "the first profes-
      sional intelligence officer" to become head of CIA, saying "No other man left such
      a mark on the Agency." Known as the "great White Case Officer," Cline says, Dulles
      spent three-quarters of his time and energy on clandestine collection and covert
      action. He loved "exoticism, the hint of danger, and the intellectual intricacy of
      overseas operations" and, in analysis, "brief, colorful, snappy items with dramatic
      quality" (152). He savored "clandestine operations for their own sake," which Cline
      saw as a flaw, and "put CIA on the map in Washington and abroad—perhaps too
      much." Dulles, he says, was "a little vain about his appearance, especially when
      women were to be in the reception line at the foot of the aircraft landing steps" (112,
      151–54, and 167).

26   **Among these was Cora Du Bois:** Susan Seymour, *Cora Du Bois, Anthropologist, Diplo-
      mat, Agent* (Lincoln: University of Nebraska Press, 2015), describes her recruitment
      and early work on 168–78.

27   **In 1944, Du Bois found herself traveling from San Francisco:** Ibid., 178–88.

27   **Known for crisp, acerbic cables:** Ibid., 187–204.

28   **During the power struggle between:** Ibid., 224–40.

28   **By the 1950s:** While the size of the CIA is secret, many sources put it at 20,000. Cline
      says that during the Korean War, with lots of demands placed on it, the CIA "grew
      by leaps and bounds" and "shot to around the 10,000 level." The intelligence direc-
      torate was about 3,000, and clandestine services was "by far the largest component."
      He says the peak was 18,000 and that half the staff was "clerical, secretarial, and
      routine." Cline, *Secrets, Spies,* 115–19.

28   **For a decade, it continued to hum:** Nicholas Reynolds describes the OSS's home on a
      "few acres of land known as Navy Hill" in a rather decrepit (at the time) Foggy Bot-
      tom, occupying "the three-story brick and limestone office buildings" clustered
      around a bucolic gardened quadrangle. During the war, Donovan occupied room
      109 of the central building, which likely accounts for why, in cables, he was referred
      to as "109." Reynolds, *Need to Know,* 74. The haphazard growth of the buildings is
      described in Clifton Berry, *Inside the CIA: The Architecture, Art & Atmosphere of
      America's Premier Intelligence Agency* (Montgomery, Md.: Community Communica-
      tions, 1997). Dewey Clarridge, who joined the CIA in the mid-1950s, recalls that
      before the move to McLean, "CIA functions were scattered all over Washington. I

reported to a cluster of wooden buildings on Ohio Drive along the Potomac, not far from the Lincoln Memorial Reflecting Pool. Little more than shacks, they were completely anonymous, each designated by a letter of the alphabet. The buildings had formerly been used as barracks by the OSS during World War II; they looked their age." He notes that these later became the Lincoln Memorial polo fields. Duane R. Clarridge, *A Spy for All Seasons: My Life in the CIA* (New York: Scribner, 1997), 41. The site where the Heurich brewery stood is now occupied by the Kennedy Center for the Performing Arts.

29   **"There seemed to be no way to jar the spinsters"**: The prevalence of women at the CIA is noted in a presumably self-published pamphlet by Thomas Bell Smith, a former case officer recruited in 1952, who notes, "Almost no writing I've seen has made any real mention of the women in CIA" and points out that "they're there, and in large numbers." While most were secretaries, "there's a whole silent army of other women doing a thousand and one tasks," including reports officers and "girls" who "kept the identification photos and other data on known Russian intelligence personnel serving abroad." He says there were "a few girl case-officers, but with rare exceptions these worked at Headquarters." Thomas Bell Smith, *The Essential CIA: A Realistic Look Inside America's Clandestine Service by a Former CIA Staffer,* 13–26. Smith also provides a good sense of the early layout, remembering that when he reported to L Building, it sat with "its interconnected sisters I, J, and K" beside the Reflecting Pool of the Lincoln Memorial, "a two-storied box in asbestos-sided, neo-concentration-camp architecture, behind a high chain-link fence." Before 1961, he says that people worked in places with "a lot more atmosphere" than could be found in McLean, with the "target intelligence people" in an old roller-skating rink with no windows or air-conditioning. The map library was in a "quaint old theater on Virginia Avenue." His invective against the spinsters continues when he describes Central Processing as "several middle-aged Southern ladies of a type you can find in many Federal agencies." Smith, *Essential CIA,* 5–6, 19. He also noted that MI6 "had more women in relatively responsible positions than any other intelligence service known to me. This was a legacy of the Second World War, when, for example, the agent documentation effort was almost entirely carried on by female personnel" (164).

29   **Recruiters for clerks and typist positions**: Patsy McCollough, who started in 1977 as an armed security guard and by the 1980s was working in the personnel office of the clandestine services, told me, "When I first came on board, the majority of women, even those with degrees, came in as clerk typists." She noted that "Pennsylvania was one of their best places to pull clerical workers, there and West Virginia," and that it was "easier to get young single women to move away from their families" if they were reasonably close by. She noted that "they actually had hotels set up in the Washington, DC, and Northern Virginia area, where the women stayed, during the 1960s and early '70s." Patsy McCollough, telephone interview, October 28, 2020.

29   **Regardless of their real name**: Susan Hasler shares the detail about the Grace Sullivans in an unpublished memoir. When she answered an ad in the early 1980s, she wrote, "First came a letter from someone called Grace Sullivan. Years later I would meet Grace, or perhaps I should say the Graces. They were elderly ladies who worked in the Public Affairs Office. None of them was actually named Grace, but they handled routine correspondence with the public and signed everything Grace Sullivan. They also answered phone calls from people who were convinced that the CIA was bugging their dental work. This was a surprisingly common complaint. The ladies would listen sympathetically, and say something along the lines of, 'You poor thing. That must be annoying. I'll make a few phone calls and take care of it for you.'"

30   **"Patience, thoroughness, skepticism, and tireless review":** Cline, *Secrets, Spies,* 63.

31   **One of the early architects of the CIA's:** Evan Thomas, *The Very Best Men: The Daring Early Years of the CIA* (New York: Simon and Schuster, 2006), 336.

31   **According to William Colby:** William Colby and Peter Forbath, *Honorable Men: My Life in the CIA* (New York: Simon and Schuster, 1978). The comment about FitzGerald is on 147; his complaint about the "macho" tenor of operations on 214; his assessment of Luce on 123; his observations on the women of Vietnam on 142.

31   **"Whether the counter-espionage file was a simple card file":** Cline, *Secrets, Spies,* 62.

CHAPTER THREE: THE CLERK

This chapter is based on personal interviews with Heidi August, by phone and in person, on August 5, 2020, September 17, 2020, October 6, 2020, November 17, 2020, March 12, 2020, July 16, 2021, and November 18, 2023, and various conversations in between.

38   **"The need for clandestine covert action to fight the Cold War":** Colby, *Honorable Men,* 107. He refers to the "explosive growth" of the 1950s and "unqualified backing" from the American public (103–5).

38   **a 1953 *Time* magazine cover story on Allen Dulles:** "The Man with the Innocent Air," *Time,* August 3, 1953, 12–15.

39   **An exposé in *Ramparts* magazine:** Sol Stern, "A Short Account of International Student Politics and the Cold War with Particular Reference to the NSA, CIA, etc.," *Ramparts,* March 1967, 29–38.

43   **The coup came as a shock to:** In M. Cherif Bassiouni, ed., *Libya: From Repression to Revolution* (Leiden: Martinus Nijhoff, 2013), a discussion of the "advent of oil," the "corruption of King Idris and his advisers," and the conversion of Libya to "an economy based purely on oil" occurs on pages 46 and 47. The book notes that Idris's government had become "a corrupt plutocracy propped up by patronage schemes in which power was controlled by a small clique," that it was "unwilling to move away from its support of the West" or to "recognize the shift toward Arab nationalism." King Idris "refused to lead as head of state," his government "repressed dissent," and there had been "long-circulating rumors of a coup." A discussion of Qaddafi's early days is on page 48: his "revolutionary ambitions developed into an international political and ideological climate defined by popular upheavals, anti-imperialism, nationalism, and pan-Arabism." On page 49, the book notes that "On 1 September 1969 a group of roughly 70 Libyan junior military officers, led by the young Mu'ammar Qadhafi, launched a bloodless coup that quickly toppled the existing government."

46   **Among the best-known Cold War station chiefs:** The power of the midcentury station chief is well described in Evan Thomas, *Very Best Men:* "The 1950s were the high age of the CIA station chief. In countries all throughout Asia, the head of state was close to the CIA chief of station, if not actually on his payroll. The same was true throughout Latin America and the Middle East." Thomas notes that "the CIA men handed out the gold, and they often had a more direct line of communication to the White House than the ambassador" (184). The curious case of the marital swap is elaborated in an evocative profile of Louis and Nancy Dupree by James Verini, "Love and Ruin," *The Atavist,* no. 34, magazine.atavist.com /loveandruin/.

48   **Helsinki Station was important:** The role of Helsinki Station is described by Jeanne Vertefeuille, who served there in the early 1960s: "Because the country bordered the USSR, the CIA in Helsinki concentrated all its efforts on the Soviet target." She helped exfiltrate a walk-in, KGB counterintelligence officer Anatoliy Mikhaylovich, and his wife and daughter, in 1961, which involved pulling "wads of currency" out of

the station strongbox, meeting the family at the airport, and getting them on to Stockholm, Frankfurt, and the United States. Sandra Grimes and Jeanne Verte-feuille, *Circle of Treason: A CIA Account of Traitor Aldrich Ames and the Men He Betrayed* (Annapolis: Naval Institute Press, 2012), 3–5.

CHAPTER FOUR: THE DIPLOMAT'S DAUGHTER

53   **Hurrying to class:** A description of the atmosphere at Brown, and Pembroke, can be found in the 1966 *Brun Mael,* the Pembroke yearbook.

55   **Lisa's parents hired a former actress:** Lisa Manfull Harper's recollections of her life and career were shared in a series of in-person interviews on February 26, 2020, May 17, 2020, October 23, 2020, March 26, 2021, and March 6, 2023, with emails in between. These are supplemented by a 1987 speech she gave to career trainees and a vivid oral history delivered to a Brown classmate, Kristie Miller, as part of an official series of oral histories of Foreign Service wives: "Kristie Miller interview of Lisa Manfull Harper," Association for Diplomatic Studies and Training, Foreign Affairs Oral History Project, Foreign Service Spouse Series, April 19, 1990.

60   **The quintessential image of the CIA officer:** Tim Weiner, *Legacy of Ashes: The History of the CIA* (New York: Anchor, 2008), notes that "Throughout 1969 and 1970, Nixon and Kissinger focused the CIA on the secret expansion of the war in Southeast Asia" and that the agency had to make payoffs to President Thieu of South Vietnam, "manipulate the media in Saigon, fix an election in Thailand, and step up covert commando raids in North Vietnam, Cambodia, and Laos" (348). William Colby warned of the strength of the North Vietnamese, but his "warning did not register anywhere in Washington, not at the White House, not with Congress, not in the Pentagon, and not in the mind of the American ambassador in Saigon" (496). Cline says "CIA was the bearer of bad tidings throughout the Vietnam war, and was not very happily received by any of the policymakers who tried to make the Vietnam intervention work" (Cline, *Secrets, Spies,* 199). He saw the CIA estimates as "soberer and less optimistic" than those of McNamara, "who was always predicting victory by the end of the year," 199.

CHAPTER FIVE: FLAPS AND SEALS

63   **According to many accounts of the Farm:** One of the best descriptions can be found in Ted Gup, "Down on 'the Farm': Learning How to Spy for the CIA, *The Washington Post,* February 19, 1980, https://www.washingtonpost.com/archive/local/1980/02/19 /down-on-the-farm-learning-how-to-spy-for-the-cia/fbe2f23c-ab8d-4fba-aab2 -1c1da55f1c53/.

64   **When Lisa started in 1968, the case officer:** When Dewey Clarridge attended Farm training in the mid-1950s, he noted that "almost all the few women" were headed for the Directorate of Intelligence. Clarridge, *Spy for All Seasons,* 41.

65   **"Not too many women are suited to the way of life":** Smith, *Essential CIA,*13.

65   **"They just didn't think a woman could run an operation":** Jonna Mendez, telephone interview, June 4, 2020.

67   **It was the women's job to make sure:** Amy Tozzi, telephone and FaceTime interviews, May 22 and 25, 2020.

68   **"Nobody wanted a female":** Janine Brookner, in-person interview, Washington, D.C., December 9, 2020.

70   **"They would kind of snatch the form from you":** Mia McCall, telephone interview, April 5, 2021.

71   **"Let's say, I met some guy":** Mike Sulick, in-person interview, Winston-Salem, North Carolina, March 21, 2022.

72 **In 1954, Lee Coyle was a graduate of Rosemont College:** Lee Coyle, telephone interview, September 9, 2020.

72 **One of her contemporaries:** Mike Kalogeropoulos, telephone interview, April 14, 2020, and in-person interview, Vienna, Virginia, June 3, 2020.

CHAPTER SIX: YOU HAD TO WEAR A SKIRT

73 **Born in 1920, Page boasted:** Eloise Page's academic career is cited in her April 2, 1976, nomination for a Federal Woman's Award, one of many documents declassified and approved for release October 30, 2013, AR 70-14. Her wartime career was discussed during an interview with Randy Burkett, CIA historian, June 21, 2021, and her work on the Sputnik program in Amy Ryan and Gary Keeley, "Sputnik and US Intelligence: The Warning Record," *Studies in Intelligence,* vol. 61, no. 3, 1–16.

75 **At a town hall meeting in 1953, a discomfited:** A study for the Center for the Study of Intelligence, by [Last Name Redacted], Jacqueline, "The Petticoat Panel: A 1953 Study of the Role of Women in the CIA Career Service, an Intelligence Monograph," Center for the Study of Intelligence, March 2003, approved for release October 30, 2013, AR 70-14.

77 **One former secretary recalled that she paid all her boss's bills:** This anecdote is related in an oral history declassified in 2013, "Secrets of the RYBAT Sisterhood: Four Senior Women in the Directorate of Operations Discuss their Careers," CIA FOIA Reading Room, approved for release October 30, 2013.

77 **And there was a lot to know:** Nicholas Reynolds points out that Douglas Waller, *Wild Bill Donovan: The Spymaster Who Created the OSS and Modern American Espionage* (New York: Free Press, 2011), "cites the claim by OSS officer Rolfe Kingsley" on page 200. Reynolds, *Need to Know,* 365.

77 **"Some women were just so tough":** Jeanne Newell, telephone interview, November 19, 2020.

78 **"When you are trying to recruit someone in sub-Saharan":** Clarridge, *Spy for All Seasons,* 304–5.

79 **In the 1980s, when a young Californian:** Pamela McMaster, in-person interview, Santa Barbara, California, September 30, 2020.

79 **Among the many published histories:** Evan Thomas recounts this anecdote being told about William Harvey, head of Berlin operations base in the mid-1950s, who "claimed to never go a day without 'having' a woman." Acknowledging that it was "probably apocryphal," Thomas says the story went that a "psywar" colleague "looking into a window one day, spotted Harvey having his way with his secretary on a desktop. The prankster picked up the phone and dialed Harvey's number. Still rutting, Harvey picked up the receiver. 'This is God,' said the psywar operative. 'Aren't you ashamed?'" Thomas, *Very Best Men,* 131. Clifton Berry cites Archie Roosevelt's memoir, *For Lust of Knowing,* as saying "One of my friends, working in his second-floor office on a weekend, happened to look down and see a colleague in an office below in the process of undressing a pretty secretary, with the obvious intention of committing a bit of unauthorized covert action. Surrendering to an irresistible impulse, my friend picked up the phone, dialed his colleague, and watched him draw away from the lady to answer it. 'This is God speaking,' said a deep commanding voice. 'I see what you are doing. It is a grievous sin.' He hung up and saw the parties separating." Berry, *Inside the CIA,* 22.

80 **At CIA headquarters, a young officer:** Bonnie Hershberg, telephone interview, May 7, 2020.

81 **Had any of them experienced sexual harassment?:** "Secrets of the RYBAT Sisterhood," 17.

81 **This dynamic was confirmed:** Patsy McCollough, telephone interview, October 28, 2020.

83 **Around this same time, another promising trainee:** Jeanne Newell, telephone interview, November 19, 2020.

83 **In July 1974, an economist named:** R. Jennine Anderson, letter to the editor, *Ms.* magazine, July 1974. The "petticoat panel" report says that in the 1950s, "it was automatically assumed that a woman was no more than an adjunct of her husband" and that "women were expected to go LWOP or resign when their spouses were transferred overseas."

CHAPTER SEVEN: HOUSEWIFE COVER

88 **Ray Close, a chief of station:** John Weir Close, "Raymond Close: CIA Veteran and Antiwar Activist," *Winchester Star,* March 3, 2021, winchesterstar.com/obituaries/raymond-hooper-close-cia-veteran-and-anti-war-activist/article_6ba5c7d4-af9f-5685-8bb5-f8aa99f6a84b.html.

88 **Director William Colby's 1978 memoir:** Colby, *Honorable Men,* 79, 87, 89, 90, and 146.

89 **"They put the pros on us":** Mike Sulick shared his memories of the contributions of his late wife, Shirley, as well as descriptions of work in Moscow, in an interview in Wake Forest, North Carolina, on March 21, 2022. Many other interviewees for this book discussed the importance of wives, especially in denied areas, including Mike Kalogeropolous, in an in-person interview on June 3, 2020.

92 **The agency had spent much of the 1950s:** Descriptions of the agency's efforts to combat Communist influence in Europe can be found in many sources, including Cline, who talks about CIA support of anticommunist groups abroad, especially in France, Italy, and Germany, using covert and psychological efforts to counter Soviet influence, assist moderate governments, and "stabilize Western Europe against the threat of Soviet assaults on Italy, France, and Germany" (Cline, *Secrets, Spies,* 99). He writes about Radio Free Europe and other psychological warfare of the 1950s and '60s as intended to bring "psychological pressures to bear on dictatorial governments" and "helping noncommunist members" of labor and youth movements "oppose heavy-handed Community efforts to seize control of all organs of mass opinion" (129). Evan Thomas describes the impact of the crushed Hungarian revolution (Thomas, *Very Best Men,* 144), and notes that Frank Wisner described the agency's propaganda war in Europe as a tune he played on his "mighty Wurlitzer" (137).

CHAPTER EIGHT: THE HEIST

103 **On her first case officer assignment:** The description of events in Geneva is taken from personal interviews with Heidi August, on August 5, 2020, September 17, 2020, October 6, 2020, November 17, 2020, March 12, 2021, July 16, 2021, and November 18, 2023, and conversations in between, as well as photographs.

104 **Heidi's reading included essays by the Italian journalist:** Ian Fisher, "Oriana Fallaci, Incisive Italian Journalist, Is Dead at 77," *New York Times,* March 3, 2021, nytimes.com/2006/09/16/books/16fallaci.html?scp=1&sq=Oriana%20Fallaci%20obituary&st=cse.

108 **During World War II, code breaking was a key to Allied victory:** The importance of World War II code breaking is told in numerous accounts, including Liza Mundy, *Code Girls: The Untold Story of the Women Code Breakers of World War II* (New York: Hachette, 2017).

CHAPTER NINE: INCIDENT MANAGEMENT

114 **"You would have thought the world:"** Eileen Martin, telephone interview, April 27, 2020.

114 **Nearing sixty years old, Eloise Page:** Mike Kalogeropoulos, telephone interview, April 14, 2020, and in-person interview, June 3, 2020. Others who shared reminis-

cences of Page were Lee Coyle and Page's former secretary, Joanne Richcreek, who recalled that Page used to leave her little notes in shorthand when she was going to lunch. Joanne Richcreek, telephone interview, February 1, 2021, and Lee Coyle, telephone interview, September 9, 2020.

118   **When Rev. Stuart Kenworthy took over Christ Church:** Rev. Stuart Kenworthy, in-person interview, Washington, D.C., November 17, 2021.

119   **Her father, an athlete at the Naval Academy:** Sue McCloud shared memories of her life and career in an in-person interview at her home in Carmel, California, on August 16, 2020.

120   **"You really don't want to go out there":** Mike Kalogeropoulos, telephone interview, April 14, 2020, and in-person interview, June 3, 2020.

121   **"My whole experience with her":** Mia McCall, telephone interview, April 5, 2021.

126   **An Egyptian plane headed from Athens to Cairo had been hijacked:** The hijacking of Egyptair Flight 648 is chronicled in the documentary *Terror in the Sky: To Catch a Hijacker,* August 5, 2017, as part of the CNN series "Declassified: Untold Stories of American Spies," which includes transcripts of the pilot's cockpit communications, collected on the Bearcat scanner, and an interview with Heidi August, imdb.com /title/tt7134324/. A contemporaneous description of events can be found in Judith Miller, "From Takeoff to Raid: The 24 Hours of Flight 648," *New York Times,* November 27, 1985, A10, nytimes.com/1985/11/27/world/from-takeoff-to-raid-the-24 -hours-of-flight-648.html. One of many tributes to Scarlett Rogenkamp can be found in Patrick McDonnell, "Lone American Killed: Hijacking Victim Buried, Awarded the Purple Heart," *Los Angeles Times,* December 1, 1985, latimes.com /archives/la-xpm-1985-12-01-me-5580-story.html. This account is also taken from many interviews with Heidi August, as well as some of her personal writings.

CHAPTER TEN: THE VAULT WOMEN REVOLT

135   **Walking down one hallway, in the 1990s:** Jonna Mendez shared her career memories in a telephone conversation on June 4, 2020.

138   **In 1974, the investigative journalist Seymour Hersh:** Seymour M. Hersh, "Huge CIA Operation Reported in US Against Antiwar Forces, Other Dissidents in Nixon Years," *New York Times,* December 22, 1974, A1, https://www.nytimes.com/1974/12/22 /archives/huge-cia-operation-reported-in-u-s-against-antiwar-forces-other.html. Evan Thomas, *Very Best Men,* reveals that the CIA tried to run a smear campaign against the publication (330). Thomas describes the Church-Pike hearings and notes that "all through the 1950s the CIA covertly tested LSD on unwitting subjects, usually drug addicts and johns," watching them through one-way mirrors. At the Addiction Research Center in Lexington, Ky., most subjects were Black men (212). Tim Weiner discusses the pressure of the Nixon administration to foment a coup against Chile's leader, and the subsequent revelations during the 1970s of attempted assassinations, spying on domestic organizations, and the drug experiments. Tim Weiner, *Legacy of Ashes: The History of the CIA* (New York: Anchor, 2008), 354–400.

139   **Reports officer Amy Tozzi:** Amy Tozzi, telephone interview, May 22 and 25, 2020.

140   **One was Lee Coyle, who in 1954:** Lee Coyle, telephone interview, September 9, 2020.

141   **One of the first real shots over the bow:** Dawn Ellison, "One Woman's Contributions to Social Change," *Studies in Intelligence,* vol. 46, no. 3 (2002), 45–53.

143   **The quintessential CIA wife, Barbara Colby:** Carl Colby shared reminscences about his mother's contributions as a CIA wife and her work securing benefits for wives, in a telephone interview on March 30, 2023. Barbara Colby is also featured in Carl Colby's documentary about his father, *The Man Nobody Knew: In Search of My Father, CIA Spymaster William Colby,* https://www.imdb.com/title/tt1931549/. Other details about Barbara Colby's life are in Emily Langer, "Barbara Colby, Wife of CIA Spymaster, Dies," *Washington Post,* July 17, 2015, washingtonpost.com/national

/barbara-h-colby-wife-of-controversial-cia-spymaster-dies-at-94/2015/07/17
/e8db91d0-2bf8-11e5-a250-42bd812efc09_story.html. The legislation is described in
Mike Causey, "Some Splitting Up After the Split-ups," *Washington Post,* October 9, 1980, washingtonpost.com/archive/local/1980/10/09/some-splitting-up-after
-the-split-ups/10abaeb6-a47f-499a-8425-21264d60c872/.

146   **Barbara enlisted Martha Peterson:** Martha Peterson Shogi shared this caper, and rem-
iniscences of her own career, in an in-person interview in Wilmington, North Carolina, on March 22, 2022, and in her book, Martha D. Peterson, *The Widow Spy: My
CIA Journey from the Jungles of Laos to Prison in Moscow* (Wilmington, N.C.: Red
Canary Press, 2012).

CHAPTER ELEVEN: MISS MARPLE OF RUSSIA HOUSE

150   **In the summer of 1985, the CIA's Moscow Station:** Most of the details in this chapter are
taken from Sandra Grimes and Jeanne Vertefeuille, *Circle of Treason: A CIA Account
of Traitor Aldrich Ames and the Men He Betrayed* (Annapolis: Naval Institute Press,
2012).

153   **"He should have been fired at once":** Tim Weiner, "C.I.A. Colleagues Call Fallen Star
a Bias Victim," *New York Times,* September 14, 1994, A1.

CHAPTER TWELVE: WHAT ARE YOU GOING TO DO WITH THE BOAT?

155   **It is hard to understand why the senators:** Liza Mundy, "The Secret History of Women
in the Senate," *Politico Magazine,* January/February 2015, https://www.politico.com
/magazine/story/2015/01/senate-women-secret-history-113908/.

157   **A report was compiled called "The Glass Ceiling Study":** CIA, "Glass Ceiling Study
Summary," FOIA reading room, approved for release April 2006; and Walter Pincus, "CIA and the Glass Ceiling Secret," *The Washington Post,* September 9, 1994,
washingtonpost.com/archive/politics/1994/09/09/cia-and-the-glass-ceiling-secret
/cea75ce0-0ed2-4914-8600-1536004c9f77/.

158   **The first involved Janine Brookner:** Tim Weiner, "Spy Sues C.I.A., Saying She Was
Target of Sexual Discrimination," *New York Times,* July 15, 1994, B7; Tim Weiner,
"C.I.A. to Pay $410,000 to Spy Who Says She Was Smeared," *New York Times,*
December 9, 1994, A1; Abigail Jones, "She Was a CIA Spy. Now She's a Lawyer
Battling Her Old Agency. This Is Her Story," *Washington Post,* June 18, 2018; Walter
Pincus, "Ex-CIA Officer Settles Sex Discrimination Suit," *Washington Post,* Decem-
ber 24, 1994.

158   **I interviewed Brookner in December 2020:** These and subsequent quotes and descriptions are from Janine Brookner, in-person interview in Washington, D.C., December 9, 2020.

161   **The CIA damage control experts fought back:** Susan Hasler, telephone interviews on
March 18 and 20, 2020, and personal writings.

163   **As Brookner was pursuing her own case:** Tim Weiner, "Women, Citing Bias, May Sue
the CIA," *New York Times,* March 28, 1994, A10; Robert Pear, "CIA Settles Suit on
Sex Bias," *New York Times,* March 30, 1995, A21, Steven A. Holmes, "Judge Approves
$1 Million Agreement in Sex Bias Case at CIA," *New York Times,* June 10, 1995, A7.

164   **Rindskopf Parker and Conway began wrestling:** *Divine Secrets of the Rybat Sisterhood,* 20.

164   **"It seemed like a bunch of angry women":** Paula Doyle, interview, Vienna, Virginia,
June 8, 2021.

165   **"The Central Intelligence Agency, in a clear admission":** John M. Broder, "CIA Will
Settle Women Agents' Bias Lawsuit," *Los Angeles Times,* March 30, 1995, https://
www.latimes.com/archives/la-xpm-1995-03-30-mn-48854-story.html.

166 **"They won, but they really didn't"**: Mike Kalogeropoulos, interview, Vienna, Virginia, June 3, 2020.

172 **"There were plenty of men who said it was because of Cat B"**: Paula Doyle, interview, Vienna, Virginia, June 8, 2021.

172 **"She was treated like garbage, from my understanding"**: Mike Sulick, interview, Wake Forest, North Carolina, March 21, 2022.

CHAPTER THIRTEEN: THE FIERCELY ARGUED THINGS

177 **As a girl growing up in the 1970s:** My account of Cindy Storer's recollections is based on a series of personal interviews, in person and over the telephone, on August 24, 2019, April 5, 2020, January 19, 2021, March 19, 2022, February 9, 2023, and other conversations, and on an oral history conducted with Cindy Storer on April 4, 2017, by Amy Weinstein of the 9/11 Museum in New York, generously shared by Amy Weinstein with Cindy Storer's permission.

185 **A day of coordinating could:** The coordination process, including the comment about eye-poking, and the notion of the agency as a greedy institution, are well evoked in Bridget Rose Nolan, "Information Sharing and Collaboration in the United States Intelligence Community: An Ethnographic Study of the National Counterterrorism Center," 2013 dissertation available from ProQuest, AAI3565195, cryptome.org /2013/09/nolan-nctc.pdf and repository.upenn.edu/dissertations/AAI3565195.

CHAPTER FOURTEEN: FINDING X

188 **The center had been created:** Apart from Cindy's own observations, the following quotations and descriptions about the culture and history of NPIC are related in an excellent cultural history of the center. Jack O'Connor, *NPIC: Seeing the Secrets and Growing the Leaders: A Cultural History of the National Photographic Interpretation Center* (Alexandria, Va.: Acumensa Solutions, 2015), 49–56 and 120–21.

191 **As one member of the quartet, Kristin Wood, remembers:** Kristin Wood, in-person interview, June 4, 2021, Reston, Virginia.

195 **"We changed the rules," as Milt Bearden, a CIA station chief, put it:** Milt Bearden oral history interview with Amy Weinstein and Katie Edgerton of the National September 11 Memorial & Museum, November 13, 2009, shared by Amy Weinstein.

196 **"When the Soviet Union fell apart"**: Mia McCall, telephone interview, April 5, 2021.

196 **"We walked away"**: Tim Weiner, *Legacy of Ashes: The History of the CIA* (New York: Anchor, 2008), 488.

198 **The eighteenth son of a wealthy engineer:** Peter Bergen, *The Rise and Fall of Osama bin Laden* (New York: Simon and Schuster, 2021), 3–53. Lawrence Wright, *The Looming Tower: Al Qaeda and the Road to 9-11* (New York: Vintage, 2007), 75–99. Steve Coll, *Ghost Wars: The Secret History of the CIA, Afghanistan, and Bin Laden, from the Soviet Invasion to September 10, 2001*, 84–88, and various.

CHAPTER FIFTEEN: YOU DON'T BELONG HERE

201 **Like Cindy, Barbara Sude had begun her career:** The information about Barbara Sude's career is drawn from telephone interviews on July 17, 2020, and April 23, 2023; an April 4, 2017, interview with Amy Weinstein and Madeleine Rosenberg for the National September 11 Memorial & Museum; and a Spycast interview with Vince Houghton of the International Spy Museum, thecyberwire.com/podcasts/spycast /225/notes.

206 **Like Cindy Storer, Gina Bennett:** The information about Gina Bennett's career is taken from in-person and telephone interviews, in Washington, D.C., and else-

where, on July 22, 2020, October 17, 2020, January 16, 2023, and February 13, 2023, and from her two books, Gina M. Bennett, *National Security Mom: Why "Going Soft" Will Make America Strong* (Deadwood, Ore.: Wyatt-MacKenzie Publishing, 2008), and Gina M. Bennett, *National Security Mom 2: America Needs a Time-Out* (Deadwood, Ore.: Wyatt-MacKenzie Publishing, 2019).

208 **As the national security expert Tom Nichols would later write:** Tom Nichols, "The Narcissism of the Angry Young Men," *The Atlantic*, January 29, 2023, theatlantic.com /ideas/archive/2023/01/lost-boys-violent-narcissism-angry-young-men/672886 /?silverid=%25%25RECIPIENT_ID%25%25&utm_source=pocket_saves.

212 **In a five-page article, Gina laid out:** United States Department of State Bureau of Intelligence and Research, Weekend Edition, "The Wandering Mujahidin: Armed and Dangerous," August 21–22, 1993, declassified November 23, 2007, 200605437 nationalsecuritymom.com/3/WanderingMujahidin.pdf.

214 **A week later, she published:** Bennett, *National Security Mom*, 19.

214 **One of Gina's State Department colleagues:** Lyndsay Howard, telephone interview, May 30, 2021.

CHAPTER SIXTEEN: A BRIGHT AND ATTRACTIVE REDHEAD

216 **Heidi's old friend Tom Twetten had done well:** Tim Weiner describes a "brilliant plot" that grew out of the counterterrorist center when, in March 1987, former president Jimmy Carter "delivered a package of intelligence on Abu Nidal" to Syrian president Hafiz Al-Assad, who expelled Abu Nidal. "Over the next two years, with the help of the PLO and the Jordanian and Israeli intelligence services, the agency waged psychological warfare against Abu Nidal. A strong and steady flow of disinformation convinced him that his top lieutenants were traitors. He killed seven of them and dozens of their underlings over the next year, crippling his organization." The organization was "shattered," in a "stirring victory" for the counterterrorist center and "the Near East division under Tom Twetten," who would be promoted to chief of the clandestine service. Tim Weiner, *Legacy of Ashes: The History of the CIA* (New York: Anchor, 2008), 485–86. Dewey Clarridge also describes the operation against Abu Nidal. Duane R. Clarridge with Digby Diehl, *A Spy for All Seasons: My Life in the CIA* (New York: Scribner, 1997), 331–37.

219 **the counterterrorism center, a unit that no CIA officer:** Clarridge, *Spy for All Seasons*, 319–46.

220 **In his 1997 autobiography:** "Upon arriving in Athens I was confronted by a group of attractive women in their early thirties." Ibid., 156. Clarridge notes that a lieutenant of Yasser Arafat "had married an extremely attractive Lebanese woman" who was "a former Miss Universe" (162) and that the Soviet KGB resident in Rome had a wife, Vera, who was "attractive" and "vivacious." Hauled before Congress, "I was accompanied by a lawyer from the Agency's Office of General Counsel named Kathleen McGinn. A bright and attractive redhead, with six-shooter eyes and tone" (375).

224 **When published—anonymously, at first—in 2002:** Michael Scheuer, *Through Our Enemies' Eyes: Osama bin Laden, Radical Islam, and the Future of America* (Washington, D.C.: Brassey's, 2002).

226 **"I am not . . . a field intelligence officer":** Michael Scheuer, *Imperial Hubris: Why the West Is Losing the War on Terror* (Washington: Potomac Books, 2004), ix.

226 **They were fans of *Buffy*:** Peter Bergen, *The Rise and Fall of Osama Bin Laden* (New York: Simon and Schuster, 2021), 106.

227 **"Most of my closest colleagues are type-A individuals":** Gary Berntsen and Ralph Pezzulo, *Jawbreaker: The Attack on Bin Laden and Al-Qaeda; a Personal Account by the CIA's Key Field Commander* (New York: Three Rivers Press, 2005), 5.

227 **"What the hell's the matter":** Ibid., 8.

227 **Scheuer said he would have gladly hung out a sign saying:** Peter Bergen, *Manhunt: The Ten-Year Search for Bin Laden from 9/11 to Abbottabad* (New York: Random House / Crown, 1994), 77.

227 **"I had enormous respect for":** Michael Scheuer, telephone interview, May 18, 2023.

228 **"People were saying, 'What's his staff?'":** Ibid., 78–79.

229 **"Not personally but in terms of his":** Ned Zaman, David Wise, David Rose, and Bryan Burrough, "The Path to 9/11: Lost Warnings and Fatal Errors," *Vanity Fair*, November 2004, 326–38, 390–400.

229 **"No one really knew":** Michael Scheuer, interview with author, May 18, 2023.

231 **"She was talking to us about this Middle Eastern guy":** Kristin Wood, interview with author, June 14, 2021.

231 **Another team member, Alfreda Bikowsky, was more vivid:** These quotations and life details are from an interview with Alfreda Bikowsky Scheuer by this author, May 11, 2023.

235 **Paula Doyle, a case officer in the Levant:** Paula Doyle, in-person interview, Vienna, Virginia, June 8, 2021.

235 **"Her hair was on fire about":** Mia McCall, telephone interview, April 5, 2021.

CHAPTER SEVENTEEN: STRESS AND A GRAY ROOM

236 **The question then became, for Cindy Storer:** Descriptions and quotations from Cindy Storer throughout this chapter are from her many personal interviews with the author.

238 **The CIA station chief was on leave:** Peter Bergen, *The Rise and Fall of Osama bin Laden* (New York: Simon and Schuster, 2021), 71.

238 **Al-Fadl soon found himself relocated:** Jane Mayer, "Junior: The Clandestine Life of America's Top Al Qaeda Source," *New Yorker*, June 8, 2021, newyorker.com /magazine/2006/09/11/junior.

240 **One CTC analyst started giving a talk to newcomers:** Susan Hasler, telephone interviews, March 18 and 20, 2020.

241 **A "hostage swap," people called it:** Ned Zaman, David Wise, David Rose, and Bryan Burrough, "The Path to 9/11: Lost Warnings and Fatal Errors," *Vanity Fair*, November 2004, 326–38, 390–400.

241 **One reason why ambitious:** Ibid.

241 **In 1994, after Aldrich Ames was arrested:** Ibid.

241 **A hard-boiled gumshoe:** Ibid.

242 **"Fuck you. I've got it. I'm keeping it":** Ibid.

243 **Clarke himself was cranky, mercurial, authoritarian:** Ibid.

245 **In an article published in the State Department's INR bulletin on July 18, 1996:** "Terrorism / Usama bin Laden: Who's Chasing Whom?" *Intelligence and Research Bulletin*, July 18, 1996, declassified July 21, 2005.

245 **At her desk in the State Department:** These observations were shared by Gina Bennett in in-person and telephone interviews, in Washington, D.C., and elsewhere, on July 22, 2020, October 17, 2020, January 16, 2023, and February 13, 2023.

246 **In 1997, CNN analyst Peter Bergen secured:** Peter L. Bergen, *The Osama bin Laden I Know: An Oral History of Al Qaeda's Leader* (New York: Simon and Schuster, 2006), xx.

248 **In 1975, *Parade* interviewed several women of the CIA:** Connecticut Walker, "Women of the CIA," *Parade*, July 13, 1975, 4–5.

249 **"The presumption was that you weren't coming back":** Sue Gordon, telephone interview, November 3, 2021.

249 **When analyst DeNeige Watson was hired:** DeNeige Watson, telephone interview, February 18, 2021.

251 **When one analyst, Diana Bolsinger:** Diana Bolsinger, telephone interview, April 27, 2021.

CHAPTER EIGHTEEN: THE NICKED EARLOBE

251   **On Friday, May 30, 1997, a year into her tenure:** This account of Kansi's capture was de-
      scribed by Heidi August in several interviews, and by Patricia Moynihan in an in-
      person interview in McLean, Virginia, on April 30, 2023. The account also draws
      from George Tenet with Bill Harlow, *At the Center of the Storm* (New York: Harper-
      Collins, 2007), 41–43, and from an interview Brad Garrett gave with Michael Morell
      on the podcast Intelligence Matters DECLASSIFIED: Former FBI Agent Bradley
      Garrett on the Global Manhunt for Mir Aimal Kansi, Intelligence Matters, on
      August 5, 2020.

257   **Alec Station noted in an internal report that this was:** Coll, *Ghost Wars*, 382.

258   **On Friday, August 7, 1998:** Barbara Sude interviews.

258   **This was the assumption of Gary Berntsen:** Gary Berntsen and Ralph Pezzulo, *Jaw-
      breaker: The Attack on Bin Laden and Al-Qaeda; a Personal Account by the CIA's Key
      Field Commander* (New York: Three Rivers Press, 2005), 14–25.

261   **The actor Will Ferrell played Reno:** Liza Mundy, "Why Janet Reno Fascinates, Con-
      founds and Even Terrifies America?," *Washington Post Magazine*, January 25, 1998,
      https://www.washingtonpost.com/wp-srv/politics/govt/admin/stories/reno012598
      .htm.

261   **Tribal assets provided what Tenet:** George Tenet with Bill Harlow, 113–15.

262   **"No capture plan before 9/11 ever again attained the same level":** *The 9/11 Commission
      Report: Final Report of the National Commission on Terrorist Attacks Upon the United
      States* (New York: W. W. Norton, 2004), 114.

262   **In the end, Tenet accepted the opinion:** Ibid.

262   **After the 1998 embassy bombing:** Ibid., 115.

262   **If anybody was weak, in the minds of the Alec women:** Alfreda Bikowsky Scheuer, inter-
      view with author.

263   **This consideration might or might not have factored:** *The 9/11 Commission Report*, 117.

263   **"It was a frustrating time":** Berntsen and Pezzulo, *Jawbreaker*, 33.

265   **The problem was obvious to Susan Hasler:** These details are taken from telephone in-
      terviews with Susan Hasler on March 18 and 20, 2020, and from personal writings
      that she shared for use in this book.

266   **"I can't believe this guy Scheuer just hired'":** John Rizzo, telephone interview, May 29,
      2020.

267   **"I was urging Tenet to get somebody to run the CTC who had balls":** Ned Zaman, David
      Wise, David Rose, and Bryan Burrough, "The Path to 9/11: Lost Warnings and Fatal
      Errors," *Vanity Fair*, November 2004, 326–38 and 390–400.

267   **Scheuer angrily reflected that he was the victim:** Ibid.

CHAPTER NINETEEN: "I'VE GOT A TARGET ON MY BACK"

271   **Richard Blee also understood the peace-dividend constraints:** Richard Blee, telephone
      interview, November 12, 2020.

276   **As Tenet noted in his memoir, by the end of 1999:** Tenet, *At the Center of the Storm*,
      124–26.

277   **Two suspected al-Qaeda members:** OIG Report on CIA Accountability with Respect
      to the 9/11 Attacks, June 2005, approved for release August 2007, xiv–xvii.

279   **By 2000, as operations officer Gary Berntsen:** Gary Berntsen, *Jawbreaker*, 67.

279   **The change of administration "had the greatest impact":** Tenet, *At the Center of the
      Storm*, 139.

280   **Tenet found Rice "remote":** Ibid., 138.

281   **Prior to taking over the analytic unit:** Pattie Kindsvater shared her experiences in tele-
      phone and in-person interviews between October 27, 2020, and October 22, 2021.

285   **In his memoir, George Tenet names:** Tenet, *At the Center of the Storm*, 147.

286 **"We continued to believe, however":** Ibid., 150.

288 **All these developments had been written:** *The 9/11 Commission Report*, 272, 276, 550.

289 **She noted that bin Laden, since as early as 1997:** "Bin Laden Determined to Strike in US," August 6, 2001, For the President Only, declassified and approved for release April 10, 2004, irp.fas.org/cia/product/pdb080601.pdf.

290 **The president later:** *The 9/11 Commission Report*, 260.

CHAPTER TWENTY: SEPTEMBER 11, 2001

294 **George Tenet had been breakfasting:** Tenet, *At the Center of the Storm*, 161.

303 **An orderly evacuation was overseen by the:** Sarah Finkel, "BU Hosts Chief of CIA, Former CIA Officer to Describe Experiences on 9-11," *The Daily Free Press*, April 25, 2017, https://dailyfreepress.com/2017/04/25/bu-hosts-chief-of-cia-former -cia-officer-to-describe-experiences-on-911/.

CHAPTER TWENTY-ONE: THE THREAT MATRIX

308 **Susan, who suffered from a family tendency:** Susan Hasler shared these details in an unpublished memoir.

308 **CIA director George Tenet observed:** Tenet, *At the Center of the Storm*, 172.

309 **Tenet inaugurated a daily "threat matrix":** Ibid., 234–57. Pattie Kindsvater also described the threat matrix meetings.

311 **By September 27, the CIA inserted:** Tenet describes the paramilitary operations in *At the Center of the Storm*, 186–88 and 207–77.

314 **The red cell had been conceived:** Ibid., 185.

315 **The commission also noted:** *The 9/11 Commission Report*, 341.

316 **The day after the attacks:** Tenet, xix.

316 **Jami Miscik, the agency's number two analyst:** Ibid., 302.

317 **In his memoir he recalls a meeting in September 2002:** Tenet, *Center of the Storm*, 343.

317 **"It was bad:"** Kristin Wood, interview with author.

318 **On August 26, 2002:** Tenet, *Center of the Storm*, 315.

318 **"It was obvious Rumsfeld and Cheney were determined":** Jeanne Newell, telephone interview, November 19, 2020.

319 **Working with Susan Hasler, she produced a compelling paper:** CIA Directorate of Intelligence, "The Appeal of the Islamic Extremist Movement: Obligation to the Umma," April 7, 2004, approved for release October 10, 2018.

321 **And the pressure would continue:** Kristin Wood, interview with author. This episode is also recounted in Bakos, *The Targeter*, 147–49.

CHAPTER TWENTY-TWO: THE NEW GIRLS

322 **On September 11, 2001, Rosa, now twenty-eight:** Rosa Smothers, telephone interview, May 5, 2020.

325 **On September 11, Holly Bond had just come back:** Holly Bond, Google Meet interview, May 11, 2020.

329 **"A lot of NSA analysts didn't want to do that":** Linda Millis, telephone interview, September 25, 2021.

329 **"If you want to be really karmic about it":** Sue Gordon, telephone interview, November 3, 2021.

CHAPTER TWENTY-THREE: PUTTING WARHEADS ON FOREHEADS

331 **The agency's "enhanced interrogation" program began:** Senate Select Committee on Intelligence, *The Senate Intelligence Committee Report on Torture: Committee Study of the*

Central Intelligence Agency's Detention and Interrogation Program (Brooklyn, N.Y.: Melville House, 2014).

332 **The spectacle of Zubaydah's waterboarding:** Ibid., 32–55. Jennifer Matthews's witnessing of Abu Zubaydah's waterboarding is related in Nada Bakos with Davin Coburn, *The Targeter: My Life in the CIA Hunting Terrorists and Challenging the White House* (New York: Little, Brown, 2019), 208.

332 **On March 1, 2003, CIA and Pakistani officers:** Ibid., 83–97.

333 **"Let's be forward leaning":** Senate Select Committee on Intelligence, *The Senate Intelligence Committee Report on Torture* (Brooklyn: Melville House, 2014), 164. Bikowsky is not named in the report, but her identity emerged in news accounts afterward, and she acknowledged her coerced interrogation work in interviews with this author and with Reuters.

334 **The detainee, Hassan Ghul, was in a safe house, "literally having tea":** *The Senate Intelligence Committee Report on Torture*, 403–4, footnote 767.

335 **"She has a caustic personality, but she is frighteningly intelligent":** Matthew Cole, "Bin Laden Expert Accused of Shaping CIA Deception on 'Torture' Program," NBC News, December 18, 2014, nbcnews.com/news/investigations/bin-laden-expert-accused-shaping-cia-deception-torture-program-n269551.

335 **Bikowsky broke her own cover:** Alfreda Bikowsky Scheuer, telephone interview with this author on May 11, 2023, and in Aram Roston, "Ex-CIA Analyst Says She 'Got Bloodied' in Tangled U.S. War on Al Qaeda," Reuters, April 20, 2022, reuters.com/world/exclusive-ex-cia-analyst-says-she-got-bloodied-tangled-us-war-al-qaeda-2022-04-20/.

336 **Darrell Blocker, a clandestine officer:** Darrell Blocker, telephone interview, May 24, 2023.

337 **"I'm not going to sit here, with the benefit of hindsight":** Pat Milton, "Gina Haspel Says She Knows 'the CIA like the Back of My Hand,'" CBS News, May 9, 2018, cbsnews.com/news/gina-haspel-says-she-knows-the-cia-like-the-back-of-my-hand/.

338 **As the excesses of the war on terror:** Rafia Zakaria, "How the War on Terror Became America's First 'Feminist War,'" *Literary Hub*, excerpted from Rafia Zakaria, *Against White Feminism: Notes on Disruption* (New York: W. W. Norton, 2021).

339 **"Didn't the CIA kill Martin Luther King?":** Nicole Ash, in-person interview, May 23, 2023.

CHAPTER TWENTY-FOUR: ESPIONAGE IS ESPIONAGE

340 **Lisa Harper, nearing sixty, was another member:** This chapter is based on author interviews with Lisa Harper.

341 **Around 2004, George Tenet noted that a stream:** Tenet, *Center of the Storm*, 246.

CHAPTER TWENTY-FIVE: I MADE BAD PEOPLE HAVE BAD DAYS

350 **Terrorists began using rape as a recruiting tool:** Bakos, *Targeter*, 131–32.

350 **Some terrorists "just need killing":** Ibid., 214.

350 **One, Lisa Rager, joined in 2002:** Lisa Rager, Zoom interview, July 11, 2021.

352 **Angie Lewis learned to live reasonably comfortably in that gray zone:** Angie Lewis, in-person interview, Burbank, California, July 5, 2021.

CHAPTER TWENTY-SIX: ANYTHING TO FIT IN

354 **Twenty-two-year-old Molly Chambers was working:** Molly Chambers shared her experiences in two in-person interviews in Washington, D.C., on July 22, 2021, and February 20, 2023.

359   **"We all took it pretty hard":** Sandy Tveit, telephone interview, May 22, 2023.

361   **Among them was general counsel John Rizzo:** Elizabeth Flock, "Former CIA Officials Who Oversaw Torture Pick Apart Inaccuracies in *Zero Dark Thirty.*" *U.S. News & World Report,* January 29, 2013, https://www.usnews.com/news/blogs/washington -whispers/2013/01/29/former-cia-officials-who-oversaw-torture-pick-apart -inaccuracies-in-zero-dark-thirty.

361   **In 2015, an anonymous CIA officer:** Jeff Stein, "The Inside Information That Could Have Stopped 9-11," *Newsweek,* January 14, 2015, https://www.newsweek.com/2015 /01/23/information-could-have-stopped-911-299148.html.

361   **Ellen Dickey, a targeter:** Ellen Dickey, in-person interview, Washington, DC, June 17, 2021.

CHAPTER TWENTY-SEVEN: LAUNDRY ON THE LINE

371   **Fran Moore had just arrived at work:** Fran Moore described her life and career in a telephone interview, September 20, 2021. And she described this moment in a public interview with the 9/11 Memorial & Museum, on October 26, 2020.

376   **Taking a lesson from Israel's experience:** Peter Bergen, *Manhunt: The Ten-Year Search for Bin Laden from 9/11 to Abbottabad* (New York: Random House / Crown, 2012), 84.

377   **suggesting a systematic focus on the people:** Ibid., 90, and Fran Moore interview.

379   **The analyst is still undercover, so let's call her Rachel:** "Rachel," in-person interview, CIA headquarters, McLean, Virginia, July 15, 2022.

381   **Analysts wrote several high-vis memos, arguing:** Bergen, *Manhunt,* 127.

381   **This is when Fran Moore got the exciting report:** Fran Moore described the events of the hunt in our telephone interview on September 20, 2021, and in a public presentation on October 26, 2021, to the National September 11 Memorial & Museum Foundation, 911memorial.org/learn/past-public-programs/pursuit-justice-integrating -intelligence. This account of the hunt also draws from another 9/11 museum presentation, "Finding Bin Laden," featuring Robert Cardillo, and a May 2021 presentation to the OSS Society, with Admiral Bill McRaven, former CIA director Leon Panetta, and CIA officer Michael Vickers.

384   **Admiral William H. McRaven, of the Joint Special Operations Command:** Walter W. Napier III, 514 AMW Historian, "OPERATION Neptune Spear: 10 year anniversary," April 30, 2021, *USAFWC & Nellis News,* https://www.nellis.af.mil/News /Article/2591901/operation-neptune-spear-10-year-anniversary/.

384   **The SEALs flew to Bagram Air Base:** Mark Owen with Kevin Mauer, *No Easy Day: The Navy Seal Mission That Killed Osama bin Laden* (New York: Penguin, 2013). His conversation with Jen takes place on page 204. Subsequent quotations are on pages 270, 278, 298, 301, 302, and 306.

EPILOGUE

390   **Ellie Duckett wanted to dip her toes:** Ruth Eleanor "Ellie" Duckett, October 22, 1948– June 21, 2016, obituary, wilmingtoncares.com/obituary/ruth-eleanor-ellie-duckett/.

BIBLIOGRAPHY

SELECTED INTERVIEWS

Ash, Nicole, in Arlington, Virginia, May 24, 2023.

August, Heidi, in Santa Barbara, California, and by telephone, August 5, 2020, September 17, 2020, October 6, 2020, November 17, 2020, March 12, 2021, July 16, 2021, and November 18, 2023, various.

Bakos, Nada, by telephone, May 21, 2021.

Bennett, Gina, by telephone and in Washington, D.C., July 22, 2020, October 17, 2020, January 16, 2023, and February 13, 2023.

Blee, Richard, by telephone, November 12, 2020.

Blocker, Darrell, by Zoom, June 14, 2021, and by telephone thereafter.

Bolsinger, Diana, by telephone, April 27, 2021.

Bond, Holly, by Google Meet, May 11, 2020.

Brookner, Janine, in Washington, D.C., December 9, 2020.

Burkett, Randy, in McLean, Virginia, June 21, 2021.

Carlson, Sarah, by telephone, April 17, 2020.

Chambers, Molly, in Washington, D.C., July 22, 2021, and February 20, 2023.

Coyle, Lee, by telephone, September 9, 2020.

Dickey, Ellen, in Washington, D.C., June 17, 2021.

Doyle, Paula, in Vienna, Virginia, June 8, 2021.

Gordon, Sue, by telephone, November 3, 2021.

Graham, Mary Margaret, by telephone, August 21, 2020.

Greenstein, Ilana, May 19, 2020.

Harper, Lisa Manfull, in Washington, D.C., and by telephone, February 26, 2020, May 17, 2020, October 23, 2020, March 26, 2021, and March 6, 2023.

Hasler, Susan, by telephone, March 18 and 20, 2020.

Hershberg, Bonnie, by telephone, May 7, 2020.

Howard, Lyndsay, by telephone, May 30, 2021.

Kalogeropoulos, Mike and Pat, by telephone, April 14, 2020, and in Vienna, Virginia, June 3, 2020.

Kenworthy, Rev. Stuart, in Washington, D.C., November 17, 2021.

Kindsvater, Pattie, by telephone and in Washington, D.C., various between October 27, 2020, and October 22, 2021.

Layton, Katherine, by telephone, August 7, 2020.

Lewis, Angie, in Burbank, California, July 5, 2021.

Martin, Eileen, by Zoom, June 4, 2021.

McCall, Mia, by telephone, April 5, 2021.

McCloud, Sue, in Carmel, California, August 16, 2020.

McCollough, Patsy, by telephone, October 28, 2020.

McMaster, Pamela, in Santa Barbara, California, September 30, 2020.

Mendez, Jonna, by telephone, June 4, 2020.

Millis, Linda, by telephone, September 25, 2020.
Moore, Fran, by telephone, September 20, 2021.
Moran, Lindsay, by telephone, June 22, 2020.
Moynihan, Patricia, in McLean, Virginia, April 30, 2023.
Newell, Jeanne, by telephone, November 19, 2020.
Pedrick, Arlin, in Burbank, California, on July 18, 2021.
Rager, Lisa, by Zoom, July 11, 2021.
Richcreek, Joanne, by telephone, February 1, 2021.
Rizzo, John, by telephone, May 29, 2020.
Shogi Peterson, Martha, by FaceTime and in Wilmington, North Carolina, May 28, 2020, and March 22, 2022.
Smith, Eileen, by telephone, April 27, 2020, and June 8, 2020.
Smothers, Rosa, by telephone, May 5, 2020.
Storer, Cindy, by telephone and in Atlanta, Georgia, August 24, 2019, April 5, 2020, January 19, 2021, March 19, 2022, February 9, 2023, April 19, 2023, various.
Sude, Barbara, by telephone, July 17, 2020, and April 23, 2023.
Sulick, Mike, Wake Forest, North Carolina, March 21, 2022.
Scheuer, Alfreda Bikowsky, by telephone, May 11, 2023.
Scheuer, Michael, by telephone, May 18, 2023.
Taylor, Pat, by telephone, June 18, 2020.
Tozzi, Amy, by telephone and FaceTime, May 22 and 25, 2020.
Tveit, Sandy, by telephone, May 22, 2023.
Walder, Tracy, by telephone, April 17, 2020.
Watson, DeNeige, by telephone, February 18, 2021.
Wood, Kristin, by telephone and in Reston, Virginia, June 14, 2021, and March 30, 2023.

GOVERNMENT PUBLICATIONS

"The Appeal of the Islamic Extremist Movement; Obligation to the Umma." Central Intelligence Agency, Directorate of Intelligence, approved for release October 10, 2018.
"Bin Laden Determined to Strike in US," August 6, 2001, For the President Only, declassified and approved for release April 10, 2004, irp.fas.org/cia/product/pdb080601.pdf.
[Last Name Redacted], Jacqueline, "The Petticoat Panel: A 1953 Study of the Role of Women in the CIA Career Service, an Intelligence Monograph," Center for the Study of Intelligence, March 2003, approved for release October 30, 2013, AR 70-14.
Michael Warner and the CIA History Staff in the Center for the Study of Intelligence, "The Office of Strategic Services: America's First Intelligence Agency," cia.gov/static /7851e16f9e100b6f9cc4ef002028ce2f/Office-of-Strategic-Services.pdf.
OIG Report on CIA Accountability with Respect to the 9/11 Attacks, June 2005, approved for release August 2007, xiv–xvii.
OSS Assessment Staff. *Assessment of Men: Selection of Personnel for the Office of Strategic Services.* New York: Rinehart, 1948.
"Secrets of the RYBAT Sisterhood: Four Senior Women in the Directorate of Operations Discuss their Careers," CIA FOIA Reading Room, approved for release October 30, 2013.
Senate Select Committee on Intelligence, *The Senate Intelligence Committee Report on Torture: Committee Study of the Central Intelligence Agency's Detention and Interrogation Program.* Brooklyn: Melville House, 2014.
"Terrorism / Usama bin Laden: Who's Chasing Whom?" *Intelligence and Research Bulletin,* July 18, 1996, declassified July 21, 2005.
The 9/11 Commission Report: Final Report of the National Commission on Terrorist Attacks upon the United States. New York: W. W. Norton, 2004.
United States Department of State Bureau of Intelligence and Research, Weekend Edi-

tion, "The Wandering Mujahidin: Armed and Dangerous," August 21–22, 1993, declassified November 23, 2007, 200605437 nationalsecuritymom.com/3/Wandering Mujahidin.pdf.

BOOKS

Abbott, Karen. *Liar, Temptress, Soldier, Spy: Four Women Undercover in the Civil War*. New York: HarperCollins, 2014.

Andrew, Christopher. *Defend the Realm*. New York: Vintage Books, 2010.

———. *The Secret World: A History of Intelligence*. New Haven: Yale University Press, 2017.

Atwood, Kathryn J. *Women Heroes of World War II: 26 Stories of Espionage, Sabotage, Resistance, and Rescue*. Chicago: Chicago Review Press, 2011.

Bakos, Nada, with Davin Coburn. *The Targeter: My Life in the CIA Hunting Terrorists and Challenging the White House*. New York: Little, Brown, 2019.

Bancroft, Mary. *Autobiography of a Spy*. New York: William Morrow, 1983.

Bassiouni, M. Cherif, ed. *Libya: From Repression to Revolution*. Leiden: Martinus Nijhoff, 2013.

Bennett, Gina M. *National Security Mom: Why "Going Soft" Will Make America Strong*. Deadwood, Ore.: Wyatt-MacKenzie Publishing, 2008.

———. *National Security Mom 2: America Needs a Time-Out*. Deadwood, Ore.: Wyatt-MacKenzie Publishing, 2019.

Bergen, Peter. *Manhunt: The Ten-Year Search for Bin Laden from 9/11 to Abbottabad*. New York: Random House / Crown, 2012.

———. *The Rise and Fall of Osama bin Laden*. New York: Simon and Schuster, 2021.

Berntsen, Gary, and Ralph Pezzulo. *Jawbreaker: The Attack on Bin Laden and Al-Qaeda; a Personal Account by the CIA's Key Field Commander*. New York: Three Rivers Press, 2005.

Berry, F. Clifton. *Inside the CIA: The Architecture, Art and Atmosphere of America's Premier Intelligence Agency*. Montgomery, Md.: Community Communications, 1997.

Carlson, Sarah. *In the Dark of War: A CIA Officer's Inside Account of the US Evacuation from Libya*. New York: Fidelis, 2020.

Clarridge, Duane R., with Digby Diehl. *A Spy for All Seasons: My Life in the CIA*. New York: Scribner, 1997.

Cline, Ray S. *Secrets, Spies and Scholars: The Essential CIA*. Washington, D.C.: Acropolis Books, 1976.

Colby, William, and Peter Forbath. *Honorable Men: My Life in the CIA*. New York: Simon and Schuster, 1978.

Coll, Steve. *Ghost Wars: The Secret History of the CIA, Afghanistan, and Bin Laden, from the Soviet Invasion to September 10, 2001*. New York: Penguin, 2004.

Crumpton, Henry. *The Art of Intelligence: Lessons from a Life in the CIA's Clandestine Service*. New York: Penguin, 2012.

Earley, Lt. Col. Charity Adams. *One Woman's Army: A Black Officer Remembers the WAC*. Texas A&M University Military History Series, no. 12, October 1, 1995.

Grimes, Sandra, and Jeanne Vertefeuille. *Circle of Treason: A CIA Account of Traitor Aldrich Ames and the Men He Betrayed*. Annapolis: Naval Institute Press, 2012.

Hasler, Susan. *Intelligence: A Tale of Terror and Uncivil Service*. Asheville, N.C.: Bear Page Press, 2010.

———. *The Flat Bureaucrat: A CIA Satire*. Asheville, N.C.: Bear Page Press. 2015.

Helm, Sarah. *A Life in Secrets: Vera Atkins and the Missing Agents of World War II*. New York: Anchor Books, 2007.

Hindley, Meredith H. *Destination Casablanca: Exile, Espionage, and the Battle for North Africa in World War II*. New York: PublicAffairs, 2017.

Holt, Nathalia. *Wise Gals: The Spies Who Built the CIA and Changed the Future of Espionage*. New York: Putnam, 2022.

Kleiman, Kathy. *Proving Ground: The Untold Story of the Six Women Who Programmed the World's First Modern Computer.* New York: Grand Central, 2022.

MacDonald, Elizabeth P. *Undercover Girl.* New York: Time Life Books, January 1, 1993.

Mayer, Jane. *The Dark Side: The Inside Story of How the War on Terror Turned into a War on American Ideals.* New York: Anchor Books, 2009.

McIntosh, Elizabeth P. *Sisterhood of Spies: Women of the OSS.* Annapolis: Naval Institute Press, 1998.

Mundy, Liza. *Code Girls: The Untold Story of the Women Code Breakers of World War II.* New York: Hachette, 2017.

Nolan, Bridget Rose. "Information Sharing and Collaboration in the United States Intelligence Community: An Ethnographic Study of the National Counterterrorism Center," 2013 dissertation, available from ProQuest, AAI3565195, cryptome.org/2013/09/nolan-nctc.pdf and repository.upenn.edu/dissertations/AAI3565195.

O'Connor, Jack. *NPIC: Seeing the Secrets and Growing the Leaders; A Cultural History of the National Photographic Interpretation Center.* Alexandria, Va.: Acumensa Solutions, 2015.

Olson, Lynne. *Madame Fourcade's Secret War: The Daring Young Woman Who Led France's Largest Spy Network Against Hitler.* New York: Random House, 2019.

Owen, Mark, with Kevin Maurier. *No Easy Day: The Navy SEAL Mission That Killed Osama bin Laden.* New York: Penguin Books, 2012.

Pearson, Judith L. *The Wolves at the Door: The True Story of America's Greatest Female Spy.* Guilford, Conn.: Lyons Press, 2005.

Peterson, Martha D. *The Widow Spy: My CIA Journey from the Jungles of Laos to Prison in Moscow.* Wilmington, Del.: Red Canary Press, 2012.

Powers, Thomas. *The Man Who Kept the Secrets: Richard Helms and the CIA.* New York: Alfred A. Knopf, 1979.

Purnell, Sonia. *A Woman of No Importance: The Untold Story of the American Spy Who Helped Win World War II.* New York: Viking, 2019.

Reynolds, Nicholas. *Need to Know: World War II and the Rise of American Intelligence.* New York: Mariner, 2022.

Rizzo, John. *Company Man.* New York: Scribner, 2014.

Roosevelt, Kermit. *War Report of the OSS.* New York: Walker, 1976.

Rose, Sarah. *D-Day Girls: The Spies Who Armed the Resistance, Sabotaged the Nazis, and Helped Win World War II.* New York: Crown, 2020.

Seymour, Susan. *Cora Du Bois: Anthropologist, Diplomat, Agent.* Lincoln: University of Nebraska Press, 2015.

Smith, Thomas Bell. *The Essential CIA: A Realistic Look Inside America's Clandestine Service by a Former CIA Staffer,* self-published pamphlet, undated.

Stevenson, William. *A Man Called Intrepid: The Incredible True Story of the Master Spy Who Helped Win World War II.* New York: Skyhorse, 2014.

———. *Spymistress: The True Story of the Greatest Female Secret Agent of World War II.* New York: Arcade, 2011.

Sulick, Michael J. *American Spies: Espionage Against the United States from the Cold War to the Present.* Washington, D.C.: Georgetown University Press, 2020.

———. *Spying in America: Espionage from the Revolutionary War to the Dawn of the Cold War.* Washington, D.C.: Georgetown University Press, 2012.

Tenet, George, with Bill Harlow. *At the Center of the Storm: My Years at the CIA.* New York: HarperCollins, 2007.

Thomas, Evan. *The Very Best Men: The Daring Early Years of the CIA.* New York: Simon and Schuster, 2006.

Thomas, Gordon, and Greg Lewis. *Shadow Warriors of World War II: The Daring Women of the SOE.* Chicago: Chicago Review Press, 2017.

Todd, Ann. *OSS Operation Blackmail: One Woman's Covert War Against the Imperial Japanese Army.* Annapolis: Naval Institute Press, 2017.

Walder, Tracy, with Jessica Anya Blau. *The Unexpected Spy: From the CIA to the FBI, My Secret Life Taking Down Some of the World's Most Notorious Terrorists*. New York: St. Martin's Press, 2020.

Waller, Douglas. *Wild Bill Donovan: The Spymaster Who Created the OSS and Modern American Espionage*. New York: Free Press, 2011.

Weiner, Tim. *Legacy of Ashes: The History of the CIA*. New York: Anchor Books, 2008.

Whipple, Chris. *The Spy Masters: How the CIA Directors Shape History and the Future*. New York: Scribner, 2020.

Wright, Lawrence. *The Looming Tower: Al-Qaeda and the Road to 9/11*. New York: Vintage, 2007.

ORAL HISTORIES, DOCUMENTARIES, AND PODCASTS

Cardillo, Robert. "Finding Bin Laden." National September 11 Memorial & Museum presentation.

Chanin, Cliff. Public interview with Fran Moore for the National September 11 Memorial & Museum, October 26, 2020, 911memorial.org/learn/past-public-programs/pursuit -justice-integrating-intelligence.

CNN. *Terror in the Sky: To Catch a Hijacker*. August 5, 2017, part of the series "Declassified: Untold Stories of American Spies."

Colby, Carl. "The Man Nobody Knew: In Search of My Father, CIA Spymaster William Colby," https://www.imdb.com/title/tt1931549/.

Garrett, Brad. Podcast interview with Michael Morell on "Intelligence Matters DE-CLASSIFIED: Former FBI Agent Bradley Garrett on the Global Manhunt for Mir Aimal Kansi," August 5, 2020.

Houghton, Vince. Podcast with Barbara Sude for the International Spy Museum, thecyberwire.com/podcasts/spycast/225/notes.

Miller, Kristie. "Kristie Miller Interview of Lisa Manfull Harper." Association for Diplomatic Studies and Training, Foreign Affairs Oral History Project, Foreign Service Spouse Series, April 19, 1990.

Weinstein, Amy. Oral history interview conducted with Cindy Storer for the National September 11 Memorial & Museum, April 4, 2017.

——— and Katie Edgerton. Oral history interview conducted with Milt Bearden for the National September 11 Memorial & Museum, November 13, 2009.

——— and Madeleine Rosenberg. Oral history interview conducted with Barbara Sude for the National September 11 Memorial & Museum, April 4, 2017.

ARTICLES

Bowcott, Owen. "Women Make Better Spies—as Long as They Forget Sex." *The Guardian*, May 20, 2004, theguardian.com/uk/2004/may/21/artsandhumanities.highereducation.

Causey, Mike. "Some Splitting Up After the Split-ups." *Washington Post*, October 9, 1980, washingtonpost.com/archive/local/1980/10/09/some-splitting-up-after-the-split-ups /10abaeb6-a47f-499a-8425-21264d60c872/.

Cole, Matthew. "Bin Laden Expert Accused of Shaping CIA Deception on 'Torture' Program." NBC News, December 18, 2014, nbcnews.com/news/investigations/bin-laden -expert-accused-shaping-cia-deception-torture-program-n269551.

Ellison, Dawn. "One Woman's Contributions to Social Change." *Studies in Intelligence*, vol. 46, no. 3 (2002), 45–53.

Fisher, Ian. "Oriana Fallaci, Incisive Italian Journalist, Is Dead at 77," *New York Times*, March 3, 2021, nytimes.com/2006/09/16/books/16fallaci.html?scp=1&sq=Oriana %20Fallaci%20obituary&st=cse.

Flock, Elizabeth. "Former CIA Officials Who Oversaw Torture Pick Apart Inaccuracies in 'Zero Dark Thirty.'" *U.S. News & World Report,* January 29, 2013, usnews.com/news /blogs/washington-whispers/2013/01/29/former-cia-officials-who-oversaw-torture -pick-apart-inaccuracies-in-zero-dark-thirty.

Gormly, Kelly B. "How Kate Warne, America's First Woman Detective, Foiled a Plot to Assassinate Abraham Lincoln." *Smithsonian,* March 29, 2022, smithsonianmag.com /history/how-kate-warne-americas-first-woman-detective-foiled-a-plot-to -assassinate-abraham-lincoln-180979829/.

Hersh, Seymour. "Huge C.I.A. Operation Reported in U.S. Against Antiwar Forces, Other Dissidents in Nixon Years." *New York Times,* December 22, 1974, A1, nytimes .com/1974/12/22/archives/huge-cia-operation-reported-in-u-s-against-antiwar -forces-other.html.

Holmes, Steven A. "Judge Approves $1 Million Agreement in Sex Bias Case at CIA." *New York Times,* June 10, 1995, A7.

Ignatius, David. "After Five Decades, a Spy Tells Her Tale." *Washington Post,* December 28, 1998, washingtonpost.com/archive/politics/1998/12/28/after-five-decades-a-spy-tells -her-tale/8bfa5aae-5527-4eb5-8e45-878f1ec823fb/.

Jones, Abigail. "She Was a CIA Spy. Now She's a Lawyer Battling Her Old Agency. This Is Her Story." *Washington Post,* June 18, 2018.

Kinzer, Stephen. "When a CIA Director Had Scores of Affairs." *New York Times,* November 10, 2012, nytimes.com/2012/11/10/opinion/when-a-cia-director-had-scores -of-affairs.html.

Langer, Emily. "Barbara Colby, Wife of CIA Spymaster, Dies." *Washington Post,* July 17, 2015, washingtonpost.com/national/barbara-h-colby-wife-of-controversial-cia -spymaster-dies-at-94/2015/07/17/e8db91d0-2bf8-11e5-a250-42bd812efc09_story.html.

Mayer, Jane. "Junior: The Clandestine Life of America's Top Al Qaeda Source." *New Yorker,* June 8, 2021, newyorker.com/magazine/2006/09/11/junior.

McDonnell, Patrick. "Lone American Killed: Hijacking Victim Buried, Awarded the Purple Heart." *Los Angeles Times,* December 1, 1985, latimes.com/archives/la-xpm -1985-12-01-me-5580-story.html.

Miller, Judith. "From Takeoff to Raid: The 24 Hours of Flight 648." *New York Times,* November 27, 1985, A10, nytimes.com/1985/11/27/world/from-takeoff-to-raid-the-24 -hours-of-flight-648.html.

Milton, Pat. "Gina Haspel Says She Knows 'the CIA like the Back of My Hand.'" CBS News, May 9, 2018, cbsnews.com/news/gina-haspel-says-she-knows-the-cia-like-the -back-of-my-hand/.

Mundy, Liza. "Jeannie Rousseau de Clarens: The Glass-Ceiling-Breaking Spy." *Politico Magazine,* December 28, 2017, https://www.politico.com/magazine/story/2017/12/28 /jeannie-rousseau-de-clarens-obituary-216181/.

———. "The Secret History of Women in the Senate." *Politico Magazine,* January/Febru-ary 2015, politico.com/magazine/story/2015/01/senate-women-secret-history-113908/.

———. "Why Janet Reno Fascinates, Confounds and Even Terrifies America." *The Wash-ington Post Magazine,* January 25, 1998. washingtonpost.com/wp-srv/politics/govt /admin/stories/reno012598.htm.

Napier, Walter W., III. 514 AMW Historian, "OPERATION Neptune Spear: 10 year An-niversary." April 30, 2021, USAFWC % Nellis News, https://www.nellis.af.mil/News /Article/2591901/operation-neptune-spear-10-year-anniversary/.

Nichols, Tom. "The Narcissism of the Angry Young Men." *The Atlantic,* January 29, 2023, theatlantic.com/ideas/archive/2023/01/lost-boys-violent-narcissism-angry-young -men/672886/?silverid=%25%25RECIPIENT_ID%25%25&utm_source=pocket _saves.

Pear, Robert. "CIA Settles Suit on Sex Bias." *New York Times,* March 30, 1995, A21.

Pincus, Walter. "CIA and the Glass Ceiling Secret." *Washington Post,* September 9, 1994, washingtonpost.com/archive/politics/1994/09/09/cia-and-the-glass-ceiling-secret /cea75ce0-0ed2-4914-8600-1536004c9f77/.

————. "Ex-CIA Officer Settles Sex Discrimination Suit." *Washington Post,* December 24, 1994.

Roston, Aram. "Ex-CIA Analyst Says She 'Got Bloodied' in Tangled U.S. War on Al Qaeda," Reuters, April 20, 2022, reuters.com/world/exclusive-ex-cia-analyst-says-she-got-bloodied-tangled-us-war-al-qaeda-2022-04-20/.

Ryan, Amy, and Gary Keeley. "Sputnik and US Intelligence: The Warning Record." *Studies in Intelligence,* vol. 61, no. 3, 1–16.

Shapira, Ian. "Decades After Duty in the OSS and CIA, 'Spy Girls' Find Each Other in Retirement." *Washington Post,* June 26, 2011, washingtonpost.com/local/decades-after-duty-in-the-oss-and-cia-spy-girls-find-each-other-in-retirement/2011/05/28/AG2xvZmH_story.html.

Stein, Jeff. "The Inside Information That Could Have Stopped 9/11." *Newsweek,* January 14, 2015, newsweek.com/2015/01/23/information-could-have-stopped-911-299148.html.

Stern, Sol. "A Short Account of International Student Politics and the Cold War with Particular Reference to the NSA, CIA, etc." *Ramparts,* March 1967, 29–38.

Unsigned. "Excerpts from Speech by Helms to Society of Newspaper Editors." *New York Times,* April 15, 1971, 30.

Unsigned. "The Man with the Innocent Air." *Time,* August 3, 1953, 12–15.

Verini, James. "Love and Ruin." *The Atavist,* no. 34, magazine.atavist.com/loveandruin/.

Walker, Connecticut. "Women of the CIA." *Parade,* July 13, 1975, 4–5.

Weiner, Tim. "C.I.A. Colleagues Call Fallen Star a Bias Victim." *New York Times,* September 14, 1994, A1.

————. "C.I.A. to Pay $410,000 to Spy Who Says She Was Smeared." *New York Times,* December 9, 1994, A1.

————. "Spy Sues C.I.A., Saying She Was Target of Sexual Discrimination." *New York Times,* July 15, 1994, B7.

————. "Women, Citing Bias, May Sue the CIA." *New York Times,* March 28, 1994, A10.

Zakaria, Rafia. "How the War on Terror Became America's First 'Feminist' War." Literary Hub, excerpted from Rafia Zakaria, *Against White Feminism: Notes on Disruption,* New York: W. W. Norton, 2021, lithub.com/how-the-war-on-terror-became-americas-first-feminist-war/.

Zaman, Ned, David Wise, David Rose, and Bryan Burrough. "The Path to 9/11: Lost Warnings and Fatal Errors." *Vanity Fair,* November 2004, 326–38 and 390–400.

PHOTOGRAPH CREDITS

INDEX

ABOUT THE AUTHOR

LIZA MUNDY is an award-winning journalist and the
New York Times bestselling author of five books, including *The Sisterhood*. A former staff writer for *The Washington Post*,
Mundy lives in Washington, DC, and Los Angeles.
She writes for *The Atlantic*, *Politico*, and *Smithsonian*, among
other publications.

lizamundy.com

ABOUT THE TYPE

This book was set in Caslon, a typeface first designed in 1722 by William Caslon (1692–1766). Its widespread use by most English printers in the early eighteenth century soon supplanted the Dutch typefaces that had formerly prevailed. The roman is considered a "workhorse" typeface due to its pleasant, open appearance, while the italic is exceedingly decorative.